BEETHOVEN

BEETHOVEN

Maynard Solomon

SCHIRMER BOOKS
A Division of Macmillan Publishing Co., Inc.
NEW YORK

Schirmer Books
A Division of Macmillan Publishing Co., Inc.
866 Third Avenue, New York, N.Y. 10022

Collier Macmillan Canada, Ltd.

Schirmer Books Paperback Edition 1979

Library of Congress Catalog Card Number: 77-5242

Printed in the United States of America

Casebound printing number

3   4   5   6   7   8   9   10

Paperback printing number

 14   15   16   17

Library of Congress Cataloging in Publication Data

Solomon, Maynard.
   Beethoven.

   Bibliography: p.
   Includes index.
   1. Beethoven, Ludwig van, 1770-1827.
2. Composers--Biography. I. Title.
ML410.B4S64   780'.92'4   (B)   77-5242
ISBN 0-02-872460-7
ISBN 0-02-872240-X pbk.

Extracts from *The Letters of Beethoven,* edited by Emily Anderson, are reprinted by permission of Macmillan London and Basingstoke.

For Eva
and for Mark, Nina, and Maury

1802, in which Beethoven apparently exorcized his suicidal impulses and declared his determination to resist adversity; his *Tagebuch* (Diary) of 1812–18, in which we may observe Beethoven in his most vulnerable and self-questioning moods; and his passionate letter to an unidentified woman (whom he called "my Immortal Beloved"), written on July 6 and 7 of an unspecified year.

It is a reasonable assumption, then, that Beethoven wished us to know something more about him than a mere chronology of his life and work. He wanted understanding as well, as though sensing that both forgiveness and sympathy inevitably follow in its train. Or perhaps Beethoven hoped that others might be able to cast light upon some of the unyielding problems of his life. As an artist and as a man, he knew the healing power of communication and the cathartic effect of shared fears. "All evil is mysterious and appears greatest when viewed in solitude," he wrote in a diary entry of 1817. "Discussed with others it seems more endurable, because one becomes entirely familiar with that which we dread, and feels as if it had been overcome." [3]

Unfortunately—and inevitably—Beethoven's hope that the facts of his life would be presented in an ungarbled and unvarnished form was not soon to be fulfilled. Before the year of his death was over, a worthless and error-filled biography—by Schlosser—was published in Prague.[4] More fatefully, Anton Schindler, his former assistant and secretary, removed many of the most important documents, which lay unguarded in Beethoven's lodgings, and converted them into his private property. In 1845 Schindler sold most of these documents and memorabilia to the king of Prussia in exchange for a lifetime annuity, but he destroyed two-thirds of the Conversation Books and may well have suppressed or discarded other valuable materials. His much-translated and often-reprinted biography of Beethoven (1840, with revised and enlarged editions in 1845 and 1860) largely shaped the nineteenth-century conception of Beethoven; and it has continued to exert its influence in our own time. It was not until the publication between 1866 and 1879 of the multivolume biography by Alexander Wheelock Thayer that Schindler's unreliable portrait was seriously challenged and the main outlines of Beethoven's life faithfully reconstructed. After Thayer's death, his biography of Beethoven was completed and revised by Hermann Deiters and Hugo Riemann (1901–17); the original English manuscript was edited and completed by Henry E. Krehbiel (1921), and was recently (1964; rev. ed. 1967) re-edited by Elliot Forbes, who skillfully incorporated into it many of the findings of modern research. Forbes's edition remains the indispensable biography of Beethoven; but Thayer's strictly chronological, year-by-year method of documentation—and his avoidance of any discussion of the music other than the details of Beethoven's productivity—did not permit him to illuminate the composer's psychological development, to deal with his personal relationships in their evolution, or to demonstrate any significant connections between his life and his works.

The reader who consults the bibliographical essay which closes this book will discover that the work of Beethoven documentation began rather than ended with the work of Thayer and his scholarly contemporaries Ludwig Nohl and Gustav Nottebohm. (Indeed, the accurate reconstruction of the chronology of Beethoven's works has been made possible only in recent decades through the careful study of his sketches and autograph manuscripts.) Scholars such as A. C. Kalischer, Theodor von Frimmel, Ludwig Schiedermair, Romain Rolland, Max Unger, Jacques-Gabriel Prod'homme, Stephan Ley, Joseph Schmidt-Görg, Georg Kinsky, Hans Halm, Donald W. MacArdle, Emily Anderson, and Alan Tyson—to name only a few—devoted decades of their lives to the accumulation of data and to the careful construction of a factual foundation for Beethoven studies.

The proper study of Beethoven is based on contemporary documents— on letters, diaries, Conversation Books, court and parish records, autograph manuscripts and sketches, music publications, reviews, concert programs, and similar materials. These may be utilized by a biographer with relative confidence as to their authenticity, although even they, as we shall see, must be approached with some caution. A second major source of material bearing significantly on Beethoven's life and personality consists of the reminiscences of his contemporaries. Here more serious questions arise as to the validity of anecdotes, reports, and memoirs that were written down long after the fact by a wide variety of individuals. The extent of the dangers involved in the use of contemporary documents was dramatically illustrated in March 1977 at the Berlin *Beethoven-Kongress*, where a long-held suspicion was finally confirmed. Working with handwriting analyses, Grita Herre and Dagmar Beck proved that Schindler had fabricated more than 150 of his own entries in the Conversation Books. Until now these entries had been unhesitatingly accepted as authentic by Beethoven scholars; some of Schindler's forgeries had formed the basis for extensive biographical and musical interpretations. It is true that Thayer had little confidence in Schindler's testimony, and ever since Thayer published his *Ein kritischer Beitrag zur Beethoven-Literatur* [A critical contribution to the Beethoven literature] in 1877, Schindler had been seen as an unreliable, biased, and self-serving witness. Nevertheless, even Thayer relied heavily on Schindler, and the latter, who was in intimate contact with Beethoven for a number of years and who personally interviewed many of his friends, cannot wholly be dismissed. It will not be an easy task to separate his facts from his fictions.

We have no such extreme problem with regard to other contemporary observers. But each of their reports must also be verified, where possible, and their reminiscences as a whole evaluated as to their reliability and possible bias. Of the leading sources, it is my judgment that the reminiscences of Ignaz von Seyfried, Carl Czerny, Gerhard von Breuning, Fanny Giannatasio del Rio, and Karl Holz are generally trustworthy insofar as they reflect personal observations, and that the *Biographical Notices* of Franz Wegeler and Ferdinand Ries reveal some curious lapses and factual errors but are in the main unbiased and accurate. More difficult to evaluate is the so-called Fischer Manuscript, which consists of the reminiscences of Cäcilia and Gottfried Fischer, written down by the latter more than a half-century after the Beethoven family had rented a flat in their parents' home. This manuscript is perhaps the most important single fund of information on Beethoven's family background and on his early years in Bonn. Thayer regarded it as somewhat suspect, but Hermann Deiters and Joseph Schmidt-Görg, each of whom published editions of portions of the manuscript, concluded that wherever parallel evidence was available from other sources, the Fischer memoirs were found to be quite reliable. Nevertheless, as I have observed elsewhere,[5] even the simple Fischers had an axe to grind—viz., the desire to prove that Beethoven had been born in thèir parents' house—and this led them into a number of deliberate falsifications concerning the dates of the Fischer family's association with the Beethovens. On the whole, however, I have accepted as valid their homely, keenly observed anecdotes concerning Beethoven's youth, his family, and his early experiences.

Another important document is the Fischhoff Manuscript, a collection of materials for a projected early biography. Along with many interesting anecdotes and letters, it contains a transcription of Beethoven's *Tagebuch* of 1812-18. This extraordinary document contains Beethoven's intimate musings during a critical period of his life, along with transcriptions from a wide variety of philosophical, literary, and theological texts that enrich our knowledge of his intellectual and religious strivings. Unfortunately, Beethoven's original manuscript has disappeared and we must rely upon copies that are inaccurate in many details, owing to the difficulty in deciphering Beethoven's handwriting.

The present book is an attempt to provide an accurate account of Beethoven's life and works based on authentic documents and reminiscences and on the accumulated discoveries of Beethoven scholarship. But no new biography of Beethoven is needed which does not also try to come to grips with at least a few of the many unanswered questions concerning his personality and his creativity. I do not entertain the illusion that it is possible to explain all such questions, or even to give more than provisional answers to the major ones. But I believe that I have successfully resisted the temptation to fashion an uncontradictory and consistent portrait of Beethoven—to construct a safe, clear, well-ordered design; for such a portrait can be purchased only at the price of truth, by avoiding the obscurities that riddle the documentary material. I will recount the salient facts and describe the significant relationships of Beethoven's life in some detail; but I will pause at those junctures where we are suddenly confronted with opaque and seemingly inexplicable events and situations—where we discover delusions and even pathological actions. "There is a grain of truth concealed in every delusion," Freud observed: "there is something in it that really deserves belief." [6] At the least, every delusion deserves an attempt—however imperfect—at clarification. In this sense, my book is an essay in interpretation and meaning: I will try to discover the meaning of several of the ambiguities and delusions in Beethoven's life and to offer some indications of their possible significance for his creative quest.

It is my belief that neither a work of art nor a man's life can be fully understood through any single category of analysis. Accordingly I have utilized a rather wide variety of categories—aesthetic, historical, psychoanalytic, sociological—in a search for the manifold origins of Beethoven's personality and of his music. And I have tried to place Beethoven simultaneously within the contexts of social events, of his family constellation, of the history of ideas, and of the evolution of musical styles and forms. The reader will soon discover which of these categories and contexts I lean most heavily upon, but he should not suppose that I regard any of these—or all of them taken together—as sufficient to exhaust the meaning of a series of creative events unique in the history of mankind.

NEW YORK
JULY 1977

Acknowledgments

Grateful acknowledgment and thanks to the following for their helpful assistance and for providing photocopies of manuscript and/or scarce materials: Columbia University libraries; New York Public Library; Library of Congress; Harvard University music library; Bibliothèque nationale, Paris; Stadtarchiv, Frankfurt; Goethe Museum (Freies Deutsches Hochstift), Frankfurt; Deutsche Staatsbibliothek, Berlin; Universitätsbibliothek, Münster; Universitätsbibliothek, Mainz; Beethovenhaus, Bonn; Mugar Memorial Library, Boston University. Thanks to George Marek for permitting me access to his photocopies of the Karlsbad guest lists and police registers for 1812 and of the *Prager Oberpostamts-Zeitung* for June–July 1812; to Ruth MacArdle for permitting the microfilming of the typescript of her late husband's monumental guide to the periodical literature, *Beethoven Abstracts*, some years before its publication; to my friend Harry Goldschmidt for a highly interesting correspondence concerning the Immortal Beloved, for guiding me to several sources that I would otherwise have overlooked, and (through his assistant Clemens Brenneis) for transcripts of hitherto unpublished sections of Beethoven's Conversation Books; to Joseph Schmidt-Görg and Hans Schmidt, formerly of the Beethovenhaus, for replying to several queries; to Joseph Braunstein, Douglas Johnson, Christa Landon, Peter Riethus, William Drabkin, and Nathan Fishman for clarifying particular factual or bibliographical questions; to Achim von Brentano for kindly permitting reproduction of the 1798 miniature portrait of Antonie Brentano; to Martin Staehelin, present director of the Beethoven-Archiv, for generously providing newly acquired materials on Frau Brentano; to Ingrid Scheib of the Goethe House, New York, for her help in deciphering and translating the Brentano manuscript correspondence; to the many antiquarian booksellers who helped me to obtain rare materials on Beethoven, and especially to Samuel Orlinick of the Scientific Library Service (New York), Theodore

Front (Los Angeles), H. Baron (London), and Walter Ricke (Munich); to Muriel Bennett for typing the manuscript; to Ken Stuart, editor of Schirmer Books, for his confidence in this project; and to Abbie Meyer, Eileen Fitzgerald DeWald, Valerie Klima, and Robert Cohen for their care in editing the typescript and seeing it through the press.

The chapter on "Haydn and Beethoven" was read by James Webster, who generously corrected a number of factual errors. The section on the Immortal Beloved was read in an earlier manuscript version by Elliot Forbes and Leon Plantinga; I have greatly benefited from their comments.

My profoundest gratitude goes to my friends Joseph Kerman, William S. Newman, Harry Slochower, and Alan Tyson—each of whom read the typed manuscript in its entirety—for their keen criticisms; their extensive corrections of fact, interpretation, and style; their insistence upon an unattainable standard of excellence; and also for their extremely lively hostilities, which confirmed my feeling (and my hope) that I had written a book that might spark some small controversies. But this does not sufficiently express my debt to each of these men. Harry Slochower set me on the path of biographical exploration and patiently provided me with the equipment to attempt the task. William S. Newman encouraged my Beethoven studies in their early stages and prompted me to deal with the nature and the causes of Beethoven's profound style shifts. Alan Tyson generously shared with me his inexhaustible store of knowledge about Beethoven. And Joseph Kerman's extremely detailed critique of the manuscript served as my indispensable guide to its final revision. Naturally, the errors of fact and extravagances of interpretation which the reader will doubtless encounter in the following pages are wholly my responsibility.

Several sections of this book appeared in different form in *The Musical Quarterly, Music Review, Music & Letters, Beethoven Studies, Telos*, and *American Imago*. I am grateful to the editors of these publications for their encouragement and for their permission to reprint these materials.

My wife, Eva, helped me to revise a number of the most problematical chapters of this book. Even more crucially, she provided a sane sounding board for my speculations on Beethoven over these past twelve years.

I
BONN

Beethoven's birthplace, Bonn.

1
Family Background

Ludwig van Beethoven was born into a family of court musicians at the electorate of Cologne, situated in Bonn. His grandfather, whose name he bore, was bass singer and *Kapellmeister* at the electoral court; his father, Johann, was a court tenor and music teacher of moderate talent. Johann married the widowed Maria Magdalena Leym (née Keverich) on November 12, 1767. Their first child, Ludwig Maria, was baptized on April 2, 1769, and lived for six days. Their second son, Ludwig, was baptized on December 17, 1770.

One would expect that so straightforward a sequence of events could generate no biographical difficulties. Yet, this tiny nucleus of incontrovertible, documented facts gave rise to a complex series of misconceptions which shaped many of Beethoven's emotional attitudes and actions throughout his life.

The first of these was so inaccessible to reason that it may well be more accurate to call it a delusion. It concerns the year of Beethoven's birth. For most of his life, Beethoven believed that he had been born in December of 1772 rather than in December of 1770. (Indeed, in his

3

Heiligenstadt Testament, written in October 1802, he implied that he was three to five years younger than his real age.[1]) Repeatedly, his friends—Ferdinand Ries, Franz Gerhard Wegeler, Wilhelm Christian Müller—provided him with copies of his baptismal certificate, but in each case he refused to accept their validity. In some obscure way, Beethoven had convinced himself that the baptismal certificates were those of his older brother, Ludwig Maria. He warned Wegeler to be on the alert for this possibility when he wrote his childhood friend on May 2, 1810, asking that he obtain a "correct" certificate of baptism:

> But one thing must be borne in mind, namely that there was a brother *born before me*, who was also named Ludwig with the addition Maria, but who died. To fix my age beyond doubt, this brother must first be found, inasmuch as I already know that in this respect a mistake has been made by others, and I have been said to be older than I am. Unfortunately I myself lived for a time without knowing my age.... I urge you to attend to this matter, to find Ludwig Maria and the present Ludwig, who was born after him.[2]

When the certificate arrived, duly signed by the "Mayor's office of Bonn," giving December 17, 1770, as the baptismal date, Beethoven still would not accept it as valid. He wrote on the back of it: "1772. The baptismal certificate seems to be incorrect, since there was a Ludwig born before me." [3]

How is this to be explained? It was long believed that Beethoven merely adopted a misconception about his age which had been current during his years in Bonn. Some biographers blamed Beethoven's father for the two-year discrepancy, claiming that he may have purposely falsified the boy's age in order to promote his possibilities as a *Wunderkind* along the lines of the Mozart children. Others gave Johann the benefit of the doubt, stressing the widespread laxity at that time in keeping family records. A hard look at the evidence, however, shows that Johann van Beethoven never deducted two years from his son's age, that at no time prior to 1790 was his age understated by two years, and that there was a consistent pattern of deductions of one year during Beethoven's first two decades.[4] Apparently Beethoven and his associates (and perhaps his parents as well) all then believed that he had been born in December 1771. Therefore, Beethoven's persistent belief that he was born in December 1772 (or later) originated in his own mind. In view of the unmistakable ways by which he could have tested and confirmed the accuracy of the baptismal certificates, it seems clear that he was unwilling or unable to subject the issue of his birth year to rational consideration. The birth-year delusion was Beethoven's own. Its possible meaning and ramifications will become clearer only after we have learned more about his life and personality.

A related matter of even greater emotional significance is Beethoven's uncertainty about the facts of his parentage itself. Reports that Beethoven was the illegitimate son of a king of Prussia—variously Friedrich Wilhelm II and Frederick the Great—first appeared in print in 1810, and were repeated in encyclopedias, music dictionaries, and music periodicals throughout the remainder of his lifetime. At precisely what date Beethoven became aware of these reports is not known; probably they came to his attention almost immediately. Beginning in 1819, his friends and his nephew Karl urged him to deny the reports. The Conversation Books repeatedly contain such entreaties as: "Such things must be corrected, because you do not need to borrow glory from the king—rather the reverse is the case"; or: "It is written that you are a bastard of Frederick the Great.... We must insert a notice in the *Allgemeine Zeitung*."[5] But the composer would not be moved to action, nor did he authorize or even permit any of his friends to refute the story of his royal ancestry, which had by this time gained wide currency in France, England, and Italy as well as in Germany and Austria. Wegeler, in a letter of December 28, 1825, sounded a note of anger and disappointment with Beethoven for having permitted the story to flourish for so long without contradiction: "Why do you not avenge the honor of your mother when, in the *Konversations-Lexikon* and in France, it is given that you are a love-child? . . . Only your natural reluctance to occupy yourself with anything other than music is the cause of this culpable indifference. If you wish, I will let the world know the truth about this. This is the least point on which you should respond to me." [6]

That neither the accusation of "culpable indifference" nor his old friend's challenge to avenge his mother's honor called forth an immediate response is in itself remarkable. It was almost a full year later, and only after the onset of the illness which was to result in his death, that Beethoven belatedly replied to Wegeler, in a letter of December 7, 1826: "You say that I have been mentioned somewhere as being the natural son of the late king of Prussia. Well, the same thing was said to me a long time ago. But I have adopted the principle of neither writing anything about myself nor replying to anything that has been written about me. Hence I gladly leave it to you to make known to the world the integrity of my parents, and especially of my mother." [7] Yet, having written the letter, he neglected to have it posted. Evidently he still had a powerful resistance to refuting the rumor. When Wegeler again wrote to him reproachfully, Beethoven replied on February 17, 1827: "But indeed I was surprised to read in your last letter that you had not yet received anything. From the letter which you are now receiving you will see that I wrote to you as long ago as December 10th of last year. . . . [It was] left lying about until today. . . ." [8]

Here, as in Beethoven's delusion about his birth year, we are confronted with a difficult question: what were the forces and events in Beethoven's life which caused him to deny his father and to dishonor his mother's memory? An interpretation of this extraordinary matter can be attempted only after we have laid a foundation of fact concerning Beethoven's earliest experiences in Bonn.

Kapellmeister Ludwig van Beethoven strongly opposed the marriage of his son Johann to Maria Magdalena Keverich Leym in 1767. He claimed to have made inquiries and discovered that she had been a chambermaid. His reproaches were sufficiently loud to reach the ears of his landlord's family, the Fischers, who lived downstairs: "I never believed or expected that you would so degrade yourself," they reportedly heard him say to Johann.[9] Such was the first confrontation between the three main characters in the early life of Ludwig van Beethoven—his grandfather, his father, and his mother.

Maria Magdalena was born on December 19, 1746, the daughter of Heinrich Keverich, chief overseer of the kitchen at the palace of the elector of Trèves at Ehrenbreitstein. She married Johann Leym (born August 9, 1733; he was a valet of the elector of Trèves) at sixteen, bore him a son who died an infant, and was widowed in 1765, before she was nineteen. Johann van Beethoven brought his intended bride home to Bonn from Ehrenbreitstein, and they were married on November 12, 1767, despite the elder Ludwig's opposition. "Madame van Beethoven later said," Gottfried Fischer tells us, "that her family would have given her a good wedding celebration, but her father-in-law stubbornly refused to be present unless the thing were quickly over with."[10]

The *Kapellmeister* was mistaken in his claim that Maria Magdalena had been a housemaid. Actually, her family included a number of wealthy merchants, court councillors, and senators. Hence, as Schiedermair remarks, it was not Johann van Beethoven but rather Maria Magdalena Keverich "who contracted a marriage beneath her station."[11] Why, then, did the elder Beethoven oppose the marriage? Perhaps because it threatened to disturb the carefully ordered, precise, and comfortable existence which he had led for many years with his son in the second-story apartment (six rooms plus a maid's room) at Rheingasse 934. The Fischer memoirs describe his apartment: "Everything was so beautiful and proper and well arranged . . . all six rooms were provided with beautiful furniture, many paintings and cupboards, a cupboard of silver service, a cupboard with fine gilded porcelain and glass, an assortment of the most beautiful linens which could be drawn through a ring; everything from the smallest article sparkled like silver."[12] A household so meticulously maintained reflected an equally well-ordered life, which brooked no interference and desired no change, especially one which might separate the father from his only son.

Ludwig van Beethoven the elder was baptized on January 5, 1712, at Malines in Belgium, the third son of Michael and Mary. At the age of five he became a student at the choir school of the church of St. Rombaut, where he remained until 1725. In that year he began to receive instruction on the organ and in the art of accompanying and realizing figured bass at the keyboard; soon he was playing at services in various churches. In 1731 he was appointed choir director at the church of St. Pierre at Louvain, and by 1732 he was singing bass at the Cathedral of St. Lambert in Liège. In March of the following year—perhaps at the request of elector Clemens August, archbishop of Cologne, who is thought to have met him in Liège—he made his way to Cologne and thence to Bonn, where he was to spend the rest of his life, first as bass soloist and singer in the choir (a post which he retained until his last year) and then as court *Kapellmeister* in charge of music at the chapel, the concert hall, the theater, and the court ballroom from 1761 until his death on December 24, 1773, of a stroke. From about 1740, he found time to establish a profitable wine business in addition to his court duties and, according to contemporary documents, became a moneylender as well.

His commercial activities were quite in the family tradition. His father, Michael (1684–1749), had been indentured as a baker's apprentice in 1700 and became a master baker in 1707; he later prospered in real estate and, after 1720, as a dealer in laces, paintings, and furniture. By 1739 his fortunes had suffered a reversal and rumors of bankruptcy spread, causing him to begin selling off his estate; by 1741 he was indeed bankrupt, with unpaid judgments of approximately 10,000 florins (an amount equivalent to a small fortune today) against him. He and his wife accordingly joined their sons, Ludwig and Cornelius, in Bonn, where they were beyond the jurisdiction of the Flemish courts and where they lived peacefully until their deaths in 1749. Cornelius (1708–64), who arrived in Bonn circa 1731–32, was a chandler by trade, and became purveyor of candles to the electoral court. He married a widow of the Bonn bourgeoisie in 1734, and from 1736 onward his name appeared on the list of the burghers of Bonn. After the death of his first wife in 1755, he married a relative of hers, Anna Barbara Marx, under a special Papal dispensation permitting marriage within the restricted bounds of consanguinity.

On September 7 or 17, 1733, Ludwig married Maria Josepha Poll (or Pols; nothing is known of her background; she was born ca. 1714), and they had three children, of whom only Johann survived. He was born in 1739 or 1740; the exact date is lacking because no record of his baptism has ever been found. Maria Josepha reportedly was an alcoholic, and her condition became such that she was placed in a cloister, where she remained until her death on September 30, 1775. The date of her removal to the cloister is not known. The Fischer memoirs describe her husband at the wedding of Theodor Fischer on June 24, 1761: "During the ceremony, tears streamed from his eyes, and when asked about it, he answered that he was thinking about his own marriage and wedding ceremony."[13] Presumably he was thinking also of his marital tragedy, and so his wife may have been absent as early as 1761. The testimony as to her alcoholism comes from the Fischer children, who would have learned of it from their parents. There is nothing to indicate that any member of the Beethoven family visited her at the cloister. In later years the composer never mentioned her existence, although her death took place when he was almost five years old. Nor is there any indication that the elder Beethoven entered into a relationship with another woman after his wife's removal; rather, he remained alone in the Fischer house with his son. His subsequent resistance to his son's marriage may have been in part an unwillingness to reintroduce a discordant, female element into his totally self-sufficient bachelor existence.

Within Maria Magdalena's family, the attitude toward the marriage was equally unfavorable; the wedding was held in Bonn rather than in the bride's hometown probably because of family opposition. Maria Magdalena's father (born January 14, 1702) had died on August 3, 1759, when she was only twelve years old. Her mother was born on November 8, 1707, was married on August 14, 1731, and had six children, of whom four seem to have died in infancy. Her mother became the family bread-winner after 1759, working as a cook at the court. Towards the year 1768 Frau Keverich suffered a psychological breakdown, to which her daughter's second marriage may have contributed. For an official document of March 26, 1768, reports that "through an ill-turned marriage of her only daughter 300 Thalers disappeared," and although one scholar generously takes this to mean that she had given her daughter a sub-stantial dowry, some observers conclude that "Johann van Beethoven relieved his mother-in-law of almost all her savings."[14] Because of her poverty, a guardian was appointed. The report continues: "She has imposed upon herself a life of such severe and unusual penitence that it is hard to understand how she can survive, living as she does in this unnatural manner, taking little food, and that of the worst quality, and sometimes lying almost the whole night through in the bitterest cold, wind, and rain, outside the churches in the open air."[15] Indeed, she did not survive for very long: she died in September of the same year.

Maria Magdalena's reaction to her mother's death and the role which her husband's avarice played in causing it is not known, but we may reasonably surmise that this was one of the first links in the "chain of sorrows" that she described to Cäcilia Fischer as constituting her married state. This came up in a discussion concerning a suitor of Cäcilia's, in which Frau van Beethoven remarked: "If you want to take my good advice, remain single, and then you will have the most tranquil, most beautiful, most pleasurable life. For what is marriage? A little joy, but then a chain of sorrows. And you are still young." Frau van Beethoven often elaborated on this theme, remarking "how thoughtlessly so many young people get married without knowing what [sorrows] await them." She knew of few happy marriages and of fewer happy women: "One should weep when a girl is brought into the world," she said.[16]

As we have seen, her first son by Johann, Ludwig Maria, was baptized on April 2, 1769, and died after six days. The next child, Ludwig, was baptized on December 17, 1770, and therefore was probably born on December 15 or 16. She had five more children, of whom two, Caspar Anton Carl, baptized on April 8, 1774, and Nikolaus Johann, baptized on October 2, 1776, survived. Anna Maria Franziska, baptized on February 23, 1779, lived only a few days; Franz Georg, baptized on January 17, 1781, survived until August 16, 1783; and Maria Margaretha Josepha, baptized on May 5, 1786, died on November 26, 1787, at the age of a year and a half.

We have, then, a sketch of the beginnings of an inauspicious marriage, which had been opposed by the parents, which was to be marked by straitened circumstances, conflict, and tragedy throughout its relatively brief span, and which was apparently regretted by the wife soon after the ceremony. Maria Magdalena's disappointment at her marriage cannot be ascribed simply to the deaths of her mother and her first child, nor to poverty. Three of her first four children survived and in the early years of the marriage her family was under the protection of the elder Ludwig, who was earning a high salary from his post as *Kapellmeister* plus a good income from his wine business, and who turned out to be not at all averse to helping his son raise a family. Clearly, the marriage did not amount to the threat that he had anticipated. His orderly existence continued as before; his daughter-in-law recognized his authority and indeed virtually exalted him as the patriarchal head of her family; his relationship to his son underwent no profound change, and he gained a grandson as well, who bore his name rather than that of the father.

Nor was Maria Magdalena's husband incapable of providing for his new family. In 1769 he had received an increase of 25 florins above his annual salary of 100 florins, and he received 50 florins more by virtue of a decree of April 3, 1772. Moreover, he was able to earn something by teaching. As there are no signs that he was anything other than a competent musician during the 1770s, we may accept Gottfried Fischer's statement that during these years Johann "performed his duties punctually; he gave clavier and voice lessons to the sons and daughters of the English, French, and Imperial embassies, to the masters and daughters of the local nobility, as well as to those of esteemed burghers; he often had more to do than he could do. . . . " [17] He was so well liked by his students that he received many favors and presents from their families. (Among the gifts were supplies of good wines; Frimmel wryly comments that even at this early time, "one must notice that the talk is already about wine.") [18] He was also frequently called on to prepare young musicians for service in the chapel. It was not, therefore, as a family provider that Johann failed in the early years.

Johann van Beethoven had received an elementary education and had been placed in a preparatory class of the College of Jesuits, where he failed to make any progress. At twelve he had entered the court chapel as a soprano. His father had taught him to sing and to play the clavier, and he learned to play the violin capably as well. After his voice changed, he was, by a decree of 1756, accepted into the electoral choir, where he remained until his last years, when his "stale voice" and notoriously drunken behavior compelled his retirement. He had faithfully followed the pattern that his father had set out for him; and he had remained under his father's wing—both at home and in the choir—evidently without demur, until (in what must have been a major act of defiance for so amiable and submissive a young man) he decided upon marriage in 1767.

Actually, he had spoken of marriage for many years prior to that time. He and Theodor Fischer, the landlord's son, were close friends, played the zither and sang songs together, and decided in approximately 1760 that the time had finally come for them to start families—to "ship out onto the sea of love." [19] Theodor Fischer was married in 1761, but "Johann der Läufer" ("Johann the sprinter"), as his father derisively called him, was off to a slow start; it would be another six years before he summoned sufficient courage. When the time finally came, he found a bride in a distant city and brought the news of his betrothal to his father as a *fait accompli*: "When Johann van Beethoven presented his loved one to his father in person," relates Fischer, "he said that this is what I wish, and he stood fast and declared that he would not be swayed from his determination that she would be his bride." [20]

Thayer believed that Johann's alcoholism was probably inherited from his mother, and Gottfried Fischer naively attributed it to the wine trade which his father maintained. Prod'homme hazards that the court tenor began to drift "little by little" into drunkenness as the family's "resources diminished, after the death of his father. . . .";[21] Schiedermair assumes that the alcoholic haze in which Johann spent his final years was intensified by the death of Maria Magdalena.

The etiology of alcoholism, however, has deeper roots than these. As Edward Glover has observed: "All the primary features of alcoholism represent fundamentally the individual's attempt to extricate himself from an impasse." [22] The alcoholic finds in drink a temporary surcease from an unhappy life situation or an unbearable psychological conflict. We may speculate that the impasse from which Johann could not extricate himself was the conflict concerning his relationship to his father, a domineering personality who brooked no opposition from either his family or his musicians. Where he could not control by persuasion he did not hesitate to seek to compel; unable to enforce obedience by his musicians on one occasion, he petitioned the elector, who thereupon commanded the unruly court musicians "to obey all the commands given by our *Kapellmeister*" upon threat of dismissal.[23] The domination of Johann by his father is clear on the surface: the elder Ludwig had chosen his son's profession, taught him music, introduced him to the court chapel, obtained his appointment as court singer, and functioned simultaneously as his employer, protector, and sole parent. The placing of Johann's mother in an institution had the effect of intensifying his domination at the hands of the only remaining parent, and perhaps gave rise to a cluster of ambivalent feelings toward him. The Fischer memoirs portray a father convinced that his son would never amount to anything, who broadcast this conviction in contemptuous tones. The elder Ludwig's opposition to his son's marriage apparently reflected his belief that Johann—who was then twenty-seven or twenty-eight years of age—was incapable of becoming a husband and a father, let alone of choosing a suitable bride. Johann's marriage, then, seems to have represented his single moment of rebellion against a relationship marked by forceful domination on one side and his own passivity on the other.

But Johann was not to find in marriage a release from the powerful influence of his father. The *Kapellmeister* moved out, it is true, but only down the street, a little way from their lodgings at 515 Bonngasse, and he remained a dominant force within Johann's new household. Johann had found his own woman, had started a family, and was carrying out his duties and obligations—he was doing the best he could. But it was still not enough. Nothing had changed, really. To his father he remained "Johann der Läufer," the Johann van Beethoven who "had a flighty spirit"; who, when his father was called away from home, would take advantage of his absence to leave Bonn, traveling to Cologne, Deutz, Andernach, Coblentz, Ehrenbreitstein, "and who knows where else." "Keep running, keep running," said his father, sarcastically. "You will some day run to your final destination." [24]

The death of his father brought Johann's hostile feelings to the surface. (Surely it was no desperate need for money which caused him to pawn his departed father's portrait.) The mediocrity of his own career should have demonstrated to Johann the gulf between his capabilities and those of his father; but his only recorded reaction to the elder Ludwig's death shows that he thought otherwise. Petitioning the elector for a salary increase in early January 1774, within two weeks of his father's death, Johann wrote:

> Will your Electoral Grace be pleased to hear that my father has passed away from this world, to whom it was granted to serve His Electoral Grace Clemens August and Your Electoral Grace and gloriously reigning Lord Lord [sic] 42 years, as *Kapellmeister* with great honor, whose position I have been found capable of filling, but nevertheless I would not venture to offer my capacity to Your Electoral Grace. . . .[25]

The thought that he could become *Kapellmeister* was doubtless only the most grandiose of Johann's notions; and it was one he would try to convert into reality a decade later. In general, however, he lacked the energy to pursue his fantasies. The Fischers remembered him often lying in the window, staring out at the rain or making faces at his drinking companion, fish dealer Klein, who was similarly wont to recline in the window across the street. He spent an increasing amount of time away from home, as well as many nights in the taverns or wandering through the town with his friends, arriving home in the middle of the night or early in the morning—a sure way of avoiding his family and conjugal responsibilities and turning the leadership of the family over to his wife. When the Rhine overflowed in 1784, flooding many sections of Bonn, it was not Johann but his wife who showed heroism and courage, calming the residents with encouraging words and waiting until others had been evacuated to make her escape into the Giergasse across the roofs and down improvised ladders.

In later years, Johann was regarded as a person of low repute. An official report to Archduke Maximilian Franz, immediately after he reached Bonn in the summer of 1784 as successor to the deceased elector Max Friedrich, reflected the general opinion: "Johann Beethoven has a very stale voice, has been long in the service, very poor, of fair deportment and married." [26] Until 1784, he had been tolerated because of the protection first of his father and then of the powerful electoral minister, Count Kaspar Anton von Belderbusch. (We may assume that Belderbusch's protection was a transference from a friendly and long-standing relationship with his court *Kapellmeister*, who was a fellow Fleming.) The count served as godfather to Johann's third son and was a frequent visitor to the Beethoven lodgings, one of the few members of the titled nobility so recorded. Johann became so closely identified as a protégé of Belderbusch that he earned the ill will of the minister's many enemies. An anonymous contemporary document prepared by opponents of Belderbusch includes Johann van Beethoven on a list of "good sleuthhounds and spies who may be hired for a cheap price," [27] suggesting that Johann may have been an agent or informer for Belderbusch.

The death of the minister in 1784, a few months after the passing of elector Max Friedrich, left Johann van Beethoven without a protector at the court or friends of influence in the new electorate. To compound his difficulties, in late 1785 or early 1786 he attempted to defraud the heirs of Belderbusch through a false claim upon their estate.[28] He claimed, in a petition to the elector, that he had given many valuable gifts to the count and to his mistress, the Abbess of Vilich, in return for an alleged promise that he would be appointed *Kapellmeister*. He demanded that the Belderbusch heirs return the gifts, which were listed under a forged signature. Though no legal action was taken against him when the scheme failed, his status in the court and in Bonn reached its nadir, perhaps hastening the downward-spiraling course of his dissolution. A report on a petition by young Ludwig van Beethoven of February 15, 1784, requesting that he receive a formal appointment as assistant court organist with increased remuneration, bluntly states that his father was no longer able to support his family. Thereafter, Johann was tolerated on the electoral rolls as an act of charity, and he became something of a comic figure. On January 1, 1793, the elector wrote to Court Marshal von Schall that "the revenues from the liquor excise have suffered a loss" by the recent death of Johann van Beethoven.[29]

At home, Maria Magdalena repeatedly complained about her husband's drinking debts and often lamented being left alone so often in the house. But it seems clear that both she and Johann were pleased to have her run the family's affairs. This is implied in an episode reported from their early married life:

> When he received his monthly salary or money from his pupils, he would play a joke upon returning home: he would throw the money at his wife's feet and say: "Now woman, manage with that." Then she would give him a bottle of wine, saying: "One cannot let men return home with empty hands." He said: "Yes, empty hands!" She responded: "Yes, but I know that you prefer a full glass to an empty one." "Yes, yes, the woman is right, she is always right." [30]

Nothing essentially changed in later years. Johann would walk conspicuously through the neighborhood drinking wine from a flask. Once Frau van Beethoven called to him from the window and he responded: "It is such hot weather that I have a great thirst." She said, "That's true, but you often have a thirst without a summer heat," to which he replied agreeably, "You are right, I agree with you. I thank you, it will soon be time to eat; don't worry, I will come right away." [31]

Maria Magdalena apparently assumed the role of the pained, suffering, righteous wife of a ne'er-do-well drunkard and played it in high tragic

style. Cäcilia Fischer could not remember ever having seen her laugh
("She was always serious"), and the widow Karth described her as "a
quiet, suffering woman." [32] She was said to be "a clever woman [who]
could give converse and reply aptly, politely, and modestly to high and
low, and for this reason she was much liked and respected." [33] Apparently she was not withdrawn, for it was reported that she became
"hot-tempered and argumentative" on occasion, and Gottfried Fischer
observed that "she knew how to give and take in a manner that is becoming to all people of honest thoughts." [34] Cäcilia also recalled that
Beethoven's mother would often speak about her travels and about the
"dangers she had undergone," [35] which, taken together with her warnings about marriage, may indicate a fearful and imaginative disposition,
perhaps one quite similar to that which we will encounter in Beethoven's
Heiligenstadt Testament, his letter to the Immortal Beloved, and elsewhere in his correspondence and diaries. We may safely assume that
Maria Magdalena imparted to her children, and particularly to her oldest son, many of the same thoughts which she passed on to Cäcilia
Fischer. Indeed, the Fischers assert that Beethoven was present when
his mother warned Cäcilia against marriage, which, if true, may explain
why we find an almost literal echo of those feelings in a report by Fanny
Giannatasio of Beethoven's opinions in 1817 on the same subject.

On Maria Magdalena's birthday the family momentarily set aside its
troubles and conflicts. The scene is described by Cäcilia Fischer:

> Each year, the feast of St. Mary Magdalene (her birthday and name
> day) was kept with due solemnity. The music stands were brought from
> the *Tucksaal* and placed in the two sitting rooms overlooking the street,
> and a canopy, embellished with flowers, leaves, and laurel, was put up
> in the room containing Grandfather Ludwig's portrait. On the eve of the
> day, Madame van Beethoven was induced to retire betimes. By ten
> o'clock all was in readiness. The silence was broken by the tuning up of
> instruments; Madame van Beethoven was awakened [and] requested to
> dress, and was then led to a beautifully draped chair beneath the can-
> opy. An outburst of music roused the neighbors, the most drowsy soon
> catching the infectious gaiety. When the music was over the table was
> spread and, after food and drink, the merry company fell to dancing
> (but in stockinged feet to lessen the noise), and so the festivities came to
> an end.[36]

No equivalent respect or honor was shown the father of the family, for
it was his role to play the amiable and ineffectual Dionysian, heir to
the weaknesses of the flesh, as a foil for Maria Magdalena's suffering
transcendence of life's tribulations.

Oedipus and the Sphinx.

"An einen Säugling," WoO 108 (1783).

2
Childhood

There is ample evidence of the crucial effect upon Beethoven's early life of the stresses and conflicts within his family constellation. In a home in which the son's natural role model—the father—had been toppled from his pedestal, the monumentalization of the grandfather took on heroic proportions, and this deeply affected Johann's attitude toward his eldest son, with, in turn, rich implications for the latter's course of development.

Beethoven's admiration for his grandfather bordered on hero worship; the resulting desire to emulate the *Kapellmeister* remained with him throughout his life. In 1801 he wrote from Vienna to Wegeler, in Bonn, asking him to forward "by the mail coach as soon as possible" [1] one object—the portrait of his grandfather, painted by Radoux—which he treasured until his death. Schlösser, who visited Beethoven in 1823, recalled that the portrait occupied a preeminent place in Beethoven's rooms, and commented on the latter's "childlike reverence" for the elder Ludwig. [2] Wegeler is, perhaps, the best witness to the earliest manifestations of this reverence: "Little Ludwig clung with the greatest ardor to the grandfather, who, we are told, was at the same time his godfather;

15

despite his tender age when he lost him, he vividly retained the early impressions. He spoke readily about his grandfather to his childhood friends, and his pious and sweet mother—whom he loved more than his harsh father—had to tell him much about his grandfather." [3] In 1816, Fanny Giannatasio wrote in her diary that Beethoven often spoke of his grandfather in glowing terms, describing "what a true and honorable man he had been." [4] The psychological identification was so powerful that on August 1, 1824, Beethoven wrote his attorney, Johann Baptist Bach: "I think that I might have a stroke some day, like my worthy grandfather, whom I take after." [5]

It was only natural that Beethoven should strive to emulate the *Kapellmeister*, who had been the most powerful force in Bonn's musical life. (As we shall see, Beethoven retained a lifelong aspiration to become a *Kapellmeister* himself.) It is worth noting, however, that a strong psychological identification with a grandfather may well reflect a repudiation of the father; the child may come to terms with an unsatisfactory image of his father by idealizing his male grandparent. In Beethoven's case, as we have seen, the *Kapellmeister's* death failed to restore Johann to a position of eminence in the household; on the contrary, Maria Magdalena evoked the memory of her father-in-law's talent, position, and power, and this painfully contrasted with her husband's hapless mediocrity. Johann's resentment against his father was already deeply rooted; now his wife was apparently attempting to mold their son in the grandfather's image, an attempt which Johann was bound to resist.

The issue was joined when Beethoven reached the age at which he could be taught music—which occurred when he was about four or five years old. Johann used the occasion as a means of establishing his supremacy in the family rather than as an opportunity to instruct a supremely gifted child in the art of playing clavier and violin. He conducted his son's musical education in a brutal and willful manner. There is unequivocal testimony on this. Head Burgomaster Windeck "saw the little Louis van Beethoven in [the] house standing in front of the clavier and weeping." [6] Cäcilia Fischer remembered him as "a tiny boy, standing on a little footstool in front of the clavier, to which the implacable severity of his father had so early condemned him." [7] Fétis interviewed a childhood companion of Beethoven's who reported that "Beethoven's father used violence when it came to making him start his musical studies, and ... there were few days when he was not beaten in order to compel him to set himself at the piano." [8] Wegeler witnessed "the same thing"; he wrote that on his visits to a neighboring house, "the doings and sufferings of Louis were visible." [9] The father was not merely strict, but cruel. "He treated him harshly . . . ," wrote Court Councillor Krupp to Simrock, "and sometimes shut him up in the cellar." [10]

After several years, Johann, finding his own knowledge insufficient to the task of Ludwig's musical education, enlisted the aid of an eccentric actor/musician, Tobias Pfeiffer, who had come to Bonn in the summer of 1779 with the Grossman and Helmuth theatrical company. Pfeiffer and Johann soon became tavern companions; Pfeiffer was invited to stay in the Beethoven apartment; and—in view of their intimacy—it evidently appeared only natural to Johann that he share his pedagogical duties with the twenty-eight-year-old Pfeiffer until the latter's departure the following spring. Mäurer, a cellist in Bonn at the time, relates the story: ". . . often, when Pfeiffer had been boozing with Beethoven's father in a wine-tavern until 11 or 12 o'clock, he went home with him, where [they found] Louis . . . in bed sleeping. The father roughly shook him awake, the boy gathered his wits and, weeping, went to the piano, where he remained, with Pfeiffer seated next to him, until morning."[11]

Johann did not try to extinguish his son's creativity; indeed, he looked upon Beethoven's talents as a means of self-glorification. Reports that he rejoiced in his son's accomplishments as a pianist indicate that he sought credit for having fathered such a son. He invited music lovers in Bonn and at court to hear the boy play at his apartment (there was often an admission charge) and in 1778 he presented him in a concert in Cologne.[12] That no further public concerts ensued may be an indication that Beethoven was not then a prodigy of the first rank. This would not be surprising in view of Johann's limitations as a musician and pedagogue. But it seems possible that Johann's goal was to train his son as a competent court musician while simultaneously limiting his attainments so as to prevent Beethoven from surpassing him—which is to say, from rising to the level of his own father. For the gifted young Ludwig may have uncomfortably reminded Johann of the *Kapellmeister*. Perhaps he supervised his son's musical training in a manner calculated to prevent this identification from bearing fruit. (At the same time he may also have been reliving his own childhood experiences and taking the role which his father had assumed toward him.) Perhaps this is why his pedagogy took an unusual turn: Beethoven's first steps toward expression of his genius were manifested in free fantasies, on the violin and clavier, improvisations which were quickly silenced by his father: "Once he was playing without notes; his father happened in and said: 'What silly trash are you scraping away at now? You know that I can't bear that; scrape according to the notes; otherwise your scraping won't be of much use.' "

This was not an isolated incident. "When Johann van Beethoven happened to have visitors and Ludwig came into the room, he was wont to edge up to the piano and play chords with his right hand. Then his father would say: 'More of your fooling around? Go away, or I'll box your ears.' " On another occasion, he was again playing according to his own invention, without notes. "His father said: 'Haven't you heard anything of what I've told you?' He played again, then said to his father: 'Now isn't that beautiful?' Whereupon his father said: 'That is something else, which you made up yourself. You are not to do that yet. . . . I won't have you doing it now, you're not ready for it yet.' "[13]

One wonders when Johann might have considered his son to be ready. Mastery of the art of improvisation was the hallmark of the eighteenth-century virtuoso and composer. At the age of six, Leopold Mozart's son created "utter amazement" with his ability to "improvise for hours on end out of his own head, now *cantabile*, now in chords, producing the best of ideas according to the taste of today."[14] A talent for improvisation manifested itself in Beethoven, too, during his first decade; his father, however, clearly opposed his son's attempts to stray from the narrow path which he had set for him.

It would be natural for a child, in confusion and despair over so tangled a relationship with his father, to turn to his mother for solace and love. However, it is nowhere recorded that Maria Magdalena protested her husband's treatment of her eldest son. (We may surmise that Johann insisted that his harsh methods were merely good pedagogy.) Furthermore, there are indications that her care for her son was insufficient to offset the negative implications of her husband's actions. Thayer found contemporary reports implying "that the mother's care in externals was not always of the best;"[15] Gottfried Fischer related that the "Beethoven children were not delicately brought up; they were often left with the maids."[16] And Cäcilia Fischer confirmed that Beethoven was "often dirty and negligent."[17] The only anecdote of Beethoven's childhood expressive of his mother's love for him dates from their 1781–82 trip to Rotterdam; Maria Magdalena told Frau Karth that during a cold spell en route she "had to hold his feet in her lap to prevent them from being frostbitten."[18] As we will see in a later chapter, Beethoven's difficulties in establishing a love relationship with a woman, as well as his tendencies toward misogyny, may have had their origin in his unsatisfying relationship with his mother.

In later years, Beethoven shrouded his first decade in a veil of silence. Schindler wrote: "Beethoven himself as a rule did not speak of his early youth, and when he did he seemed uncertain and confused."[19] At the same time, he protected himself from his memories of childhood trauma by repeated expressions of love and respect for his mother, and avoidance of derogatory remarks about his father. All who knew Beethoven agree that he remembered his mother "with filial affection and fervent gratitude" and always referred to her "with love and feeling, calling her often an honest, good-hearted woman."[20] The first preserved letter by Beethoven, dated September 15, 1787, to an acquaintance in Augsburg, surely expresses deep feelings of love for his mother, who had died on July 17: "She was such a good, kind mother to me and indeed my best friend. Oh! who was happier than I, when I could still utter the sweet name of mother and it was heard and answered; and to whom can I say it now? To the dumb likenesses of her which my imagination fashions for me?" [21]

As for his father, we will soon encounter the eruption of Beethoven's rage against Johann in the late 1780s. However, though the material we have bearing on Beethoven's relationship to his father is extremely meager, it is sufficient to indicate the presence of a strong tender strain in the son's attitude. Johann's three sons, led by Beethoven, would go in search of their drunken father and "induce their papa to go quietly home with them"; [22] and Stephan von Breuning saw Beethoven "desperately" intervene with the police to prevent his father's arrest.[23] Ries related that "he spoke seldom and with reluctance" about his father, "but any harsh word by a third person made him angry." [24] And, although he complained about the inadequacy of his early musical training, Beethoven never directly criticized his father.[25] Thayer noted the paucity of references by Beethoven to his father: "The only reference to his . . . father made by Beethoven in all the manuscripts [I] examined . . . , an official document or two excepted, is written in Beethoven's hand upon an unfinished copy of one of Emanuel Bach's cantatas . . . : 'Written down by my dear father.'" [26] It was Beethoven's misfortune that his deep love for his parents apparently called forth few corresponding expressions of love on their part.

We have, then, a matrix of family circumstances, actions, and attitudes which might well have led to permanent disillusionment and despair. It is testimony to Beethoven's strength and resiliency of character that he was able to withstand these stresses. Nevertheless, their effects were readily discernible to all of his contemporaries. Apparently abandoning any hope of establishing warm and loving relationships, Beethoven largely withdrew from the society of his fellows and playmates, and from his parents as well. Gottfried Fischer reports that Beethoven's "happiest hours were those when he was free from the company of his parents, which was seldom the case—when all the family were away and he was alone by himself." [27] "He remained shy and monosyllabic," wrote W. C. Müller, "because he had little thought of communication with others." [28] Mäurer also noticed the early signs of withdrawal in Beethoven, who "remained indifferent to all praise, retreated, and practiced best when he was alone, when his father was not at home." [29] Thayer, summarizing his researches among Beethoven's schoolmates, wrote: "Of those who were his schoolfellows and who in after years recorded their reminiscences of him, not one speaks of him as a playfellow, none has anecdotes to relate of games with him, rambles on the hills, or adventures upon the Rhine and its shores in which he bore a part." [30]

Even the most withdrawn child, of course, has his bright moments: we hear a few pathetic tales of young Beethoven stealing Frau Fischer's chicken eggs and a neighbor's hen, or reacting with excitement to piggy-back rides by his cousins. But essentially his was a lonely, withdrawn childhood. Mäurer described him in the year 1780: "Outside of music he understood nothing of social life; consequently he was ill-humored with other people, did not know how to converse with them, and withdrew into himself, so that he was looked upon as a misanthrope." [31] His schoolmates recalled him as isolated and neglected. Electoral Councillor Würzer, who attended public school (the Bonn *Tirocinium*) with him in the 1770s, wrote these devastating words in his memoirs: "Apparently his mother was already dead at the time, for Luis v. B. was distinguished by uncleanliness, negligence, etc." [32] It is possible that Beethoven's unclean and uncared-for appearance was a mute cry for help, an expression of an anguish which he could not express in words.

Another distress signal was his inability to make progress at school. (Most unusual was his lifelong inability to learn arithmetic beyond addition.) Funck, another classmate at the *Tirocinium*, wrote bluntly: "What was striking about Louis, to which I can testify, is that he learned absolutely nothing in school." [33] The Fischers remember Johann saying that Beethoven "wasn't learning very much in school." [34] And Wurzer marveled that "not a sign was to be discovered in him of that spark of genius which glowed so brilliantly in him afterwards." [35]

Now, the child of genius or potential genius is inevitably said to be a lonely child, for "he is a child who senses his own difference [and] feels isolated and inferior thereby." [36] In his second decade, strengthened by the constantly growing consciousness of his creative powers, Beethoven emerged from his isolation, with the assistance of teachers and patrons. In the 1770s, however, when his creativity itself and his emotional survival were at stake, he seems to have found sustenance in fantasy. Cäcilia Fischer recalled Beethoven "leaning in the window with his head in both hands and staring fixedly at one spot." He said: "I was just occupied with such a lovely deep thought, I couldn't bear to be disturbed." [37] In the attic of the Fischer house on the Bonngasse were two telescopes, with which one could see twenty miles. It was Beethoven's delight to seclude himself in the attic and look out across the Rhine toward the Seven Mountains.

The center of Beethoven's fantasy life, however, was his music, which occupied virtually all his waking hours. School and friendship counted for little compared with the gratification and sense of accomplishment which he received from his playing. He told his student, Carl Czerny, that he practiced "prodigiously," usually until well past midnight, perfecting the technique which was to mark him as one of the outstanding keyboard virtuosos of his day, testing and expanding his improvisatory powers, giving expression in his solitude to his luxuriant musical imagination, tapping creative currents which must have stirred their originator as deeply as they did his listeners in later years. He hungered for instruction and sought it outside his home. Court organist Gilles van den Eeden (ca. 1710–82) taught him briefly (perhaps in composition as well) in the late 1770s; according to tradition, he had organ lessons from Friar Willibald Koch and from Zenser, organist of the Münsterkirche. Van den Eeden is said to have sent the boy to play organ at High Mass, and one Pater Hanzmann arranged for him to play at six o'clock morning Mass at the cloister of the Minorites. Nor were his musical interests limited to the keyboard: he had lessons on violin from his relative Franz Rovantini and, later, from Franz Ries; later, too, he studied horn with Nikolaus Simrock.

With the aid of his music, Beethoven had wrapped himself in a protective cloak of his own daydreams. Freud writes that "unsatisfied wishes are the driving power behind fantasies; every separate fantasy contains the fulfillment of a wish, and improves on unsatisfactory reality." [38] And Beethoven's reality paled in comparison with his ideal world. When Cäcilia Fischer reproached him: "How dirty you are again—you ought to keep yourself clean," he replied: "What's the difference—when I become a Lord no one will pay that any mind." [39] We seem to be in the presence of a fantasy life of rich and unusual dimensions.

Under ordinary circumstances, the topography of this fantasy life could not be mapped. However, Beethoven left us several trails to his psychic interior in his birth-year delusion and in his refusal to deny the reports of his royal parentage. Perhaps we are now in a position to offer several highly tentative interpretations of these matters.

In the fantasy which Freud and Otto Rank named the "Family Romance," the child replaces one or both of his parents with elevated surrogates— heroes, celebrities, kings, or nobles.[40] Freud found that this fantasy, which is universal in myth, religion, fairy-tale, and imaginative fiction, was widespread in the daydreams of ordinary people, and appeared in a more intense and enduring form among the creative and the talented.[41] Usually it is a fantasy which arises during childhood or adolescence and thereafter recedes into an amnesia, from which it can be recovered only by analysis. With Beethoven it if anything gained in strength and tenacity as he grew to maturity. But its roots were in the conditions of his childhood.

In Beethoven's Family Romance, as with many others, only the father is replaced by an elevated substitute, while the mother is retained. This is so for several reasons, but primarily because the identity of the mother is, as a rule, readily ascertainable, whereas, as Bachofen wrote, "the father as begetter presents an entirely different aspect. Standing in no visible relation to the child, he can never, even in the marital relation, cast off a certain fictive character." [42] *Pater semper incertus est.* Or, in Telemachus's words to Athene, which Beethoven underscored in his copy of *The Odyssey* and transcribed on another occasion.

> My mother saith that he is my father;
> For myself I know it not,
> For no man knoweth who hath begotten him.[43]

For this reason, the Family Romance fantasy may readily be implanted in a child by his mother, especially by one who is dissatisfied in marriage, who demeans her husband in the presence of the child, and who feels that she deserved a more worthy mate. Maria Magdalena's frequent, and justified, complaints about Johann's alcoholism and ineffectuality may well have had an unexpected effect upon her son. Moreover (perhaps without malice, for sorrow was her *métier*), each time she lauded her father-in-law's qualities and accomplishments, she was by contrast criticizing Johann, baring his inadequacies as a father and a husband. At some point her son may have come to feel: "Another man was (or should have been) my father," ultimately leading to Johann's indeed being supplanted as the father in Beethoven's inner world. For the denial that Johann van Beethoven was his real father is the central "fact" in Beethoven's Family Romance.

The ramifications of the Family Romance are extremely tangled, and its possible meanings cannot be exhausted. The father is at once slain and elevated; the mother is retained, raised to the rank of king's mistress, but simultaneously degraded for her infidelity. The father may be removed in order to give the child access to the mother; siblings may be illegitimized to assuage incestuous impulses. The Family Romance permits the imaginary seizure of parental power, a seizure which we will encounter on more than one occasion in Beethoven's later life. Patricidal implications are on the surface: the Family Romance neutralizes the father's power by setting a more powerful figure in his place. At the same time it relieves guilt at the death of the father. ("The man whose death I desired was not my father; it was a stranger who was slain.") In a sense, Beethoven had split his father into real and illusory images, suppressing the all-too-painful knowledge of his father as wastrel, second-rate musician, toady, probable informer and police agent, drunkard, inadequate provider, and hapless extortionist and resurrecting him as a noble or royal figure. In the recesses of Beethoven's mind, his real father vied for supremacy with his desired, ideal father.

Beethoven was forced to carry a multiple burden, consisting of not only the patterns of father rejection which his mother's attitudes and his father's actions had instilled in him, but a matrix of negative feelings toward his mother as well, for splitting him from his father and causing him to participate in Johann's downfall. Yet he could not identify with his father, for this would have entailed, in addition to a rejection of his grandfather's example and his mother's precepts, the suppression of his genius. (Otto Rank wrote: "There seems to be a certain necessity for the prophet to deny his parents." [44]) Surely, as he began to grow up, Beethoven must have wondered about the disparity between his own creative gifts and his father's mediocrity. Perhaps this is why he underlined a meaningful passage in the *Odyssey:*

> Few sons are like
> Their fathers; most are worse, a very few
> Excel their fathers.[45]

The creative genius finds it difficult to reconcile his gifts with his parentage. He is imbued with a sense of his "superiority" over others, even over those who gave him life. This may lead him toward a narcissistic self-sufficiency, a feeling of omnipotent self-creation; or it may result in fantasies that he was begotten by more suitable—noble, royal, even divine—parents. The fantasy of royal descent satisfied Beethoven's passion for grandeur, his hunger for greatness.

Let us consider the simplest, the most touching, and, I believe, the deepest level of Beethoven's Family Romance: the fantasy that he was an illegitimate child. Beethoven's Family Romance was fed by, and perhaps had its origin in, his birth-year delusion. This, too, was a fantasy of illegitimacy. Let us recall the confusion concerning his birth year and particularly the widespread belief that he was born in December 1771. Beethoven's difficulty was this: if he was born in December 1771 at the earliest, then the certificate documenting the baptism of a Ludwig van Beethoven on December 17, 1770, must have belonged, as in fact he insisted it did, to his older brother, Ludwig Maria. And if this were the case, Beethoven's own, "true" baptismal certificate had disappeared from the archives. It could not be found by Beethoven or by any of his friends—Wegeler, Ries, Müller—all of whom had procured copies of the "wrong" certificate. Therefore, his own baptismal certificate—the evidence of his birth and the proof of his parentage—either never existed or had been concealed or destroyed. What (he thought) could have been the reason for this mysterious suppression of the facts of his birth?

Following from this, other crucial questions arose, focusing, superficially, on the mystery of his correct age, but in fact, and more poignantly, centering on the impenetrable secret: "Who is my real father?" The text of what was perhaps Beethoven's first song, "An einen Säugling" [To an infant], WoO 108,* written when he was but twelve years old, holds out the hope of an answer:

---

* WoO is an abbreviation for "work without opus number," according to the numerical listing of such works in the standard catalog of Beethoven's completed compositions by Kinsky and Halm (see bibliography).

You still do not know whose child you are. You do not know who prepares the swaddling clothes, who it is that warms you and gives you milk. You grow in peace nevertheless. Within a few years, among all those who have cared for you, you will learn to distinguish your mother. Nonetheless there is some occult giver who cares for all of us—our thanks go to him—with food and drink. My dim intelligence does not yet comprehend this; but after the years have gone by, if I am pious and a believer, even he will be revealed.

From here it was but a short step to the Family Romance fantasy.

The fantasy can take deep root, however, only when the child is (or imagines himself to be) neglected, maltreated, and unloved. The rarely assuaged, tragic family circumstances of his youth placed Beethoven's personal "golden age" not in his earliest childhood but in the period before he was born, immediately after the marriage of his parents in 1767 and up to the death of their first son, Ludwig Maria. "What is marriage?" his mother asked, as Beethoven overheard: "A little joy, and then a chain of sorrows." Surrounded by sadness, withdrawing into isolation and daydreaming, Ludwig van Beethoven may have inwardly felt that the first link in that chain of sorrows was forged at the time of his own conception and birth. He looked back in anguish to an Eden which he could not reach except by sharing the identity of his more favored older brother.

Ultimately, Beethoven's Family Romance signified his belief that he was the "false" son, who could never take the place of his dead brother. His fantasy of ennoblement was not merely the assertion of a desired nobility, or the delusory rejection of his humble parents, but, most of all, the admission of a pathetic longing to have been the first-born, who was mourned but not forgotten by his parents. All of his fantasies, then, may have a single, transparent source: they may be the expression, denial, and symbolic transcendence of the feeling that he was unloved and unwanted. They are the rectification of a presumed illegitimacy. They are the heartfelt—and unanswered—cry of a child for his parents' love.

Beethoven. Silhouette by Joseph
Neesen (ca. 1786).

3
Beethoven's Second Decade

At the beginning of his second decade, Beethoven's career as a musician began to establish itself. Though he was not to be a prodigy like Mozart, at a respectably early age he was seen to be an able young professional. He took great pride in his new status. The Fischers describe him when he "came forward as a composer and . . . organist, and in token of rank wore a sword on his left side when he went up to the rood loft in the court church with his father." No longer unkempt and ill-clothed, he wore the gala dress of the court musician: "Sea-green frock coat, green knee breeches with buckles, stockings of white or black silk, shoes with black bowknots, embroidered vest with pocket flaps, the vest bound with real gold cord, hair curled and with queue, crush hat under the left arm, sword on the left side with silver belt." [1]

Beethoven was now engaged in the work of the world and was seeking a firmly delineated niche in his community, hoping to establish for himself a determinate place in society. A new sense of his inner worth was a necessary precondition for this process. Indeed, it was of this time that Fischer reported that Beethoven "now believed himself to be the equal of his father in music." [2] The relationship between father and son was undergoing a realignment. We find here the final separation of Beethoven's musical education from his father's supervision as well as the beginning of his training in composition. Shortly thereafter, Beethoven's musical abilities expanded to the point where he became assistant court organist (without salary) in 1782 and "cembalist in the orchestra" in 1783. In June 1784 he received an official appointment as deputy court organist, at a salary of 150 florins. These events mark the end of Beethoven's childhood and the beginning of his "first period" as a composer.

The pivotal figure in this transition was Christian Gottlob Neefe (1748–98), the German composer, organist, and conductor, who came to Bonn in October 1779 to join the Grossman and Helmuth theatrical company and was named successor to van den Eeden as court organist on February 15, 1781. He became Beethoven's composition instructor in 1780 or 1781 and remained his only significant teacher until Beethoven left Bonn in November 1792.

Neefe at once recognized and encouraged Beethoven's genius and provided him with his earliest professional experience. He trained him as assistant court organist and left him temporarily in full charge as early as June 1782; shortly thereafter he turned over to his twelve-year-old student his position as "cembalist," which involved direction of the orchestra from the keyboard and playing at sight from the score. Furthermore, and indicative of the quality of his concern for the young composer, he arranged for publication of Beethoven's early works, and he wrote the first public notice about him, a communication of March 2, 1783, to Cramer's *Magazin der Musik*:

> Louis van Betthoven [sic.], . . . a boy of eleven years and of most promising talent. He plays the clavier very skillfully and with power, reads at sight very well, and—to put it in a nutshell—he plays chiefly *The Well-Tempered Clavichord* of Sebastian Bach, which Herr Neefe put into his hands. Whoever knows this collection of preludes and fugues in all the keys—which might almost be called the *non plus ultra* of our art—will know what this means. So far as his duties permitted, Herr Neefe has also given him instruction in thoroughbass. He is now training him in composition and for his encouragement has had nine variations for the pianoforte, written by him on a march—by Ernst Christoph Dressler—engraved at Mannheim. This youthful genius is deserving of help to enable him to travel. He would surely become a second Wolfgang Amadeus Mozart were he to continue as he has begun. [3]

Beethoven wrote appreciatively (if rather stiffly) to Neefe from Vienna in 1793: "I thank you for the advice you have very often given me about making progress in my divine art. Should I ever become a great man, you too will have a share in my success." [4] Clearly, Neefe hoped to be associated with the discovery of a second Mozart; and, in fact, his lasting fame partly rests on his tutelage of Beethoven.[5] Whatever his motivations, Neefe's teaching and encouragement provided the springboard for Beethoven's rapid development in the early 1780s. Moreover, by virtue of his own intellectual background and moral code Neefe was someone whom Beethoven could look up to, and even emulate, at this critical juncture of his life. During his Leipzig years, Neefe had been drawn toward the German *Sturm und Drang* movement, to Gellert, Klopstock, and the young Goethe; and he became sympathetic to the ideals of the German Enlightenment (*Aufklärung*) as well. In Bonn, he was a leader of the Order of Illuminati, which was closely related to the Masonic movement. Although there is no direct evidence of his influence on Beethoven's subsequent attraction to Enlightenment literature and ideals, it is probable that it was at least partially through Neefe that Beethoven first made their acquaintance.

Neefe's ethical outlook was evidently shaped by his own early conflicts with his father, who wished his son to follow him in the legal profession. It was as a student of jurisprudence that he enrolled in 1769 at the University of Leipzig, where he was ridden with hypochondria and thoughts of suicide. His dissertation was, transparently, devoted to the question of whether a father could disinherit a son who wanted to enter the theater.[6] Neefe opted for the negative on this issue, and turned from law to music in 1771. His moral code, as revealed in his *Autobiography*,[7] was marked by a striving for ethical perfection and for the suppression of sensual desire through sublimated activity. Clearly, Beethoven had found a kindred spirit and a moral mentor in Neefe, whose puritanical presence and ethical imperatives were a superb counterbalance to the behavior and character of Johann van Beethoven.

Beethoven's first known compositions were produced under Neefe's guidance. From 1782 to 1785 his works include a set of Variations on a March by Dressler, WoO 63 (1782); three Sonatas for Piano dedicated to Elector Max Friedrich, WoO 47 (1782–83); a Piano Concerto in E-flat major, WoO 4 (1784); three Quartets for Piano and Strings, WoO 36 (1785); as well as several songs and small keyboard works. The variations, sonatas, and *Lieder* were quickly published, with attention pointedly drawn to his tender age. He was a young would-be prodigy, industriously applying himself to a composer's vocation.

Until recently, it was believed that his progress as a composer continued uninterruptedly throughout these early years. However, the fact of the matter is that past the compositions already mentioned, the dates of Beethoven's Bonn compositions are very inexactly known. A cold look at the evidence reveals that not a single one of the thirty-odd later Bonn pieces can with certainty be placed in these middle years.[8] All the facts suggest that Beethoven composed at most a handful of small works and one more-extended composition in a period of about four years after 1785. He resumed composition with renewed seriousness and a high level of productivity only as he was entering his twentieth year, in late 1789 or early 1790.

The discovery of this compositional hiatus helps to answer a number of questions about the graph of Beethoven's productivity and perhaps explains why his grasp of the techniques of composition was insufficient until a rather advanced age, so that he found it obligatory to study counterpoint after his arrival in late 1792 in Vienna, where it took the combined efforts of a number of teachers to ground him in the rudiments of the art. The hiatus itself, however, which delayed his development as a composer during the crucial adolescent years, remains unexplained.

External factors surely played some role. Beethoven's first publications evidently failed to create sufficient interest to warrant the assumption that he would emerge as a major composer. A devastating contemporary notice in Forkel's *Musikalischer Almanach* of 1784 unfavorably compared several of Beethoven's first publications with the work of beginning students (". . . perhaps could be respected as the first attempts of a beginner in music, like an exercise by a third- or fourth-form student in our schools").[9] By the time the three piano quartets were completed in 1785, it is possible that Beethoven's sponsors had given up hope of creating a prodigy of Mozartian proportions; perhaps this is one reason why the quartets remained unpublished. In fact, it is noteworthy that from 1784 until his departure from Bonn, there was only one publication —in 1791—of a Beethoven work.[10] The successive deaths of Elector Max Friedrich and Minister von Belderbusch in 1784 deprived the young composer of those who undoubtedly had been his most powerful friends at Bonn. A mid-1784 report to the new elector, Max Franz, does not even refer to Beethoven as a composer, but merely as a young keyboard player of "good capability."[11] Beethoven had lost much ground at the electoral court.

Moreover, his relationship with Neefe may well have gone through something of a crisis in mid-1784. As a foreigner, a radical, and a Protestant, Neefe was considered dispensable, and efforts were made to effect economies by replacing him with Beethoven. Neefe's wages were, in fact, halved in June; as Forbes noted, Beethoven's first payments "had clearly been taken out of the salary of his teacher."[12] The matter was resolved in early 1785, however, with the restoration of Neefe's full salary.

The catastrophes which enveloped Beethoven's family during the second half of the 1780s did increase Beethoven's responsibilities as financial provider and virtual head of the family; moreover, he was occupied with multiple activities as court musician and as teacher. From 1788, he had additional duties as violist in the court and theater orchestras.

But it was not the pressure of these activities that barred composition; Beethoven found much time for leisure, social contact, and entertainment during precisely this period. And in the subsequent, very productive years of 1790–92 he found it possible to combine essentially identical duties as court musician and family provider with a very respectable output as a composer.

Beethoven's abandonment of composition, then, cannot in the main be attributed to external circumstances. Perhaps this was a necessary moratorium, permitting Beethoven's creative powers to lie fallow for a while; his career contains several such "silent" periods, which were followed by heightened creativity. His withdrawal from composition, however, inevitably carried overtones of defeat. And these implications were reinforced by the failure of Beethoven's journey to Vienna in the spring of 1787. It is thought that he was sent there by the elector to enable the Viennese to hear and judge a promising Bonn pianist, and perhaps to play for (or even to take lessons from) Mozart. But his stay lasted not more than two weeks, for almost immediately following his arrival in early April his father notified him that his mother's consumptive condition had worsened and requested that he return to Bonn at once. Beethoven immediately set out; yet even as he was on his way home his father urged him on: ". . . the nearer I came to my native town, the more frequently did I receive from my father letters urging me to travel more quickly than usual, because my mother was not in very good health. So I made as much haste as I could." [13] He had not remained in Vienna long enough to accomplish his purpose, and he did not return there after his mother's death to take up where he had left off. The trip to Vienna, as the elector later pointed out to Haydn, was a total failure, with Beethoven bringing back "nothing but debts." [14]

These events would have been sufficient to wound the self-esteem of any adolescent. The death of his mother in July, followed by that of his baby sister in November, was of a different order: these losses and the ensuing mourning process may well have blocked Beethoven's creative development and contributed to the prolongation of his moratorium. Moreover, his mother's death had the effect of placing Beethoven in charge of the family, a responsibility that soon became a restrictive factor in his development.

After a parent's death, the child's relationship to the surviving parent usually undergoes a radical change, and often there is a desperate, pathetic attempt by the survivors to put the child in the place of the missing parent. It was now Beethoven rather than Maria Magdalena who was in charge of the family finances, Beethoven who suffered the full consequences of Johann's alcoholism, Beethoven who had to intervene with the police to prevent his father from being taken into custody. Events had combined to compel Johann van Beethoven's eldest son to

assume the role which first the *Kapellmeister* and then Maria Magdalena had played in relation to Johann throughout his childhood and
manhood. Beethoven became his father's guardian, thus restoring the
infantile relationship of domination and care from which Johann had
never been able to free himself.

During these last years, Johann van Beethoven largely gave up his
grip upon reality and abandoned himself to a narcotized existence.
Nevertheless, he was now able to exercise an even more profound control over his son's life, based upon his ability to manipulate Beethoven's
sense of pity and guilt, which apparently grew as Johann's fortunes declined. In fact, it seems that Johann's strength lay in his very weakness,
in his ability to compel others—successively his father, his wife, and his
eldest son—to rescue him from himself. He had become Anchises on the
back of Aeneas. (Ernest Simmel wrote of the alcoholic that "by his
alcoholism he tortures those who care for him. . . . His addiction is
chronic murder and chronic suicide." [15]) In this case, of course, Johann's
weight would ultimately become insupportable. Beethoven would have
to set aside the parasitical father whom he simultaneously loved and
despised, who had transformed him into a surrogate wife and father, and
who was preventing him from achieving fulfillment as a composer and
as a man.

The turning point in this poignant entanglement occurred in late 1789,
when Beethoven addressed a petition to the elector asking that half his
father's salary be paid to him, and evidently requesting that his father
be retired from service and perhaps exiled from Bonn as well. Beethoven's petition has disappeared, but the answering decree of November
20, 1789, survives:

> His electoral Highness having graciously granted the prayer of the pe-
> titioner and dispensed henceforth wholly with the services of his father,
> who is to withdraw to a village in the electorate, it is graciously com-
> manded that he be paid in accordance with his wish only 100 rthr.
> [Rheinthalers] of the annual salary which he has had heretofore, begin-
> ning with the approaching new year, and that the other 100 thlr.
> [thalers] be paid to the supplicating son, besides the salary which he now
> draws and the three measures of grain for the support of his brothers.[16]

Thayer refers to Beethoven's petition as "the extraordinary step of placing himself at the head of the family." [17] Actually, that step had been
taken long before. Now he was attempting to free himself from a para-
lyzing embrace.

In order for the decree to become effective, Beethoven was to present the document to the elector's Inland Revenue Office and Exchequer
(*Landrentmeisterei*). He did not do this during his father's lifetime, be-

cause, as Beethoven wrote in a petition to the elector in the spring of 1793, "my father earnestly besought me not to do this, lest he should be publicly regarded as incapable of supporting his family by his own efforts. He added that he himself would pay me the 25 Rhein-thalers every quarter; and this was always punctually done." [18] Beethoven's 1789 petition had clearly been warranted by circumstances; but he was incapable of fully carrying through the action, perhaps because of its patricidal implications. It is a measure of his devotion to his father (and of his inner strength) that Beethoven granted Johann's plea that he be permitted to retain a fragment of personal dignity.

That Beethoven was ridden with conflicts concerning this momentous event in his life is shown by the remainder of his 1793 petition to the elector. It is the only record we have of Beethoven's reaction to his father's death:

MOST WORTHY AND MOST EXCELLENT ELECTOR:
  MOST GRACIOUS LORD!

A few years ago Your Electoral Excellency was pleased to retire my father, the court tenor van Beethoven, and by a most gracious decree to allow me out of his salary 100 Reichsthalers so as to enable me to have my two younger brothers clothed, fed, and educated and also to discharge the debts which our father had incurred. . . .

After his death, which took place in December of last year, I wanted to avail myself of your most precious favor by presenting the afore-mentioned most gracious decree. I was horrified, however, to find that he had suppressed it.

Hence with the most dutiful reverence I beg Your Excellency graciously to renew this decree and also to instruct Your Excellency's *Landrentmeisterei* to send me the previous quarterly amount which fell due at the beginning of February.

> Your Electoral Excellency's
> most humble and most faithfully
> obedient
> LUDWIG VAN BEETHOVEN,
> Court Organist [19]

It is striking that here, as in Johann's petition to the elector of January 1774, in which he had asserted his ability to take his father's place as *Kapellmeister*, there is not the slightest hint of filial piety, let alone of grief. Instead, Beethoven expresses his "horror" that his father had done away with the electoral decree. This does not mean that Beethoven did not love his father. In earlier years, he had gathered pleasure from summer journeys with his father visiting music lovers in the Rhine country-side. In later years, he had favored his father with the opportunity to bask in the reflection of his son's abilities, permitting him to realize

vicariously some of his own frustrated ambitions, and listening with un-
doubted embarrassment to the sentimental and drunken cadences in
which Johann boasted: "My son Ludwig, he is now my only joy, he has
become so accomplished in music and composition that he is looked
upon with wonder by everyone. My Ludwig, my Ludwig, I foresee that
he will in time become a great man in the world." [20]

It was not the absence of love which prevented Beethoven from revealing either his grief or his love; rather, I believe that it was his
inability to complete the process of mourning so necessary in freeing an
individual from his emotional ties to a lost loved one. As Helene Deutsch
has written: "As long as the early libidinal or aggressive attachments
persist, the painful affect continues to flourish, and vice versa, the attachments are unresolved as long as the affective process of mourning has
not been accomplished." [21] We will have occasion to observe that the
inability to verbalize his sense of loss at the deaths of those he loved—such
as certain of his patrons, friends, and teachers—was characteristic of
Beethoven throughout his life.

Be that as it may, the audacious petition of 1789 coincided with the
liberation of Beethoven's creative force as a composer. The period of his
suppressed creativity was over. A sudden and sustained burst of activity
began around late 1789 or in the first months of 1790 and continued
until Beethoven's departure for Vienna in November 1792. Among the
many works composed in this period were four or five sets of piano
variations (WoO 64, WoO 65, WoO 66, WoO 67, and perhaps WoO 40
as well); two full-scale cantatas (WoO 87 and WoO 88); incidental music
for a ballet (WoO 1); a number of works for piano solo and for various combinations of wind instruments; and a piano trio (WoO 38),
along with other chamber music, several concert arias, and a substantial
number of songs, including almost all of the eight *Lieder* which were
published in 1805 as opus 52.

Simultaneously, we begin to find, after 1790, Beethoven's first glowing
notices as an interpreter and improviser on the keyboard. In 1791, he
improvised with great effect for the famous pianist, Abbé Sterkel; later
in the year, a report by Carl Junker in an important contemporary
journal, Bossler's *Musikalische Correspondenz*, described the high esteem
in which Beethoven was held: "I heard also one of the greatest of
pianists—the dear, good Bethofen. . . . Even the members of this remarkable orchestra are, without exception, his admirers, and all ears
when he plays." [22]

Beethoven's emergence from the relative obscurity of the court orchestra and his resumption of composition occurred, therefore, at approximately the same time. His long creative pause was at an end.

Maximilian Franz, elector of Cologne.

4
Last Years in Bonn: Enlightenment

Germany in the eighteenth century was loosely organized into a multiplicity of small feudal territories and dominions, the so-called *Kleinstaaterei*, ruled by hundreds of lesser and greater sovereigns. This splintered, motley, decaying confederation consisted of nearly 300 territories, which orbited around the twin centers of Berlin and Vienna. Bonn, which housed the court of the elector of Cologne, owed its allegiance to Vienna, seat of the Holy Roman Empire and headquarters of the Habsburg monarchy. Bonn's prince electors were simultaneously the ecclesiastical and secular rulers of the small territory on the Rhine, bordering France. A contemporary traveler, Baron Caspar Riesbeck, described Bonn in 1780 as "the largest and handsomest town betwixt Coblentz and Cologne." [1] As for its political and cultural life, he reported: "The present government of the archbishoprick of Cologne and the bishoprick of Münster is without a doubt the most active and most enlightened of all the ecclesiastical governments of Germany. The ministry of the court of Bonn is excellently composed.... The cabinet of Bonn is singularly happy in the establishment of seminaries of education, the improvement of agriculture and industry, and the extirpation of every species of monkery." [2] Riesbeck was writing of the Bonn of Maximilian Friedrich, who was elector from 1761 until his death in 1784. Under his rule the Jesuits were suppressed (1774), an academy was founded (1777), and despite the harsh economies of Minister von Belderbusch in so many areas, cultural activities, especially theater and opera, flourished. There was a remarkably broad dissemination of Enlightened literature and thought in Bonn. Booksellers in the 1770s and 1780s sold the latest editions of the works of Rousseau and Montesquieu alongside the writings of Klopstock, Herder, Schiller, and Goethe.

But it was under the rule of Elector Maximilian Franz, which began in 1784, that the ideas of the Enlightenment virtually became the official principles of the electorate. Max Franz's regime was the reflection in Bonn of the attitudes and ideology of his brother Emperor Joseph II, a follower of Voltaire, Frederick the Great, and the encyclopedists. Upon the death of his mother, Empress Maria Theresa, in 1780, Joseph launched a headlong and unparalleled program of internal reform which included steps towards the emancipation of the serfs, the spread of education, secularization of church lands, tax and juridical reforms, and the founding of numerous charitable institutions. It was a program which brought him into conflict with the high clergy and segments of the nobility as well as with neighboring states and sovereigns; and ultimately, in 1790, major portions of his reforms were retracted, although the land reforms remained relatively intact. Riesbeck noted that Joseph's "principles of government [were] as republican as those of most of the states who at this day call themselves republics." [3] The historian A. J. P. Taylor calls his work "an astonishing achievement of Enlightened philosophy, witness to the force of the Imperial structure"; but he also remarks that "his revolutionary policy did not have the support of a revolutionary class. . . . His aim could be completed only by revolution; and revolution would destroy the dynasty." [4]

In Bonn, Max Franz tried to keep pace with Viennese developments, and enlarged the scope of intellectual freedom in his tiny electorate. Wilhelm von Humboldt, a distinguished scholar who visited Bonn in October 1788, noted that the court library contained "the best periodical writings as well as learned and political newspapers and books." [5] Of great significance was the decree of August 9, 1785, raising the Bonn academy to the rank of university—a university at which Kantian philosophy was taught by van der Schüren and Johannes Neeb, and at which such men as the revolutionary Eulogius Schneider and Schiller's friend Bartholomäus Ludwig Fischenich lectured on Greek literature and on natural and human rights, respectively.

Despite the receptivity to Enlightenment ideas, advanced and radical thinkers were constantly on the alert for signs of repression. A Freemason's lodge had been founded in 1776 but it soon disappeared, perhaps because Maria Theresa had suppressed Freemasonry within the Austrian territories.[6] Its place was taken by a secret, anticlerical Order of Illuminati, founded in 1781, which combined Enlightened notions of "progress through reason" with quasi-Masonic ritual. Its members included many who were associated with Beethoven: Neefe, Nikolaus Simrock, Franz Ries, von Schall, Johann Peter Eichhoff, Johann Joseph Eichhoff.[7] Neefe was one of the leaders of the group (its *Lokaloberer*), which published its own weekly newspaper beginning in April 1784. The order was uncovered and suppressed in Bavaria—its headquarters— in 1784–85, and the Bonn Illuminati, fearing a prohibition, dissolved their group in favor of a less dangerous forum, the *Lese-Gesellschaft* (Reading Society), which was founded in 1787 by thirteen "friends of literature," who included most of the former Illuminati.[8] Soon its membership numbered 100, including Neefe, Eichhoff, Ries, Count Waldstein, Malchus, Schneider, and other associates and friends of Beethoven.

Ultimately, as we know, the representatives of Enlightened thought were hounded in and out of the capitals of anti-Napoleonic Europe by many of the former adherents of Enlightened despotism. In the later 1780s, however, there were few hints of future repression, nor were there premonitions that the dissolution of the electorate itself would take place in 1794, following the occupation of the Rhineland by the French armies.

It was within this atmosphere that Beethoven's social and cultural attitudes took shape. He adopted as his own the leading principles of the European Enlightenment under conditions in which it was unnecessary for him to step outside of society as rebel or apostate. As far as we know, his behavior at Bonn was that of an exemplary young court musician, a dutiful servant of the electorate. An official report of 1784 described him from the court's viewpoint as being "of good capability" and "of good and quiet deportment." [9] There is no recorded instance of his dissatisfaction with or rebellion against the requirements of Bonn's feudal aristocratic patronage. Perhaps he was grateful to the court, which acted favorably on his various petitions for partial amelioration of his family's financial situation. (As late as 1801, long after he had left the court's service, Beethoven intended to dedicate a major work, his First Symphony, to Max Franz.) It was surely a mark of extreme favor that the elector twice underwrote Beethoven's journeys to Vienna; from afar he observed his court organist's progress with a nice mixture of concern and irony. The elector's "favorite and constant companion," [10] Count Ferdinand Waldstein (1762–1823), who arrived in Bonn in 1788, also became Beethoven's patron, and was the first to link his name with those of Mozart and Haydn.

Beethoven's daily routine reflected his conformity to an exemplary standard. In addition to fulfilling his family responsibilities and court duties he gave lessons to augment the family income, suppressing to some degree what Wegeler calls his "extraordinary aversion" to teaching.[11] In overcoming this aversion, he had the assistance of the widowed Frau Helene von Breuning, to whom he clearly seems to have turned as a mother surrogate in these years. She knew, said Beethoven, "how to keep the insects away from the blossoms"—that is, explains Schindler, how to protect him from "fawning flattery" and from his own tendencies toward vanity.[12] She possessed the power, as Thayer wrote with such approval, to "compel him to the performance of his duties."[13]

It is a striking fact that in later years Beethoven repeatedly recalled his dedication to virtue as emanating from his childhood. Thus: "From my earliest childhood my zeal to serve our poor suffering humanity in any way whatsoever by means of my art has made no compromise with any lower motive."[14] Or: "Since I was a child my greatest happiness and pleasure have been to be able to do something for others."[15] Finally: "*Never, never* will you find me dishonorable. Since my childhood I have learnt to love virtue—and everything beautiful and good."[16] It would appear, then, that virtue and service to humanity became Beethoven's conscious goals from a very early age.

These private imperatives readily found ideological clothing in the humanistic and virtuous precepts of Enlightened thought. In the later 1780s, Beethoven came into contact with the most distinguished minds of Bonn. His participation in Bonn's intellectual life took place on many levels; the tendency of biographers (following Wegeler, who introduced Beethoven to the Breuning family and who himself married into the family) to ascribe his cultural growth primarily to his relationship with the Breunings is surely exaggerated. Beethoven was in close contact with, although not actually a member of, the *Lese–Gesellschaft;*[17] its commission from Beethoven of a cantata on the death of Emperor Joseph II in 1790 was clearly a sign of his close connection with the society as well as of the high regard in which he was held. In his later years at Bonn, Beethoven spent many of his evenings at the *Zehrgarten,* a tavern with an adjoining bookshop run by the widowed Anna Maria Koch, which was the favorite meeting place for radicals, university professors, and intellectuals of all classes and ages, without regard to rank. And in 1789, together with his close friends Anton Reicha and Karl Kügelgen, he actually enrolled at the university. What lectures he attended and how long his matriculation continued are not known.

This university experience was not to be repeated. Wegeler tells us that when a series of lectures on Kant was organized in Vienna in the 1790s, "Beethoven didn't want to attend even once, even under my urging."[18] Rather, Beethoven preferred self-education through voracious reading in popularizations of the works of the major thinkers; through rich encounters with poetry, drama, and opera; and, most happily, through discourse and conversation with good minds in pleasant sur-roundings—whether in the salon or the tavern, the palace or the coffee-house. In 1809 he wrote to the Leipzig music publisher Breitkopf & Härtel: "There is hardly any treatise which could be too learned *for me*. I have not the slightest pretension to what is properly called erudition. Yet from my childhood I have striven to understand *what the better and wiser people* of every age were driving at in their works." [19] This is no pose, even if the first sentence may be overstated. In the Conversation Books of his last years, he jotted down the titles of scores of books which he wished to buy or consult.

As for his unwillingness to attend lectures on Kant in Vienna, this should not be regarded as minimizing Kant's impact upon Beethoven. Indeed, Kant's impact extended to all of his educated contemporaries. Heine wrote: "In the year 1789 . . . nothing else was talked of in Germany but the philosophy of Kant, about which were poured forth in abundance commentaries, chrestomathies, interpretations, estimates, apologies, and so forth." [20] Beethoven's was, of course, a popularized conception of Kant—one which had no room for Kant's epistemology or his exploration of the faculties of knowledge. Beethoven had no training or aptitude for discussions of the distinctions between the world of phenomena and the world of "noumena"; the Kantian idea of time and space as *a priori* forms of perception was beyond the grasp and probably beyond the interest of the teen-age composer who had never gone past grade school and had been a backward student there. As did most of his contemporaries, Beethoven understood Kant in a sloganized and simplified form; his was the Kant of the "categorical imperative," who wrote in a paraphrase of the "golden rule": "Act so that the maxim of thy action may be a principle of universal legislation"; the Kant of "Two things fill the soul with ever new and increasing wonder and reverence the oftener the mind dwells upon them—the starry sky above me and the moral law within me," which found its way into Beethoven's Conversation Book of February 1820 as "The moral law in us, and the starry sky above us—Kant!!!" [21] Beethoven was surely familiar with the opening words of Kant's preface to *Religion in the Light of Reason Alone:* "So far as morality is based upon the conception of man as a free agent who, just because he is free, binds himself through his reason to unconditioned laws, it stands in need neither of the idea of another Being over him, for him to apprehend his duty, nor of an incentive other than the law itself, for him to do his duty."

We know very little about the nature or extent of Beethoven's re-ligious beliefs during his Bonn years. However, there is no hint that Beethoven at this time was religious, let alone that he practiced the Catholic religion into which he had been born. Apart from neighbor's conventional references to his mother's piety there are no reports that his parents were active Catholics, or that they instilled any of their sons with religious feeling. It seems clear that Enlightened and especially Kantian conceptions of morality served Beethoven and many of his compatriots in Bonn as a substitute theology during this period. True, the external forms of Catholicism were observed at court. But this Enlightened "electoral Catholicism" was really a compromise ideology that permitted a relatively peaceful coexistence between the Church and Enlightened rationalism. Bonn's leading intellectuals and artists were not avowed atheists by any means: Neefe, after a period of youthful questioning, had returned to belief in God; even Eulogius Schneider argued against hierarchical religion not as a disbeliever but as a proponent of a rationalist portrait of Christ in which Jesus is seen as a teacher of mankind. Nevertheless, few intellectuals would acknowledge faith in traditional religion as a revealed faith during this period, or indeed until a variety of neo-Christian forms and beliefs revived in the aftermath of the Napoleonic Wars. As a practical matter, religion was relegated to a subordinate position, and where it was not altogether rejected as inimical to reason, it was viewed as but a special case of the Kantian moral law.

Beethoven's superficial Kantianism and his worship of Schiller were fully consistent with service to the nobility and the court. Even sympathy with the French Revolution (and—apart from his subscription to a volume of Eulogius Schneider's poems—there is no sure sign of such sympathy on Beethoven's part) was not inconsistent with acceptance of the given state of affairs at home. Such men as Schneider, who took up the cause (and fell in the Terror) were rare indeed. Most German intellectuals hailed the Revolution but condemned its consequences. Germany fought its revolutionary battles not in the political arena but on the stage and in the study. Germany's philosophers occupied themselves with the notion of freedom at the very moment that the French were bloodying their streets and their soil in search of the reality of freedom. But this political somnolence was not without its compensations. Marcuse observed that the isolation of the educated classes from practical affairs may have rendered them impotent to reshape their society, but that it simultaneously led to extraordinary achievements in science, art, and philosophy. "Culture," he wrote, "set freedom *of thought* before freedom *of action*, morality before practical justice, the inner life before the social life of man. This idealistic culture, however, just because it stood aloof from an intolerable reality and thereby maintained itself intact and unsullied, served, despite its false consolations and glorifications, as the repository for truths which had not been realized in the history of mankind." [22]

The *Sturm und Drang* movement, which briefly dominated German drama of a somewhat earlier period, had occasionally inveighed against absolutism as such, but as Paul Henry Lang has remarked, "its revolutionary tendencies usually flickered out with the exhaustion of the pathos that engendered them." [23] Beethoven, too, despised tyranny, but he did not visualize—let alone advocate—the abolition of kingship. His reverence for Schiller was primarily for the author of *Die Räuber* and *Don Carlos,* which center upon class and Oedipal conflicts between prince and monarch. Beethoven's Schiller heroes are those princes who struggle with oppressive absolutism as representatives of Enlightened monarchy, whose goal is not conquest but reconciliation. The historical Saint Joan gives way to Schiller's (and Beethoven's) Johanna, who rises from defeat on the battlefield not to face inquisition and immolation, but rather to receive ennoblement by the king, quite in the tradition of Enlightened despotism and archaic wish fulfillment:

> Kneel down! and rise
> A Noble! thy monarch, from the dust
> Of thy mean birth exalts thee.
> (Act III, Scene 4)

And, at bottom, Beethoven's Schiller is the Schiller of "An die Freude," that elevated *Trinklied* of 1785 which so profoundly captured the composer's imagination that he planned to set it to music even before his departure from Bonn. In 1793, Fischenich wrote to Schiller's wife Charlotte: "He intends to compose Schiller's '*Freude*' verse by verse." [24] It was a long way from the conception to the fulfillment of the "Ode to Joy" project, whose musical setting in the Ninth Symphony perhaps represents the clearest statement of Beethoven's desire for harmony and reconciliation.

Utopian currents of the eighteenth century revolved around the idea of a *bon prince,* a wish-fulfilling hero who could dissolve the tangled problems of the relations between masters and men. It was such heroes—represented in German drama by Wallenstein, Karl Moor, Egmont—who bore the accumulated weight of Messianic hopes and strivings. We will meet their counterparts in Beethoven's *Fidelio* and *Egmont,* and perhaps in the symphony which he intended to call *Bonaparte.* Those who shared the hope for a noble savior did not serve the aristocracy as servants did their masters; rather, they wished to preserve aristocratic ideals through the realization of their notion of Enlightened rule. Their desire was to purge society of those elements within the absolutist framework that were base and "ignoble." Even Frederick the Great himself, in his *Considérations sur l'état du corps politique de l'Europe,* insisted upon the necessity for the Enlightened leader to reform the tyrannical princes. (That Frederick's version of the Social Contract did not altogether square with the realities of his own rule is attested to by Lessing, who wrote,

"Let some one appear in Berlin and raise his voice for the rights of the subjects and against exploitation and despotism . . . and you would find out very soon which is the most enslaved country of Europe." [25])

It is of course fitting that the figure of a princely savior should enter Beethoven's music with a cantata composed in 1790 in mournful celebration of Joseph II, the *Aufklärer*/Emperor whose idealized memory was cherished for decades thereafter by many of his subjects. But reliance upon the notion of an aristocratic redeemer remained central to Beethoven's beliefs until his last years—which observation may enable us to understand some of the contradictions in his later political utterances, which embraced Caesaristic formulations along with lofty humanistic statements, apparent support of Napoleon during the Consulate along with glorification of the monarchs assembled at the Congress of Vienna, and condemnation of the restoration of hereditary monarchy under the French Imperium along with his admiration of constitutional monarchy on British lines.[26] We will see later that Beethoven's veneration for ideal Enlightened leaders—be they prince, king, or first consul— is countered by a process of disillusionment with such leaders in reality. In his early years, however, this tendency has yet to make its appearance.

Beethoven had found his place in society and had accepted—probably without question—the current, advanced ideology of his community. Throughout his life he was to be unfailingly guided by a conscious belief in the principles of political liberty, personal excellence, and ethical action. His devotion to art and beauty and his acceptance of the main notions of the Enlightenment—virtue, reason, freedom, progress, universal brotherhood—served, perhaps, to contain the eruptive forces within him that were engendered by the conditions of his childhood and the serious difficulties of his adolescent years.

These forces, however, could not be wholly contained. It seems to be in the nature of adolescence that the personality undergoes a liquefying process, in the course of which the individual strives to discover new creative goals and seeks their realization. Forces previously bound up within the personality structure are liberated, new identifications and interests are formed, and hidden potentialities rise to the surface. At the same time, regressive features may well emerge, and there may be a bewildering dissolution of prior identifications and beliefs. Surely we can make out Beethoven's silhouette, if not his portrait, in Anna Freud's sketch of the mood swings characteristic of the creative adolescent: "the height of elation or depth of despair, the quickly rising enthusiasms, the utter hopelessness, the burning . . . intellectual and philosophical preoccupations, the yearning for freedom, the sense of loneliness, the feeling of oppression by the parents, the impotent rages or active hates directed against the adult world, the erotic crushes . . . the suicidal fantasies." [27]

We cannot fail to note the conflict-ridden side of Beethoven's character during his adolescent years. "Since my return to Bonn I have as yet enjoyed very few happy hours," he wrote to von Schaden in September 1787. "I have been suffering from melancholia, which in my case is almost as great a torture as my illness." [28] To Frau von Breuning he revealed "his obstinate and passionate moods," his occasional willfulness or irrationality. "He has his *raptus* again," she would say with a shrug of her shoulders.[29] More painfully, the young Beethoven was unable to establish a love relationship with any woman—in part, perhaps, because he was invariably drawn to women who were attached or pledged to others. This pattern—of intense passion for the unavailable—we will observe later on in his life. According to Wegeler, Beethoven's first love, Jeannette d'Honrath, who was also loved by Stephan von Breuning, was already devoted to an Austrian recruiting officer. Romberg described Beethoven's passion for his student, Maria Anna von Westerholt, as a hopeless attachment like that of Goethe's Werther for Lotte; Fräulein Westerholt married a member of the nobility in 1792. Beethoven also appears to have been drawn to Eleonore von Breuning, who later became Wegeler's wife; his letters to her reveal a strong mixture of affection and hostility. He may also have been attracted to Barbara, daughter of the widow Koch; but she neglected to answer his letters from Vienna, and later married a nobleman.

Beethoven's sexual timidity made him the unhappy target of the younger orchestra members on at least one occasion. While dining in a restaurant in 1791, several musicians prompted the waitress "to play off her charms upon Beethoven. He received her advances and familiarities with repellent coldness; and as she, encouraged by the others, still persevered, he lost his patience and put an end to her importunities by a smart box on the ear." [30] It must have been a desperate trial of his chastity that caused Beethoven to strike a woman.

Beethoven nevertheless formed many rich relationships during his later Bonn years. Among his intimate friends were the brothers Christoph, Lorenz, and Stephan von Breuning; Franz Gerhard Wegeler; the twins Gerhard and Karl Kügelgen; the cousins Andreas and Bernhard Romberg; Karl August von Malchus; and Anton Reicha. And he was fully at home among the members of the court orchestra. Simrock, a horn player who later became Beethoven's Bonn publisher, told Junker that "the utmost harmony reigns among us, and we love each other as brothers." [31] On the two-month stay of the electoral orchestra in Mergentheim in the fall of 1791, the twenty-year-old Beethoven and cellist Bernhard Romberg happily served as scullions for their fellows in the orchestra, and this journey remained for Beethoven a "fruitful source of loveliest visions." [32] Indicative of his friends' warm affection for him are the fifteen entries in an autograph album dating from October 24 to November 1, 1792, on the eve of Beethoven's departure for Vienna.

His situation at Bonn gave Beethoven a relative freedom from material want. His family was poor but not poverty-stricken. Its annual income from the mid-1780s on of more than 450 florins was exceeded only by the salaries of the *Kapellmeister* and the *Kapelldirektor* and was more than double the salary of the lowest paid musicians. Beethoven also earned something from teaching. The family employed maids throughout the Bonn period, and after the mother's death, a housekeeper was hired to attend to the younger children.

Feudal patronage provided artists with the necessities of life, with fine clothing and powdered wigs which engendered illusions of social superiority, and with a relative peace of mind which would rarely have been obtained in a "free" marketplace. But the circumstances of musical patronage in Bonn made it difficult for Beethoven to venture outside the bounds of conventional musical expression. Viewing Beethoven's career in retrospect, it seems clear that such a rupture with or radical reshaping of tradition was to be a necessary precondition for the emergence of his genius.

A crucial figure in this development was to be Franz Joseph Haydn, who was himself newly liberated from the more extreme modes of feudal patronage. In 1790, following the death of his patron, Prince Nicholas Esterházy, Haydn accepted an offer from the Bonn-born London impresario, Johann Peter Salomon, to visit England. In December he set out for England, where for the first time he was to achieve a full consciousness of standing upon the world musical stage. On the way to London, accompanied by Salomon, he stopped at Bonn, arriving during Christmas. He was feted by the elector and the leading musicians—perhaps including Beethoven and certainly including Neefe, who was a keen admirer of Haydn's music. He is reported to have stopped in Bonn once more, en route to Vienna, on his return from his triumphal English stay, in the late spring of 1792. [33] It was on one of these occasions that Beethoven showed him one of his cantatas (it is not known which one). Haydn was sufficiently impressed to accept Beethoven as a student upon the request of the elector. Fischenich wrote to Charlotte von Schiller from Bonn on January 26, 1793, of Beethoven: "a young man of this place whose musical talents are universally praised and whom the elector has sent to Haydn in Vienna.... Haydn has written here that he would put him at grand operas and soon be obliged to [himself] quit composing." [34]

Beethoven set out for Vienna a day or two after November 1, 1792. On December 18, barely seven weeks later, Johann van Beethoven died.

Until recently the specific cause of his death was unknown, but the publication in 1971 of a new edition of the Fischer memoirs revealed that "in 1792, Johann van Beethoven . . . lay sick with dropsy of the chest [*Brustwasser*]," probably a reference to heart failure.[35] How long he lay dying we do not know, but it now seems clear that Beethoven was aware of his father's terminal illness. We cannot tell whether Beethoven's departure in these circumstances is to be regarded as an abandonment or as a means of absenting himself because he could not face the prospect of his father's death; perhaps both factors were at play. In any event, this separation, however poignant, was a necessary stage in the process by which Beethoven passed from adolescence to maturity.

It was no doubt Beethoven's intention to return to Bonn and to take a leading role in Bonn musical life (perhaps as *Kapellmeister*) following the completion of his course of study with Haydn.[36] He never fulfilled this wish, however. Despite repeated declarations of his desire to visit his birthplace and the graves of his parents, Beethoven never saw Bonn again. But he was to make a symbolic, spiritual return to Bonn in his last years, in which he once again took up the unsolved problems of his youth and arrived at a new mode of self-understanding.

Title page of the "Electoral"
Sonatas, WoO 47 (1783).

5
The Music

Bonn's musical life in the 1780s was that of a miniature Vienna, a cosmopolitan crossroads in which early-Classic and Classic styles competed freely and without restriction. Beethoven had an opportunity to hear or perform the widest imaginable variety of the most important secular works of the age, from the solo sonata and chamber music repertory to large-scale compositions for the stage. Operas by Mozart, Gluck, Cimarosa, Sacchini, Benda, Neefe, Salieri, Paisiello, Grétry, Pergolesi, Gossec, and many others were staged in the early 1780s. The repertory of the four seasons from 1789 through 1792 similarly included music from the leading schools of the day, excepting that of Berlin, with a heightened concentration on the operas of Mozart, plus works by such men as Paisiello, Dalayrac, Cimarosa, Holzbauer, Dittersdorf, and Pergolesi. As for instrumental music, publications by most of the outstanding contemporary composers were on sale in Bonn, including many symphonies, sonatas, concertos, and chamber works by Haydn and Mozart, and even more by Haydn's pupil, the popular and accessible Ignaz Pleyel. Furthermore, the electoral court library contained a vast amount of religious music, along with symphonic and chamber music by many composers.[1]

It was a characteristic of Neefe that he apparently made no special attempt to impose upon his student his own predilections for the music of the North German masters, but instead permitted or even encouraged him to absorb influences from a variety of sources. Beethoven's Bonn works, although they do not yet reflect an achieved personal style, reveal a broad-ranging eclecticism in which French, Franco-Rhenish, North German, South German, Viennese, and Italian influences are at play. Scholarship has succeeded in tracing many of the musical sources of his early style, but has always failed to establish a single, dominant influence, partly because of the intermingling of styles in his early music and also because the elements of the Classical style appeared simultaneously and pervasively in many European centers.

In any event, Beethoven's music from this period shows the almost unvarying adoption of conventional formulas. He fully accepted the language and styles of his contemporaries and predecessors. Nor did his first compositions impress his peers as the works of an exceptional composer. As late as mid-1791 he does not even appear as a composer on the list of "Cabinet, Chapel, and Court Musicians of the Elector of Cologne" printed in Bossler's *Musikalische Correspondenz*, although Joseph Reicha, Andreas Perner, and the Romberg cousins are so listed.[2]

Beethoven's Bonn works explore a good many of the standard genres of his time. The piano music includes at least five sonatas, several sets of variations, and a concerto, along with rondos and miscellaneous compositions. His chamber music consists of three quartets for piano and strings; a trio for piano, violin, and cello; and a number of works for various combinations of wind instruments. He also composed a good deal of vocal music, including about eighteen *Lieder*, three concert arias, and two full-scale cantatas for soloists, chorus, and orchestra. Finally, there was incidental music to a ballet and fragments of a violin concerto and of a C-minor symphony. In all there were more than fifty separate works, two-thirds of which were composed between 1790 and 1792.

The works for winds, such as the Octet, op. 103, the Rondino, WoO 25, and the Trio for Piano, Flute, and Bassoon, WoO 37—all heavily indebted to Mozart—were quite unabashedly music for court entertainment. Max Franz's digestion evidently was helped by wind instrument ensembles, for he was regularly entertained at table (as was his brother, Emperor Joseph) by a small band consisting of two oboes, two clarinets, two horns, and two bassoons. It was for this combination that Beethoven scored the Octet and the Rondino. The Octet is a diverting and agreeable work, with an Andante lightly touched by melancholy, a graceful Minuet, and a cheerful Finale. The Rondino, a one-movement work that leans on Mozart's melodic invention, shows equal sureness in its handling of the instrumentation. (It was probably intended as the original finale of the Octet.) Yet Beethoven was either content with his easy mastery of this genre or dissatisfied with its potentialities, for he wrote little music for winds alone in later years.

The potentialities of the variation form were far greater; but the courtly pursuit of pleasure together with Enlightenment music theory encouraged a fashionable, *galant* style of variation characterized by pleasing but superficial embroideries of the thematic material. Beethoven's Bonn variations are largely in this prevailing manner. The Variations on a March by Dressler, WoO 63, are figural variations of a simple kind. The variations for piano on a theme from Dittersdorf's opera, *Das rote Käppchen*, WoO 66; for piano and violin on Mozart's "Se vuol ballare," WoO 40 (completed later in Vienna?); and for piano four-hands on a theme by Count Waldstein, WoO 67, are characteristic and charming ornamental variations, although the Waldstein set is also of interest for its quasi-orchestral colors and the Dittersdorf set contains fine humorous moments as well as a beautiful slow variation (no. 6), which plumbs the inner structure of the theme. (These last variations are said to be modeled upon a set by Neefe on another theme from Dittersdorf's opera.) The brilliant set of variations on Righini's "Venni Amore," WoO 65, is of superior quality, so much so that some earlier scholars thought (wrongly) that it had been thoroughly recomposed prior to its Vienna publication in 1802.

None of Beethoven's Bonn works in sonata form are studied as landmarks in the development of the form. They are essentially imitative examples of contemporary Classic sonata-style works, to which we listen in the hope of catching a glimpse of the mature Beethoven, a motif utilized in a later work, an intimation of future greatness. Nor are we disappointed in these respects. The three "Electoral" Sonatas for Piano, WoO 47 (1782–83), are unadventurous three-movement works, with little development, utilizing simple rondo and variation techniques. Some claim they are modeled on the music of C. P. E. Bach; others hear in them echoes of Neefe, Haydn, Stamitz, or Sterkel. However, in the Sonata in F minor can be heard anticipations of the Sonata, op. 13 (*Pathétique*), of 1798–99, and Schiedermair noted that the main theme of its third movement contains an idea that reappears in the Sonata, op. 10 no. 2, as well as in the scherzos of the Third and Fifth Symphonies.[3] In the third "Electoral" sonata, in D, Prod'homme observed a motif reminiscent of the introduction to the Seventh Symphony of three decades later.[4] The later, fragmentary Sonata in C, WoO 51, composed for Eleonore von Breuning, makes little attempt at thematic development; it is transparent and undemanding, with the lovely ornamental passagework of its Allegro reminiscent of the Italian style of Galuppi or Domenico Scarlatti. The graceful Adagio, however, recalls the early sonatas of the Viennese school.

The three Quartets for Piano and Strings, WoO 36 (1785), are in the style of Mozart, whose music became increasingly popular after the installation of Max Franz in 1784. The Quartet in E-flat is frankly modeled on, and owes some of its most beautiful passages to, Mozart's Violin Sonata, K. V. 379; while, according to Douglas Johnson, those in C and D are more subtly based on Mozart's K.V. 296 and K.V. 380 sonatas, respectively.[5] Each of the quartets is in three movements, with quick outer movements enclosing a slow movement in the dominant or subdominant key. The closing movements are in rondo form. Beethoven never published these works, possibly because of their indebtedness to Mozart and possibly because the piano dominates the scoring so completely. He evidently held them dear, however, for they contain a number of original melodic ideas upon which he drew in Vienna for the Sonatas, op. 2 nos. 1 and 3, the *Sonate pathétique*, op. 13, and the finale of the Sonata, op. 27 no. 1. The cheerful Trio in E-flat for Piano, Violin, and Cello, WoO 38 (1791), may, as Deiters says, be more advanced than the quartets (it is Beethoven's first work with a scherzo and the first to use a coda in a sonata-form movement), but it is lacking in depth and character.

Rounding out Beethoven's instrumental music from this period are fragments of a violin concerto and two other orchestral works. The Concerto for Piano and Orchestra, WoO 4, of 1784 is formally diffuse and melodically uninteresting despite moments of folklike gaiety in the closing movement; although composed in emulation of the early Classic style of J. C. Bach and the South Germans, it lacks their craftsmanship and elegance. The incidental music for a *Ritterballett* ("Knight's Ballet"), WoO 1, is of interest largely for extramusical reasons, for at its performance on March 6, 1791, Count Waldstein was named as its composer. It is unlikely that Beethoven resented this appropriation of his work by his patron; more likely he agreed to act as Waldstein's ghostwriter, in conformity with the hierarchical relationship between patron and artist. (Even Mozart's *Requiem* similarly was presented at first as the composition of the nobleman who had commissioned it.)

Beethoven's propensity for instrumental music is often exaggerated: more than 40 percent of his Bonn works are for voice. This percentage corresponds closely to the proportion governing his entire output: approximately half of his 600 works are vocal.[6] Naturally, statistics do not properly express the relative importance of different works, but they do give some indication that Beethoven was drawn to the voice throughout his career. His *Lieder* compare favorably with those of his contemporaries, although, as with most pre-Romantic *Lieder*, few have entered the modern repertory. Most of them are in simple strophic form, but several—perhaps through absorption of style elements from Italian opera—utilize contrasting sections, recitative passages, and through-composed techniques. Especially touching are the "Elegie auf den Tod eines Pudels" [Elegy on the death of a poodle], WoO 110, and "Klage" [Lament], WoO

113, the latter featuring contrasting major and minor sections and touches of chromaticism. The songs are important in revealing Beethoven's literary leanings, which largely reflect the tastes of the intellectual circles in which he moved. He set to music poems by Hölty, Pfeffel, Gleim, Matthisson, Sophie Mereau, Goethe, Lessing, and Bürger, many of which he found in contemporary almanacs and journals. Two concert arias for bass and orchestra, WoO 89 and 90, in the Italian *opera buffa* style are characterized by touches of humor, expressive writing for the voice, and skillful orchestration. Of equal facility is "Primo Amore," WoO 92, for soprano and orchestra, which has recently been established as a Bonn work.[7]

In these works Beethoven remained within the traditional patterns of musical expression. His Bonn compositions rarely penetrate the surface of the emotions, perhaps precisely because they correspond so harmoniously with the ideal of the benevolent principality in which they were created—an untroubled aestheticism which exalted abstract beauty and found pleasure in the constant repetition of gracefully predictable patterns and forms.

All of this would make for a straightforward and wholly consistent view of Beethoven's music during the Bonn period were it not for the existence of the *Funeral Cantata on the Death of Joseph II,* WoO 87, and its companion work, the *Cantata on the Elevation of Leopold II to the Imperial Dignity,* WoO 88. These works, especially the *Joseph* Cantata, reveal what would otherwise be quite unexpected—the existence, even in this early period, of many of those revolutionary and transcendent elements which were to form the basis of Beethoven's post–1800, "heroic" style. It is as though the elements of the "heroic" manner existed embryonically and were waiting only for the processes of time—the conjunction of outward events and inner daring—to manifest themselves.

The news of Emperor Joseph's death on February 20, 1790, reached Bonn within a few days. Severin Anton Averdonk's text for a memorial cantata was soon completed, and at a meeting of the *Lese–Gesellschaft* Eulogius Schneider proposed that it be set to music by Beethoven. The *Funeral Cantata on the Death of Joseph II* was probably completed sometime in March; the *Cantata on the Elevation of Leopold II* followed shortly after Leopold's election as emperor on September 30, 1790. Neither work was performed during Beethoven's lifetime. A memorial meeting of the *Lese–Gesellschaft* was held as scheduled on March 19, but the minutes of a March 17 meeting state that "for various reasons the proposed cantata cannot be performed."[8] One of the cantatas (probably the *Joseph* Cantata) was also rehearsed for a proposed performance at

Mergentheim in the fall of 1791, but the performance was cancelled because of performance difficulties. "We had all manner of protests over the difficult places [in the score]," wrote Simrock, "and [Beethoven] asserted that each player must be able to perform his part correctly; we proved we couldn't, simply because all the figures were completely unusual... and so it was not performed at court, and we have never seen anything more of it since." [9]

Beethoven did not bring the cantatas to public notice or offer them for publication; the music remained unknown until the rediscovery of copies of the scores at auction in 1884. In a letter to Hanslick in May 1884, Brahms wrote of the *Joseph* Cantata: "Even if there were no name on the title page, none other could be conjectured—it is Beethoven through and through! The beautiful and noble pathos, sublime in its feeling and imagination; the intensity, perhaps violent in its expression; moreover, the voice leading and declamation, and in the two outer sections all the characteristics which we may observe in and associate with his later works." [10]

The significance of the cantatas lies not so much in their quality as independent works but rather in the clues they provide as to the formation of Beethoven's musical vocabulary. A number of motifs, passages, and dramatic ideas from the *Joseph* Cantata recur in the middle-period symphonies—the *Eroica*, the Sixth, and the Seventh—and in the overtures to *Coriolan* and *Egmont*. Of particular interest are several anticipations of passages in the funeral march of the *Eroica* Symphony which reveal Beethoven's association of certain musical ideas with the concept of death. For example, the extramusical meaning of the "disintegrating" passage in the closing measures of the funeral march movement is confirmed by Beethoven's use of a similar passage in the cantata to accompany the word *"Todt"* (dead). [11] Beethoven used one section of the cantata—the soprano aria with chorus, "Then mankind mounts toward the light"—as the basis for the second finale of *Fidelio*. The beautiful, arched melody of the aria has been called Beethoven's *Humanitätsmelodie*, his "humanity melody," expressive of his yearning for freedom and brotherhood. [12] These anticipations even reach beyond Beethoven's middle years: the opening of the cantata's second section, preceding the words "A monstrous creature, named Fanaticism, rose up from the caverns of Hell," finds its fulfillment in the finale of the Ninth Symphony, and in both cases the passages are followed by bass recitatives of quite similar shape and purpose.

The *Leopold* Cantata is not equally inspired—although the addition of trumpets and drums to the scoring and the martial and festive character of several sections provide a propulsive dimension significantly lacking in the earlier work—nor does it contain as many notable foreshadowings of the later Beethoven. But where the funeral cantata is so important in the formation of Beethoven's musical vocabulary for the portrayal of death, sorrow, strife, heroic defiance, grief, and tranquility, the *Leopold* Cantata is significant in that it deals with the representation of victory and joyful conclusion—which was all the more important in that this was one of the major musical problems for which Beethoven could find no single adequate solution. The *Joseph* Cantata avoids this issue by repeating the opening "death" chorus as its finale; the *Leopold* Cantata, because of its affirmative subject matter, is forced to come to grips with it. Its final section, "*Stürzet nieder, Millionen*" [Prostrate yourselves, ye multitudes], anticipates in rudimentary form that section of the finale of the Ninth Symphony in which the chorus interrupts the variations and intones "*Seid umschlungen, Millionen*" [Embrace, ye multitudes].

Numerous influences upon the *Joseph* Cantata can be traced: that of Gluck, in the orchestral timbres and the character of the writing for strings and winds; that of Mozart, whose style is apparent in both the soprano and bass arias; and that of the school of Rameau, with its *tombeaux* and *apothéoses* for deceased composers. Schiedermair has noted the influence of the Mannheim composer Ignaz Holzbauer in the introductory unison chords and in the second soprano aria, as well as in several sections of the *Leopold* Cantata. These influences are far outweighed, however, by the uniquely Beethovenian elements: the orchestral underlinings, the dynamic contrasts, the sudden *pianissimos* or *fortissimos*, and, above all, the first emergence of Beethoven's special kind of "absolute melody," which Hans Gál described as characterized by broad rhythms, eight-measure groupings, clear melodic curves, and diatonic movement without suspensions.[13] These *cantabile*, expressive, *legato*, sustained melodies appear in the soprano aria with chorus of the *Joseph* Cantata and reappear in *Fidelio*, the *Missa Solemnis*, the adagios of the greater instrumental works, and the "Ode to Joy" of the Ninth Symphony. They signify Beethoven's emancipation from the Mannheim style and his sublimation of the Classic melodic style of Mozart and Haydn.

The stunning importance of these cantatas, then, lies in the light which they cast upon the unfolding of style elements of unmistakable Beethovenian cast. It is not far-fetched to see in the *Joseph* Cantata one of those extraordinary leaps in Beethoven's creative powers such as we see in the *Eroica* Symphony of 1803–04 and the *Hammerklavier* Sonata of 1817–18. Ultimately, such an event is not fully explicable, but it may be worthwhile to sketch the confluence of biographical and historical factors which played some role in its genesis.

The form in which the work is cast is essentially a product of the Enlightenment. For this is not a cantata in Bach's sense nor an echo of the early eighteenth-century French cantata in neoclassic style. In the late eighteenth century, the cantata was revived as a large-scale secular hymn of virtuous character for public celebration. Examples of the form, such as the *Cantata for the Funeral of Gustavus III of Sweden* by the German-Swedish composer Joseph Martin Kraus confirm its function as a secular requiem for Enlightened leaders. Cantatas of this type were evidently current in European courts of the 1780s, but the form was later taken up by the composers of the French Revolution, who created its main examples.

The Revolution sought to transform French music into a moral weapon in the service of a historic mission. The frivolities and sensuousness of *galant* music were abjured; the "scholastic" contrivances of Baroque and Classic forms were done away with; and music was assigned, in Combarieu's words, "a serious character which it had not had since antiquity outside of the Church." [14] In brief, the Revolution introduced an explicit ideological and ethical function into music which was later to become one of the characteristics of Beethoven's "public" compositions. Revolutionary music was utilized in official ceremonies, public events, and celebrations of various abstract revolutionary ideals. And one of its major functions was the apotheosis of its fallen heroes through funeral hymns, funeral marches, and funeral cantatas. The French were ever ready to compose such works on short notice. Cherubini, for example, wrote a work entitled "Mirabeau on his Death Bed" in 1791, a *Hymne funèbre sur la mort de général Hoche* in 1797, and even a premature *Cantata on the Death of Haydn,* inspired by a false rumor in 1805. Gossec and Méhul, among others, wrote similar works, with Gossec creating what was perhaps the best title: *Chant funèbre sur la mort de Féraud, représantant du peuple, assassiné, l'an II, dans la convention nationale* [Funeral chant on the death of Féraud, representative of the people, assassinated in the Year Two in the National Convention].

The death of the hero—a theme which was to become a prime component of Beethoven's musical vocabulary—was central to the subject matter of Revolutionary music. This theme, which we will meet in the slow movement of the Piano Sonata, op. 26 (*Funeral March on the Death of a Hero*); *Christ on the Mount of Olives,* op. 85; the *Eroica* Symphony ("Composed to Celebrate the Memory of a Great Man"); *Fidelio;* and the Incidental Music to Goethe's *Egmont,* makes its first major appearance in Beethoven's funeral cantata. Intimations that Beethoven may have been attracted to the subject of death itself were evident in several Bonn *Lieder* and perhaps in the choice of a pathetic funeral march as a theme for his first published work, the Variations on a March by Dressler. This inclination may even have been present in Beethoven's first reported composition, the lost "funeral cantata" of 1781, said to have been written in memory of George Cressener, the English ambassador to the electoral court who was a friend of the Beethoven family.[15] (This work, which was composed before Beethoven had learned the rudiments of composition, was probably an extended song such as the similarly titled "cantata," "Adelaide," op. 46, of 1795–96. Some scholars have doubted its existence.)

The *Joseph* Cantata's dramatic theme—the death of a good prince—seems also to have permitted Beethoven to here express deeper feelings than those possible within the manner and modes of his imitative and "obedient" instrumental music. The cantata speaks of shared grief, of the love between a ruler and his subjects, of the battle of reason against ignorance and fanaticism, of a hero who dies in humanity's service. Moreover, it was a commissioned work, sanctioned and approved by Beethoven's patrons, teachers, and social superiors; a work consciously dedicated to a collective and humanistic purpose. Hence Beethoven could freely give expression to his deepest impulses, including his passion for heroism. And indeed, he could simultaneously appear as a devoted son honoring his father—the Kaiser being the ultimate authority figure of the Habsburg realms—and as a mournful but triumphant disciple who has survived to tell the tale. Therefore, the *Joseph* Cantata perhaps also expresses Beethoven's conflict-ridden feelings toward his father, who was at this time reduced to a shadowy and feeble existence.

But apart from the speculative question of Beethoven's psychological predisposition to this subject matter, there is a striking timeliness about the appearance of his first major work. The *Joseph* Cantata came into existence at a critical juncture in European history, one which would soon have fateful consequences for the electorate in which it was created. Until the French Revolution, the chief German courts, whether at Berlin, Vienna, Bonn, or Weimar, had for some years presented a relatively placid and harmonious surface; the aristocracy was imbued with an unshakable belief in its own benevolence and in the value of its way of life and its culture. Above all, it was persuaded of the immutability of its future. The storming of the Bastille effectively disposed of this pervasive confidence. The Revolution inaugurated an era in which one of the dominant trends was the desire to restore an earlier historical condition. This trend deepened as the destructive Napoleonic Wars continued well into the nineteenth century. An image of an idealized aristocratic "golden age" of heroism and beauty came into being. The Germans, of course, were not unique in this: all societies undergoing disintegration, violent transformation, or repression tend to proliferate such mythic periods in their national past. (For segments of the French aristocracy, the seventeenth century became "*le grand siècle*.") For the inhabitants of Bonn it was only natural that they should fix upon the pre-Revolutionary period, before the currents of history washed away the electorate itself. And for many Enlightened members of the Habsburg monarchy, including Beethoven, the "golden age" was now seen as the period of the reign of Emperor Joseph II. Enlightened despotism was converted from "reality" into wish. The actualities of the past were submerged in a golden glow of mythological re-creation. Beethoven's personal mythology—his revision of the facts of his own parentage—seems here to have found its social equivalent.

Whatever its biographical and historical sources may have been, the *Cantata on the Death of Emperor Joseph II* inaugurated a new and highly productive phase in Beethoven's career as a composer. However, despite the grandness of its conception, the rhetorical dynamism of its style, and the beauty of many of its details, the work has little impact today. The loosely structured cantata form was sufficient to strike ideological poses and to express unmediated feelings, but it proved inadequate to explore the concepts of heroism or tragedy. The incipient "heroic" style elements themselves disappeared from Beethoven's musical palette for more than a decade, while he developed the technical and formal equipment necessary to adequately express these new contents. Belatedly, Beethoven now had to master counterpoint and the forms and styles of the Viennese school.

II
VIENNA
Early Years

Prince Karl Lichnowsky and Princess Marie Christiane Lichnowsky. Anonymous portraits in oils.

6
A Pianist and His Patrons

Where Beethoven's earlier journey to Vienna had been an abject failure, his second was an unqualified success. His first decade in Vienna consisted of an unbroken series of professional triumphs. He arrived in the second week of November 1792, bearing introductions from Count Waldstein along with the invitation to study with Haydn. Through Waldstein's family connections and Haydn's musical connections he gained access to the houses of the hereditary nobility, including several which had played significant roles in furthering the careers of Gluck, Haydn, and Mozart. Moreover, his reputation as a notable pianist in the employ of the uncle of Habsburg Emperor Franz had preceded him. He was received in the palaces and salons of aristocratic connoisseurs, amateurs, and music lovers, who sought to nourish and encourage the young Beethoven as a worthy successor to the masters of the Viennese musical tradition. Upon Beethoven's departure from Bonn, Waldstein had written in his autograph album: "The Genius of Mozart is mourning and weeping over the death of her pupil. She found a refuge but no occupation with the inexhaustible Haydn; through him she wishes to form a

57

union with another. With the help of assiduous labor you shall receive *Mozart's spirit from Haydn's hands.*" [1] This prophecy was fulfilled more rapidly than could have been expected.

Beethoven was initially regarded primarily as a virtuoso pianist; he was seen as only a student of composition, despite the rather large body of works which he had created during his last years in Bonn. He arrived in Vienna at a propitious moment for a virtuoso pianist. Clementi and Johann Baptist Cramer had settled in London; Joseph Wölffl was just beginning his career in Warsaw. Mozart, who in his later years devoted himself to keyboard performance less than previously, had been dead for twelve months, leaving no pianistic successor of the first rank in Vienna. From all accounts, Beethoven was a remarkable pianist, whose historic importance is that he bridged the Classic and late-Classic styles of performance. His powerful, brilliant, and imaginative style contrasted strongly with the fashionably sweet and delicate style of earlier keyboard virtuosos, although when he wished to, Beethoven could imitate their cloying and effeminate manner with devastating accuracy.[2] Romberg, Cherubini, and others who were attached to the earlier style found his playing rough and harsh, but most musicians and connoisseurs, especially those of the younger generation, were profoundly moved. His extraordinary effect upon audiences was described by Carl Czerny:

> In whatever company he might chance to be, he knew how to produce such an effect upon every hearer that frequently not an eye remained dry, while many would break out into loud sobs; for there was something wonderful in his expression in addition to the beauty and originality of his ideas and his spirited style of rendering them. After ending an improvisation of this kind he would burst into loud laughter and banter his hearers on the emotion he had caused in them. "You are fools!" he would say. . . . "Who can live among such spoiled children!" he would cry.[3]

Beethoven was concerned to maintain his preeminent position and regarded any accomplished pianist as a potential rival. In mid-1794 he wrote to Eleonore von Breuning of his "desire to embarrass" and "revenge myself on" the "Viennese pianists, some of whom are my sworn enemies." [4] Vienna was a city of pianists. In the 1790s there were more than 300 pianists there, most of whom were engaged in teaching piano to the children of the best families. (According to Arthur Loesser, there may have been as many as 6,000 piano students in Vienna at the time.) Beethoven feared that other pianists might hear him extemporize and then copy down the "several peculiarities of my style and palm them off with pride as their own." [5] A few years later he indeed encountered contenders for his position as the leading pianist of Vienna. These included

Wölffl, Cramer, Johann Nepomuk Hummel, Abbé Joseph Gelinek, and Daniel Steibelt. So keen were several of these rivalries that patrons and devotees of these men formed opposing camps and set their favorite pianists against each other in competitions. Gelinek remembered one such pianistic duel, in which he was quickly bested by "that young fellow, [who] must be in league with the devil." [6] In 1799 a series of contests between Beethoven and Wölffl was held at the villa of Baron Raymond von Wetzler, a member of a banking family who was Wölffl's patron. The conductor, Ignaz von Seyfried, described the duels between the two "athletes" as though he were reporting one of those contests between wild animals at the Hetz Amphitheater which had been a favorite amusement of the Viennese until the mid-1790s. (The virtuoso was indeed considered something of a freak of nature, and eighteenth-century fairs in the major cities of Germany featured virtuosos and musical child prodigies alongside itinerant jugglers and rope walkers.) In 1800, a similar contest took place between Beethoven and the flamboyant Daniel Steibelt at the home of Count Fries; and shortly thereafter—when the young Hummel began to reach the peak of his pianistic proficiency—Czerny wrote that the general public preferred him to Beethoven. "Soon," he reported, "the two masters formed parties which opposed one another with bitter enmity." [7] That Beethoven was willing to participate in these events is indicative of the strength of his patronage ties as well as of the symbolic importance to him of his virtuosity.

Beethoven's reputation as a virtuoso performer soon spread beyond the confines of the aristocratic salons, although these remained his primary forum. From March 1795 to October 1798 he made eleven public appearances in Vienna, mostly in concerts given by another musician (Haydn, the Rombergs, the singers Josefa Duschek and Maria Bolla) or in benefit concerts. [8] His name was prominently featured at several of these, and the reviews were favorable. From February to July 1796 he undertook a tour to Prague, Dresden, Leipzig, and Berlin, where he performed at the Prussian court for Friedrich Wilhelm II. Along with the famed cellist Jean-Louis Duport, he played his two Sonatas for Cello and Piano, op. 5, for the king, who was himself an amateur cellist. Beethoven was delighted when the king gave him a gold snuffbox filled with louis d'ors; he "declared with pride that it was not an ordinary snuffbox, but such a one as it might have been customary to give to an ambassador." [9] Later in the same year he performed at Pressburg and perhaps at Pesth as well, although it is probable that his only concert performance there dates from 1800. He also gave several successful concerts in Prague in 1798.

If Beethoven's initial reputation rested on his abilities as a performer, it was not long before he made his presence felt as a composer. His first major Viennese compositions began to appear in 1795, and within a few years several of his early publications—such as "Adelaide" (later numbered op. 46), the *Sonate pathétique*, op. 13, and many of his sets of variations— achieved a wide sale, inaugurating competitive bidding by music publishers for his future works. By 1799 his music was being circulated by five publishers, with others waiting in the wings. Beethoven was rapidly gaining a consciousness of addressing a continental audience and achieving a measure of international fame. "My art is winning me friends and renown, and what more do I want?" wrote Beethoven to his brother Nikolaus Johann on February 19, 1796, adding, on a blunter note, "And this time I shall make a good deal of money." [10]

Czerny reported that as a youth, Beethoven "received all manner of support from our high aristocracy and enjoyed as much care and respect as ever fell to the lot of a young artist." [11] Beethoven himself "frequently declared," Schindler wrote, "that at this time he was best appreciated, and best comprehended as an artist, by noble and other high personages." [12] And we can accept this statement by an otherwise often unreliable witness, for, indeed, Beethoven was lionized by the aristocracy, petted and spoiled by the sensitive and the wealthy. So great was their passion for music, and so important was it to their sense of social status that they be known as patrons of an important artist, that they lavished money and gifts upon him. During the initial Vienna years, he was simultaneously patronized by a number of individual nobles. Several of these, including Prince Joseph Lobkowitz (1772–1816), Count Andreas Razumovsky (1752–1836), and Count Moritz Fries (1777–1826) ("Good Count Fries," Beethoven called him), began to play a more significant role in his commissions and performances during the following decade. The most influential of the earlier patrons were Baron Gottfried van Swieten (1733 or 1734–1803), Count Johann Georg von Browne-Camus (1767–1827), and, above all, Prince Karl Lichnowsky (1756–1814) and his wife, Princess Christiane (1765–1841).

Swieten, formerly of the imperial diplomatic service and later director of the Imperial Library and president of the Education Commission, was a musical connoisseur of the first order. He founded and (rather autocratically) presided over a musical society of nobles dedicated to the performance and preservation of "old" music, particularly the choral music of Handel, Bach, and the Renaissance masters. He figured prominently in the biographies of C. P. E. Bach, Mozart, and Haydn, and is best remembered as the librettist for Haydn's *Seasons* and *Creation*, as well as for the vocal version of the "Seven Last Words from the Cross." He organized frequent concerts, usually held at his residence in the Renngasse or in the great hall of the Court Library, which were high points of Viennese musical life. Swieten, who had the demeanor of a "grand seigneur" and who, according to Haydn, wrote symphonies "as stiff as he himself," [13] became one of Beethoven's staunchest supporters. Schindler records that Beethoven "carefully preserved" notes which

Swieten wrote to him, which suggests real affection on the composer's part. One of these notes hints at a whimsicality (lightly concealed behind a peremptory facade) not otherwise attributed to the old connoisseur, who was to receive the dedication of Beethoven's First Symphony, op. 21:

> Herr Beethoven in Alstergasse, No. 45, care of Prince Lichnowsky. If you have no other engagement, I should like to have you at my house next Wednesday with your nightcap in your bag. Please reply immediately. Swieten.[14]

The Count von Browne-Camus, descended from an old Irish family, was in the Russian Imperial Service at Vienna. Though extremely wealthy from landholdings in Livonia, he squandered his income, as did many others of Beethoven's patrons. His generosity toward Beethoven between 1797–98 and 1803 was rewarded by Beethoven's dedication to him of the String Trios, op. 9 (which Beethoven referred to in 1798 as "la meilleure de [mes] oeuvres"); the Sonata in B-flat major, op. 22; and the six Gellert *Lieder*, op. 48. In addition, Beethoven dedicated to the Countess Browne the three Sonatas, op. 10, and the Variations for Piano on a Russian Dance, WoO 71. In his dedication of the String Trios, Beethoven called Browne "the foremost Maecenas of my muse." [15]

Karl Lichnowsky was Beethoven's foremost patron, however, and remained so for more than a dozen years. His home was the center of a circle of musicians, composers, and connoisseurs, and it was at his musical parties that many of Beethoven's works were first performed. At the Lichnowsky home Beethoven met those youthful musicians who were to become famous as the outstanding players of the day, including the members of the Schuppanzigh Quartet (later renamed the Razumovsky Quartet). There he formed lifelong friendships with the prince's brother, Count Moritz, and with Baron Nikolaus von Zmeskall, who remained Beethoven's most constant Viennese friend.

After a brief stay, upon his arrival in Vienna, in a small attic room, where "he had a miserable time," [16] Beethoven was invited to live with the Lichnowskys, and he remained with them as "a member of the family" [17] for several years. So close were his ties to the prince that for many years after he took his own, separate lodgings, he chose his rooms with a view to remaining in close proximity to the Lichnowskys.[18] According to Carl Czerny, Lichnowsky treated Beethoven "as a friend and brother, and induced the entire nobility to support him." [19]

This was quite a coup on Beethoven's part, for the Lichnowsky family had been a leading force in Viennese musical life for several generations. The prince's mother-in-law, Countess Maria Wilhelmine Thun, had been a patron of Gluck, Haydn, and Mozart, who wrote, on March 24, 1781: "She is the most charming and most lovable lady I have ever met, and I am very high in her favor." [20] Two of her daughters married patrons of Beethoven—Lichnowsky and Count Razumovsky—and she was herself one of his devotees. Lichnowsky was both a pupil and a patron of Mozart; in 1789 he had organized for Mozart a tour of Bohemia and Germany almost identical to that which he arranged for Beethoven in 1796. Lichnowsky's wife, Princess Christiane, was one of the better pianists of the Viennese nobility.

Lichnowsky himself gained Beethoven's deepest affection and gratitude, and his wife, although she was only five years older than Beethoven, became a "second mother" to him.[21] The prince and the princess also earned the unusual (perhaps unique) right to suggest and even demand changes or improvements in his compositions, including *Fidelio*. They were utterly persuaded of Beethoven's genius, so much so that in 1804–1805 the prince interfered in Beethoven's love affair with Countess Josephine Deym, apparently on the grounds that it would have a detrimental effect on the composer's career.[22]

In return for his patronage, Lichnowsky received the dedications of Beethoven's first major Vienna works, the Trios, op. 1, and later those of the *Sonate pathétique*, op. 13, the Sonata, op. 26, the Second Symphony, op. 36, and the Variations on "Quant' è più bello," WoO 69. His wife was honored with the dedication of the Variations on a Theme from *Judas Maccabeus*, WoO 45, and that of Beethoven's ballet score, *The Creatures of Prometheus*, op. 43. In addition, Beethoven dedicated his Rondo in G, op. 51 no. 2, to the prince's sister, Countess Henriette, and the Variations and Fugue, op. 35, as well as the Sonata, op. 90, to Count Moritz Lichnowsky. The Clarinet Trio, op. 11, he dedicated to Countess Thun.

But the depth of their association went far beyond dedications, nor can their relationship be considered typical of that obtaining between patron and composer. For it seems clear that the Lichnowsky couple regarded Beethoven as a substitute son [23] and that he in turn experienced considerable emotional conflict in relation to them. At the heart of this conflict was his desire to receive their affection and favor, on the one hand, along with an equally strong wish to be free of their domination, which in this case took the form of a protectiveness as suffocating in its effect as it was comforting as an expression of love. His every need or want was anticipated, including (and this must have been infuriating) his desire to liberate himself from their protectiveness. The prince, Wegeler recalled, "once directed his serving man that if ever he and Beethoven should ring at the same time the latter was to be first served. Beethoven heard this, and the same day engaged a servant for himself." [24] On another occasion, when the stable of the prince was offered Beethoven while he was learning to ride horseback, he bought a horse of his own to avoid the feeling of dependency which came with the acceptance of a gift freely offered. (In a parallel incident, Count Browne gave him a horse, which he then abandoned.) Sometimes gifts were concealed in order to avoid Beethoven's rejection. Lichnowsky seems to have secretly subsidized the publication of the Trios, op. 1, on which Beethoven made a profit of 843 florins—equivalent to almost two years of his Bonn salary.

Beethoven was evidently unable freely to accept these evidences of favor and affection. He would eat away from home in order to assert his independence: "The dinner hour at the prince's was four o'clock. 'Am I supposed,' said Beethoven, 'to come home every day at half-past three, change my clothes, shave, and all that? I'll have none of it!' And so he would very often eat at a tavern." [25] Yet, at the same time, he delighted in their gifts. Lichnowsky gave him a quartet of rare Italian instruments (preserved in the Beethovenhaus at Bonn), which he prized throughout his life; and in 1800, perceiving Beethoven's need to be both secure and independent, he granted him an annuity of 600 florins, to be continued for an indefinite period (it was paid at least until 1806). Beethoven's gratitude is evident in several letters of later years. He wrote in 1801 to Wegeler: "Lichnowsky, who, although you may find it hard to believe what I say, was always, and still is, my warmest friend (of course we have had some slight misunderstandings, but these have only strengthened our friendship), has disbursed for my benefit a fixed sum of 600 gulden, on which I can draw until I obtain a suitable appointment"; [26] and in 1801 to Karl Amenda: "I may say that of all of them Lichnowsky has best stood the test." [27] There were other gifts as well, of a more personal nature. Resting on Beethoven's desk until his death was a pendulum clock in the shape of an inverted pyramid, on which was engraved in alabaster the head of a woman; it had been given to him by the Princess Lichnowsky. And perhaps most important of all was a bust of the prince, which Beethoven kept in a place of honor in his lodgings until 1806.

If we can believe a report by Schindler, the difficulty of the matter was summed up by Beethoven himself, when he said: "They treated me like a grandson. The princess's affection became at times so oversolicitous that she would have made a glass shade to put over me, so that no unworthy person might touch or breathe upon me." [28] To be put under glass was to be made a passive object—carefully preserved and beloved, true, but an object nevertheless—whereas it was Beethoven's need to become an active force impinging on the outside world. It would be some time, however, before Beethoven would be able to loosen this bond.

Similar conflicts developed between Beethoven and many of his other patrons and friends. It troubled him that his acceptance by others appeared to derive from his talents rather than from his qualities as a person. When Countess Susanna Guicciardi gave him a gift, he took this as "payment" for his lessons to her daughter, and was deeply hurt: "I'm not exaggerating when I say that your present gave me a shock. . . . It immediately put the little I had done for dear [Giulietta] on a par with your present." [29] Typifying his anxieties on this point, he once wrote angrily to a friend: "Am I then nothing more than a music maker for yourself or the others?" [30]

This may be why Beethoven developed a strong resistance to playing the piano for his patrons. Wegeler wrote that "his aversion to playing for an audience had become so strong that every time he was urged to play he would fly into a rage. He often came to me then [1794–96], gloomy and out of sorts, complaining that they had made him play, even though his fingers ached and the blood under his nails burned." [31] It even became his custom to play in a room adjoining the main salon, where he could be heard but not observed. On one such occasion, when a member of the audience tried to look into the room, Beethoven promptly "left the piano, took his hat, and ran out without yielding to pleas and importunities." [32] Wegeler writes that Beethoven's resistance to playing "was frequently the source of bitter quarrels with his closest friends and patrons." [33] One of the most startling of these incidents was recounted by Frau von Bernhard as having taken place at the Lichnowskys in the late 1790s: she witnessed the elderly Countess Thun "on her knees in front of Beethoven who reclined on the sofa, begging him to play something, which he refused to do." [34]

Ernest Newman thought of such incidents as "exhibitions of ill-breeding" rather than as "evidences of a noble democratic spirit." [35] Certainly, Beethoven was not an English gentleman; but neither was he a Jacobin teaching dissipated nobles a lesson. To explain his apparent boorishness, his *hauteur*, and his many eccentricities in terms of his need to demonstrate his independence and assert his equality with his patrons as a human being is not sufficient; the matter is more complex. The very nature of personal patronage seems inevitably to arouse in all artists contradictory emotions of gratitude and resentment, submission and rebelliousness, love and hostility. Where the tie is of so intimate a nature— as was the case with Beethoven and patrons such as the Lichnowskys— these conflicts naturally become intensified. Moreover, several of Beethoven's patrons were hardly free of neurotic and even psychopathological symptoms themselves. Count Browne was described by his tutor, Johannes Büel (a warm friend of Beethoven's), as "one of the strangest men, full of excellent talents and beautiful qualities of heart and spirit on the one hand, and on the other full of weakness and depravity." [36] He suffered a mental breakdown and was committed for a time to an institution. According to one source, Prince Lobkowitz was also highly eccentric: he would leave his correspondence unanswered, even unopened, for years, and he would on occasion spend weeks in absolute seclusion. He had installed in his room a great mirror opposite the window so that he could watch passersby without himself being seen, and he is reported to have gazed into this mirror for hours on end.[37]

The Lichnowskys, too, were hardly a normal couple. Lichnowsky, a Freemason and a follower of Voltaire, was described by a contemporary as "a cynical lecher," while the princess, whose breasts had been surgically removed, was "very withdrawn" and anguished by doubts concerning her husband's fidelity. She accused him of fathering an illegitimate daughter and insisted upon adopting the child as her own. And, however unlikely, it was rumored by a contemporary scandalmonger that she once disguised herself as a prostitute and arranged to meet her own husband at a brothel.[38] ("They did not seem to live happily together," Frau von Bernhard wrote. "Her face always bore such a melancholy expression." [39])

At this time, powerful economic pressures were placing great strains upon the finances of the nobility, and its drive toward ostentation and luxury was now being slowed, with a consequent dwindling of the more lavish forms of patronage of the arts. Especially in the years following the French Revolution, there were attempts to restrict expenditures on music at the palaces and the courts; these led to the dismissal of many private standing orchestras and theater or opera companies. When Beethoven arrived in Vienna, only a handful of the numerous orchestras formerly employed in aristocratic houses remained; instead, the higher nobility kept groups of chamber players and instrumental soloists, some of whom doubled as servants. Beethoven's patrons were among those who were affected by economic pressures. Count Browne squandered his fortune; Count Waldstein died in povery; Prince Lobkowitz and Count Fries went bankrupt; Prince Kinsky became financially embarassed. Even Prince Lichnowsky was reported by Frau Bernhard to have lived well beyond his means. These impoverishments, however, belong to a somewhat later period; in Beethoven's early years in Vienna, the aristocratic houses were relatively intact despite the encroachment of debts and the necessity of liquidating portions of their landed estates.

On the whole, the feudal mold was not broken with Beethoven's arrival in Vienna; rather, it was altered through the transfer of patronage from the electorate to segments of the Viennese nobility. Beethoven was now a "free-lance" semifeudal composer and virtuoso, moving toward relative independence from aristocratic patronage. He had to come to terms with the partial freedom from patronage which was accruing to him by accidents of time, place, and personality. But accompanying the growth of Beethoven's personal freedom was the loss of much of the security which had nourished three generations of musicians in his family. Hence, throughout his life, Beethoven never abandoned the hope of obtaining a permanent court position which would relieve his ever-increasing—if often baseless—financial anxieties. His expectation of soon returning to Bonn evaporated with the French occupation of the Rhineland in 1794; whatever hopes he may have entertained of receiving an appointment at the Prussian court failed to materialize. Thereafter, it remained one of his most profound wishes to obtain an imperial post in Vienna. We may speculate that this desire was impelled not only by needs for security and status but by his desire to emulate the great *Kapellmeister* of his childhood. In any event, it was not to be fulfilled; nor, as we shall see, was Beethoven altogether free of internal resistance with respect to obtaining the position to which his father had aspired. In the last analysis, Beethoven's desire to be his own master remained in perpetual and irreconcilable conflict with his desire for status and financial stability.

Half a century earlier, in 1749, following his expulsion from the choir of St. Stephen's Cathedral because his soprano voice was changing, Joseph Haydn had become a "free" musician, earning a living by playing at dances, writing arrangements, giving music lessons, and participating in street serenades. After a decade of economic uncertainty, Haydn was relieved to secure a regular post, first as *Kapellmeister* to Count Morzin, and, in 1761, as assistant *Kapellmeister* to the court of Esterházy at Eisenstadt. He remained there, as Esterházy's leading musician, for almost thirty years, under conditions which permitted the full development of his creativity. Haydn was well aware of the advantages of court patronage. He told Griesinger: "My prince was always satisfied with my works. Not only did I have the encouragement of constant approval, but as conductor of an orchestra I could make experiments, observe what produced an effect and what weakened it, and was thus in a position to improve, to alter, make additions or omissions, and be as bold as I pleased. I was cut off from the world; there was no one to confuse or torment me, and I was forced to become original." [40] In his autobiographical sketch of 1778 he described himself as *"Kapellmeister* to his Highness Prince Esterházy, in whose service I hope to live and die." [41]

In the service of the Esterházys he retained his nimble ability to weather all kinds of storms. "Haydn did not fight," says Geiringer; "he was apparently never in opposition; nevertheless, he succeeded in having things done exactly the way he wanted." [42] By 1790, however, he began to chafe at the restrictions and isolation of life at the Esterházy palace. He wrote: "I am doomed to stay at home. It is indeed sad always to be a slave." [43]

Now, in the closing days of 1792, just returned from his first, triumphal London residence, Haydn was charged with completing the musical education of a brilliant, sensitive, and uncontrollable composer from the Rhineland.

Joseph Haydn. Portrait in oils by Thomas Hardy
(1791).

7
Haydn and Beethoven

It is said that Haydn, in a fit of pique, once called Beethoven an atheist.[1]
Although Haydn's statement possibly reflected the then prevailing view
of Beethoven's religiosity, it probably merely expressed his resentment at
his pupil's reluctance to acknowledge a musical rather than a heavenly
deity. Haydn was agreeable to training a disciple who would ultimately
equal or transcend him (and he surely knew this) but, for understandable reasons, he wanted to obtain from him the frank concession
that he was a "pupil of Haydn." Indeed, Ries reported that Haydn asked
Beethoven to place those very words on the title page of his first works,
but that Beethoven disdainfully refused to do so. (When Ries questioned
him about this, Beethoven became so angry—even in retrospect—that he
exclaimed that "he had never learned anything from [Haydn]." [2]) Recognition of his master was precisely what Beethoven could not grant Haydn.
Perhaps he did not wish to be regarded as another Ignaz Pleyel, who
remained a "pupil of Haydn" throughout his life. Even Pleyel was evidently not content with this designation, for when Haydn arrived in
London he found that Pleyel had consented to compete with him under

the auspices of a rival musical society. "So now a bloody, harmonious war will commence between master and pupil," Haydn wrote from London.[3] On the surface, they remained friends, but on one occasion when Pleyel was being praised, Haydn burst out: "But I hope it will be remembered that he was my pupil"; and he wrote to Marianne von Genzinger: "Pleyel's presumption is criticized everywhere." [4]

The relationship between Haydn and Beethoven took on a complex and tangled character from the very start. Beethoven almost immediately conceived the notion that Haydn was envious of him, or unconcerned about his progress. Whether this was his motivation or not (and I believe there is a better explanation), he commenced secret lessons in early 1793 with another teacher, Johann Schenk (1761–1830). Schenk tells the story, unfortunately in somewhat garbled form:

> Towards the end of July [sic!], Abbé Gelinek informed me that he had made the acquaintance of a young man who displayed extraordinary virtuosity on the pianoforte, such, indeed, as he had not observed since Mozart. In passing he said that Beethoven had been studying counterpoint with Haydn for more than six months [sic!] and was still at work on the first exercise; also that His Excellency Baron van Swieten had earnestly recommended the study of counterpoint and frequently inquired of him how far he had advanced in his studies. As a result of these frequent incitations and the fact that he was still in the first stages of his instruction, Beethoven, eager to learn, became discontented and often gave expression to his dissatisfaction to his friend. Gelinek took the matter much to heart and came to me with the question whether I felt disposed to assist his friend in the study of counterpoint.[5]

A meeting was arranged, at which Beethoven improvised to great effect for Schenk and then showed him his first exercise in counterpoint, which "disclosed the fact that... there were mistakes in every mode." [6] Schenk agreed to help him. Naturally, it was all-important that Haydn not find out. Schenk wrote, quite candidly: "I recommended that he copy every exercise which I corrected in order that Haydn should not recognize the handwriting of a stranger when the exercise was submitted to him." [7] (It seems possible that Beethoven engaged Schenk, not only to check on Haydn, but to help him with his homework.) According to Schindler, Beethoven and Schenk met in 1824 and merrily reminisced about the secret instruction: they "burst out laughing to think how they had fooled Haydn, who never once had guessed what was going on." [8]

Nottebohm, who reviewed the exercises which Beethoven had written under Haydn's supervision, came to the conclusion that Haydn was not a systematic or sufficiently-interested teacher. Only a sixth of the exercises had been to any extent corrected, numerous errors remained uncorrected, and in some cases Haydn, while attempting to correct one error, would make another in his own solution.[9] These lapses are perhaps understandable, given Haydn's circumstances at the time. The deaths of Mozart in 1791 and of his esteemed friend Marianne von Genzinger in 1793 had affected him deeply. Furthermore, Haydn was conducting more-or-less simultaneous love affairs with a London widow, Rebecca Schroeter, and with the singer Luigia Polzelli. He had returned from the heady English experience to the usual and painful relationship with his wife, whose death he wished for in a most candid way; writing to Luigia Polzelli from London, he congratulated her on the death of her husband: "Dear Polzelli, perhaps, perhaps the time will come, which we both so often dreamt of, when four eyes shall be closed. Two are closed, but the other two . . ." [10] Haydn was, moreover, preoccupied with preparations for a return trip to London in early 1794, for which he was commencing six new symphonies, and for which, in 1793, he wrote the set of six String Quartets, opp. 71/74. And perhaps Haydn somehow resented Beethoven because he obtained such immediate and easy access to the highest plane of Viennese society. It should be remembered that although Haydn had influential early supporters among the nobility and its connoisseurs, it was not until after his London triumphs that his music met with universal admiration in the Habsburg capital. True, he had achieved a considerable reputation even in the 1770s, but Emperor Joseph II had described his work as "tricks and nonsense," and in 1778–79 his application for membership in the charitable organization for musicians—the *Tonkünstlersocietät*—had failed to find a hospitable reception. Geiringer dates the apotheosis of Haydn by the Viennese from the second London residence, and he observes—perhaps with some degree of exaggeration—that even as late as the years 1792–95 he still was regarded by some as "nothing more than the court conductor of a Hungarian magnate." [11] Hence, there may have been some simple jealousy on Haydn's part toward the pianist/composer who was so quickly accepted and adored by the Viennese nobility. But this is conjectural, for we also know that it was substantially through the influence of Haydn that Beethoven was able to make his initial impact upon Vienna. Many of Haydn's pupils became Beethoven's friends or patrons, including Countess Thun, the Erdödy family, Pleyel, Krumpholz, Anton Kraft, Wranitsky, and Seyfried. And Haydn apparently presented Beethoven to Esterházy at Eisenstadt in 1793, surely a sign of pride in his pupil.

In any event, Nottebohm's conclusion about the insufficiency of Haydn's instruction of Beethoven is at best a partial view of the matter.[12] There were countless schoolteachers and *Kleinmeister*, proficient in the craft of counterpoint, who could have corrected the infringements of the rules in Beethoven's studies; it did not require a Joseph Haydn to point out parallel fifths in Beethoven's exercises. And if we look at the development of Beethoven's music during the period immediately following his studies with Haydn, we see that this was not Haydn's main function or contribution. Furthermore, the fact that errors in the exercises examined by Nottebohm remained uncorrected does not mean that Haydn did not correct them verbally or urge Beethoven (who was in his twenty-third year and already the composer of numerous works) to uncover his own errors and correct them. To study with Haydn was to learn not merely textbook rules of counterpoint and part writing, but the principles of formal organization, the nature of sonata writing, the handling of tonal forces, the techniques by which dynamic contrasts could be achieved, the alternation of emotional moods consistent with artistic unity, thematic development, harmonic structure—in short, the whole range of high-Classic musical ideas and techniques. There is no evidence that Haydn formally instructed Beethoven in such matters; he did not need to, for Beethoven took Haydn as his musical model and absorbed these lessons by his presence and his example.

There was no shortcut from the *Joseph* Cantata to the *Eroica* Symphony. Schenk and Albrechtsberger could teach Beethoven counterpoint, but they could not convey to him the heritage of Mozart and Haydn. Beethoven's difficulty with Haydn was that he learned too much from him—more than he could acknowledge. And this may partly explain why he was less than forthright in his dealings with the older man. First there was the secret instruction with Schenk, which was not kept from Haydn for very long: "After a year," wrote Schenk, "Beethoven and Gelinek had a falling out. . . . As a result, Gelinek got angry and betrayed my secret. Beethoven and his brothers made a secret of it no longer." [13] But this was not the only reason for Haydn's disenchantment with his student during the fourteen months of his formal instruction (which lasted until January 1794). Beethoven took cash advances from his teacher, misinformed him about the amount of his subsistence allowance from Bonn, and led him to believe that a number of works written before his departure from Bonn were new compositions.

Beethoven's motives in this last regard were by no means malevolent. Perhaps he was trying to impress Haydn with his productivity. For he had not been able to complete a single work of importance during 1793; [14] the year had been almost wholly given over to revisions of such Bonn compositions as the Octet and the Piano Concerto No. 2. Although it was long believed that the Trios, op. 1, had been written or completed in 1793 and performed for Haydn prior to his departure for London in January 1794, it now seems clear from the investigations of Douglas Johnson that no. 1 was written in Bonn and touched up in 1793, while nos. 2 and 3 were first sketched and composed after Haydn's departure.[15] The only other works which were completed in 1793 were the Variations for Piano and Violin on "Se vuol ballare," WoO 40, and a few *Lieder;* begun in 1793 and completed in 1794 was the Rondo in G for Piano and Violin, WoO 41.

The year 1793, then, showed a drop in Beethoven's output reminiscent of the post-1785 years, in which his productivity came to a virtual halt. My guess is that the move to Vienna, the death of his father, and his deep ambivalence toward Haydn had blocked Beethoven's creativity as a composer. Perhaps it was this creative impasse which led Beethoven to pretend that some Bonn works (perhaps partly rewritten in some cases) were new compositions. In his last years, Beethoven came to realize that occasional periods of standstill were to be expected. ("Many times I haven't been able to compose for long periods of time, but it always comes back sooner or later," he said.[16]) But the young Beethoven was doubtless deeply troubled by such creative difficulties.

On November 23, 1793, almost one year after his work with Beethoven had begun, Haydn wrote a letter to Elector Max Franz on behalf of his student which reveals his paternal affection for Beethoven, the high regard in which he held him as a composer, the pride which he took in being his teacher, and his total unawareness that Beethoven was anything other than a devoted pupil:

MOST REVEREND ARCHBISHOP AND ELECTOR,

I am taking the liberty of sending to your Reverence in all humility a few pieces of music—a quintet, an eight-voice "Parthie," an oboe concerto, a set of variations for the piano, and a fugue—composed by my dear pupil Beethoven, who was so graciously entrusted to me. They will, I flatter myself, be graciously accepted by your Reverence as evidence of his diligence beyond the scope of his own studies. On the basis of these pieces, expert and amateur alike cannot but admit that Beethoven will in time become one of the greatest musical artists in Europe, and I shall be proud to call myself his teacher. I only wish that he might remain with me for some time yet.

While I am on the subject of Beethoven, may your Reverence permit me to say a few words concerning his financial affairs. For the past year he was allotted 100# [ducats]. That this sum was insufficient even for mere living expenses your Reverence will, I am sure, be well aware. Your Reverence, however, may have had good reasons for sending him out into the great world with so small a sum. On this assumption and in order to prevent him from falling into the hands of usurers, I have on the one hand vouched for him and on the other advanced him cash, so that he owes me 500 fl., of which not a kreutzer has been spent unnecessarily. I now request that this sum be paid him. And since to work on borrowed money increases the interest, and what is more is very burdensome for an artist like Beethoven, I thought that if your Reverence would allot him 1000 fl. for the coming year, your Reverence would be showing him the highest favor, and at the same time would free him of all anxiety. For the teachers which are absolutely indispensable to him and the expenses which are unavoidable if he is to be admitted to some of the houses here, take so much that the barest minimum that he needs comes close to 1000 fl. As to the extravagance that is to be feared in a young man going out into the great world, I think I can reassure your Reverence. For in hundreds of situations I have always found that he is prepared, of his own accord, to sacrifice everything for his art. This is particularly admirable in view of the many tempting opportunities and should give your Reverence the assurance that your gracious kindness to Beethoven will not fall into the hands of usurers. In the hopes that your Reverence will graciously accept this request of mine in behalf of my dear pupil, I am, with deepest respect, your Reverence's most humble and obedient servant

JOSEPH HAYDN
Kapellmeister of Prince Nicholas Esterházy

Vienna, November 23, 1793 [17]

The elector's reply was, at the very least, disillusioning:

The music of young Beethoven which you sent me I received with your letter. Since, however, this music, with the exception of the fugue, was composed and performed here in Bonn before he departed on his second journey to Vienna, I cannot regard it as progress made in Vienna.

As far as the allotment which he has had for his subsistence in Vienna is concerned, it does indeed amount to only 500 fl. But in addition to this 500 fl. his salary here of 400 fl. has been continuously paid to him; he received 900 fl. for the year. I cannot, therefore, very well see why he is as much in arrears in his finances as you say.

I am wondering, therefore, whether he had not better come back here in order to resume his work. For I very much doubt that he has made any important progress in composition and in the development of his musical taste during his present stay, and I fear that, as in the case of his first journey to Vienna, he will bring back nothing but debts.[18]

Knowing that a storm was impending, Beethoven wrote to the elector on the same day that Haydn's letter was dispatched, begging "that your Electoral Highness will not deprive me of the kindness once granted" and assuring him of his eternal respect for his "kindness" and "nobility." [19] We have no record of what steps he took to try to patch it up with Haydn. Perhaps it was as a result of this episode that Haydn's reported plan to take Beethoven to London with him was abandoned, and that there was no formal resumption of lessons after Haydn returned from London in August 1795. Haydn arranged for the continuation of Beethoven's studies in counterpoint with the composer and renowned pedagogue Johann Georg Albrechtsberger (1736–1809); this course of instruction began soon after Haydn's departure and continued until approximately the spring of 1795.

Beethoven's tendency to arouse in his Vienna teachers conflicting reactions—compounded of affection and resentment, admiration and enmity—was not restricted to Haydn. The noted Italian opera composer and Imperial *Kapellmeister*, Antonio Salieri (1750–1825), was Beethoven's teacher in dramatic and vocal composition for a number of years (starting perhaps as early as 1798) in Vienna. The young Moscheles remembered "how astonished I was one day when calling upon *Hofkapellmeister* Salieri, who was not at home, to see on his table a sheet of paper on which was written, in large, bold characters, 'The pupil Beethoven has been here.'" [20] This evidently took place in 1808 or 1809 and seems to indicate a warm relationship between the teacher and his former student; yet in January of 1809 Beethoven described Salieri as his enemy: "Herr Salieri, being my most active opponent, played me a horrible trick." [21] In 1799, Beethoven dedicated to Salieri his three Sonatas for Violin and Piano, op. 12; but when his teacher criticized *Fidelio*, Beethoven refused to make the suggested changes and remained angry for some time. For his part, Salieri could not accept Beethoven's later music, and it was perhaps partly through his tutelage of Schubert that the young composer became for a time an opponent of Beethoven's music. [22]

Albrechtsberger, too, seems to have had mixed feelings about Beethoven. He wrote three extremely friendly letters to Beethoven in 1796 and 1797; [23] but a contemporary musician (whom Thayer considered a reliable witness) reports that Albrechtsberger called one of Beethoven's opus 18 quartets "trash" and advised him not "to have anything to do with [Beethoven]; he learned absolutely nothing and will never accomplish anything decent." [24] For his part, Beethoven referred to Albrechtsberger as a "musical pedant" and creator of "musical skeletons"; but he cherished Albrechtsberger's course of instruction, returned to it for self-study, and in later years rendered assistance to his teacher's nephew. Nottebohm reports on Albrechtsberger's instruction in a totally favorable light.

Beethoven's difficulty in crediting his teachers was also not limited to Haydn. Ries wrote: they "valued Beethoven highly, but were also of one mind touching his habits of study. All of them said Beethoven was so headstrong and self-sufficient that he had to learn much through harsh experience which he had refused to accept when it was presented to him as a subject of study. Particularly Albrechtsberger and Salieri were of this opinion." [25]

In any case, whatever the reason for Haydn's empathy with Beethoven, he appears to have forgiven him and to have continued—after his return from the second residence in London—to associate with him and perhaps even to instruct him and criticize his works informally. Beethoven played one of his own piano concertos at a Haydn concert of December 18, 1795, surely a sign of great favor by Haydn and an indication that he considered Beethoven his protégé. And Beethoven in turn dedicated to Haydn his important Sonatas, op. 2, in 1796, and improvised publicly on Haydn themes. In addition, he scored one of Haydn's quartets (op. 20 no. 1, in E-flat major) and in later years obtained and carefully preserved the autograph of one of his London symphonies.

Why, then, do we find Beethoven expressing hostility toward his former teacher? Ries related that "Haydn seldom escaped without a few digs in the ribs, for Beethoven cherished a grudge against him from earlier days." [26] Beethoven evidently told Ries that the reason for his "grudge" against Haydn was that Haydn had severely criticized the third of the opus 1 Trios:

> This astonished Beethoven, inasmuch as he considered the third the best of the Trios, as it is still the one which gives the greatest pleasure and makes the greatest effect. Consequently, Haydn's remark left a bad impression on Beethoven and led him to think that Haydn was envious, jealous, and ill-disposed toward him. I confess that when Beethoven told me of this I gave it little credence. I therefore took occasion to ask Haydn himself about it. His answer, however, confirmed Beethoven's statement; he said he had not believed that this Trio would be so quickly and easily understood and so favorably received by the public. [27]

Despite the reasonableness of Haydn's explanation, Beethoven did not forgive the criticism, which he perhaps interpreted to mean that his teacher had set boundaries upon his creativity.

Thayer marked 1800 as a critical year for Beethoven: "It is the year in which, cutting loose from the pianoforte, he asserted his claims to a position with Mozart and the still living and productive Haydn in the higher forms of chamber and orchestral composition—the quartet and the symphony." [28] It is therefore not very surprising to find that Beethoven's conflicts with Haydn reached their peak at around this time. Ries's report of Beethoven's "grudge" against Haydn is post–1800, as is a famous anecdote which indicates how strained relations between them had become at this time. Haydn, meeting Beethoven on the street, complimented him on his ballet music for *The Creatures of Prometheus.* "Oh, dear Papa," Beethoven responded, "you are too good; but it is no *Creation* by a long shot." Startled by the unnecessary comparison with his own masterpiece, Haydn retorted: "You are right. It is no *Creation,* and I hardly think it ever will be!" [29] Beethoven made no secret of his competition with Haydn at this time. Doležalek reports that when the Septet (completed in 1799) was first played Beethoven exclaimed: "This is my *Creation.*" [30]

It seems possible, then, that by the turn of the century Beethoven felt the weight of Haydn's influence (as well as of that of the Viennese school, of which Haydn was the greatest surviving representative) as an impediment to the growth of his own musical individuality.[31] We may well be exaggerating somewhat the degree of Beethoven's reliance upon Haydn in order to make this point, for although Haydn was clearly Beethoven's major (though far from his only) musical influence, in addition to being his teacher, there are many wholly individual characteristics in Beethoven's more important compositions of this period. In any event, it seems to have been necessary for Beethoven's further development that—having absorbed the lessons of Mozart and Haydn—he now begin to move toward a new synthesis of styles which would make his future works a thoroughgoing departure from the Viennese high-Classic style.

To be sure, this process had already begun in the later 1790s. Indeed, some connoisseurs refused to fully accept the early Beethoven as an authentic inheritor of the Mozart–Haydn tradition. If we are to believe the recollections of Carl Czerny, it was at this very time that "all the followers of the old Mozart–Haydn school opposed [Beethoven] bitterly." [32] We know that this is not altogether accurate, for Lichnowsky, Thun, Lobkowitz, Apponyi, Swieten, and other patrons of Beethoven were also among the significant enthusiasts of his predecessors' music. But it was surely a source of disappointment to Beethoven that Swieten, writing in the first volume of the *Allgemeine musikalische Zeitung* in 1799, failed to mention his name among those contemporary composers "who tread firmly in the footsteps of the truly great and good...." [33] Furthermore, early critics were apparently more sensitive than we are to the extent of Beethoven's departures—and especially those of a harmonic nature—from the tradition. Reviewers in the *Allgemeine musikalische Zeitung* complained of "clumsy, harsh modulations" in his early sets of variations, and they found in his elegant Violin Sonatas, op. 12, "a forced attempt at strange modulations, an aversion to the conventional key relationships, a piling up of difficulty upon difficulty." [34]

If these signs of Beethoven's revolutionary style shift were perceptible to Beethoven's contemporaries several years before the *Eroica* Symphony, they certainly had long been apparent to Joseph Haydn. Thus it became evident to Beethoven that, unless he were willing to write numerous Septets and First Symphonies, his "new path" (as he termed it) would mean creating music that could not be to Haydn's taste and would not meet with his approval. Seyfried, who was close to both Beethoven and Haydn during this period, makes this explicit when he writes that Beethoven suffered from "a sort of apprehension, because he was aware that he had struck out a path for himself which Haydn did not approve of." [35] To protect himself from the feelings of sorrow and guilt which accompanied this process of separation, Beethoven began to break the personal tie as well, and he visited the increasingly infirm Haydn "less and less." [36]

Haydn missed Beethoven. Seyfried writes that he frequently inquired

after him, asking, "Well, how goes it with our Grand Mogul?" and knowing that Seyfried would tell his friend that Haydn had asked after him.[37]
In 1803, he (almost humbly) submitted a text to Beethoven through
Griesinger, asking for his opinion as to whether it was a fit subject for
an oratorio setting. Griesinger wrote to Breitkopf & Härtel: "Papa's
[request] will surprise you not less than it did me; but that is really what
happened! ... It is likely that Haydn's decision will depend on Beethoven's
pronouncement." [38] Beethoven reported unfavorably on the text, but of
course it was not the text that primarily concerned Haydn, who "was delighted that Beethoven was so well disposed toward him, for he had
the feeling that Beethoven was guilty of a great arrogance toward him." [39]
He wanted contact and friendship with Beethoven, and one would like to
believe that Beethoven's desire was equally great, that his withdrawal
from Haydn was painful to him, arousing feelings of remorse over being
young and productive at a time when Haydn was unable to work and
was approaching death.

Beethoven attended the March 27, 1808, concert in honor of Haydn's
seventy-sixth birthday, which featured a performance of *The Creation*.
He stood with members of the high nobility "at the door of the hall of the
university to receive the venerable guest on his arrival there in Prince
Esterházy's coach" and accompanied him as he was carried in an arm-
chair into the hall, to the sound of trumpets and drums.[40] It is said that
Beethoven "knelt down before Haydn and fervently kissed the hands and
forehead of his old teacher." [41] After Haydn's death, which is nowhere
mentioned in Beethoven's correspondence, all traces of resentment and
bitterness disappeared, to be replaced by unlimited praise and affection.

In later years, Beethoven unfailingly referred to his old master in
terms of reverence, regarding him as the equal of Handel, Bach, Gluck,
and Mozart. And on one occasion he even refused to acknowledge that he
himself merited a place alongside these men. "Do not rob Handel, Haydn
and Mozart of their laurel wreaths," he wrote to a young admirer in 1812;
"They are entitled to theirs, but I am not yet entitled to one." [42] But in
his earlier years he had not yet achieved this level of confidence, and he
felt the need to insist upon his equality with the Viennese masters; writing
to Breitkopf & Härtel about Haydn's and Mozart's talent for arranging
their own sonatas, he observed: "Without wishing to force my company
on those two great men, I make the same statement about my own
pianoforte sonatas also ... I am quite convinced that nobody else could
do the same thing with ease." [43]

Viewed in the light of the conflict both of generations and of styles,
it is not surprising that Haydn should have been unable to follow Beethoven beyond the limits of the high-Classic style which he himself had
perfected. There are a number of reports alleging that Haydn was hostile
to Beethoven's post–1800 music. For example, one contemporary musi-

cian recalled that Haydn "could not quite reconcile himself with Beethoven's music"; [44] and an Italian music dictionary quoted Haydn as saying of his pupil's compositions: "The first works pleased me very much; but I confess that I do not understand the later es. It seems to me that he writes more and more fantastically." [45] No single one of these reports can be confirmed by documentary evidence, and the reliability of the most detailed of them has been questioned.[46] But the sheer number of these recollections—and the total absence of reports of praise by Haydn for any of Beethoven's compositions following the Septet and *The Creatures of Prometheus* [47]—makes it rather probable that Haydn was unable or unwilling to comprehend Beethoven's greater achievements. This must have been a source of pain to the younger man. Certainly it reinforced his feeling that he had to make his own way—even without the appreciation and encouragement of the man whom he venerated above all other living composers.

Beethoven. Engraving by Johann Neidl
after a drawing by Stainhauser (1801).

8
Portrait of a Young Composer

Beethoven was short of stature, with a large head and thick, bristly coal-black hair framing a pockmarked and ruddy-complexioned face. His forehead was broad, and heavily underlined by bushy eyebrows. Some contemporaries report that he was "ugly" and even "repulsive," but many remarked the animation and expressiveness of his eyes, which reflected his inner feelings to an extraordinary extent—now flashing and brilliant, at other times filled with an indefinable sadness. His mouth was small and delicately shaped. He had white teeth, which he habitually rubbed with a napkin or handkerchief. His chin was broad and divided by a deep cleft. He was powerfully built, with broad shoulders, strong hands overgrown with hair, and short, thick fingers. It was to be some years before his frame filled out and became robust; he remained lean until his mid-thirties. He was wholly lacking in physical grace: his movements were awkward and clumsy, and he constantly overturned and broke things and tended to spill his inkwell into the piano. Ries wondered how Beethoven ever managed to shave himself, for his cheeks were filled with cuts. Although upon his arrival in Vienna he noted down in his diary the name and address of a dancing-master, he never learned to dance in time to music. His "entire deportment," Frau Bernhard wrote, "showed no signs of exterior polish; on the contrary he was unmannerly in both demeanor and behavior." [1]

His outer dress was altogether variable and generally reflected his inner moods. As the years progressed he tended to go about, as Grillparzer noted, "dressed in a most negligent, indeed even slovenly way," [2] but in the early Vienna years he was neatly and, on occasion, even modishly dressed. Naturally he abjured the pre-1789 courtly gentleman's costume, with its knee breeches and wigs, which by the 1790s had become a mere anachronism. Frau Bernhard vividly remembered a study in contrasts at the Lichnowsky residence: "Haydn and Salieri sat on the sofa on one side of the little music room, both most carefully dressed in the old-fashioned style with bagwig, shoes, and silk stockings, while Beethoven used to appear even here in the freer, ultra-Rhenish garb, almost carelessly dressed." [3] In accord with the imitation of Roman styles under the influence of the French, Beethoven at this time wore his hair cut "à la Titus." Later, he let it grow as it would.

In the company of strangers, Beethoven was "reserved, stiff, and seemingly haughty."[4] Haydn was not the only one who regarded him as arrogant and overbearing. One report spoke of his "studied rudeness" and thought this suggested that he was "acting a part." [5] Beethoven's defensive exterior masked a fragile sensitivity to slights, real or imagined. He would storm away from an aristocratic dinner in fury because he had not been granted a setting at the main table. Exaggerated (or false) attentiveness equally disturbed him; on one occasion he suddenly quit the country house of a certain baron because the latter "annoyed him with his excessive politeness, and he could not bear to be asked, every morning, if he were quite well." [6] Cherubini called him "an unlicked bear"; Goethe later called him "an utterly untamed personality." [7] His closest friends suffered his moods and sudden rages, which, most often, were followed by expressions of boundless penitence. Occasionally his temper crossed the boundary into physical violence. He was seen to throw an unwanted entrée at a waiter's head, and to pelt a housekeeper with eggs which he found insufficiently fresh.

Among his close friends, however, he could be, according to Schindler, "comical, lively, and sometimes even loquacious"; [8] and Rochlitz wrote that "once he is in the vein, rough, striking witticisms, droll conceits, surprising and exciting paradoxes suggest themselves to him in a continuous flow." [9] These reports refer to later times, but Czerny confirmed that in the early years too, apart from his inevitable melancholic moods, Beethoven was "always merry, mischievous, full of witticisms and jokes." [10] His correspondence with certain friends crackles with zany metaphors, satire, exuberant jests, and occasionally scatalogical word play. In company, or when listening to mediocre music, he would often unaccountably break into a loud, hearty laugh, as though he had attained a Homeric insight into an indefinable drollery. His friends, wrote Seyfried, "seldom learned the why and wherefore of an explosion of this kind, since as a rule he laughed at his own secret thoughts and imaginings without condescending to explain them." [11] Rarely, however, could he sustain a single mood for any extended time. He wrote to Bettina Brentano that he had attended "a bacchanalia, where I really had to laugh a great deal, with the result that today I have had to cry as heartily." "Exuberant jollity," he explained, "often drives me back most violently into myself." [12]

Beethoven's daily life was organized so as to maximize his creative productivity. He arose at daybreak, breakfasted, and went directly to his desk, where he normally worked—with occasional time out for a short walk—until midday. His dinner concluded, he generally took a long walk ("twice around the city," according to Seyfried [13]), which could occupy much of the afternoon. Toward nightfall he often repaired to a favorite tavern to meet with friends and read the newspapers. Evenings were typically spent in company, at the theater, or making music. He retired early, usually at ten o'clock, but would sometimes continue to write for many more hours until a creative surge was exhausted. He sketched musical ideas constantly, whether at home, on the street, in a tavern, lying on his side in a meadow, or perched in the crook of a branched tree. "I always have a notebook ... with me, and when an idea comes to me, I put it down at once," he told Gerhard von Breuning.[14] "I even get up in the middle of the night when a thought comes, because otherwise I might forget it." He filled a large number of sketchbooks during his lifetime, and retained them for very occasional reference (and perhaps because he hesitated to discard any evidence of his creativity) until his death. "I dare not go without my banner," he said, quoting Schiller's Joan of Arc, when asked why he always carried a sketchbook with him.[15]

Beethoven's productivity was generally richer during the warmer months, which he spent, as did most Viennese of means, outside the capital. In the 1790s he probably spent the summers at the country estates of his patrons and admirers. After becoming financially more secure, he took his own summer lodgings, with rare exceptions, each year from 1800 on. In the countryside he was better able to find tranquillity, seclusion, and contact with nature, which he worshipped in an almost religious fashion: "It seems as if in the country every tree said to me 'Holy! Holy!'— Who can give complete expression to the ecstasy of the woods?" [16] In a letter of 1810 he wrote that he looked forward to the country with "childish excitement": "How delighted I shall be to ramble for a while through bushes, woods, under trees, through grass and around rocks. No one can love the country as much as I do. For surely woods, trees, and rocks produce the echo which man desires to hear." [17] Beethoven's creativity required peaceful, conflict-free external surroundings. This may be why he wrote in his diary that "calm and liberty are the most precious of all possessions." [18]

Perhaps in the pursuit of an unattainable tranquillity, Beethoven changed his lodgings almost as readily as his moods. "Scarcely was he established in a new dwelling," Seyfried wrote, "when something or other displeased him, and he walked himself footsore to find another." [19] The slightest provocation led him to pack his belongings, and at times it became difficult to find an apartment for so unreliable a lodger. (This is especially true of 1799–1804 and of Beethoven's last decade, for he remained at lodgings at the Pasqualati house—with only several interruptions—from late 1804 until 1814.) Beethoven's restlessness perhaps reflected his unsatisfied desire to establish a real home, a desire unrealizable in view of his bachelorhood, to which he never became fully reconciled.

If he could not have his own family, he repeatedly attempted to participate, by reflected light as it were, in the family life of others. One of the basic patterns of Beethoven's life until his final decade consisted of his attaching himself to a series of families as a surrogate son or brother. This began in Bonn, with the Breuning, Koch, and Westerholt families. After his arrival in Vienna, the Lichnowskys played this role for some years, as we have seen. They were followed in succession by the Brunsvik, Guicciardi, and Deym families, the Bigots, the Erdödys, the Malfattis, the Brentanos, the Giannatasios, and the Streichers. It can fairly be said that Beethoven's happiest personal moments—music making aside—were spent in these home settings, where he could experience some of the joys, pleasures, and fellowship of family life. It was at the hearths of these surrogate families that Beethoven—sometimes unwittingly—kindled most of his love interests. It is not surprising, in view of this, that each of these relationships developed stresses which fundamentally altered or dissolved it, whereupon Beethoven, after a period of mourning mingled with distress, would take up his peregrinations in search of another "ideal" family or a reasonable facsimile thereof.

Of his own family, only his two brothers, Caspar Carl and Nikolaus Johann, remained. The former arrived in Vienna in 1794 and, after a brief career as a music teacher, obtained a minor position as bank cashier in the state bureaucracy, which he held until his death in 1815. He occasionally served his brother—rather ineptly, and perhaps dishonestly, it was said—as unpaid secretary and business agent. Beethoven had less contact during the early years with Nikolaus Johann, who followed his brothers to Vienna in 1795; he was employed as a pharmacist's assistant in Vienna until 1808, when he started a shop of his own in Linz and became wealthy, largely as a result of war profiteering during the French occupation of 1809. Beethoven's relations with his brothers alternated freely between effusive familial affection and fraternal rivalry, which on more than one occasion led to physical violence. It never occurred to him that his brothers knew how to conduct their own lives: he repeatedly interfered in their affairs, asserting his supposed prerogatives as the eldest brother and guardian.

Perhaps in partial compensation for his fraternal conflicts, Beethoven entered into intimate association with a series of idealized brother figures. This, too, was a continuation of a Bonn pattern, which began with the von Breuning brothers, Anton Reicha, Karl August von Malchus, and others. Typifying the tone of these relationships is Malchus's entry in Beethoven's farewell autograph album, upon the composer's departure from Bonn:

> The heaven of my deep love ties our hearts with bonds which cannot be untied—and only death can sunder them.—Reach out your hand, my beloved, and so until death
>
> THY MALCHUS [20]

In Vienna, this series of exaggeratedly romantic friendships continued, first with Lorenz von Breuning (1777–98), who arrived there in 1794 for a stay of three years, and then with Karl Friedrich Amenda (1771–1836), a violinist and theology student who arrived in the spring of 1798, just in time to fill the void left by Lorenz's departure the previous fall. As tutor to the children of Prince Lobkowitz he quickly made Beethoven's acquaintance and soon, in the words of a contemporary document, "captured Beethoven's heart." They became such inseparable companions that when one was seen alone people would call out, "Where is the other one?" [21] Beethoven gave Amenda a manuscript copy of the Quartet in F, op. 18, no. 1, with a warm dedicatory message, and prior to Amenda's departure from Vienna in 1799, he played the Adagio of the quartet for him. "It pictured for me the parting of two lovers," said Amenda. "Good!" said Beethoven, "I thought of the scene in the burial vault in *Romeo and Juliet.*" [22] For Amenda it was a parting; for Beethoven the music symbolized, perhaps, the death of their relationship. However, Amenda's faithfulness (and, we may surmise, his permanent absence) permitted his elevation to the rank of the ideal. As Beethoven wrote of him to Ries in 1804, "Although for almost six years neither of us has had news of the other, yet I know that I hold the first place in his heart, just as he holds it in mine." [23]

Amenda was succeeded by Stephan von Breuning, who took up residence in Vienna around 1801, and, to a lesser extent, by Count Franz von Brunsvik, recipient of the dedication of the *Appassionata* Sonata, op. 57. Breuning remained Beethoven's closest friend until 1808 or 1809; subsequently, after a long hiatus, they resumed their friendship in Beethoven's last year. In 1807, perhaps in anticipation of Breuning's impending marriage to Julie von Vering, Beethoven began to transfer his affection to Baron Ignaz von Gleichenstein (1778–1828), and this young cellist who hailed from Freiburg im Breisgau became Beethoven's most important friend for several years. He handled many of Beethoven's business affairs during these years, and received in return the dedication of the Cello Sonata, op. 69. In 1809, Beethoven enlisted Gleichenstein's aid in his marriage project: "Now you can help me to look for a wife. Indeed you might find some beautiful girl at F[reiburg]....If you do find one, however, please form the connection in advance." [24] Later in that year, indeed, we find both of them courting the Malfatti sisters, Gleichenstein successfully and Beethoven unsuccessfully. The strains of their intimacy, along with Gleichenstein's decision to marry, ended the relationship in ca. 1810 or 1811. (He reappeared only when Beethoven was on his deathbed.) "Again and again your friendship only causes me fresh irritation and pain," wrote Beethoven. "My cold friend, I send you all good wishes—Whatever is wrong with you you are not really my friend—not by far as much as I am yours." [25]

Beethoven's early difficulties in establishing a love relationship with a woman carried over into his early Vienna period. He wrote home to Nikolaus Simrock in 1794: "If your daughters are now grown up, do fashion one to be my bride. For if I have to live at Bonn as a bachelor, I will certainly not stay there for long—Surely you too must now feel rather anxious." [26] Beethoven's own anxiety may be operating here, mingled with the desire that the older man assist him in entering the forbidding world of marriage.

His first known "flame" of the Vienna period was the singer Magdalena Willmann, whose Bonn origin may have constituted part of her attraction, as she provided a link to Beethoven's childhood home. She arrived in Vienna in 1794. Beethoven is said to have proposed marriage to her unsuccessfully—evidently without any encouragement or preparation. She refused him, it was said, because he was "ugly and half-crazy." [27]

Beethoven's name has also been loosely, and unconvincingly, linked with several other women whom he knew during the early Vienna years—with Countess Josephine Clary, an amateur singer, who married Count Christian Clam-Gallas in 1797; with Christine Gerhardi, another singer whom Beethoven frequently accompanied on the piano, who married Joseph Frank in 1798; with Anna Luise Barbara Keglevich, who became Princess Odeschalchi in 1801 and who received the dedications of four of Beethoven's significant piano compositions. But there is no hard evidence of an attachment to any of these, and in any event it certainly makes a meager list for a young man in his twenties. This makes it difficult to accept Wegeler's oft-quoted statement: "In Vienna, at all events so long as I lived there, Beethoven was perpetually engrossed in a love affair, and occasionally he made conquests which an Adonis would have found difficult if not impossible." [28] Wegeler was in Vienna for about eighteen months, ending in mid-1796, and therefore was probably present during Magdalena Willmann's rebuff of Beethoven. Evidently it took more (or less) than an Adonis to win her. As we will see, it was not until after 1800 that Beethoven began a more determined pursuit of what Goethe called the "eternal feminine." As for less ethereal relationships, Beethoven during this period seems to have had a powerful aversion to prostitutes. He warned his brother, Nikolaus Johann, in 1794, "Do be on your guard against the whole tribe of bad women." [29] We may assume that he, too, was on his guard. It was said that the Falstaffian violinist Ignaz Schuppanzigh "once, after a merry party, took Beethoven to a girl, and then had to avoid Beethoven for weeks." [30]

This surely represents the continuation of a pattern which had been formed years earlier. As we saw, from his Bonn days onward Beethoven was imbued with the ideal of exemplary behavior, and he consciously patterned his life in emulation of a noble ideal. He proudly told his friends that he had been educated with proverbs; in a Conversation Book he wrote: "Socrates and Jesus were my masters." [31] Seyfried summed up Beethoven's moral outlook: "Rectitude of principle, high morality, propriety of feeling, and pure natural religion were his distinctions. These virtues reigned within himself, and he required them at the hands of others. 'As good as his word' was his favorite saying, and nothing angered him more than a broken promise." [32]

Naturally, few people could live up to Beethoven's high standards of morality, and many of his relationships were undermined by a suspiciousness which in later years took on a somewhat ominous cast. To overemphasize the latter aspect of the young Beethoven's personality, however, would be a serious mistake. His trusting qualities predominated to such an extent that when Himmel slyly wrote him from Berlin that a lamp for the blind had been invented, Beethoven unhesitatingly broadcast the remarkable news to all his friends. As Wilhelm Rust observed, Beethoven was "very childlike and certainly very sincere. He is a great lover of truth and in this goes too far very often." [33] It is the child in Beethoven which emerges in these early Vienna years, the child whose desires for self-indulgence and play had been largely suppressed by the conditions of his life in Bonn.

Overall, Beethoven's first Vienna decade was a period of growth, challenge, and triumph. He had carried the Viennese salons and concert halls as a virtuoso, launched a major career as a composer, and forged for himself a significant place in the greatest musical tradition of his time. Whatever fears he might have entertained of a repetition of the failure of 1787 proved unfounded; Beethoven had left home, traveled to the city of the emperor, and conquered it. He exulted in his liberation, both from the rigors of feudal service and from the heavy weight of family responsibilities which had been his in Bonn. He had loosened the reins upon his creative powers and attained a consciousness of his own potentialities. With all due allowance for those elements in his life and character which would inexorably lead to crisis, these years were marked, in the main, by an essential contentment as well as by great outward accomplishment, public appreciation, and financial reward. It was a period of "play," the first years in which Beethoven could unrestrainedly take pleasure in friendships and his newfound fame and try to become, as he wrote Eleonore von Breuning, "a happier man, from whose visage time and a kindlier fate shall have smoothed out all the furrows of a hateful past." [34]

During this period, then, Beethoven appears to have temporarily lightened for himself (he would never be altogether free of it) the burden of the categorical imperative, which required of him that he subordinate his own normal drives for self-gratification to the needs of others. Beethoven's main impulse was now toward self-fulfillment. Around January 1, 1794, he wrote in his diary: "Courage! In spite of all bodily weaknesses my spirit shall rule. . . . This year must determine the complete man. Nothing must remain undone." [35] He had acquired an unshakable faith in his ability and become imperiously aware of the quality of his genius. As early as 1793, in a letter to Neefe, he wrote (immodestly) of "my divine art." [36] On one occasion in his early Vienna years he exhibited withering scorn toward a man who would not automatically grant him a place beside Handel and Goethe in the pantheon of genius. In later years, on hearing that one of his works had failed to please, he impatiently responded: "It will please one day," a remark which, as Ernest Walker noted, would have been difficult to imagine coming from Haydn or Mozart. [37] Nevertheless, the desire for recognition was as deeply rooted in Beethoven as in any man, and he took unalloyed pleasure at receiving the accoutrements of accomplishment—medals, honors, money, fame, and applause. As Thayer gently noted, "Beethoven was not always as indifferent to distinctions of all kinds as he sometimes professed." [38] Nor was he unconcerned about reviews. He wrote to Breitkopf & Härtel on April 22, 1801, broadly intimating that he expected better treatment (it was indeed forthcoming) in their influential music journal:

Advise your reviewers to be more circumspect and intelligent, particularly in regard to the productions of younger composers. For many a one, who perhaps might go far, may take fright. As for myself, far be it from me to think that I have achieved a perfection which suffers no adverse criticism. But your reviewer's outcry against me was at first very mortifying. . . .[39]

But these are minor elements in Beethoven's character and do not touch on the central motivations of his creativity. Beethoven was possessed of an unswerving sense of "mission," of "vocation," and filled with a deep conviction as to the significance of his work and of his art. All else was subordinated to the fulfillment of this mission. Clearly, the categorical imperative is not absent here, but rather has taken a new and proudly exultant form. Whereas in early 1793 Beethoven could write that his precepts were "To do good whenever one can, to love liberty above all else, never to deny the truth, even though it be before the throne," [40] by 1798 an elitist, almost Caesarist element has entered his thought; in that year, he wrote to Zmeskall: "The devil take you. I refuse to hear anything about your whole moral outlook. *Power* is the moral principle of those who excel others, and it is also mine." [41] And in 1801, he referred to two of his friends as "merely . . . instruments on which to play when I feel inclined. . . . I value them merely for what they do for me." [42] One need not take such utterances literally, but in them one may see the strengthening of a narcissistic tendency which was, I believe, a necessary precondition for the formation of Beethoven's sense of mission and, consequently, of his "heroic" style.

Though we have no reason to believe that Beethoven inwardly abandoned his beliefs in Enlightened and humanistic principles, it is a curious fact that there is virtually no reflection of these beliefs in his actions, correspondence, or music during the first years in Vienna. Nor is there any manifestation of Beethoven's sympathy with the French Revolution, apart from his supposed—and unconfirmed—friendship with the French ambassador, General Bernadotte, for two months in 1798. Beethoven's radicalism, it seems, was strongly tempered by discretion after his arrival in Vienna. In 1794 he wrote to Simrock, who, we recall, was a member of the Illuminist order in Bonn:

> We are having very hot weather here; and the Viennese are afraid that soon they will not be able to get any more *ice cream*. For, as the winter was so mild, ice is scarce. Here various *important* people have been locked up; it is said that a revolution was about to break out—But I believe that so long as an Austrian can get his *brown ale* and his *little sausages,* he is not likely to revolt. People say that the gates leading to the suburbs are to be closed at 10 P.M. The soldiers have loaded their muskets with ball. You dare not raise your voice here or the police will take you into custody.[43]

Beethoven was one of those who did not raise his voice—nor, I believe, did he feel any powerful compulsion to do so. During these years there is no expression of his dissatisfaction with the imperial court or with the repressive regime of the Habsburg Kaiser Franz. Just as in Bonn he had readily adopted as his own the advanced ideology and outlook of his society, in Vienna he tended to merge his views and interests with those of his patrons and with those of Vienna as a whole. Beethoven's ambivalence with respect to Vienna, his rages against his adopted city, begins to emerge in the following decade. In these early years, the desire to "belong" was ascendant. In 1796 he set to music a patriotic anti-Napoleonic text by Friedelberg: the following year he wrote music for another war song, "Ein grosses, deutsches Volk sind wir" [We are a great German people]. In 1800 he dedicated to Empress Maria Theresia his Septet, op. 20; and on April 5, 1803, he closed his triumphal concert with a series of improvisations on Haydn's "Gott erhalte Franz den Kaiser" [God save Emperor Franz].

Just as we should not exaggerate Beethoven's radicalism, however, perhaps we should beware of overstressing his conformity, for, fundamentally, it is a tension between obedience and rebellion which characterized Beethoven throughout his life. If Beethoven's allegiance to Enlightened ideals was not altogether apparent during these years, this does not mean that his faith in reason and freedom had given way to cynicism or that his ethical precepts had yielded to self-serving conformity.

In this sketch of Beethoven's character during the first Vienna years, we can readily see both the modification and the continuation of patterns of thought and behavior that had been established in Bonn. There is one significant matter, however, which at first glance has no readily apparent Bonn antecedents and which provides a dramatic insight into Beethoven's personality. This is the certainty that he encouraged, or at the very least permitted to pass unchallenged, the widespread Viennese assumption that he was of noble birth. This "nobility pretense" was accepted as valid for more than a quarter of a century after his arrival in Vienna until December 1818, when the composer, in a moment of "confusion," confessed his lack of a patent of nobility in a legal proceeding held before a court reserved for the nobility and brought the deception to an end.[44]

We have no way of knowing if Beethoven set out upon a deliberate imposture. Most likely, the nobility pretense was tacitly inaugurated when he permitted this assumption, which flowed from the "van" in his name, to pass unchallenged. The "van," no sure sign of nobility in the Netherlands, was transformed into the unimpeachable "von" on numerous occasions, even in the early years. For example, the announcements and a review of the March 29, 1795, benefit concert for the widows of the Musicians' Society refer to "Herr Ludwig von Beethoven," as does the announcement of the Romberg concert at which Beethoven appeared in 1797. Later, in a letter to his wife, Goethe wrote of "von Beethoven," and during the Congress of Vienna the police filed a secret report on this same "Herr von Beethoven." [45] There was, then, a ready and widespread belief in Beethoven's presumed nobility, though naturally this did not extend to those who had known him in Bonn, raising the ever-present possibility of exposure and embarrassment. Soon it was too late, and too inconvenient, to correct the belief.

There was surely no economic necessity involved in this deception. Haydn had risen to the rank of a revered national composer despite his humble origins, and without benefit of nobility patent. It was not necessary for Beethoven to pretend to nobility in order to gain entrée as a musician and composer to the homes and salons of the nobility, for these were open to those of less than noble rank.[46] But if the pretense was "unnecessary" to him from an economic viewpoint, it was clearly a matter of some psychological urgency. It seems probable that Beethoven's growing confidence in his genius and in his personal worth could have overcome any sense of social inferiority based upon ancestry had not his identification with the aristocracy been deeply rooted.

This is not to say that Beethoven viewed those aristocrats with whom he associated in any idealized fashion. Quite the contrary. Beethoven repeatedly criticized his aristocratic friends, often in the most impolite and scornful language. And in later years he railed imprudently—but with impunity—against the Imperial Court and even against the Kaiser. Clearly, Beethoven idealized, not actual nobles, but the concept of nobility itself. Conversely, he despised the common citizen—the burgher—with an aristocrat's disdain for the lowborn and the money-grubbing. One day in 1820 his friend Karl Peters wrote in a Conversation Book: "You are as discontented today as I." Beethoven took up the pencil and responded: "The burgher ought to be excluded from the society of higher men, and here am I fallen among them." [47] When his deception was exposed in 1818, the nobles' court—the Landrecht—transferred Beethoven's legal proceeding to the Magistrat, a civil court with jurisdiction over issues involving commoners. This had a devastating effect upon the composer. He wanted nothing to do with such lower courts, which were suited, he wrote, only for "innkeepers, cobblers, and tailors." [48]

The equation of power and nobility was inevitable to one who had grown up in a hierarchical German principality. The nobility did, in fact, hold the power in Habsburg society: it controlled the means by which one made a living, and it daily demonstrated its omnipotence in relation to those—Beethoven's father and grandfather, his teachers—who were Beethoven's authority figures. As the psychologist Otto Fenichel has observed, "Human beings have only two ways of facing a power which restricts them: revolt; or else a (more or less illusory) participation, which makes it possible for them to bear their suppression." [49] Beethoven, through his nobility pretense, was able to put himself in the place of the mighty, to partake of aristocratic power, to share the insignia of its supremacy, and to "conquer" the nobility by pretending to be of it. (As he once said to the Giannatasios: "It is good to go around with the nobility, but one must have something with which to impress them." [50]) At the same time, he was asserting his equality with the aristocrats. In this he comes close to a number of contemporary thinkers—typified by Rousseau in France and August von Kotzebue in Germany—who maintained that aristocracy should be elective rather than hereditary, based on merit rather than birth; and Beethoven (who owned Kotzebue's book on the subject) probably held this view. In a letter to Schindler of 1823 he wrote, "As for the question of 'being noble,' I think I have given sufficient proof to you that I am so on principle." [51] Actually, Schindler's famous though discredited tale of Beethoven defying the Landrecht with the words "My nobility is *here* and *here*," as he pointed to his head and heart,[52] comes quite close to reflecting the psychological truth of the matter.

Central to the nobility pretense is the need for acceptance by those in command of society: the leaders and shapers, the royalty and nobility. That Beethoven felt he had to pretend nobility in order to obtain such acceptance may be a poignant indication of the depth of this need in him. The matter only begins here, however. For not even his own "confession" before the Landrecht in 1818, when he acknowledged his lack of an aristocratic genealogy, was able to persuade Beethoven that he did not indeed belong to the nobility. His claim of nobility was no simple pretense, nor did it rest upon a theoretical definition of nobility. At bottom, it was a claim of equality of birth. Moreover, Beethoven seemed to be genuinely unsettled about the facts of the matter. In a Conversation Book of 1820, he wrote that the courts had "learned my brother was not of the nobility" and added, in a note of puzzlement: "It is singular, as far as I know, that there is a hiatus here which ought to be filled, for my nature shows that I do not belong with this plebeian M[agistrat]." [53] In thus acknowledging his brother's non-nobility and simultaneously stating that his own "nature" was that of a noble, Beethoven seems here to have expressed the fantasy that the two brothers had different fathers; for this is the only way in which the "singular hiatus" could have been filled.

The nobility pretense, then, may lead us back to Beethoven's Family Romance. Through the pretense, he sought transcendence of his parentage and his humble origins; through it, he could, perhaps, pursue his quest for a mythical, noble father to replace the mediocre court tenor who had begotten him. The nobility pretense, then, may well have been a form through which Beethoven "lived out" his Family Romance. Perhaps we have here the materialization of an archaic daydream, an attempt to transform reality as the only "sure" way of fulfilling a deeply held wish.

The mythic hero fulfills his quest in a distant city—in Thebes, Troy, Jerusalem, or Rome. Similarly, the creative genius often must leave home in order to find his destiny. Bach travels to Weimar and Leipzig, Handel to London; Mozart must dissolve the ties which bind him to Salzburg; Chopin and Stravinsky settle in Paris; Beethoven and Brahms leave Germany for Vienna. Perhaps certain forms of genius can flower only under conditions of exile or alienation. Perhaps, too, the genius needs to take on a new identity congruent with his creative accomplishments and capabilities, an identity possible only in a city of strangers who are unaware of the facts of his birth and the circumstances of his past. In the new city his origins are clouded, thus becoming the subject first of speculation and then of a variety of legends. With Beethoven, the conquest of the new city—Vienna—was accompanied by his adoption of a new persona and by the fabrication of a noble lineage.

On some level, the nobility probably sensed all along that Beethoven was not one of them; for his manners, education, and speech surely marked him as a commoner, despite his best efforts to achieve an aristocratic polish through dancing lessons, horseback riding, and self education. It is conceivable that members of the aristocracy tolerated the great composer's pretense with a fine combination of tact and secret amusement.

But Vienna would have tolerated much more from Beethoven. For he and his music played an increasingly important role not only in Viennese musical life but in the shaping of a people's image of itself at a crucial moment in its history.

Michaelerplatz, Vienna. Colored engraving by Karl Postl (1810).

9
Vienna: City of Dreams

The death of Emperor Joseph II in 1790, followed by the reversal of most of his Enlightened, anticlerical, and antifeudal reforms, resulted in the withdrawal of Austria from the evolutionary currents of European history. Long before Metternich and von Gentz developed police surveillance and political repression into a fine art, Colloredo and Franz I had established a regime wholly devoted to the preservation of privilege. One leading historian calls the empire of Franz I "the classic example of the police state." [1] There was an official, controlled press; correspondence was monitored; passports were required for travel within the Austrian realm; a network of spies penetrated all levels of society, inhibiting the expression of criticism and of "dangerous thoughts"; there was heavy censorship of all reading matter and an arbitrary prohibition of all manner of foreign books. The secret police kept guard against all signs of social ferment; the execution of leaders of dissident groups of officials and officers early in the 1790s stifled vocal criticism. These measures, however, did not create a sullen, rebellious, seething populace. The fortunes of the trading middle class were bound up with the welfare of the court and the imperial administration. As for Vienna's so-called "sub-nobility"—the hardworking, well-educated state bureaucracy and the professionals who rendered personal or cultural services to the high aristocracy—its members felt excluded from the main circles of power and resented imperial privilege but nonetheless cherished their position in the social fabric and maintained as their ideal an empire organized upon Enlightened principles.[2] (Many of Beethoven's closest friends are to be found among these lesser aristocrats.) Their egalitarianism did not extend very far; they had no discernible sympathy for the artisans and unskilled workers who from time to time after 1792 demonstrated, struck, rioted, and were flogged and jailed by "Papa" Franz's armed forces. Nor did the industrial and financial classes seriously challenge existing privilege; rather, their goal was to emulate the high aristocracy and share in its prerogatives. The wholesale ennoblement of bankers and financiers was sufficient to defuse most resentments based on caste differences. As for the peasantry, which constituted more than 60 percent of the Austrian populace, it lived securely on the fertile agricultural lands of the entailed estates.

The Austrian national character had been imbued with a spirit of outward piety leavened by prudent conformism ever since the savage suppression of the Reformation in the sixteenth and seventeenth centuries. Actually, the regimes of Maria Theresa and Joseph II, however benevolent, had also been despotisms which conditioned most Austrians to accept arbitrary government. A German visitor in 1780 wrote that there were then six hundred spies in Vienna, and that "the police of this place [are] entirely taken up with the object of suppressing everything that indicates vigor and manly strength." [3] Nevertheless, the decade of the 1780s had been a liberating experience for many Viennese, who glimpsed the possibilities of a more humane and rational organization of society. For them the reinstitution and intensification of repressive measures of rule were all the more devastating, because such measures were seen against the background of those hopeful possibilities.

Though the portrait of sybaritic Vienna painted by prudish English and German observers in the later eighteenth century may have been overdrawn, it is largely true that the Viennese gave the impression of a people dedicated to entertainment rather than enlightenment, to escapism rather than involvement in the affairs of the world. "What succeeds most here is buffoonery, and even the bettermost part of the reading public is satisfied with plays, romances, and fairy tales," wrote Riesbeck in 1780,[4] while Owen noted in 1792 that "good cheer is, indeed, pursued here in every quarter, and mirth is worshipped in every form." [5] "Serious" subjects were generally avoided in conversation by most Viennese. Too *"traurig"* (too sad), they were wont to say, as they turned to topics of amusement and gossip. "Desperate but not serious" became the unofficial

Viennese motto. Rope dancers and jugglers, puppeteers and charlatans competed for attention on the public squares. The theaters were filled with entertainments of the widest variety, while at the Hetz Amphitheater equestrians and acrobats served as curtain raisers for the main events: bloody battles to the death between wild animals for the diversion of the populace. In fair weather, the people walked upon the ramparts which surrounded the inner city or strolled in the Prater or the Augarten; and always they gathered in the lavish coffeehouses and beer halls which proliferated throughout Vienna. Dancing was a universal amusement, and there were numerous houses appropriate to this purpose at which members of all classes mingled, often wearing masks to disguise their identity and increase their fascination. It was said that "many of these dancing halls are institutions for infamous purposes." [6] Whether this was true or not, prostitution was widespread in Vienna. When it was proposed to Joseph II to construct licensed brothels, he replied: "The walls would cost me nothing, but the expense of roofing would be ruinous, for it would just be necessary to put a roof over the whole city." [7] The number of illegitimate births was not far short of the number of those within wedlock.

Another British visitor to Vienna may well have exaggerated when he wrote, "No city perhaps can present such scenes of affected sanctity and real licentiousness," [8] but it surely is not unfair to assert that most Viennese had accepted a life of bread and circuses rather than one of high principle and deep feeling. Nor were the police unaware of the pacifying advantages of these Viennese proclivities. A police memorandum preventing the closing of the Theater-an-der-Wien in 1805 observed: "The people are accustomed to theatrical shows.... In times like these, when the character of individuals is affected by so many sufferings, the police are more than ever obliged to cooperate in the diversion of the citizens by every moral means. The most dangerous hours of the day are the evening hours. They cannot be filled more innocently than in the theater." [9] If the police winked at the political jokes that were frequently interspersed in popular farces they did so because they understood that popular diversion was an escape valve for social resentments and pressures.

Viennese life presented a surface of gaiety; "At its heart," wrote A. J. P. Taylor, "was a despairing frivolity." [10] The determination to savor the present masked a desire to forget or revise the past and a hopelessness concerning the future. The vaunted Viennese idealization of womanhood went hand in hand with a pernicious, commercialized view of sex and marriage. The easy rejections of *"traurig"* politics arose from fear of reprisal; love for the Kaiser was thoroughly interwoven with dread of his secret police. And for many members of Viennese society—those who had not forgotten the Josephinian ideal of a benevolent monarchy devoted to rationality and social advancement—the reversion to irrationality and terror interwoven with hedonistic gratification was grossly unsatisfying.

In some ultimately inexplicable way, the high-Classic style of the late Mozart, the later Haydn, and the early Beethoven seemed perfectly to embody and to crystallize the moods and sentiments of such Viennese during the post-Josephinian period. If the conditions of Viennese life in the Napoleonic era had led to a failure of political nerve, to a withdrawal from philosophical inquiry, and to a diminution in avowedly humanistic concerns, Enlightened sentiments and rational tendencies nevertheless had to find their outlet. Apparently they found one in the realm of Viennese instrumental music—the most immediate, most abstract, and least censorable of the arts. In a sense, we may view the masterpieces of the high-Classic style as a music into which flowed the thwarted impulses of the Josephinian *Aufklärung*, a music of meditative cast which refuses to give way to superficiality and pretense, a music which is "classic" by virtue of its avoidance of the extremes of triviality and grandiosity. At the same time, this music expressed a utopian ideal: the creation of a self-contained world symbolic of the higher values of rationality, play, and beauty. In the greater works of Mozart, Haydn, and the early Beethoven are condensed some of the contradictory feelings of Viennese life. Gaiety is undermined by a sense of loss, courtly grace is penetrated by brusque and dissonant elements, and profound meditation is intermingled with fantasy.

The obvious pretenses and deceptions of ritual opera had long since worn out their effectiveness through overuse; Rococo aestheticism, the *galant* style, and overworked early Classic formulas had too large an admixture of transparent narcoticism to satisfy the needs of the more liberated and enlightened members of society. Within a few short years, Viennese music underwent a stunning alteration through the crystallization of the high-Classic style and the beginnings of its functioning as a "national" art. Mozart, who had labored so painfully to make his mark in Vienna, was suddenly (and posthumously) its favorite son, and both his person and his works were lauded as the embodiment of the Viennese spirit. Haydn was now monumentalized by the city which had rather neglected him for several decades.

At first, Beethoven deliberately chose for himself the role of their successor, mastering their genres, styles, and tradition and bringing them to completion. Beethoven's role in Viennese life, however, was to be quite different from that of his predecessors. Despite, or perhaps because of, his iconoclasm and rebelliousness, Vienna was to find in Beethoven its myth-maker, the creator of its new "sacred history," one who was prepared to furnish it with a model of heroism as well as beauty during an age of revolution and destruction and to hold out the image of an age of reconciliation and freedom to come. In the 1790s Beethoven was merging his most intimate desires with the collective strivings of Vienna and its aristocracy, finding collaborators in what Hanns Sachs terms a "mutual daydream." Later he would supply citizens of his adopted city with a consistent body of emotional attitudes, and with a conception of the world that would symbolically legitimize their very existence and give them hope of a future in which their place might be secure.

Title page of the Trios, op. 1 (1795).

(Gesellschaft der Musikfreunde, Vienna)

10
The Music

Beethoven's early Vienna works continued to absorb influences from a wide variety of sources. These influences, however, do not here lead to an unfocused eclecticism—as was the case with his Bonn music—but are increasingly under the control of an emerging, forceful musical personality. Beethoven's receptivity was now combined with a capacity to resist other influences which, however appealing, were not useful to the main lines of his development. He listened to, and studied, an enormous amount of the music of his contemporaries, sometimes with adoration, sometimes bursting into laughter when he heard bad music—perhaps because he perceived missed connections and unfulfilled possibilities; but always he was receptive to new ideas, trying to master—as he wrote in another connection—"what the better and wiser people of every age were driving at in their works." [1]

Although scholars have long delighted in tracing Beethoven's style to a wide variety of sources, his primary influences were, of course, those emanating from the Viennese Classical style. He revered Gluck as one of the greatest of composers, ranking him with Handel, Bach, Mozart, and Haydn. Rolland rightly says that insufficient attention is paid to Gluck's influence on the young Beethoven with respect to "dramatic expression, energy of accent, concision of musical speech, breadth and clarity of design. . . ." [2] Tovey, however, did not overlook Gluck's significance; he wrote that the whole of Beethoven's "aesthetic system has arisen from the sonata style, which is . . . intimately connected with the revolution, or rather the birth, of dramatic music style in the operas of Gluck." [3] Mozart's influence, which had permeated many of the Bonn works, remained strong during the early Vienna years, especially in Beethoven's chamber music for strings and for winds. The absence of personal competition vis-à-vis Mozart permitted Beethoven to express sublimated adoration for the Salzburg master, while still sensing the futility of striving after a perfection that had already been attained. On hearing a performance of Mozart's C-minor Piano Concerto, K.V. 491, Beethoven exclaimed to a fellow pianist and composer: "Cramer! Cramer! We shall never be able to do anything like that!" [4]

As for the influence of Haydn, we saw earlier that Beethoven was seeking to find a personal voice in a world spiritually dominated by the older master. He apparently had some difficulties with Clementi as well: on Clementi's visit to Vienna in 1804 Beethoven refused to make a first call on the older master, leaving the two studiously avoiding each other. Ries remembered that the composers, along with their respective pupils, would eat in a tavern at the same table, but that "the one did not speak to the other, or if he did, he confined himself to a greeting." [5] Still later, we will find an anxiety over Cherubini's influence as well; this lasted until he mastered Cherubini's rhetorical "grand manner," and eventually subsided following his clear transcendence of the French master.

The primary genres which Beethoven explored during his first Vienna period, which lasted until about 1802, are the piano sonata, the duo sonata, the piano trio, the string trio, the string quartet, chamber music for winds, the concerto, and the symphony. In addition he wrote a good many occasional pieces (mostly dance music), almost two dozen *Lieder*, several arias, a concert scene, and a large number of sets of variations. Conspicuously absent (or minimally present) are choral music, music for the church, and, with one exception, which we shall treat in a later chapter, music for the stage. The major forms to which Beethoven devoted himself were the sonata form in three- and four-movement cycles and, continuing the Bonn trend, variation form, both within and outside of the sonata cycle.

As has long been recognized, the piano was the central vehicle of Beethoven's musical development during the first Vienna years, both as composer and as virtuoso. With his removal to Vienna, his emergence as a virtuoso, and his tutelage under Haydn, he became aware of the expressive possibilities of the piano in contrast to those of earlier keyboard instruments. From early on, he interested himself in piano manufacture, seeking instruments of increased range, heavier action, bigger tone, and more versatile pedals. "One can also make the pianoforte sing," he wrote around 1796 to his piano manufacturer friend Johann Andreas Streicher; "I hope the time will come when the harp and the pianoforte will be treated as two entirely different instruments." [6] By 1802, he wrote to Zmeskall that piano manufacturers were "swarming around me in their anxiety . . . to make me a pianoforte exactly as I should like it." [7]

There was a ready market for piano variations among Vienna's multitude of pianists and piano students. Beethoven wrote more than a dozen sets of variations for piano (some with accompanying violin or cello) between 1793 and 1801. Each of them was promptly published, usually within a few months of its composition. They were for the most part skillfully wrought sets of ornamental variations on themes from popular or familiar operas—entertaining, brilliant, and deliberately superficial, although few are without beautiful moments. Meanwhile, in slow movements of sonata-cycle works such as the Trio, op. 1 no. 3; the String Quartet, op. 18 no. 5; the Septet, op. 20; the Sonata, op. 14 no. 2; and the first movement of the Sonata, op. 26, Beethoven was progressing from the external variation manner to more complex and imaginative principles of variation technique. The Variations on Salieri's "La stessa, la stessissima," WoO 73, written in 1799, still rely on ornamental techniques, but their harmonic plan and carefully designed tempo alternations create a more organic structure. The significant advance in this form, which constitutes part of the transition to Beethoven's next style period, took place in 1802 with the Variations on an Original Theme in F major, op. 34, and the Fifteen Variations and Fugue in E-flat major, op. 35, later known as the "Eroica" Variations. Beethoven wrote to Breitkopf & Härtel asking that the printed edition include an introductory note, composed by himself, calling attention to their innovative character:

> As the v[ariations] are distinctly different from my earlier ones, instead of indicating them like my *previous ones* . . . I have included them in the proper numerical series *of my greater musical works,* the more so as the themes have been composed by me.[8]

The opus 35 Variations are of special interest by virtue of their use of compositional procedures—fugue, chaconne, harmonic variation—identified with the Baroque composers. Wrote Beethoven: "The introduction to these grand variations . . . begins with the bass of the theme and eventually develops into two, three, and four parts; and not till then does the theme appear, which again cannot be called a variation." [9] To the listener, it is unclear as to whether the grotesque bass melody is the theme or the harmony of the theme, an ambiguity which creates great interest.

Beethoven's first works to bear an opus number were the three Trios for Piano, Violin, and Cello, op. 1, published in 1795. They were a great success, commanding "extraordinary attention" and receiving—except for Haydn's caveat concerning the C-minor Trio—the "undivided applause" of connoisseurs and music lovers.[10] (Yet, a few arrangements aside, Beethoven did not return to the form until his Trios, op. 70, in 1808.) Like Beethoven's first Viennese piano sonatas, the opus 1 Trios are fashioned on a grand scale, each being in four movements and each being of great length, averaging almost 1,100 measures per trio. Beethoven was from the first thinking in terms of formal expansion within the standard parameters of high-Classic sonata form. The third trio, in C minor, is the outstanding work of this set, illustrating what Nigel Fortune calls "the most epoch making of his creative conquests: the expansion of long-range tonal drama, intensified by the nature of the material, dynamic contrasts and the generation of momentum." [11] Noteworthy in the trios is the independent and occasionally florid writing for the cello. In this Beethoven had considerable precedent in Mozart's trios, but little in Haydn's. In the Cello Sonatas, op. 5, written in 1796 for Jean-Louis Duport to play for Friedrich Wilhelm II of Prussia, Beethoven had no such precedent, for neither Mozart nor Haydn had composed sonatas for the cello, which was only recently emancipating itself from its traditional role as a continuo instrument and beginning to assert its prerogatives as a virtuoso vehicle. Beethoven's were the first important sonatas for this combination to contain a fully written-out piano part. These ambitiously scaled, sonorous sonatas, with their spacious Adagio introductions, opened the era of the Classic–Romantic cello sonata. Beethoven's next effort in this genre dates from 1807–08; in the early Vienna years, however, he also wrote three sets of variations for cello and piano, op. 66, WoO 45, and WoO 46.

Beethoven's ten sonatas for violin and piano have always been cornerstones of the sonata duo repertory, though they have received far less critical attention than the piano sonatas. Beethoven, himself a violinist in Bonn, took lessons with Schuppanzigh and Krumpholz after arriving in Vienna and had, if no special skill, a special love for the instrument, composing for it some of his most contented, graceful, and perfectly proportioned music. All but two of the sonatas were composed within the five years ending in 1802. The set of three Sonatas, op. 12, dates from 1797–98; the Sonatas, op. 23 and op. 24 (*Spring*), from 1800–1801 (they were originally intended to be published [and perhaps played] together); and the three Sonatas, op. 30, dedicated to Czar Alexander, from 1802. Of these, only opus 24 and opus 30 no. 2 are in four movements, the others adhering to the standard three-movement cycle. Riezler writes of the first five sonatas that, in contrast to the piano sonatas, they "showed less evidence of mental struggle and were therefore . . . in many respects more perfect, but at the same time less individual." [12] Nevertheless, there are innovative and even experimental touches—especially in opus 23, with its unusual Presto first movement, foreshadowing the *Kreutzer* Sonata, op. 47, and in the rondo-finale of opus 24, with its unexpected digressions into distant tonalities, preceding the fourth refrain. The Sonatas, op. 30, are a clear advance, with an expansion of tonal sonorities, and moments of heroic pathos which clearly signal that Beethoven was arriving at the outer limit of the high-Classic style. Indeed, what is now the finale of the *Kreutzer* was originally intended for the finale of opus 30 no. 1. Beethoven had by this time dramatically extended the expressive range of his piano writing. Now he was in the process of shaping a new, dynamic, and declamatory voice for the violin to balance this unprecedented pianistic style.

Beethoven's chamber music for strings, which includes three string trios, six string quartets, and two string quintets, marks a stage in his gradual liberation from reliance upon the piano as the anchor of his compositional style. The String Trios, op. 9, were sketched as early as 1796 or 1797 and were published in 1798. As we noted earlier, in his dedicatory message to Count Browne, Beethoven called them "the best of my works" up to that point, and more than one critic has agreed with his judgment. Like the Piano Trios, op. 1, each of them is in four movements and each elaborates somewhat different possibilities of the sonata cycle. Opus 9 no. 1 opens with an Adagio introduction and closes in sonata form rather than the usual rondo form. Opus 9 no. 2 substitutes an Andante quasi allegretto for the traditional slow movement, a shift in balance which recurs in the Eighth Symphony in 1812. Where the first two trios are expansive and luxuriant, the third, in C minor, is considerably condensed, striving for the sense of inevitability and logic which characterizes Beethoven's later symphonic C-minor projects. Beethoven never returned to the string trio in later years, perhaps because of the tonal superiority and greater expressiveness and flexibility of the string quartet, which ultimately superseded other chamber-music genres for him.

It was to the set of String Quartets, op. 18, that Beethoven turned for the most ambitious single project of his early Vienna years. This set was begun in 1798, composed primarily in 1799 and 1800, and published in 1801 with a dedication to Prince Lobkowitz. The string quartet was one of the favored media of the Viennese salons, Vienna was a world center of string-quartet composition, and Haydn had been the supreme master of the form. During the years 1793–99, Haydn composed fourteen of his sixty-eight quartets, dedicating them to members of the same group of aristocratic patrons whose names are frequently encountered in Beethoven's early biography: Count Apponyi (op. 71 and op. 74), Count Erdödy (op. 76), and Prince Lobkowitz (op. 77). As Haydn usually composed his quartets in groups of six, Beethoven's opus 18 carried overtones of both emulation and competition.[13]

The probable original order of composition of the opus 18 Quartets was established (somewhat erroneously) by Nottebohm and more recently clarified by Brandenburg: [14] nos. 3, 1, 2, 5, 4, and 6. Several were partially rewritten prior to publication. All of them essentially accept the usual four-movement structure and all reflect the Viennese Classic style, with an occasional admixture of Italianate melody—perhaps under the influence of Salieri, to whom Beethoven had just dedicated his Sonatas, op. 12.

The adherence to tradition is more evident in the first three quartets, for in the later ones Beethoven began to alter the weights and textures of the movements within the usual structure. Kerman writes that in these, "Beethoven seems suddenly to have thrown the classical framework in doubt. These pieces all entertain experiments with different types and arrangements of movements." [15] The opening movements are lightened, and since the finales are composed in sonata form rather than in the characteristic rondo form, the climax of each cycle tends to be transferred to the close of each work. The Andante scherzoso quasi Allegretto of no. 4, like the similarly designated second movement of the String Trio, op. 9 no. 2, signals Beethoven's willingness to dispense with the traditional slow movement. The insertion of an Allegro in the Adagio cantabile of no. 2—this apparently occurred late in the compositional process—is another example of the flexibility with which Beethoven was now handling the traditional forms. Most striking, perhaps, is the mystical 44-bar second Adagio entitled "La Malinconia" that prefaces the finale of no. 6 and returns briefly to arrest the climax of the Allegretto quasi Allegro before the final statement and coda. This is not to say, however, that the opus 18 Quartets can be regarded as experimental works comparable to Beethoven's most impressive contemporary piano sonatas. Many of Beethoven's "unusual" touches—the reversal of the inner movements in no. 5 and the use of variation form in the Andante cantabile of the same work—have precedents in Haydn and Mozart. If there are occasional intimations of Beethoven's later quartet styles in these works, and if, as Radcliffe notes, Beethoven here uses "a rhetoric more emphatic and vehement than that of Haydn or Mozart," [16] the quartets essentially remain traditional and even conservative, reflecting Beethoven's main ambition—to achieve mastery of a major medium of the high-Classic tradition.

Beethoven mastered the string quintet (quartet, with added viola) with only two efforts. In 1795–96 he arranged for string quintet his then unpublished Octet for Winds (later published as opus 103), with revisions sufficient to warrant calling it a new composition (opus 4). It is, however, the String Quintet, op. 29, written in 1800–1801 and published the following year, that is his masterpiece in this genre, worthy of a place alongside Mozart's magnificent works for this combination of instruments. It is a characteristically spacious, sonorous, and fully controlled work, with smoothly flowing thematic development, a lyrical Adagio, an inventive and unflagging Scherzo and—with much tremolo accompaniment—one of the most successful "stormy" finales (the first was in opus 2 no. 1) of Beethoven's early years.

Completing this brief survey of Beethoven's chamber music are three works for piano and winds: the Quintet for Piano and Winds, op. 16, written in 1796–97 and modeled on Mozart's quintet for the same instrumentation, K.V. 452; the Sonata for French Horn (or Cello) and Piano, op. 17, written in haste (according to Ries, in one day) for performance by Beethoven and Johann Wenzel Stich at the latter's concert of April 18, 1800 (it was repeated at another concert shortly thereafter in Pesth); and the Trio for Clarinet, Cello, and Piano, op. 11, composed in 1798. Beethoven also wrote several works for winds and strings: the slight Serenade, op. 25, for flute, violin, and viola; and the popular Septet, op. 20, for clarinet, horn, bassoon, and strings, written for Empress Maria Theresia at the turn of the century. Also composed during this period, but kept from publication until 1810, were a Sextet for String Quartet and Horns, op. 81b, and a Sextet for Clarinets, Horns, and Basoons, op. 71. Rosen makes the interesting point that works such as the Septet and the Quintet are "classicizing" rather than "classic" in style: "They are reproductions of classical forms . . . based upon the exterior models, the results of the classical impulse, and not upon the impulse itself." [17] This style also leads, however, toward the tenuous and amiable pre-Romantic, Biedermeier manner of Spohr and other composers of the following decades.

Beethoven's chamber music for winds, or for winds supported by strings or piano, did not survive the century that adored such combinations. In terms of Beethoven's further development, these works may be regarded as preparations for his long-delayed entry into symphonic music.

Beethoven composed three concertos for piano and orchestra in these years. The Concerto no. 2 in B-flat, although of Bonn origin, and perhaps first drafted as early as 1785, was probably rewritten at least twice in Vienna; it was published in 1801 as opus 19. The sparkling Concerto no. 1 in C, op. 15, also published in 1801, bears an earlier opus number than the Concerto no. 2 but was written later, certainly by 1798, for full orchestra, including trumpets and kettledrums. Perhaps to forestall negative criticism in Breitkopf & Härtel's *Allgemeine musikalische Zeitung,* Beethoven warned the Leipzig publisher that neither work was among his better compositions in the form.[18] He wrote out three cadenzas for the First Concerto, the last of which dates from 1804 or later. Both concertos reflect Mozart's example in formal organization, in the balance between piano and orchestra, and in the nature of the pianistic writing. The Concerto no. 3, op. 37, which was completed in 1800, represents a marked advance over its predecessors, and it became the established model of Classic–Romantic concerto form for the nineteenth century. Where the First Concerto has elements of what Tovey calls the Classic "comedy of manners," and the Second reveals a more intimate, if not fully realized, chamber-music quality, the Third represents Beethoven's first effort in this genre to record something far beyond merely exterior wit or refinement, and to move toward dramatic oratory. Beethoven had earlier (e.g., opus 1 no. 3; opus 9 no. 3; opus 10 no. 1; opus 13; opus 18 no. 4) enlisted the key of C minor in his search for the expression of *"pathétique"* sentiments; in his middle Vienna years, C minor would become his "heroic" key, as in the Fifth Symphony, the funeral march of the *Eroica* Symphony, and the Overture to *Coriolan.* This direction is foreshadowed to some extent in the Third Piano Concerto as well as in the Violin Sonata, op. 30 no. 2.

Sketches from the mid-1790s for an unwritten Symphony in C major survive,[19] but it was not until 1800 that Beethoven ventured to complete his First Symphony, op. 21. It was then five years after Haydn's final effort in the form, and twelve years after Mozart's *Jupiter* Symphony. In the interim, numerous symphonies by such composers as Wranitsky, Eybler, and Cartellieri—none of which made any lasting impression—had found their way onto concert programs in Vienna.[20] In light of the risks involved, as well as the newness of the task, it was natural that Beethoven's First Symphony, scored for the standard orchestra of Haydn and Mozart, with clarinets added, should lean heavily on the traditional inheritance. Perhaps this is why it became one of the most popular of Beethoven's symphonies during his lifetime. Tovey, who calls it Beethoven's "fitting farewell to the eighteenth century," stresses that it "shows a characteristic caution in handling sonata form for the first time with a full orchestra." [21] However, contemporary critics did not by any means regard it as a timid or imitative work. The reviewer in the *Allgemeine musikalische Zeitung* spoke of its "considerable art, novelty and . . . wealth of ideas," [22] thinking no doubt of the audacious "off-key" opening; the striking use of the timpani in the Andante cantabile, which foreshadows similar solos in Beethoven's later works; and the teasing scale passage which initiates the closing Allegro.

Completed in 1802, during a turbulent period in Beethoven's life, the

Second Symphony, in D major, op. 36, is already the work of a mature master who is settling accounts—or making peace—with the high-Classic symphonic tradition before embarking on an unprecedented musical voyage. It is a work which has both retrospective and prospective characteristics: it is firmly rooted in Mozart's and Haydn's last symphonies while anticipating Beethoven's later development by its dynamic contrasts, unexpected modulations, and propulsive movement, all of which are controlled by a confident and flowing Classicism.

Thirty-two piano sonatas bear Beethoven's opus numbers. The first twenty were composed in the eight years ending 1802, and it is in them that Beethoven's first unquestioned masterpieces are to be found. These sonatas fall readily into two groups: thirteen sonatas written prior to 1800—opus 2 to opus 22, plus two "easy sonatas," opus 49—which explore and expand the possibilities of sonata form; and seven sonatas—opus 26 to opus 31—which are simultaneously an epilogue or farewell to the standard high-Classic sonata and a transition toward a new line of development, whose potentialities would be realized in the works of Beethoven's later years. Beethoven's earliest sonatas, broadly conceived, spacious in design, rich in detail and invention, were clearly intended as major efforts. Where Haydn and Mozart had relied almost exclusively on the three-movement design, six of Beethoven's first sonatas (including his first four) used the four-movement scheme usually reserved for symphonies and quartets, through the addition of a minuet or scherzo; these sonatas were, on the average, almost one and a half times as long as those of his predecessors. The sonatas run the full gamut of *Sturm und Drang* sentiment—passion, reverie, exuberance, heroism, solemnity, nobility, and dramatic pathos— but they are also full of abrupt harmonic and dynamic effects, piquant episodes, unusual rhythms, syncopations, and brief departures for distant keys, all of which signify that this young composer was not content merely to remain a dutiful exponent of a great tradition. Tovey observes that Beethoven's "epigrammatic" manner was characteristic "not of immaturity, but of art in which problems are successfully solved for the first time." [23] It is Beethoven's unification of two opposing trends—the epigrammatic tendency along with an overall striving for spaciousness—that is a distinguishing characteristic of his early Vienna style.

Riezler calls the Sonata, op. 7, Beethoven's "first masterpiece," [24] and Beethoven may have had a similar feeling about it, for he entitled the work "Grande Sonate" and issued it as a separate opus rather than as one of a set. The first two of the set of three Sonatas, op. 10, are filled with imaginative ideas, but are overshadowed by the particularly important third sonata (also designated "Grande" by the composer), with its eloquent and sombre Largo e mesto, which forecasts the disintegrating passage at the close of the *Eroica* funeral march. The *Sonate pathétique*, op. 13, of 1798–99 has had a great popularity partly on account of its romantic title, but this does not diminish its real importance. It is the most dynamically propulsive of Beethoven's piano sonatas thus far, the first sonata to utilize a slow, dramatic introduction, and the first whose movements are clearly and unmistakably linked through the use of related thematic material and conscious reminiscences. In its ardent, youthful way, it opens up the path to the "fantasy sonatas" of the following years.

The two Sonatas, op. 14, mark a turn toward less dramatic subject matter. The "Grande Sonate," op. 22, closes out this high-Classic phase of Beethoven's sonata development on a note of absolute confidence in his mastery of the form. Beethoven was especially proud of it: "This sonata is really something," he wrote to his publisher.[25] William S. Newman finds in it "a new pre-Mendelssohnian charm and grace and an Italianate lyricism." [26]

With the next group of sonatas, opus 26 (*Funeral March*) and opus 27 nos. 1 and 2 (*Moonlight*), Beethoven appeared to take leave of the traditional sonata-cycle form in favor of a more flexible construction—the "fantasy sonata"—which permitted the freer expression of improvisatory ideas and displaced the climax of the cycle to the final movement. Beethoven gave the title "Sonata quasi una Fantasia" to each of the two Sonatas, op. 27, a designation which has no readily apparent precedent in the later Classic era. The unusual innovation is that none of these three sonatas contains an opening sonata-form allegro movement. Bekker, who analyzed this important stage in Beethoven's sonata evolution, wrote that Beethoven must have found first-movement sonata form a hindrance to his desire "to give free rein to his fancy, to improvise, not only in a single movement, but with absolute freedom throughout a multiple form." The opening sonata-allegro movement, writes Bekker,

> gave the work a definite character from the beginning . . . which succeeding movements could supplement but not change. Beethoven rebelled against this determinative quality in the first movement. He wanted a prelude, an introduction, not a proposition. He did not wish to commit himself in the first movement to a certain sequence of thought.[27]

Nor, we may add, did he wish to exhaust the dramatic essence of the cycle in its first movement. The Sonata, op. 26, initiates this development with its opening Andante con variazioni movement, but fails thereafter to pursue its architectural implications; it remained for the opus 27 Sonatas to bring it to fruition. Each work begins with a slow introductory movement which has the character of a dreamlike improvisation, followed by a scherzo interlude (and, in opus 27 no. 1, a lyrical Adagio movement);

and each closes with a climactic fast movement. In opus 27 no. 2 the finale is no longer a rondo, but a fully developed sonata-form movement.

Beethoven's exploration of the possibilities of expressing new impulses and ideas in the fantasy sonata did not end in 1801; he would once again take up this thread in his later years. At this moment in his creative journey, however, Beethoven was setting himself other tasks. With the calm and reflective Sonata, op. 28 (*Pastorale*), Beethoven reverted, for the last time in his life, to the normal four-movement sonata form, with a traditional distribution of emotional weight and emphasis. Like so many of Beethoven's works which follow hard upon a dramatic achievement, opus 28 celebrates the peace that comes from the fulfillment of a difficult creative effort and withdraws to a relative traditionalism, from which Beethoven will gain strength for a new creative surge.

It is difficult to say whether the three Sonatas, op. 31 (composed in 1802; published 1803–04 by Nägeli in Zürich), opened an era or closed one. Bekker saw the first two sonatas as the culmination of the fantasy-sonata form, and the third as the beginning of a new virtuoso style which would later come to fruition in the *Waldstein* and *Appassionata* sonatas. Blom calls the first—a three-movement piece in G major—"a somewhat reactionary work for its time" and one which leans heavily on pianistic devices.[28] The cheerful and witty third sonata, in E-flat major, is in four movements, using both a scherzo and a minuet between the two sonata-form outer movements. But it is the impassioned second sonata, in D minor and in three movements, which is the best known of the set. The first movement of the D-minor Sonata opens with an unusual alternation of an arpeggiated recitative-Largo and an agitated Allegro and omits the traditional second theme; this has given rise to debate as to its underlying structural principle. Ludwig Misch believes that the Largo and the Allegro, taken together, constitute the theme, and he finds in this mixture a daring innovation, "far more novel and simple, more daring and logical" than had previously been supposed.[29] The dancing, triumphant Allegretto is one of Beethoven's most successful finales, perhaps foreshadowing the transfigured waltz movement which closes the String Quartet in A minor, op. 132.

One senses during these years, and especially in the years 1798 to 1802, Beethoven's determination to achieve a mastery of the Viennese high-Classic style within each of its major instrumental genres. The challenge of the piano trio was met earliest, with opus 1 in 1795; the string trio with opus 9 in 1798; the string quartet with opus 18 in 1799 and 1800; the string quintet with opus 29 in 1801; the Classic piano concerto with the Third Concerto in 1800; the duo sonata with opuses 23, 24, and 30 in 1801–02; the piano sonata with opuses 22 and 28 in 1800 and 1801; the symphony with the D major in 1802. It was Beethoven's tendency, having mastered a genre, to withdraw for a time from a further expansion of the implications of his advance and turn elsewhere. It seems that until 1802, Beethoven restrained the pull of his imagination each time it threatened to move him beyond the limits of the Classic tradition and, with what appears to have been conscious deliberation, occupied himself in less dangerous terrain. This may be why several works of this period— such as the two symphonies and the sonatas, op. 28 and op. 31 no. 1— have a somewhat conservative cast when viewed alongside several of the String Quartets, op. 18, and the sonatas, op. 27 and op. 31 no. 2.

Beethoven had gained the high ground of the Viennese tradition; he was now faced with the choice of endless repetition of his conquests or casting out in an uncharted direction. According to Czerny, it was soon after the composition of the Sonata in D major, op. 28, that Beethoven said to his friend Krumpholz: "I am only a little satisfied with my previous works. From today on I will take a new path." [30] Several paths lay open before Beethoven. One of these lay in the direction of Romanticism, toward the loosening and imaginative extension of Classic designs and the consolidation of an internal, probing, transcendent style. For reasons which are necessarily obscure, Beethoven chose to delay this stage of his development, perhaps because in the years around 1801 and 1802 he found within sonata form new, unexplored possibilities—thematic condensation; more intense, extended, and dramatic development; and the infusion of richer fantasy and improvisatory materials into an even more highly structured Classicism.

Beethoven was now well launched upon his "new path"—a qualitative change in his style which would become a turning point in the history of music itself. It is hard to imagine that a transformation of this magnitude could occur without an accompanying biographical crisis of major proportions.

III
THE HEROIC PERIOD

Beethoven. Miniature on ivory by
Christian Horneman (1803).

11
Crisis and Creativity

The years 1800 and 1801 marked an important advance in Beethoven's career. In 1800 he began to receive the sizable annuity from Prince Lichnowsky, which gave him a relative degree of independence from the more restrictive forms of aristocratic patronage. On April 2, 1800, he gave the first public concert (*Akademie*) for his own benefit, at which was performed, in addition to works by Mozart and Haydn, his First Symphony, the Septet, and his Piano Concerto, op. 15. True, the Viennese critics inexplicably ignored the concert, and a review in Breitkopf & Härtel's music journal was not altogether favorable, but it was an event which symbolized Beethoven's emergence as a major creative personality. Shortly thereafter, his ballet score, *The Creatures of Prometheus*, was a resounding success; it was to be performed twenty-three times in 1801–02. Foreign publishers increasingly began to bid for his works (which clearly had enjoyed an excellent sale in Viennese editions), thereby giving Beethoven a sense of his international importance and, perhaps, a glimpse of the possibilities of immortality as well. The year 1801 saw the richest publishing harvest of his career to that time, both in quantity and in musical scope.

Beneath this surface of accomplishment, however, inner conflicts were converging to form a crisis of major proportions. Beethoven was fulfilling many of his most deeply rooted wishes. Why, then, do we now find an undercurrent of malaise, a feeling of anxiety mingled with the apprehension of some unknown yet dreaded catastrophe? It is as though he were about to be destroyed by success itself. (Indeed, he once wrote to Zmeskall: "Sometimes I feel that I shall soon go mad in consequence of my unmerited fame; fortune is seeking me out and for that very reason I almost dread some fresh calamity." [1])

This contradiction in Beethoven's existence—an outward appearance of accomplishment, productivity, and gratification permeated by a sense of impending personal tragedy and despair—is reflected in his famous letter of June 29, 1801, to Franz Wegeler in Bonn:

> You want to know something about my present situation. Well, on the whole it is not at all bad. . . . My compositions bring me in a good deal; and I may say that I am offered more commissions than it is possible for me to carry out. Moreover for every composition I can count on six or seven publishers, and even more, if I want them; people no longer come to an arrangement with me, I state my price and they pay. So you see how pleasantly situated I am. For instance, I see a friend in need and it so happens that the state of my purse does not allow me to help him immediately; well then, I have only to sit down and compose and in a short time I can come to his aid. Moreover, I live more economically than I used to; and if I remain in Vienna for good, no doubt I shall contrive to obtain one day for a concert every year. I have given a few concerts.

Now Beethoven changes his mood and goes into a long account of his medical symptoms, perhaps hoping to obtain some advice from his physician friend:

> But that jealous demon, my wretched health, has put a nasty spoke in my wheel; and it amounts to this, that for the last three years my hearing has become weaker and weaker. The trouble is supposed to have been caused by the condition of my abdomen, which, as you know, was wretched even before I left Bonn, but has become worse in Vienna, where I have been constantly afflicted with diarrhea and have been suffering in consequence from an extraordinary debility. Frank tried to *tone up* my constitution with strengthening medicines and my hearing with almond oil, but much good did it do me! His treatment had no effect; my deafness became even worse and my abdomen continued to be in the same state as before. Such was my condition until the autumn of last year; and sometimes I gave way to despair. Then a medical ass

advised me to take cold baths to improve my condition. A more sensible doctor, however, prescribed the usual tepid baths in the Danube. The result was miraculous, and my insides improved. But my deafness persisted—or, I should say, became even worse. During this last winter I was truly wretched, for I had had really dreadful attacks of colic and again relapsed completely into my former condition. And thus I remained until about four weeks ago when I went to see *Vering*. For I began to think that my condition demanded the attention of a surgeon as well; and in any case I had confidence in him. Well, he succeeded in checking almost completely this violent diarrhea. He prescribed tepid baths in the Danube, to which I had always to add a bottle of strengthening ingredients. He ordered no medicines until about four days ago, when he prescribed pills for my stomach and an infusion for my ear. As a result I have been feeling, I may say, stronger and better; but my ears continue to hum and buzz day and night. I must confess that I lead a miserable life. For almost two years I have ceased to attend any social functions, just because I find it impossible to say to people: I am deaf. If I had any other profession I might be able to cope with my infirmity; but in my profession it is a terrible handicap. And if my enemies, of whom I have a fair number, were to hear about it, what would they say? In order to give you some idea of this strange deafness, let me tell you that in the theater I have to place myself quite close to the orchestra in order to understand what the actor is saying, and that at a distance I cannot hear the high notes of instruments or voices. As for the spoken voice, it is surprising that some people have never noticed my deafness; but since I have always been liable to fits of absentmindedness, they attribute my hardness of hearing to that. Sometimes, too, I can scarcely hear a person who speaks softly; I can hear sounds, it is true, but cannot make out the words. But if anyone shouts, I can't bear it. Heaven alone knows what is to become of me. *Vering tells me that my hearing will certainly improve, although my deafness may not be completely cured.* Already I have often cursed my Creator and my existence. *Plutarch* has shown me the *path of resignation*. If it is at all possible, I will bid defiance to my fate, though I feel that as long as I live there will be moments when I shall be God's most unhappy creature. . . . Resignation, what a wretched resource! Yet it is all that is left to me. . . .[2]

Two days later, on July 1, Beethoven wrote a similar letter to Karl Amenda:

How often would I like to have you here with me, for your B[eethoven] is leading a very unhappy life and is at variance with Nature and his Creator. Many times already I have cursed Him for exposing His creatures to the slightest hazard, so that the most beautiful blossom is thereby often crushed and destroyed. Let me tell you that my most prized possession, *my hearing*, has greatly deteriorated. When you were still with me, I already felt the symptoms; but I said nothing about them. Now they have become very much worse. . . . You will realize what a sad life I must now lead, seeing that I am cut off from everything that is dear and precious to me . . . I must withdraw from everything; and my best years will rapidly pass away without my being able to achieve all that my talent and my strength have commanded me to do. Sad resignation, to which I am forced to have recourse. Needless to say, I am resolved to overcome all this, but how is it going to be done? [3]

Despite the ominous portents in these letters, Beethoven's anxiety receded in the subsequent months. This was partly due to his good fortune in obtaining a new physician, with whom he developed a strong personal bond. The first symptoms of deafness had given rise to panic, sending Beethoven from one doctor to another in search of relief. But shortly after mid-1801 he turned to Johann Adam Schmidt, professor of general pathology and therapy at the Josephine Academy, who inspired Beethoven's confidence and allayed his fears to an extraordinary extent. Replying to Wegeler's inquiry about the state of his health, Beethoven wrote, on November 16, 1801: "True enough, I cannot deny it, the humming and buzzing is slightly less than it used to be, particularly in my left ear, where my deafness really began." Fearful of overstating the improvement, he continued: "But so far my hearing is certainly not a bit better; and I am inclined to think, although I do not dare to say so definitely, that it is a little weaker." However, optimism then gets the better of Beethoven's caution: "I am now leading a slightly more pleasant life, for I am mixing more with my fellow creatures. . . . This change has been brought about by a dear, charming girl who loves me and whom I love. After two years I am again enjoying a few blissful moments; and for the first time I feel that marriage might bring me happiness. Unfortunately she is not my class, and at the moment I certainly could not marry—I must still bustle about a good deal." (The reference is almost certainly to Countess Giulietta Guicciardi, one of Beethoven's piano students—aged sixteen—to whom he was drawn at this time.) And finally, he abandons the pessimistic tone: "For some time now my physical strength has been increasing more and more, and therefore my mental powers also. Every day brings me nearer to the goal which I feel but cannot describe. . . . I will seize Fate by the throat; it shall certainly not bend and crush me completely." [4] Resignation was now tempered by the determination to resist.

We gather, then, that Beethoven had endured several years of considerable anguish. Yet these were years of extremely high productivity and creative accomplishment, years which gave rise to those works which exhibit Beethoven's greatest mastery of the high-Classic style as well as the clearest signs that he was in transition toward a radically new style. Unlike the Bonn moratorium of 1786–89, the brief creative impasse of 1793, and the long crisis which would inaugurate his last period, there was here no interruption of productivity, but rather a remarkable acceleration in Beethoven's stylistic evolution, in which the new and the superseded styles thoroughly intermingled. "I live entirely in my music," he wrote to Wegeler, in the very same letter that announced his deafness, "and hardly have I completed one composition when I have already begun another. At my present rate of composing, I often produce three or four works at the same time." [5] His July 1, 1801, letter to Amenda was even more exuberant on this score: "Why, at the moment I feel equal to anything. Since your departure I have been composing all types of music, except operas and sacred works." [6] One begins to suspect that Beethoven's crisis and his extraordinary creativity were somehow related, and even that the former may have been the necessary precondition of the latter.

In 1800, Beethoven completed the six Quartets, op. 18; the First Symphony, op. 21; the Septet, op. 20; the Third Piano Concerto, op. 37; and the Sonata, op. 22, as well as a number of lesser works. The compositions completed in 1801 were even more impressive, including *The Creatures of Prometheus,* op. 43 (originally numbered op. 24); the String Quintet, op. 29; the Violin Sonatas, opp. 23 and 24; and four Piano Sonatas, op. 26, op. 27 nos. 1 and 2, and op. 28. As for the year 1802, its major works included the Second Symphony, op. 36; the three Violin Sonatas, op. 30; the sets of Variations, opp. 34 and 35; and the three Piano Sonatas, op. 31. Clearly there is no sign of a creative slowdown.

At this time, too, Beethoven was apparently leading an active social life. He was increasingly on close terms with his brother Caspar Carl. Stephan von Breuning had arrived from Bonn in 1801, and he and Beethoven met almost every day. Beethoven wrote of him to Wegeler: "It does me good to revive the old feelings of friendship." [7] Another Bonn friend, the composer Anton Reicha, arrived from Paris in 1802 to resume an intimate friendship ("like that of Orestes and Pylades," Reicha claimed). Beethoven continued to spend much time in Zmeskall's company and kept up his amusing correspondence with this friend whom he variously dubbed "Most Excellent Count of Music," "Baron Muck-Driver," and "Plenipotentiary of Beethoven's Kingdom." Moreover, it was precisely during these years of crisis that Beethoven's close friendship with the Brunsvik and Guicciardi families developed. He gave piano lessons to Josephine and Therese Brunsvik, as well as to their cousin, the above-mentioned Giulietta Guicciardi; he was a frequent guest at the Brunsvik's Vienna home and visited their Hungarian estates. Their brother Franz "adored" Beethoven, and the composer became close friends with him and with Josephine's husband, Count Joseph Deym.

Nevertheless, it appears that Beethoven's malaise had returned by the spring of 1802. Certainly his deafness was the prime factor in this discontent, but impediments to the progress of his career also played some part. He had hoped to give a major *Akademie* during the previous winter but had been unable to obtain the use of the court theater for a concert. And his approaches to the Imperial Court had not brought his desire for a permanent court position any closer to fruition. In a letter of April 8 he expressed his anger in surprisingly strong—and even dangerous—terms: "There are rascals in the Imperial City as there are at the Imperial Court—"[8] A few weeks later he wrote to Breitkopf & Härtel: "A good deal of business—and also a great many worries—have rendered me for a time quite useless for some things."[9] Dr. Schmidt recommended seclusion in the countryside as a shield against the vexations of ordinary life. Accordingly, Beethoven repaired to the quiet village of Heiligenstadt, probably in late April, and seems to have remained there for a full half year, an unusually extended vacation for him. His student, Ferdinand Ries—son of his Bonn neighbor, Franz Ries—who had visited Vienna in the spring of 1800 and returned there from Munich in late 1801 or early 1802,[10] came to see him in Heiligenstadt, and described both his apparent deafness and his moods: "I called his attention to a shepherd who was piping very agreeably in the woods on a flute made of a twig of elder. For half an hour Beethoven could hear nothing, and though I assured him that it was the same with me (which was not the case), he became extremely quiet and morose. When occasionally he seemed to be merry, it was generally to the extreme of boisterousness; but this happened seldom."[11] Perhaps these swings between melancholic and manic behavior reflected the depths of the pain which he was enduring—which was sufficient to cause him to consider ending his life. We learn of this from a celebrated document that was found among his papers after his death and that is now known as the Heiligenstadt Testament. Beethoven addressed his brothers on October 6 and October 10:

FOR MY BROTHERS CARL AND   BEETHOVEN

Oh you men who think or say that I am malevolent, stubborn, or misanthropic, how greatly do you wrong me. You do not know the secret cause which makes me seem that way to you. From childhood on, my heart and soul have been full of the tender feeling of goodwill, and I was ever inclined to accomplish great things. But, think that for six years now I have been hopelessly afflicted, made worse by senseless physicians, from year to year deceived with hopes of improvement, finally compelled to face the prospect of *a lasting malady* (whose cure will take years or, perhaps, be impossible). Though born with a fiery, active temperament, even susceptible to the diversions of society, I was soon compelled to withdraw myself, to live life alone. If at times I tried to forget all this, oh how harshly was I flung back by the doubly sad experience of my bad hearing. Yet it was impossible for me to say to people, "Speak louder, shout, for I am deaf." Ah, how could I possibly admit an infirmity in the *one sense* which ought to be more perfect in me than in others, a sense which I once possessed in the highest perfection, a perfection such as few in my profession enjoy or ever have enjoyed.—Oh I cannot do it; therefore forgive me when you see me draw back when I would have gladly mingled with you. My misfortune is doubly painful to me because I am bound to be misunderstood; for me there can be no relaxation with my fellow men, no refined conversations, no mutual exchange of ideas. I must live almost alone, like one who has been banished; I can mix with society only as much as true necessity demands. If I approach near to people a hot terror seizes upon me, and I fear being exposed to the danger that my condition might be noticed. Thus it has been during the last six months which I have spent in the country. By ordering me to spare my hearing as much as possible, my intelligent doctor almost fell in with my own present frame of mind, though sometimes I ran counter to it by yielding to my desire for companionship. But what a humiliation for me when someone standing next to me heard a flute in the distance and *I heard nothing,* or someone heard a *shepherd singing* and again I heard nothing. Such incidents drove me almost to despair; a little more of that and I would have ended my life—it was only *my art* that held me back. Ah, it seemed to me impossible to leave the world until I had brought forth all that I felt was within me. So I endured this wretched existence—truly wretched for so susceptible a body, which can be thrown by a sudden change from the best condition to the very worst.—*Patience,* they say, is what I must now choose for my guide, and I have done so—I hope my determination will remain firm to endure until it pleases the inexorable Parcae to break the thread. Perhaps I shall get better, perhaps not; I am ready.—Forced to become a philosopher already in my twenty-eighth year,—oh it is not easy, and for the artist much more difficult than for anyone else.—Divine One, thou seest my inmost soul; thou knowest that therein dwells the love of mankind and the desire to do good.—Oh fellow men, when at some point you read this, consider then that you have done me an injustice; someone who has had misfortune may console himself to find a similar case to his, who despite all the limitations of Nature nevertheless did everything within his powers to become accepted among worthy artists and men.—You, my brothers Carl and   , as soon as I am dead, if Dr. Schmidt is still alive, ask him in my name to describe my malady, and attach this written document to his account of my illness so that so far as is possible at least the world may become reconciled to me after my death.—At the same time, I declare you two to be the heirs to my small fortune (if so it can be called); divide it fairly; bear with and help each other. What injury you have done me you know was long ago forgiven. To you, brother Carl, I give special thanks for the attachment you have shown me of late. It is my wish that you may have a better and freer life than I have had. Recommend *virtue* to your children; it alone, not money, can make them happy. I speak from experience; this was what upheld me in time of misery. Thanks to it and to my art, I did not end my life by suicide—Farewell and love each other—I thank all my friends, particularly *Prince Lichnowsky* and *Professor Schmidt*—I would like the instruments from Prince L. to be preserved by one of you, but not to be the cause of strife between you, and as soon as they can serve you a better purpose, then sell them. How happy I shall be if I can still be helpful to you in my grave—so be it.—With joy I hasten to meet death.—If it comes before I have had the chance to develop all my artistic capacities, it will still be coming too soon despite my harsh fate, and I should probably wish it later—yet even so I should be happy, for would it not free me from a state of endless suffering?— Come *when* thou wilt, I shall meet thee bravely.—Farewell and do not wholly forget me when I am dead; I deserve this from you, for during my lifetime I was thinking of you often and of ways to make you happy—please be so—

Ludwig van Beethoven
(seal)

Heiglnstadt, [Heiligenstadt]
October 6th,
    1802

For my brothers Carl and [...] to be read and executed after my death.

Heiglnstadt, October 10th, 1802, thus I bid thee farewell—and indeed sadly.—Yes, that fond hope—which I brought here with me, to be cured to a degree at least—this I must now wholly abandon. As the leaves of autumn fall and are withered—so likewise has my hope been blighted—I leave here—almost as I came —even the high courage—which often inspired me in the beautiful days of summer—has disappeared—Oh Providence—grant me at last but one day *of pure joy*—it is so long since real joy echoed in my heart—Oh when—Oh when, Oh Divine One—shall I feel it again in the temple of nature and of mankind—Never?—No— Oh that would be too hard.[12]

The Heiligenstadt Testament is the most striking confessional statement in the biography of Beethoven. But the testament's emotional tone is curiously uneven, alternating between touching expressions of Beethoven's feelings of despair at his encroaching deafness and stilted, even literary formulations emphasizing his adherence to virtue. There are passages of real pathos, but these are so intertwined with self-conscious dramatics that one begins to realize that this neatly written document is a carefully revised "fair copy" which has been scrubbed clean of much of its original emotion. In particular, one remains unpersuaded by the references to suicide: "I would have ended my life—it was only *my* art that held me back"; "Thanks to [virtue] and to my art, I did not end my life by suicide." It is as though Beethoven were being deliberately laconic in order to avoid reviving distressful feelings. Probably the testament was written after the passions which gave rise to it had begun to cool.

Nevertheless, these underlying passions are evident despite Beethoven's redrafting; and they are so because Beethoven failed in his apparent goal—to present a coherent and "rational" explanation of his troubled state. For three years, perhaps more, he had been subject to attacks of severe anxiety, bordering on panic; he sought in the Heiligenstadt Testament to explain this suffering and anguish, which, he avowed, left him lonely, discontented, and suicidal. He believed that he had found the sole "secret cause" of his torments—in his deafness—and he offered the testament as an essay in self-justification, asking that after his death it be made public so that "the world may become reconciled to me" and will understand why he was thought to be "malevolent, stubborn, or misanthropic."

But, of course, we know that this is a great oversimplification, for these traits in Beethoven's character existed long before the onset of his deafness. Frau von Breuning was already familiar with his stubbornness and wayward moods in Bonn; his tendencies toward misanthropy and withdrawal were also evident in his earliest years; and patrons, teachers, and rival pianists had felt the force of his aggressiveness long before this time. Naturally, the consciousness of advancing deafness had a traumatic effect, but one senses that there is much more at work here than a mere reiteration of sentiments he had already voiced to Wegeler and Amenda fifteen months earlier.

It is both singular and striking, as biographers have not failed to observe, that Beethoven three times left portentous blank spaces in the testament where the name of his youngest brother should have appeared. But no one has seriously tried to explain these omissions.[13] Seemingly, some peculiarity in Beethoven's relations with his brothers is involved. But is it? Was the testament indeed intended only for his brothers? There is more than a little ambiguity here, for several times Beethoven addresses not his brothers, but mankind at large: "Oh you men who think or say that I am malevolent"; "Oh fellow men, when at some point you read this, consider then that you have done me an injustice." This confusion is further compounded in the postscript, where, as George Grove observed, the change from "you" to "thee" would "seem to indicate that Beethoven is there addressing a single person."[14] Is there, we wonder, another, perhaps unspecified, addressee?

Clearly there is no way of determining Beethoven's inner motives for omitting his brother's name. But it may be helpful in coming to a preliminary understanding to observe that it was not merely here that he failed to give the name of his youngest brother. Of the hundreds of references to Nikolaus Johann in Beethoven's letters and Conversation Books, there are only two in which his name is written. The first is on the address of Beethoven's letter of February 19, 1796: "To my brother Nikolaus Beethoven, to be delivered at the chemist's shop near the Kärntnertor." [15] The second comes on March 6, 1823, in a legal document addressed to and prepared under the supervision of Beethoven's attorney, Johann Baptist Bach: "You are entitled and requested to find for my beloved nephew . . . a guardian, who must not be, however, my brother Johann van Beethoven." [16] In the former instance the name is given not in the letter but only in the address on the verso; in the second, Beethoven, seeking to exclude his brother from the guardianship of their nephew, could not legally avoid writing the name "Johann van Beethoven." Even then, the sentence which includes his name was added as an afterthought, at the foot of the page.

Beethoven addressed his youngest brother by every imaginable circumlocution. At best he called him "my brother the chemist," "my brother, the bearer of this letter," or "the civil pharmaceutical chemist"; at worst, "pseudobrother," "brother Cain," "brain eater," "my ass of a brother," or "Signor Fratello." In some instances Beethoven managed to avoid the use of the name only with great effort. May we conclude from this that he had a powerful reluctance to use his brother's name? I think so. And this reluctance extended to Caspar Carl as well; for, apart from the Heiligenstadt Testament, his name is given only in four legal documents pertaining to the guardianship of his son,[17] as well as in the aforementioned letter of February 19, 1796, where his name is written ("My greetings to our brother Caspar") and then obliterated, followed by "stet." Here, too, there are several known instances in which Beethoven had to go to some lengths to avoid naming him, as for example in a letter to Nikolaus Johann, where Beethoven wrote: "If only God would give to our other worthy brother instead of his heartlessness—some feeling." [18] Surely it would have been more natural to have used Caspar Carl's name here.

Beethoven apparently was loath to grant either of his brothers a name. And it is tempting to connect this with his disinclination to accept their independence from him—which is strikingly illustrated in later years by his interference in Nikolaus Johann's marriage and by his forcible alteration of Caspar Carl's last will.

Of course, there is a possible common sense explanation of the omission of Nikolaus Johann's name—that Beethoven was unsure, perhaps for legal purposes, whether to call him by his first, by his middle name, or by both. For, as Ludwig Nohl observed, upon his arrival in Vienna Nikolaus Johann dropped his first name and began to call himself "Johann." [19] And Beethoven may have been equally unsure about his other brother's name, for a close examination of the testament shows that the spaces for Caspar Carl's name also were originally left blank both in the heading and on the last page of the testament. They were later filled in by Beethoven and, as Tyson observed, in a different script.

Beethoven *was* able, however, to write the name of one brother four times in the Heiligenstadt Testament. It does appear, therefore, that Beethoven specifically could not there bring himself to write the name "Johann." Did Beethoven perhaps regard his brother's adoption of this name as an audacious usurpation of the name of their father? We cannot tell, but our speculations would be incomplete if we failed to mention that nowhere in the surviving documents does Beethoven refer to his father by either his first or his full name. Only one document, indeed, includes even a portion of his name, and it contains a most curious and offhand reference to the composer's departed father. This is the already cited petition of May 3, 1793, to the elector, which begins: "A few years ago Your Electoral Excellency was pleased to retire my father, the court tenor van Beethoven. . . . " [20] Here too the name "Johann" is omitted.

The possibility emerges, then, that the name which is really omitted from the Heiligenstadt Testament is that of Johann van Beethoven, *père*. His very name may still have aroused such powerful feelings that Beethoven could not bring himself to inscribe it on paper. Is this Johann, perhaps, the enigmatic "thee" of the postscript, from whom Beethoven now takes his leave?

"Thus I bid thee farewell." The Heiligenstadt Testament is a leave-taking—which is to say, a fresh start. Beethoven here enacted his own death in order that he might live again. He recreated himself in a new guise, self-sufficient and heroic. The testament is a funeral work, like the *Joseph* Cantata and *Christ on the Mount of Olives*. In a sense it is the literary prototype of the *Eroica* Symphony, a portrait of the artist as hero, stricken by deafness, withdrawn from mankind, conquering his impulses to suicide, struggling against fate, hoping to find "but one day of pure joy." It is a daydream compounded of heroism, death, and rebirth, a reaffirmation of Beethoven's adherence to virtue and to the categorical imperative.

In view of its centrality in the Heiligenstadt Testament, this may be the place to review briefly the history of Beethoven's deafness. The autopsy report stated that "the auditory nerves . . . were shriveled and destitute of neurina; the accompanying arteries were dilated to more than the size of a crow quill and cartilaginous." [21] Specialists disagree as to a diagnosis—some lean toward "otosclerosis;" others claim that it was a disease of the inner ear ("neuritis acoustica" or "labyrinthitis"); while still others favor "otitis media," a disease of the middle ear. [22] The earliest onset of his hearing difficulty dates from approximately 1796, and the first troublesome symptoms appear in 1798 or 1799. In the years of the crisis, 1801–02, the fact is that Beethoven's physical deafness had not progressed very far. There were intermittent symptoms of "tinnitus," such as humming, ringing, buzzing, and other noises in the ears; there was a partial loss of the ability to distinguish high frequencies; and sudden loud noises caused discomfort and even pain. Beethoven sought treatment from various doctors—Johann Peter Frank, Gerhard von Vering, Pater Weiss, and an unknown whom he dubbed a "medical ass"—before he found the firmly sympathetic Dr. Schmidt in 1801. Czerny, observed that in that year "he did not give the least evidence of deafness." [23] Seyfried, who between 1803 and 1806 lived for long periods of time in the same building as Beethoven and often dined with him, confirms: "No physical ill had then afflicted him; no loss of the sense which is peculiarly indispensable to the musician had darkened his life." [24] Even Ries, who learned of Beethoven's deafness in 1802, believed that "the trouble soon disappeared again." [25]

To be sure, there is a report that Beethoven had difficulty hearing the wind instruments during an 1804 rehearsal of the *Eroica* Symphony; and in the same year Stephan von Breuning wrote to Wegeler: "You cannot believe, dear Wegeler, what an indescribable—I should say terrifying—impression the waning of his hearing has had upon him. . . . He has become very withdrawn and often mistrustful of his best friends, and irresolute in many things!" [26] But Beethoven was far from incapacitated: in 1805 he conducted rehearsals of *Fidelio*, and in 1808 he called attention to subtle nuances in Rust's playing, indicative of the sharpness of his hearing. By the decade's end he no longer performed in concerts as a solo pianist; by 1814 his hearing was only barely adequate for him to participate in performances of the *Archduke* Trio, op. 97. It was actually after 1812 that his deafness progressed more rapidly, and it then became more and more difficult to speak to him without shouting. However, Czerny told Jahn that "it was not until 1817 that the deafness became so extreme that he could no longer hear music either." [27] Beethoven began to use an ear trumpet around 1816, and by 1818 the Conversation Books came into existence, so that visitors could communicate with him through writing.

In his last decade, Beethoven became more markedly deaf, and he was apparently totally so in his right ear. Even then, traces of hearing persisted throughout the 1820s. Several visitors in 1822 and 1823 were able to converse with him, and Schindler described Beethoven listening intently to the overture to Cherubini's *Medea* on a music box. On October 3, 1822, he conducted (with assistants) at the opening of the Josephstadt Theater, but the following month he attempted in vain to conduct a revival of *Fidelio* and was forced to quit the theater. As late as 1825 and 1826, Sir George Smart, Stephan von Breuning, and Samuel Spiker reported that Beethoven could occasionally still understand loud speech. Holz confirmed that "Beethoven undertook the rehearsals of his quartets up to the last." He could hear high tones: "When one yelled powerfully into his left ear one could make oneself understood." [28] He could also still distinguish certain low frequencies, such as the clatter of wagon wheels, the sounds of thunder, and gunfire.[29]

We have, then, a pattern of progressive, though uneven, deterioration of Beethoven's hearing, which reached a state of almost total deafness only in his final decade. This pattern is clearly quite different from the popular conception, which, taking the 1801 letters and the Heiligenstadt Testament at face value, gave currency, in Thayer's words, "to a very exaggerated idea of the progress of his infirmity." [30] Beethoven shared that idea: the terrifying anxieties that were generated by the probability that he would ultimately become totally deaf led him into a self-perceived intensification of his deafness. In his despair and panic he felt himself to be more deaf than his actual condition warranted at the time.

Throughout his life Beethoven and his friends were mystified as to the cause of his deafness. They attributed it to a wide variety of possibilities—to the violent digestive disorders which plagued him; to a "frightful attack of typhus"; to his having become soaked while composing music outdoors during a driving rain; to exposure in a draft on a hot summer day; to rheumatism; and to a congenital "weakness" in his auditory canals.[31] At one time, however, Beethoven thought his deafness had been induced by frustration and rage. An English pianist, Charles Neate, who visited Beethoven in 1815, urged him to come to England to seek treatment for his deafness. Neate gave Thayer the following account of Beethoven's strange reply:

> **BEETHOVEN:** No; I have already had all sorts of medical advice. I shall never be cured—I will tell you how it happened. "I was once busy writing an opera. . .
> **NEATE:** *Fidelio?*
> **BEETHOVEN:** No. It was not *Fidelio.* I had a very ill-tempered, troublesome *primo tenore* to deal with. I had already written two grand airs to the same text, with which he was dissatisfied, and now a third, which, upon trial, he seemed to approve and took away with him. I sat down immediately to a work which I had laid aside for those airs and which I was anxious to finish. I had not been half an hour at work when I heard a knock at my door, which I at once recognized as that of my *primo tenore.* I sprang up from my table under such an excitement of rage that, as the man entered the room, I threw myself upon the floor as they do upon the stage, coming down upon my hands. When I arose I found myself deaf and have been so ever since. The physicians say the nerve is injured.[32]

One would love to interpret this fascinating story (or fantasy), which Thayer rightly calls "extraordinary and inexplicable," but this might lead us into speculative regions from which we could return only with difficulty to the known facts of Beethoven's life. This much, at least, can be said: Beethoven imagined (though there was, and is, no evidence to this effect) that he had induced his own deafness, and he attributed it to his own rage in response to what he considered persecutory behavior by a *primo tenore*. (One cannot help wondering if this tenor is not a screen for another *primo tenore* in Beethoven's earlier life.)

The gradual closing off of Beethoven's aural contact with the world inevitably led to feelings of painful isolation and encouraged latent tendencies in him toward misanthropy and suspiciousness. But there may be a sense in which deafness played a positive role in his creativity, for we know that deafness did not impair and indeed may even have heightened his abilities as a composer, perhaps by its exclusion of piano virtuosity as a competing outlet for his creativity, perhaps by permitting a total concentration upon composition within a world of increasing auditory seclusion. In his deaf world, Beethoven could experiment with new forms of experience, free from the intrusive sounds of the external environment; free from the rigidities of the material world; free, like the dreamer, to combine and recombine the stuff of reality, in accordance with his desires, into previously undreamed-of forms and structures.

Perhaps this is a clue as to why the Heiligenstadt Testament expresses Beethoven's acquiescence in his deafness. Surely, his encroaching deafness was not a condition to be desired; he regarded it as a retaliation, a curse visited upon him by his Creator, or by "Fate." But one finds throughout the testament a note of acceptance: "Patience, they say, is what I must now choose for my guide, and I have done so"; or, to Wegeler: "Resignation, what a wretched resource! Yet it is all that is left to me." Beethoven once referred to his hearing as "my noblest faculty," and to its deterioration he attributed his withdrawal into a self-imposed isolation. "If I approach near to people," the testament reads, "a hot terror seizes upon me and I fear being exposed to the danger that my condition might be noticed." The void was filled by his music: "Live only in your art!" he wrote on a leaf of sketches in 1816.[33] This may partly explain his striking remark to Amenda: "When I am playing and composing, my affliction . . . hampers me least; it affects me most when I am in company." [34]

All of Beethoven's defeats were, ultimately, turned into victories. Like Henry James's "secret wound" and Dostoevsky's "holy disease," even his loss of hearing was in some obscure sense necessary (or at least useful) to the fulfillment of his creative quest. The onset of his deafness was the painful chrysalis within which his "heroic" style came to maturity. "I am staying in the country and leading a rather lazy life," he wrote to his publisher Franz Anton Hoffmeister from Heiligenstadt, "in order, how-ever, to lead again later on—an all the more active one." [35] As his shift in style asserted itself and the revolutionary advance in his art was consolidated, the symptoms themselves receded for him into a different perspective and were no longer the subject of lamentation. Between the writing of the Heiligenstadt Testament and 1810 there are only two or three passing references to his deafness in Beethoven's correspondence, along with one revealing note on a leaf of sketches for the *Razumovsky* Quartets in 1806: "Let your deafness no longer be a secret—even in art." [36] Beethoven had come to terms with his deafness.

Beethoven. Portrait in oils by Joseph Willibrord Mähler (ca. 1804).

12
The Heroic Decade (I)

Throughout the course of Beethoven's life, each of his psychological crises was followed by a period of reconstruction. He could not permanently rid himself of deep internal conflicts, but he was repeatedly able to temporarily avert the most serious emotional consequences through immersion in his work and through the posing and solution of increasingly intricate and profound creative problems. The end of the Heiligenstadt crisis in late 1802 ushered in a long period of relative equilibrium and of the highest order of creativity, which remained remarkably secure for a full eight years and was not wholly undermined until 1813. Beethoven attained an awesome level of productivity during these years: his works included an opera, an oratorio, a mass, six symphonies, four concertos, five string quartets, three trios, three string sonatas, and six piano sonatas, plus incidental music for a number of stage works, many *Lieder*, four sets of piano variations, and several symphonic overtures. Every year saw the completion of a cluster of masterpieces, each of a highly individual character; only toward the end of this period did the quality of Beethoven's output falter somewhat, a situation impressively repaired in 1812 with the composition of the Seventh and Eighth Symphonies and the Violin Sonata, op. 96.

This steady and rich productivity took place against a background of expanding reputation and international fame. So innovative a composer necessarily met resistance in quarters that were emotionally bound to familiar and less demanding musical styles, but even these resistances were broken down by what Moscheles called the "Beethoven fever" which raged among connoisseurs and especially among musicians and music lovers of the younger generation.[1] There were many among the older composers and music pedagogues who could not readily accept what appeared to them "fantastic" (Haydn) and "hare-brained" (Moscheles's teacher, Dionys Weber) departures from tradition. Czerny reported that the *Eroica* Symphony was "considered too long, elaborate, incomprehensible, and much too noisy," and the *Allgemeine musikalische Zeitung* wrote of the symphony that it contained "an excess of whimsicalities and novelties."[2] (Beethoven angrily responded: "If you fancy you can injure *me* by publishing articles of that kind, you are very much mistaken. On the contrary, by so doing you merely bring your journal into disrepute."[3])

Arthur Loesser may well be correct that "for most people, Beethoven's fame was an article of superstition; for the most part they much preferred the works of his less assertive, less inspired contemporaries."[4] However, as early as 1804 Beethoven's music was more widely circulated in the Habsburg realms than that of any other young composer, and within a few years his works were so much in demand that they appeared on concept programs as frequently as those of Mozart and Haydn. Thayer wrote that, by 1808, "it was Beethoven's popularity that must insure success to the Grand Concert for the public charities; it was his name that was known to be more attractive to the Vienna public than any other, save that of the venerable Haydn."[5] True, Beethoven was able to obtain only two public orchestral concerts for his own benefit during this period—those of April 5, 1803, and December 22, 1808—but major public concerts in Vienna increasingly scheduled his music. An average of two concerts featured his works during the years 1803 to 1806; there were three such concerts in 1807 and six in 1808. In that year, Beethoven's music was heard at five major benefit or charity concerts, climaxed by the concert of December 22, 1808, for his own benefit. In addition, during the winter of 1807–08 leading music lovers (*Liebhaber*) formed an orchestra and gave twenty concerts reserved for audiences of the aristocracy and foreign notables, at which Beethoven's works were performed, often under his own direction. The number of performances declined somewhat during 1809 and 1810, only to increase once again in the years 1811 and 1812. Meanwhile, performances in other Habsburg cities—Graz, Prague, Pesth—became commonplace.

Abroad, Beethoven's music was rapidly making its way in several major countries. In Germany, his earlier piano concertos quickly entered the repertory, and the Septet and the First Symphony had a sensational success. He especially found a welcome reception in his native Rhineland. It was in England, however, that Beethoven gained his greatest popularity outside of Austria. There the Septet was performed several times in 1801, and two performances of Beethoven symphonies took place in 1803. In 1804–05 there were ten performances of major Beethoven works in England, and thereafter an increasingly larger number of his compositions was heard.[6] Beethoven was much impressed by his British reception. Was it partly in gratitude that in 1803 he wrote his Variations on "God Save the King," WoO 78, and on "Rule Britannia," WoO 79?

France, however, long proved insusceptible to Beethoven's innovations. ("The French find my music beyond their powers of performance," remarked the composer.[7]) Following a few performances at the Paris Conservatory in 1802, his music went unheard until 1807, and thereafter there were but a few performances until the late 1820s. Only one Beethoven symphony—the First—was performed in France before 1811. Nevertheless, many of Beethoven's earlier works were rapidly published there, indicating at least that amateur performers found his music to their liking.

Of course, public performances were not a wholly accurate index of a composer's popularity, for public concerts featuring solo keyboard and chamber music were then in their infancy. Such music was usually performed in salons and at private concerts. Thus it is not really surprising that there were only two known public performances of Beethoven piano sonatas during his lifetime—of opus 90 or opus 101 in Vienna in 1816 and of the *Funeral March* Sonata, op. 26, in Boston in 1819.[8]

New publications of Beethoven's music continued to be issued at a very strong rate, including editions of all of his major symphonic works, for which there was a smaller market than for piano sonatas and variations. In the years between 1803 and 1812 an average of almost eight separate new publications appeared annually, from publishers in Vienna, Bonn, Leipzig, and Zürich. New editions of previously published works appeared in other countries. In England, half a dozen of Beethoven's works were published prior to 1810; in that year, Clementi published thirteen works, including two concertos; the String Quartet, op. 74; the "Choral Fantasia," op. 80; a number of *Lieder*, and several piano works.[9] And there were very many unauthorized English reprints of his works during this same period.

Naturally, Beethoven also encountered disappointments during this productive decade. Many of his works did not please, and others essentially disappeared from the repertory during his lifetime. As we shall see, the early failure of his only opera was an especially bitter disappointment.

Conflicts with both of his brothers also marked this decade. Caspar Carl's marriage in 1806 led to a partial estrangement, and Nikolaus Johann's insistence in 1807 that Beethoven return to him a loan of 1,500 florins was met with angry resistance by the composer, so that Nikolaus Johann's departure for Linz in 1808· was not the occasion for a fond, fraternal separation. As we shall see later on, the vicissitudes of Beethoven's amorous life—or, more precisely, the absence of one—were a constant source of pain. Beethoven also had his normal share of bad notices, quarrels with patrons, perpetual postponements of his cherished benefit concerts, delayed publications, and contract difficulties; and he could not have remained unaffected—though he is essentially silent on the matter—by the progress of his deafness throughout this period. Nevertheless, his personality was now sufficiently resilient that he could withstand these and other pressures with relative equanimity.

Following his stay in Heiligenstadt in 1802, Beethoven returned to Vienna by mid-October—bearing a thick sheaf of manuscripts, for it had been a remarkably productive summer. Almost immediately he became involved in a quarrel with Artaria & Co., his most devoted Viennese publisher, concerning its publication of his Quintet, op. 29, which he had sold to Breitkopf & Härtel. He thus inaugurated the series of legal entanglements which drained his energies (and worked off his aggressions?) during the next two decades. Despite his later admission that he himself had corrected Artaria's proofs, he accused the firm of having stolen the Quintet; and in February 1803, Artaria filed a court petition demanding a public apology. Beethoven stubbornly refused to issue a retraction, however, even in the face of a court order.[10]

At the beginning of 1803, Emanuel Schikaneder's lavish new Theater-an-der-Wien, which had opened in June 1801 in competition with the Court Theater, engaged Beethoven to compose an opera, and he and his brother Caspar Carl soon took up their lodgings at the theater. Beethoven remained occupied with other matters until late in the year, however, probably because of the late delivery of the opera text by Schikaneder (librettist of Mozart's *Magic Flute*). His oratorio *Christus am Oelberge* (*Christ on the Mount of Olives*), op. 85, was written out in a few weeks during March 1803 and performed, along with the First and Second Symphonies and the Third Piano Concerto, at Beethoven's successful *Akademie* on April 5. Immediately after the completion of *Christus*, Beethoven sketched and rapidly completed the *Kreutzer* Sonata, op. 47, for a performance by himself and the violinist, George Bridgetower, on May 24. The months from May until November—a good portion of which were spent at Baden and Oberdöbling—were devoted to the composition of the first draft of the *Eroica* Symphony.

Beethoven's correspondence for this year reflects little of his inner life; most of his letters are devoted to negotiations with publishers, rehearsals, performances, copying, proofreading, and other business details. One letter, however, written in September to Hoffmeister, shows that, despite his burgeoning success, he was far from reconciled to his freelance existence in Vienna: "Please remember that all my acquaintants hold appointments and know exactly what they have to live on," he wrote. "But Heaven help us! What appointment at the Imperial Court could be given to such a *parvum talentum com ego* [mediocre talent like myself]?" [11]

His dissatisfaction was such that he now considered leaving Vienna. On August 6, 1803, Ries wrote to Simrock that "Beethoven will stay here [in Vienna] at most for another year and a half. He is then going to Paris, which makes me extraordinarily sorrowful." [12] On October 22, Ries wrote again to advise Simrock that Beethoven wanted to title his new symphony *Bonaparte* and that he also wanted to dedicate his new sonata for violin and piano jointly to Rodolphe Kreutzer and Louis Adam, "as the first violinist and pianist in Paris." He added the news that Beethoven would soon begin work on his opera and would leave Vienna upon its completion. By December, Beethoven had decided not to permit publication of the new symphony prior to his Paris trip: "He now doesn't want to sell it and will reserve it for his journey." We can only speculate on the motives behind this intended move (or lengthy visit). Clearly Beethoven felt that he deserved a position commensurate with his talents; perhaps, too, he had received some indication that his arrival in Paris would be warmly welcomed. And perhaps his disappointment at Giulietta Guicciardi's impending marriage to Count Gallenberg was greater than has been supposed.

In November Beethoven commenced work on Schikaneder's *Vestas Feuer* [*The vestal flame*], and by year's end he had almost completed the first scene. Not finding the libretto to his liking, however, he returned the text and settled instead upon a more sympathetic topic— the rescue of an imprisoned husband by his loving wife—to be adapted and translated by Joseph Sonnleithner from J. N. Bouilly's French libretto, *Léonore; ou, l'amour conjugal*. He began work on the first act, but a change in February in the ownership of the theater led to the annulment of his contract, which was not reinstated until late in 1804. In the intervening months, Beethoven revised the *Eroica* Symphony in time for its first performance at Prince Lobkowitz's palace; completed the Triple Concerto, op. 56; composed the Piano Sonatas, op. 53 (dedicated to his Bonn patron, Count Waldstein) and op. 54; and began planning, if not actually sketching, the Sonata, op. 57 (*Appassionata*).

Although he wrote to a German musician, Gottlob Wiedebein, on July 6, "I shall probably leave here next winter," [13] the Brunsvik correspondence toward year's end reveals that he now intended not to move to Paris, but merely to visit there with Prince Lichnowsky. [14]

Beethoven's decision to remain in Vienna is closely related to the most dramatic incident of 1804, an incident which bears upon his political and ideological outlook. It is the famous story of Beethoven's destruction of the "Bonaparte" inscription of the Third Symphony upon hearing the news, in May 1804, that Napoleon had proclaimed himself emperor.

Napoleon Bonaparte. Portrait in oils by
Anne Louis Girodet-Troison.

13
Bonaparte: The Crisis of Belief

In this symphony Beethoven had Buonaparte in mind, but as he was
when he was First Consul. Beethoven esteemed him greatly at the time
and likened him to the greatest Roman consuls. I as well as several of
his more intimate friends saw a copy of the score lying upon his table
with the word "Buonaparte" at the extreme top of the title page, and at
the extreme bottom "Luigi van Beethoven," but not another word.
Whether and with what the space between was to be filled out, I do not
know. I was the first to bring him the intelligence that Buonaparte had
proclaimed himself emperor, whereupon he flew into a rage and cried
out: "Is he then, too, nothing more than an ordinary human being? Now
he, too, will trample on all the rights of man and indulge only his ambition. He will exalt himself above all others, become a tyrant!" Beethoven went to the table, took hold of the title page by the top, tore it
in two, and threw it on the floor. The first page was rewritten and only
then did the symphony receive the title *Sinfonia eroica*.[1]

This simple anecdote, told by Ferdinand Ries, is one of the more Promethean of the Beethoven legends, popular with chroniclers of Romanticism

and Revolution. Although it describes a largely rhetorical and wholly symbolic action, it has, with the passage of time, become a monumentalized example of the artist's resistance to tyranny, of the antagonism between art and politics, of the individual against the state. But a closer examination reveals that the process by which the French leader's name was removed from Beethoven's Third Symphony was more complex than has been supposed. Furthermore, and more importantly, it shows that a crisis of belief was centrally involved in the crisis which precipitated and accompanied Beethoven's "new path."

The accuracy of Ries's account of Beethoven's reaction to the news that Napoleon had been proclaimed emperor is not in question.[2] Obviously, we may make allowances for Ries's rendering of Beethoven's actual words, and we know he was incorrect in saying that the symphony was thereupon or shortly thereafter retitled *Eroica,* for this name was not used before October 1806, when the first edition of the orchestral parts was published by the Bureau des Arts et d'Industrie in Vienna.[3] But what Ries did not know was that Beethoven soon decided to restore Bonaparte's name to the symphony. On August 26, 1804, Beethoven wrote to Breitkopf & Härtel:

> I have now finished several compositions . . . my oratorio—a *new grand symphony*—a concertante for violin, violoncello, and pianoforte with full orchestra—three new sonatas for pianoforte solo. . . . The title of the symphony is really *Bonaparte.*[4]

Perhaps even more significant in illuminating Beethoven's indecision is the title page of his own copy of the score of the symphony. It is filled with erasures and corrections in Beethoven's hand:

[AT THE TOP]
N.B. 1. Cues for the other instruments are to be written into the first violin part.

[1]	Sinfonia Grande
[2]	Intitulata Bonaparte
[3]	[1804] im August
[4]	Del [or de] Sigr.
[5]	Louis van Beethoven
[6]	Geschrieben
[7]	auf Bonaparte
[8]	Sinfonia [or Sinfonie] 3 Op. 55

[AT THE BOTTOM]
    N.B. 2. The third horn [part] is so written that it can be played by a primario as well as a secundario.

The original title consisted of lines 1, 2, 4, and 5, written by the copyist; lines 3 and 8 were added by unknown hands.[5] Line 2—*Intitulata*

Bonaparte—was later crossed out, so that it is barely legible, but lines 6 and 7—*Geschrieben auf Bonaparte*—were added in pencil by Beethoven and were never erased.

Actually, even while he was writing the symphony, Beethoven had begun to dilute his commitment to France's First Consul. Ries wrote to Simrock on October 22, 1803: "He wants very much to dedicate it to Bonaparte; if not, since Lobkowitz wants [the rights to] it for half a year and is willing to give 400 ducats for it, he will title it Bonaparte." [6] It seems then that Beethoven initially planned to dedicate the symphony to Bonaparte. However, finding that this would deprive him of a large fee, he conceived the alternative idea of entitling it "Bonaparte," and it was this alternative that he confronted in May 1804 when Ries arrived, bringing the latest news from Paris. But Bonaparte was to receive neither the dedication to nor the inscription of the *Eroica* Symphony.

To its participants, the central issue of the post-Revolutionary age appeared to be the issue of Bonapartism, around which ideological responses to historical movements revolved. Zola, in his essay on Stendhal, wrote that "Napoleon's destiny acted like a hammer-blow on the heads of his contemporaries. . . . All ambitions waxed large, all undertakings took on a gigantic air . . ., all dreams turned on universal kingship." [7] For Beethoven's German and Austrian contemporaries, the Napoleonic image was especially potent: Bonaparte's admirers included Kant, Herder, Fichte, Schelling, Hegel, Schiller, Goethe, Hölderlin, Wieland, and Klopstock. Grillparzer, in his *Autobiography* wrote, "I myself was no less an enemy of the French than my father, and yet Napoleon fascinated me with a magic power. . . . He put me under a spell, as a snake does a bird." [8] Goethe, who kept a bust of Napoleon in his room, said to Eckermann in 1829: "Napoleon managed the world as Hummel his piano; both achievements appear wonderful, we do not understand one more than the other, yet so it is, and the whole is done before our eyes." Hegel, in 1806, called Napoleon a "soul of worldwide significance . . . an individual who . . . encompasses the world and rules it." [9]

Soon, however, the difficulty of reconciling the Napoleonic ideal with the French wars of conquest, or with the Napoleonic substitution of permanent war for permanent revolution, led to confusion if not disillusionment among many European intellectuals and artists. Heinrich Heine observed that the German democrats "wrapped their thoughts in profound silence," being "too republican in their sentiments to do homage to Napoleon, and too magnanimous to ally themselves with a foreign domination." [10] Napoleon himself noted that "everybody has loved me and hated me: everybody has taken me up, dropped me, and taken me up again.

. . . I was like the sun, which crosses the equator as it describes the ecliptic; as soon as I entered each man's clime, I kindled every hope, I was blessed, I was adored; but as soon as I left it, I no longer was understood and contrary sentiments replaced the old ones." [11]

Bonaparte's coronation was widely regarded as a subordination of principle to personal ambition. Beethoven's dismay was shared by intellectuals everywhere. Shelley wrote, in his introduction to *The Revolt of Islam,* that "the revulsion occasioned by the atrocities of the demagogues and the reëstablishment of successive tyrannies in France was terrible, and felt in the remotest corner of the civilized world." [12] But where Shelley optimistically continued to listen to Reason's plea for political and economic justice, and Goethe and Jefferson maintained an aloof objectivity which forbore to take sides on issues where morality was unable to choose, others, such as Coleridge and Wordsworth, became obsessed with fears of the Jacobin danger and opted for a restoration of the *ancien régime.* For his part, Beethoven neither gave way to spiritual melancholia over this issue nor abandoned his belief in the secular, fraternal utopia which Bonaparte—one *bon prince*—had betrayed.

The Revolution was over, dissolved in war and petrified in the stultifying bureaucratic forms which sooner or later overtake all social transformations. But this was a process that had begun well before 1804. Beethoven's rending of the title page therefore cannot be accepted as a simple act of angry defiance at a new development in Napoleonic politics, for these regressive tendencies had been at work for some years, and Beethoven was aware of them. His equivocal attitude toward the French leader neither started nor ended with the Imperium. His composition of two patriotic songs in 1796 and 1797 was inspired by Habsburg anti-Napoleonic campaigns; and Beethoven had even explicitly expressed his disillusionment with Napoleon in 1802, when Hoffmeister, the Leipzig publisher, forwarded a suggestion that Beethoven compose a sonata in celebration of Napoleon or of the Revolution. Beethoven's reply of April 8, 1802, indicates that even then—shortly before the *Eroica* Symphony was begun—he considered Bonaparte to have betrayed the Revolution by virtue of his Concordat with the Vatican (signed in July 1801) which reestablished Catholic worship in France:

Has the devil got hold of you all, Gentlemen?—that you suggest that *I should compose such a sonata.* Well, perhaps at the time of the Revolutionary fever—such a thing might have been possible, but now, when everything is trying to slip back into the old rut, now that Buonaparte has concluded his Concordat with the Pope—to write a sonata of that kind? . . . But good Heavens, such a sonata—in these newly developing Christian times—Ho ho—there you must leave me out—you won't get anything from me—. . . .[13]

Why, then, did Beethoven decide to write a *Bonaparte* symphony shortly after this letter to Hoffmeister?

Beethoven's projected move to Paris provides an apparently simple motive: the *Bonaparte* Symphony and the proposed dedication of the Violin Sonata, op. 47, to Adam and Kreutzer may have been intended to smoothe Beethoven's entry into the French capital.[14] And the cancellation of the tour coincided rather closely with the final removal of Bonaparte's name from the Third Symphony.

Yet we must resist the temptation to counter the Promethean interpretations of this story by reducing the entire matter to a musician's desire to advance his career. And there is no need to do so, for this would be to omit the political and personal implications of Beethoven's identification with Bonaparte in the first place, as well as of the intended move to Paris. It is surely meaningful that during this period we see Beethoven begin to reaffirm Enlightened ideals and ethical norms, for these had almost disappeared from his correspondence and his music for some years. The composition of nationalist battle songs in 1796–97, the dedication of the Septet to Empress Maria Theresia in 1800, the improvisation on "God Save Emperor Franz" in April 1803—these had not been the actions of an independent and defiant thinker, but of an apparently faithful servant of the state. Private acts of rebellion against his patrons were insufficient to offset the implications of such public avowals. True, Beethoven was reported by Schindler—and there is no confirmation of this—to have associated with the circle that gathered at the house of French Ambassador Bernadotte between February and April of 1798. If this association indeed had political overtones, it may have been a sign of the chaotic nature of Beethoven's allegiances, of the depth of his conflict with Vienna, and perhaps even of his vacillation between opposing political forces. It was only after 1800, however, that the first indications appear of a rehabilitation of his political and ideological independence. In 1801 he wrote to Wegeler that he wished his art to be "exercised only for the benefit of the poor," [15] and to Hoffmeister in the same year he proposed a quasi-socialist patronage of the artist: "There ought to be in the world a *market for art [Magazin der Kunst]* where the artist would only have to bring his works and take as much money as he needed. But, as it is, an artist has to be to a certain extent a businessman as well." [16] Remarkably, the 1802 letter to Hoffmeister concerning the proposed "Revolutionary sonata" is the first seriously political reference in his correspondence in eight years.

Beethoven evidently wished to emerge from a period of apparent ideological quiescence. Perhaps this is one reason why, in the opening years of the nineteenth century, he began a series of apparently disinterested dedications of his works to leading adherents of Enlightened positions. Thus the revered Austrian-Jewish *Aufklärer* and Freemason Joseph von Sonnenfels (favorite of and adviser to Joseph II) received the dedication of the Piano Sonata in D, op. 28, in 1801, and the young Czar Alexander—who had instituted a program of reform in the tradition of Enlightened despotism—received that of the Sonatas for Violin and Piano, op. 30, in 1803. Since dedications for Beethoven were either a major source of patronage and income or a means of expressing gratitude or friendship, these unpaid, honorary dedications are all the more significant.

The culmination of this series was the proposed dedication to Bonaparte of the Third Symphony. This dedication, along with the consideration of a move to Paris, may, therefore, have been a dramatic sign of Beethoven's desire to break with Habsburg Vienna and its political system as well as with its modes of musical patronage. If this is true, then the rending of the inscription may constitute an equally dramatic turning point—Beethoven's abandonment of his identification with France and his decision henceforth to view himself as a citizen of Vienna.

The idea of a symphonic apotheosis of Napoleon had been worked out during the relatively long period of peace which followed the defeat of Austria in late 1800, as codified by the February 9, 1801, Treaty of Lunéville. That peace was unraveling in 1804, and war was to erupt once again in 1805. To have kept "Bonaparte"—either as title or as dedication—at a moment when renewed war between France and Austria was imminent would have marked Beethoven as a philo-Jacobin, a supporter of a radical cause and of a hostile power. It would have led not merely to the loss of a patron—for Lobkowitz was an ardent patriot who later raised a battalion of troops to fight the French—but to the probability of reprisals in anti-Revolutionary Austria as well.

Of all the European nations, writes Hobsbawm, "Austria, whose family links with the Bourbons were reinforced by the direct French threat to her possessions and areas of influence in Italy, and her leading position in Germany, was the most consistently anti-French, and took part in every major coalition against France." [17] Austria suffered heavier defeats and territorial losses than any other continental power during the Napoleonic wars. We saw earlier how the Viennese authorities kept constant watch upon all expression of social or political dissent. And of all forms of dissent, support for France was considered the most dangerous.

Beethoven's passport to Viennese citizenship was the rending of the Bonaparte inscription and the consequent merging of his heroic ideal with the national outlook of the Viennese populace.

Beethoven needed musical collaborators to help create his revolutionary, "heroic" music. The high-Classic Viennese style, as we have previously noted, had essentially been completed (or exhausted) with Mozart,

Haydn, and the early Beethoven. It would require an infusion of fresh elements from a previously untapped source to transcend this style and to open up new avenues for exploration. Beethoven discovered some of these elements in contemporary French music.

The influence of French Revolutionary music upon Beethoven was no secret to his contemporaries and early admirers. E. T. A. Hoffmann noted Cherubini's presence in the Overture to *Coriolan;* Amadeus Wendt likewise heard echoes of Cherubini in the *Leonore* overtures; and Schumann recognized the influence of Méhul's Symphony in G minor upon Beethoven's Fifth Symphony. That *Fidelio* was adapted from a French post-Revolutionary opera subject, and that the opera was a German example of French "rescue opera," has long been well known. But it took the researches of twentieth-century scholars—Kretzschmar, Bücken, Botstiber, Sandberger, Schiedermair, Schmitz, Einstein, Boris Schwarz, and others—to establish and trace in some detail the breadth of these influences in the formation of Beethoven's post–1800 style. For example, Schmitz offers many examples of parallels between Beethoven's music and the works of Gossec, Grétry, Kreutzer, Berton, Méhul, Catel, and Cherubini and devotes an important study to "The Influence of Cherubini on Beethoven's Overtures." [18] He documents the clear use of French material in such works as Beethoven's First, Fifth, and Seventh Symphonies, the *Egmont* and *Leonore* overtures, the *Funeral March* Sonata, op. 26, and the Violin Sonata, op. 30 no. 2. Schwarz reveals the surprising origins of many of Beethoven's stylistic idiosyncrasies in the violin music of the French masters, and he documents the influence of Kreutzer, Rode, Baillot, and Viotti upon the middle-period Violin Concerto, op. 61.[19]

The highly ordered yet flexible structure of sonata form readily expanded to embrace the driving, ethically exalted, "grand style" elements of French music, which itself had hitherto lacked that kind of formal concentration and intensive development.[20] In a number of his "public" compositions over the next decade, Beethoven would continue to explore the potentialities of this mixture of styles. Ironically, Beethoven's heroic style, which came into being as a collaboration between Vienna and France, expired in the years 1813–14 as a vehicle celebrating the conquest of Bonaparte and France.

Beethoven's conflicts with Napoleon did not end with the *Eroica* incident. In succeeding years he became well known as a Francophobe, who was given to expressions of defiance against France and Napoleon. After Bonaparte's victory at Jena, Beethoven reputedly said to the violinist Wenzel Krumpholz, "It's a pity that I do not understand the art of war as well as I do the art of music. I would conquer him!" [21] Nevertheless, the astute Baron de Trémont, member of Napoleon's Council of State, became friendly with Beethoven in 1809 and noted Beethoven's preoccupation "with the greatness of Napoleon." Trémont observed that "through all his resentment I could see that he admired his rise from such obscure beginnings; his democratic ideas were flattered by it. One day he remarked, 'If I go to Paris, shall I be obliged to salute your emperor?' I assured him that he would not, unless commanded for an audience. 'And do you think he would command me?'" This caused Trémont to conclude that Beethoven "would have felt flattered by any mark of distinction from Napoleon." That Beethoven welcomed a member of Napoleon's council at the very moment that Napoleon was bombarding Vienna was itself a curious matter, and Trémont reported that everyone "was astonished." [22]

At about the same time, Napoleon's brother Jerôme, whom he had installed as king of the newly created kingdom of Westphalia, offered Beethoven the post of *Kapellmeister* at a substantial salary. Despite his anti-Bonapartist views, Beethoven was at one point on the verge of accepting the post. The entire affair remains clouded in ambiguities. Thayer wondered what "could have induced this half-educated, frivolous, prodigal and effeminate young satrap and sybarite to sanction an invitation" to Beethoven, and comments that it "is one of those small mysteries which seem impenetrable." [23] On Beethoven's side, we shall see that he used the offer as a lever to acquire an annuity from Archduke Rudolph and the princes Lobkowitz and Kinsky which guaranteed him lifelong financial support in return for his promise to make his domicile in Vienna a permanent one. The matter is surely more complex than this, however, and among the factors involved may have been Beethoven's desire for just that "mark of distinction from Napoleon" of which Baron de Trémont wrote. Later, in 1813, we will find Beethoven once again hoping for some "reward" from a Bonaparte—this time Louis, another brother of Napoleon, who was appointed king of Holland. He is rather abashed and defensive about it, when he writes to Varena: "I thought perhaps that the third person you mentioned was the former *king of Holland,* and—well, after all, from him, who has perhaps taken a good deal from the Dutch in a less legitimate way, I would not have scrupled to take something on account of my present situation." [24]

From May 13 to November 20, 1809, Vienna was occupied by the French. Napoleon's eagle perched on the masthead of the *Wiener Zeitung;* a cantata, *Sieg der Eintracht,* was written by Castelli and Weigl to celebrate the marriage of Napoleon to the Habsburg Princess Maria Louise; the best artists of Vienna were called to Schönbrunn to perform for Bonaparte. Beethoven was not called. On September 8, he conducted his *Eroica* Symphony at a charity concert for the theatrical poor fund. Thayer asks: "Was this selected, in the expectation that Napoleon would be present, to do him homage? If so it failed of its aim. The day before,

Napoleon journeyed from Schönbrunn. . . . Or was it in bitter sarcasm that Beethoven chose it?" [25] The latter possibility is unlikely, for Max Unger has turned up Beethoven's extraordinary note to himself of October 8, 1810: "The Mass [in C major, op. 86] could perhaps be dedicated to Napoleon." [26] It is a pity that we have only the insufficient word "ambivalence" to describe such total reversals of emotional attitude—surely too tame a word for so turbulent a set of feelings. What is involved, actually, is not merely a series of reversals but an insoluble conflict which can be resolved only through a change in the balance of forces. This was to come later, with Napoleon's defeat at Waterloo, his exile to St. Helena, and his death.*

Perhaps it is in Beethoven's ambivalence itself that we have a clue to a deeper understanding of Bonaparte's connection with the *Eroica*. As we have seen, it is a curious fact that there is no evidence whatever that Beethoven had anything other than negative feelings toward Bonaparte prior to 1803. His reported brief association with the French ambassador Bernadotte in 1798 does not contradict this, for Bernadotte was himself on extremely bad terms with Bonaparte. (Schindler, who mistakenly believed that Bernadotte was still ambassador in 1804, was perhaps equally mistaken in claiming that Bernadotte suggested that Beethoven write a composition in honor of Bonaparte.[29]) The *Eroica* Symphony, therefore, may not, after all, have been conceived in a spirit of homage, which was then superseded by disillusionment; rather, it is possible that Beethoven chose as his subject one toward whom he already felt an unconquerable ambivalence containing a strong element of hostility. The symphony, with its Funeral March, is centrally concerned with the death of the hero as well as with his birth and resurrection: "Composed," Beethoven wrote on the title page, "to celebrate the memory of a great man." Striving to free himself from his lifelong pattern of submission to the domination of authority figures, Beethoven was drawn to the conqueror who had confounded the venerable leaders of Europe and set himself in their place. If homage is on the surface, the underlying themes are patricide and fratricide, and these are mingled with the survivor's sense of triumph. As in the *Joseph* Cantata, piety toward the departed hero may mask feelings of an opposite kind.

According to one of his physicians, Andreas Bertolini, Beethoven's original plan had been to compose the Funeral March of the *Eroica* on a British topic, either the wounding of Nelson at the Battle of the Nile in 1798 or the death of General Ralph Abercromby at Alexandria in 1801.[30] In view of Beethoven's steadfast admiration for the British (which

---

* On hearing of Napoleon's death on May 5, 1821, Beethoven remarked, "I have already composed the proper music for that catastrophe"; [27] and in 1824 he said to Czerny: "Napoleon, I could not tolerate him earlier. Now I think quite differently." [28]

dated back to his family's friendship with Cressener, the British ambassador to Bonn), Nelson or Abercromby could not serve as appropriate subjects of the conflicting emotions which are condensed in the *Eroica*. And so Beethoven may have fixed upon one towards whom he had mixed feelings, one whom he had already rejected as an ideal prince/legislator. Thus the choice of Bonaparte as his subject and the rending of the inscription were part of the same process. Beethoven disposed of Bonaparte twice—once in composing the symphony and again in removing his name from the title.

Brandes described German Romanticism's glorification of desire, of wish, as "impotence itself conceived as a power." [31] A sense of national impotence lay just behind the facade of Viennese life after the death of Joseph II, with whom were interred the thwarted hopes of Enlightened despotism; these feelings of futility were reinforced by the Habsburgs' abject submission to Napoleon following the succession of crushing military defeats between 1797 and 1809.

That Beethoven was capable of producing the ultimate musical definition of heroism in this context is itself extraordinary, for he was able to evoke a dream heroism which neither he nor his native Germany nor his adopted Vienna could express in reality. Perhaps we can only measure the heroism of the *Eroica* by the depths of fear and uncertainty from which it emerged.

We have seen that there was a component of caution, an excess of discretion, even a failure of nerve, in Beethoven's removal of the Bonaparte inscription. This should not lead us to reject other levels of motivation and meaning, however. As we have seen, Beethoven regarded Bonaparte as an embodiment of Enlightened leadership; but, simultaneously, he felt betrayed by Bonaparte's Caesaristic actions. Beethoven's ambivalence mirrored a central contradiction of his age. It is this contradiction that finds expression in the *Eroica* Symphony. The *Eroica* arose from the conflict between Enlightened faith in the savior/prince and the reality of Bonapartism. Bonaparte—whose image replaced Christ's in myriads of European homes—had inherited the displaced Messianism of his time; Beethoven, who rejected blind faith and hierarchical orthodoxy in his personal theology, now rejected its secular equivalents. As an artist and a man, Beethoven could no longer accept unmediated conceptions of progress, innate human goodness, reason, and faith. His affirmations were now leavened by an acknowledgment of the frailty of human leadership and a consciousness of the regressive and brutalizing components in all forward-thrusting stages in social evolution.

Beethoven, ever-questioning, spurred by doubt, rejecting the passivity of superstition and the false confidence of ideological certainty, never abandoned his central faith in the values of the Enlightenment—altruistic love, reason, and humanistic ideals. The Enlightenment abjured superstition and dogma and supplanted theological formulations which negated the possibilities of earthly salvation with a harmonious and optimistic view of man's freedom to develop his potentialities within a framework of natural law and political reconstruction. This is not to say that its philosophers were unaware of the problem of evil or that its views were predicated upon a banal rejection of skepticism. Nevertheless, as Cassirer observed: "This era is permeated by genuine creative feeling and an unquestionable faith in the reformation of the world." [32] As Voltaire wrote: "*Some day all will be well*, is our hope; *all is well today*, is illusion." Beethoven rejected the latter illusion, and cleaved to the principle of hope.

Beethoven could not have gone over to the Revolution ("journey to Paris," so to speak), even had he so desired, without becoming a musical conformist working in conventional formulas, as Gossec, Méhul, and Spontini had done. French Revolutionary music (and painting) largely ignored both the Revolution and the Terror, stressing instead nobility of motivation and action and substituting heroic portraiture and triumphal rhetoric for conflict and tragedy. Idealism and simple faith alone, however, are insufficient grounds for greatness. Conflict is absent from ideological statements, and the resultant artwork accordingly requires no formal containment, but merely craftsmanlike expression. For it is the conflict between faith and skepticism, the struggle between belief and disbelief—which Goethe described as the most important theme of world history—that creates those dynamic tensions which tend to expand and threaten to burst the bonds of form. The *Eroica* is Beethoven's elaboration of that theme in the closing hours of the Enlightenment.

Beethoven. Portrait in oils by Isidor
Neugass (ca. 1806).

14
The Heroic Decade (II)

It was toward the end of 1804 that Beethoven resumed his lodgings at
the Theater-an-der-Wien and wrote to his librettist asking that he complete the text of his opera before the next April. Beethoven hoped that
the opera could be produced "in June at latest," [1] after which he planned
to be on his way to Paris. The trip never took place, however, and the
composition of the first and second versions of *Leonore* (retitled *Fidelio*
by the theater management) became Beethoven's main—virtually his
sole—project between the last months of 1804 and April 1806. Beethoven
sketched the balance of the opera by June 1805 and completed its composition at Hetzendorf, where he spent the summer. It was ready for
rehearsal early in the fall, but difficulties with the censor occasioned a
postponement. In the interim, Napoleon's armies occupied Vienna, so
that *Fidelio* received its premiere under extremely inauspicious conditions on November 20. According to the tenor Joseph August Röckel,
"only a few friends of Beethoven had ventured to hear the opera," [2] and
the presence of French officers in the audience was an inhibiting factor.

After repetitions on the 21st and 22nd, *Fidelio* was withdrawn. A visiting Englishman left a record of the November 21 performance in his journal:

> Went to the Wieden Theatre to the new opera *Fidelio*, the music composed by Beethoven. The story and plan of the piece are a miserable mixture of low manner and romantic situations; the airs, duets, and choruses equal to any praise. . . . Intricacy is the character of Beethoven's music, and it requires a well-practised ear, or a frequent repetition of the same piece, to understand and distinguish its beauties. This is the first opera he ever composed, and it was much applauded; a copy of complimentary verses [by Breuning] was showered down from the upper gallery at the end of the piece. Beethoven presided at the pianoforte and directed the performance himself. He is a small dark young-looking man [who] wears spectacles. . . . Few people present, though the house would have been crowded in every part but for the present state of public affairs.[3]

The critics did not respond favorably to the opera, and Beethoven's friends, led by the Lichnowskys, urged drastic revisions—especially in the long, undramatic first act—preparatory to a revival. Beethoven and Breuning now took up the libretto and, as Breuning recalled, "remodeled the whole book . . . quickening and enlivening the action." [4] (Beethoven later claimed the entire credit for the libretto's revision.) Acts 1 and 2 were combined; several numbers were omitted and others abridged. Winton Dean writes: "While the effect of these alterations must have been beneficial in speeding up the action, they did not go to the root of the problem, the undue prominence of Marzelline, and some of them were ill-judged." [5] The new version was performed on March 29, 1806, and repeated on April 10. According to Röckel, who sang the role of Florestan, it was well received "by a select public." [6] It did not find favor, however, with such eminences as Cherubini and Salieri; and we may assume that Beethoven himself was not pleased, for he undiplomatically accused the theater management of cheating him on the receipts and—following a quarrel with the theater director, Baron Peter von Braun—peremptorily withdrew the opera from production. A private performance may have been given at the Lobkowitz palace toward midyear. Lichnowsky sent the score to the queen of Prussia for a proposed Berlin production; and there was talk of a Prague production in 1807. But these did not materialize, and the opera was set aside until 1814. It was only then that Beethoven finally completed it to the public's satisfaction, if not to his own; for even after the last revision he wrote to his new librettist, Georg Friedrich Treitschke: "Let me add that this whole opera business is the most tiresome affair in the world, for I am dissatisfied with most of it, and there is hardly a number in it which *my present dissatisfaction would not have to patch up here and there with some satisfaction."* [7]

The explosive inauguration of Beethoven's post-Heiligenstadt style gave rise to a multitude of ideas for compositions. Sketches of ideas for the Fifth and Sixth Symphonies appear in the *Eroica* sketchbook of 1803–04; several string quartets were apparently germinating as early as the fall of 1804.[8] The termination of Beethoven's long operatic labors unleashed a flood of important instrumental compositions, which were now written out simultaneously or in rapid succession during the remainder of 1806. As though to make up for lost time, Beethoven rapidly completed the Fourth Piano Concerto, op. 58; the Fourth Symphony, op. 60; Thirty-two Variations for Piano in C minor, WoO 80; the Violin Concerto, op. 61; and the three Quartets, op. 59. (In this year, too, he put the finishing touches on his *Appassionata* Sonata, op. 57, which had been started in 1804.) On the autograph of opus 59 no. 1 he wrote, "begun on the 26th of May–1806." [9] On May 25, Beethoven's brother Caspar Carl married Johanna Reiss, who was then three months pregnant, and at least one commentator [10] believes that this accounts for the strange inscription on a leaf of the sketches for the very emotional Adagio of this quartet: "A weeping willow or acacia tree on my brother's grave."

The quartets were dedicated to Count Razumovsky, who in 1808 took over Lichnowsky's patronage of Schuppanzigh's quartet. Razumovsky–Lichnowsky's brother-in-law, the czar's envoy to Vienna, and a friend of Mozart and Haydn—at this time became one of Beethoven's leading patrons, sharing with Prince Lobkowitz the dedications of the Fifth and Sixth Symphonies. According to Seyfried, "Beethoven was as much at home in the Razumovsky establishment as a hen in her coop. Everything he wrote was taken warm from the nest and tried out in the frying pan." [11] In contrast to his pattern of familiar intimacy with Lichnowsky and Lobkowitz, however, Beethoven maintained a rather formal reserve vis-à-vis the Russian music lover and art collector, whom Prod'-homme succinctly described as "enemy of the Revolution, but good friend of the fair sex." [12] (It may have been of some importance to Beethoven that Razumovsky was intimate with such powerful figures as the ministers Metternich and von Gentz.) Apparently at Razumovsky's request, Beethoven included a *thème russe* in at least two of the quartets. Extramusical factors may also have been operative here, for there had been great battles between the French and the Russians at Austerlitz in the last months of 1805, and thousands of Russian prisoners ("poor, miserable, ragged, wretched objects," a contemporary wrote [13]) filled Vienna's hospitals, convents, and schools.

The composer's patronage relationships had continued their rapid evolution. Ties based on his pianistic virtuosity had largely disappeared, and he had achieved an unusual degree of independence from traditional forms of aristocratic patronage. New forms of patronage—by the public theater, by members of the financial nobility, by groups of connoisseurs—had emerged. Beethoven had been catapulted into the unaccustomed and, for him, burdensome role of business entrepreneur—seeking and sifting offers, negotiating fees and contracts, shipping merchandise, and collecting past-due accounts.

Although other aristocrats—especially Lobkowitz, Razumovsky, Franz von Oppersdorff, and young Archduke Rudolph—were playing important roles in Beethoven's career, Prince Lichnowsky, who surely regarded his guardianship as indispensable to Beethoven's welfare, was not ready to yield his prerogatives. As we mentioned earlier, he had meddled in Beethoven's love affair with Josephine Deym, and he and his wife compelled Beethoven to make changes in *Fidelio* that were not necessarily beneficial. Beethoven tried to loosen the tie: Röckel was present on one occasion in 1805 when the prince and princess were refused admission to the composer's lodgings, and it was only after much urging—and with a gloomy countenance—that Beethoven agreed to accompany them on a drive in the country.

The matter came to a head in late October or early November 1806, when Beethoven refused Lichnowsky's request that he perform for a group of French officers at his Silesian country estate. Beethoven "grew angry and refused to do what he denounced as menial labor," and there ensued a violent confrontation. Count Oppersdorff may have made his greatest contribution to Beethoven's welfare on that occasion, for he threw himself between the two combatants, one of whom "had picked up a chair and was about to break it over the head of Prince Lichnowsky, who had had the door forced of the room in which Beethoven had bolted himself." [14] Beethoven angrily left the estate, returned to Vienna, and dashed the bust of his patron to the floor. The personal rupture was soon healed—within a year, indeed, Beethoven considered dedicating the String Quartets, op. 59, to Lichnowsky—but the relationship had now been restructured. In later years, Lichnowsky would visit Beethoven in his room, quietly sit watching his protégé at work, and then depart with a brief "Adieu." On occasion Beethoven would lock him out, and the prince, uncomplaining, would descend the three flights of stairs to the street.

Until 1806 Beethoven had undoubtedly continued to receive his annuity from Lichnowsky, and he had augmented his income not only by sales of his works to a wide variety of publishers, but also by selling major new works to leading noblemen for a fixed sum, in return for which they received dedications and exclusive performance rights for a number of months. He was, therefore, making an extremely good living up to this time, and this permitted him to almost entirely give up teaching and to avoid composing ephemera or potboilers. (He had long since ceased devoting his time to teaching piano to young aristocratic ladies; and whereas his compositions before 1800 had included many frankly ephemeral works—contredanses, *Ländler*, and minuets for orchestra; pieces for mandolin or for mechanical instruments—his music thereafter, with only minor exceptions, assiduously avoided these categories.) However, Beethoven's violent break with Lichnowsky, which followed hard upon his rupture with the Theater-an-der-Wien, must surely have led to the termination of the prince's annuity. The state of Beethoven's finances therefore had become a matter of great concern to him. Perhaps this accounts in part for Stephan von Breuning's remark to a Bonn friend in the fall that "Beethoven's frame of mind is generally of a melancholy turn." [15] In the spring of 1807 Beethoven concluded an advantageous contract with Clementi for the British publication of a number of his works, but the guaranteed payment of £200 was not made for three years. In 1807, probably early in the year, Beethoven addressed a formal petition to the Royal Imperial Court Theater, which was now headed by a directorate of nobles (including princes Lobkowitz, Schwarzenberg, and Esterházy, among others), in which he applied for an employment contract at a fixed annual income of 2,400 gulden, in return for which he would undertake to compose one opera per year, plus other works. In this petition, Beethoven threatened to leave Vienna in the absence of a favorable guaranteed position:

> Admittedly the undersigned may flatter himself that so far during the period of his stay in Vienna he has won a certain amount of favor and appreciation not only from the distinguished aristocracy but also from the rest of the public, and that his works have been given an honorable reception both at home and abroad.
>
> Nevertheless, he has had to contend with all kinds of difficulties, and as yet he has not been fortunate enough to establish himself here in a position compatible with his desire to live entirely for art, to develop his talents to an even higher degree of perfection, which must be the aim of every true artist, and to secure for an independent future the advantages which hitherto have been merely incidental.
>
> Since on the whole the aim which he has ever pursued in his career has been much less to earn his daily bread than to raise the taste of the public and to let his genius soar to greater heights and even to perfection, the inevitable result has been that the undersigned has sacrificed to the Muse both material profit and his own advantage. Nevertheless, works of this kind have won him in distant countries a reputation which in several important centers guarantees to him the most favorable reception and a future suited to his talents and his knowledge.
>
> Yet the undersigned must confess that the many years he has spent in Vienna, the favor and appreciation of high and low which he has enjoyed, his desire to see completely fulfilled the expectations which hitherto he has been so fortunate as to awaken, and, he ventures to add,

the patriotism of a German make his present place of residence more to be valued and desired than any other.[16]

So far as is known, there was no written reply to this petition. In any event, Beethoven's application was not accepted. In May he wrote to Franz Brunsvik: "I shall never come to an arrangement with this princely rabble connected with the theaters."[17] Beethoven's urgent request for a benefit concert in 1807 was denied, increasing his malaise. Another disappointment was the failure of the Mass in C, op. 86, which was written in the hope of obtaining favor from Prince Nikolaus Esterházy at Eisenstadt, and was performed for the first time on September 13, 1807. Esterházy's casual rejection of the work (he reportedly said, "But, my dear Beethoven, what is this that you have done again?"[18]) led Beethoven to leave Eisenstadt in anger.

Meanwhile, Beethoven's productivity continued unabated. The years 1807 and 1808 saw the completion of the Fifth and Sixth Symphonies, the Mass in C, the *Coriolan* Overture, and the "Choral Fantasia," op. 80. The last work was hastily composed as a finale for his already overlong *Akademie* of December 22, 1808, at which virtually all of the above works were programmed, along with the Fourth Piano Concerto for good measure. ("There we sat from 6:30 till 10:30 in the most bitter cold, and found by experience that one might have too much even of a good thing," wrote Reichardt.[19]) Important chamber-music compositions—the two Piano Trios, op. 70, and the Cello Sonata, op. 69—also were completed in 1808.

Beethoven often insisted during 1808 that he would soon quit Vienna. "They are forcing me to it," he told the organist Wilhelm Rust.[20] In the summer, he wrote to Breitkopf & Härtel: "For the last two years I have suffered a great many misfortunes, and, what is more, here in V[ienna]. . . . "[21] And he wrote to the poet Heinrich Collin: "The thought that I shall certainly have to leave Vienna and become a wanderer haunts me persistently."[22]

The issue was joined in October, when King Jêrome Bonaparte invited Beethoven to Cassel in Westphalia as his *Kapellmeister* at a salary of 600 ducats. As we noted earlier, Beethoven used this offer to conclude an agreement—negotiated on his behalf by Gleichenstein and Countess Erdödy—with three young members of the high nobility (princes Lobkowitz and Kinsky and Archduke Rudolph) under which he pledged himself to permanently "make his domicile in Vienna" or "one of the other hereditary countries of His Austrian Imperial Majesty" in return for which they bound themselves to pay to him the sum of 4,000 florins annually "until Herr van Beethoven receives an appointment which shall yield him the equivalent of the above sum"—or, in the absence of such an appointment, for life. The aristocrats wrote:

As it has been demonstrated that only one who is as free from care as possible can devote himself to a single department of activity and create works of magnitude which are exalted and which ennoble art, the undersigned have decided to place Herr Ludwig van Beethoven in a position where the necessaries of life shall not cause him embarassment or clog his powerful genius.[23]

The annuity agreement was dated March 1, 1809. With it Beethoven had attained the highest degree of independence and security possible within a semifeudal mode of patronage. There was no longer a personal bond or commitment involving the slightest element of subservience. Indeed, the contract did not even require that Beethoven compose a given number of works, or that he perform services of any kind as a musician. (His work as Archduke Rudolph's teacher was unrelated to the annuity.) Beethoven hoped, vainly, that an appropriate title would follow—"the title of an Imperial *Kapellmeister* would make [me] very happy," he wrote [24]—but this was a comparatively small disappointment. (Later, Beethoven's dream of lifelong security was temporarily shattered, first by the March 15, 1811, devaluation of the Austrian currency, which reduced by 60 percent the real value of the annuity, and still later by the bankruptcy of Lobkowitz and the death of Kinsky. These events led to a tangle of threatened legal actions which were not resolved until early 1815—and then almost wholly in Beethoven's favor.) A tone of elation entered Beethoven's correspondence in 1809, and his thoughts turned to the possibilities of travel and marriage. In March he wrote to Gleichenstein, enclosing a copy of the annuity agreement:

You will see from the enclosed document, my dear, kind Gleichenstein, how honorable my remaining here has now become for me. Moreover, the title of Imperial *Kapellmeister* is to follow, and so forth. Now let me know as soon as possible whether you think that in the present warlike conditions I ought to travel. . . . Now you can help me to look for a wife. Indeed you might find some beautiful girl at F[reiburg] where you are at present, and one who would perhaps now and then grant a sigh to my harmonies.[25]

Neither hope was to be fulfilled, however. The siege and renewed occupation of Vienna by Napoleon's armies intervened, beginning in May 1809. Those who could—including the entire nobility, their entourages, and many public officials—fled the capital. Of the composer's close friends, it is said that only Breuning remained in Vienna. Beethoven himself took refuge in the house where his brother Caspar Carl and his wife lived with their two-year-old son, Karl. Apropos of his state of mind during the occupation, on July 26 he wrote to Breitkopf & Härtel:

You are indeed mistaken in supposing that I have been very well. For in the meantime we have been suffering misery in a most concentrated form. Let me tell you that since May 4th I have produced very little coherent work, at most a fragment here and there. The whole course of events has in my case affected both body and soul. . . . The existence I had built up only a short time ago rests on shaky foundations. . . . What a destructive, disorderly life I see and hear around me: nothing but drums, cannons, and human misery in every form. . . .[26]

The deaths of his physician Johann Schmidt on February 19 and of Haydn on May 31 surely deepened Beethoven's gloom.

In September Beethoven conducted the *Eroica* Symphony at a charity concert. Vienna gradually returned to relative normalcy; on October 14 Austria concluded a peace treaty with France. Writing once again to his Leipzig publishers, on November 2, Beethoven noted:

We are enjoying a little peace after violent destruction, after suffering every hardship that one could conceivably endure. I worked for a few weeks in succession, but it seemed to me more *for death* than for *immortality.* . . .
    What do you say to this *dead peace?* I no longer expect to see any stability in this age. The only *certainty* we can rely on is *blind chance.*[27]

Despite his somber mood, and an indisposition to work seriously which lasted several months, Beethoven was able to compose several major works during the invasion year, including the Fifth Piano Concerto, op. 73, the String Quartet, op. 74 (*Harp*); and three piano sonatas, opp. 78, 79, and 81a, plus a number of *Lieder* and some lesser works. Beethoven's productivity fell off somewhat in 1810, a year whose main completed works were the Incidental Music to Goethe's *Egmont,* op. 84, and the String Quartet, op. 95. One senses not that Beethoven was slowing down, but that he no longer felt driven to compose at so prodigious a pace.

Beethoven proposed marriage to young Therese Malfatti (who was then nineteen) early in 1810, his first such known offer since that made to Magdalena Willmann in the mid-1790s. It, too, was rejected. Despite the proposal, however, Therese Malfatti was not the most significant of Beethoven's romantic attachments during this decade.

To retrace our steps a bit: at the beginning of the decade, Beethoven's friendly contacts with women were largely confined to the Brunsvik and Guicciardi families. Contrary to legend, there was no romantic involvement with Therese Brunsvik. Beethoven first settled his affections upon Countess Guicciardi. From her correspondence and from a drawing which she made picturing Beethoven as a lovestruck Romeo who gazed up at her balcony while she peeked out from behind a curtain, it is evident that she delighted in her control over Beethoven, knowing that she could coax him through scolding and flirtation into becoming her gallant servant. "I have spoken to Beethoven about his variations for four hands," she wrote to her cousin Therese. "I scolded him over them; and then he promised me everything." [28]

At the same time that she was flirting with Beethoven, Guicciardi was involved on a more serious level with a young composer, Count Wenzel Robert Gallenberg, with whom she had been intimate since soon after her arrival in Vienna, and whom she married in November 1803. Beethoven was well aware of her affair with Gallenberg. In a Conversation Book entry of 1823, he revealed to Schindler the triangular nature of the relationship: "She loved me very much, far more than ever she did her husband. He, however, rather than I was her lover, but I learned of his poverty from her, and I found a rich man who gave me the sum of 500 florins to relieve him. He was always my enemy; it is for that reason that I was as good to him as possible." [29] We have, then, in sharply delineated form, an example of the standard pattern of Beethoven's love affairs: his attraction to a woman who is firmly attached to another man, so that he may participate vicariously in their relationship. The unacknowledged libidinal ties with Gallenberg (his "enemy," whom he lavishly assisted) implicit in this triangle may have placed great strains on Beethoven's perception of his own sexuality. And Giulietta's rejection of him in favor of Gallenberg may well have revived Oedipal issues—thwarted desires for his mother's love, submissive attitudes toward his father, resentment of more "favored" siblings—which intensified Beethoven's anxieties during this critical period.

The pursuit of the unattainable woman, however, had great advantages to one for whom bachelorhood was apparently a necessary (though painful) condition of creative achievement. (As Brahms quipped of his own bachelorhood: "Unfortunately I never married and am, thank God! still single.") For Beethoven regarded love relationships as impediments to his creative mission. He wrote to Wegeler in 1801: "I certainly could not marry. . . . For to me there is no greater pleasure than to practice and exercise my art." [30] In his conversation with Schindler about Giulietta Guicciardi, he wrote that she "sought me out, crying, but I scorned her." Schindler tritely but accurately observed: "Hercules at the crossroads!" whereupon Beethoven closed the conversation with the pungent observation: "And if I had wanted to sacrifice my vital powers and my life in such a way, what would have remained for the nobler, the better?" [31]

It was not long before Giulietta's place was taken by her cousin Josephine Brunsvik. In 1799, she had been compelled by her mother to marry Count Deym, thirty years her senior. In January 1804 Deym died; Josephine gave birth to their fourth child a few weeks thereafter. Later in the year she suffered a mental collapse; her sister Charlotte wrote to Therese Brunsvik of Josephine's "dreadful nervous breakdown; sometimes she laughed, sometimes wept, after which came utter fatigue and exhaustion." [32] It is shortly after this, in late 1804, that we first hear of Beethoven's love for her. Charlotte wrote on December 19: "Beethoven comes very often, he gives lessons to Pepi [Josephine]—that's just a little dangerous, I confess to you." Therese wrote to Charlotte on January 20, 1805: "But tell me, Pepi and Beethoven, that's something. May she be on her guard. . . . Her heart must have the strength to say no!" [33]

Therese's diaries imply that she and Josephine alternated between extremes of chastity and promiscuity, but that whereas she was evidently overwhelmed by feelings of guilt following her encounters, Josephine was able to give herself "freely and unconcernedly," as Therese wrote in her diary on April 19, 1809.[34] A police report on Josephine dated July 12, 1815, reads: "The morality of the Countess does not appear to enjoy a good reputation, and it is stated that she cannot be absolved from having given ground for conjugal quarrels." [35] But these refer to later times. She did not give herself to Beethoven: she claimed to have taken vows of chastity after her husband's death. Evidently Beethoven pressed her rather urgently, though unavailingly, on this issue. This is clear from the following undated letter to him which she drafted:

> This favor which you have accorded me, the pleasure of your company, would have been the finest ornament of my life if you had been able to love me less sensuously. That I cannot satisfy this sensuous love, does this cause you anger? I would have to break holy vows were I to listen to your desire. Believe me—it is I, through the fulfillment of my duty, who suffer the most—and my actions have been surely dictated by noble motives.[36]

It seems that Josephine did not fully reciprocate Beethoven's love, preferring "the pleasure of [his] company" to a fulfilled relationship. Her letters speak of her "affection," her "deep interest," her "enthusiasm" for Beethoven, but rarely of her love, and never of that in an unqualified way. But if Beethoven's desire for Josephine was of a passionate nature at the beginning, he nevertheless readily withdrew in the face of her resistance. He advised her that he was content with the relationship: "Oh, beloved J[osephine], it is no desire for the other sex that draws me to you, no *it is just you, your whole self* with all your individual qualities— this has compelled my regard." [37] He acquiesced in a spiritual relationship in which he was able to pour out his heart to her, seeking solace and comfort: "As soon as we are together again with no one to disturb us, you shall hear all about my real sorrows and the struggle with myself between death and life, a struggle in which I was engaged for some time." [38] The goals of physical gratification and marriage were set aside. He regarded himself as her possession—"you have conquered me"—and he accepted the relationship on her terms, best expressed in her draft letter: "I love you inexpressibly—like one devout mind loves another." [39]

Soon, however, Beethoven began to torment Josephine with suspicions that she was carrying on a secret affair. "*Do not doubt me*," she wrote; "I cannot express how deeply wounding it is to be equated with low creatures, even if only in thought and slight suspicion. . . . This suspicion which you impart to me so frequently, that is it which pains me beyond all expression." [40] Josephine was no stranger to this pattern; Deym, according to Therese, "watched her every turn with the greatest jealousy." [41] Hence she was once again subjected to morbid suspicion, at a time when she was recovering from an emotional breakdown.

By the summer of 1805, Beethoven's letters took on an aloof, and somewhat false, character. He asked for the return of music which he had given or lent to her; and when "An die Hoffnung," op. 32, which he composed for her, was published in September, her name had been removed from the dedication. In the fall Josephine left Vienna with her children, returning sometime in 1806. By the winter of 1805–06, Josephine had turned away from Beethoven and was being courted by Count Wolkenstein.[42] She moved to Budapest in the latter portion of 1806.

Some months after her return to Vienna in mid-1807 Beethoven attempted to renew their friendship, but was refused admittance to her house by her servants ("I was not so fortunate as to see you—That hurt me deeply" [43]). Finally, he acknowledged that it would be wiser if they were no longer to meet: "How sorry I am not to be able to see you. But it is better for your peace of mind and mine not to see you." [44] As Forbes notes, Beethoven's extremely reserved final letter ("I thank you for wishing still to appear as if I were not altogether banished from your memory" [45]) provides "a wistful close to the affair." [46]

Nor was this the only rebuff that Beethoven received at this time. Early in the same year, he invited the pianist Marie Bigot and her infant daughter for a drive, in her husband's absence. This invitation, which probably merely expressed Beethoven's yearning to join the Bigots' family circle, was misread by them as an attempted seduction of Frau Bigot, leading to a painful rejection and calling forth two heartfelt and heavily underlined letters of apology and explanation:

It is one of my chief principles *never to stand in any other relationship than that of friendship with the wife of another man. For I should not wish by forming any other kind of relationship to fill my heart with distrust of that woman who some day will perhaps share my fate.* . . .

Possibly once or twice I did indulge with Bigot in some jokes which were not quite refined. But I myself told you that sometimes I am very naughty. . . .

If I said that *something dreadful* would result from my going to see you, that was certainly meant rather as a *jest*, the purpose of which was to show you that everything connected with you attracts me more and more, so that my dearest wish is to be able to live with you both for ever. That too is the truth. . . . For *never, never* will you find me dishonorable. Since my childhood I have learnt to love virtue—and everything beautiful and good.[47]

Whether or not Marie Bigot should be tentatively listed as the successor to Josephine Deym in the chronology of Beethoven's love interests, [48] it is clear that any love he may have had for her was not reciprocated. Beethoven's association with the Bigots soon came to an end. They lived in Paris after 1809.

These rejections may have caused Beethoven to avoid any further love relationships with women during the remainder of 1807 and 1808. His attachment to Julie von Vering was primarily an attempt to share, by reflected light as it were, the love between Julie and his dear friend, Stephan von Breuning. "Often," wrote Stephan's son Gerhard, "Beethoven improvised for the young couple until deep into the night." [49] Julie and Stephan were married in April 1808. She died, aged nineteen, on March 21, 1809. In later years, Beethoven—whether truthfully or as fantasy we will never know—told the Giannatasio del Rio family "about one of his friends, who loved the same girl as he did, but the girl preferred Beethoven. . . . Beethoven left the field to his friend and retired. The girl did not live very long. I believe she died soon after marrying Beethoven's friend." [50]

In the fall of 1808, Beethoven took lodgings with his friend Countess Marie Erdödy at 1074 Krugerstrasse. (The Lichnowskys lived upstairs in the same building.) It is doubtful that there was any romantic element in his relationship with the countess, whom he called his "father confessor" (*Beichtvater*) and who was his adviser in personal and business affairs. (In addition to the Trios, op. 70, he dedicated to her the Sonatas for Piano and Cello, op. 102, in 1817.) His experiment as Countess Erdödy's lodger ended in failure, however. Early in 1809, he learned that the countess secretly had been paying not inconsiderable sums of money to his manservant. As I reconstruct the matter, Beethoven apparently believed that the countess, or her close associate, Joseph X. Brauchle, was paying his servant for sexual favors. On leaves of sketches for the Fifth Piano Concerto, then in progress, he wrote: "What more can you want? You have received *the servant* from me instead of *the master*. . . . What a substitution! ! ! ! What a glorious exchange! ! ! !" "Beethoven is no servant. . . . You wanted a servant, now you have one." [51] In a rage,

Beethoven moved out and took rooms at 1087 Walfischgasse, which he knew to house a brothel. It seems that he had seen in the countess's behavior some affront to his sexuality. The breach with the countess was soon healed by her assurance that she had given the money only "in order that he shall stay with me." "I am now *compelled* to believe in this generosity," he wrote, unconvincingly, to Zmeskall.[52]

Beethoven's courtship of Therese Malfatti was a hopeless one—opposed by her parents, conducted through an unwilling intermediary (Gleichenstein), and encouraged by not the slightest indication that Therese was drawn to him. In his only surviving letter to her, the rather embarrassed Beethoven wished to close the unsuccessful affair on a friendly note:

> By chance I have an acquaintance in your neighborhood; perhaps you will see me at your home early some morning for half an hour and then I'll be off. You see, I wish to be as little tedious as possible to you. Commend me to the good will of your father, your mother, although I have no right as yet to ask it of them; also to your cousin M. Farewell, honored T[herese], I wish you all that is good and beautiful in life. When you think of me, think of me cheerfully—forget the wild goings-on.[53]

The courtship had probably run its course by the spring of 1810. (Later, in August, Stephan von Breuning wrote to Wegeler: "I believe his marriage project has fallen through." [54])

As always when wounded, Beethoven retreated to a defensive and self-sufficient posture. Resigned to Therese Malfatti's rejection, he wrote to Gleichenstein:

> I can therefore seek support only in my own heart; there is none for me outside of it. No, nothing but wounds have come to me from friendship and such kindred feelings—So be it then: for you, poor B[eethoven], there is no happiness in the outer world, you must create it in yourself. Only in the ideal world can you find friends.[55]

From then until his love affair with the Immortal Beloved, Beethoven's only approaches to women were a flirtation with Bettina Brentano for a few weeks in the spring of 1810 and, perhaps, several days of affectionate teasing with Amalie Sebald at Teplitz in the summer of 1811.

Perhaps in connection with his marriage plans, Beethoven wrote to Wegeler, in Coblenz, for the first time since 1801, asking that he furnish a copy of Beethoven's baptismal certificate (see Chapter 1) from neighboring Bonn. And perhaps it was the pain associated with the revival of his birth-year mystery and the thoughts of his older brother, Ludwig Maria, which led Beethoven to speak once more of suicide:

For about two years I have had to give up my rather quiet and peaceful way of life and have been forced to move in society. So far I have noticed no *beneficial* result; on the contrary, perhaps a rather unfavorable one—But who can escape the onslaughts of tempests raging around him? Yet I should be happy, perhaps one of the happiest of mortals, if that fiend has not settled in my ears—If I had not read somewhere that a man should not voluntarily quit this life so long as he can still perform a good deed, I would have left this earth long ago—and, what is more, by my own hand. Oh, this life is indeed beautiful, but for me it is poisoned for ever.[56]

Simultaneously Beethoven wrote a letter to his dear friend Zmeskall which has a pathetic and despairing quality:

DEAR Z,

Don't be vexed with me for sending you this little sheet of paper— Are you not aware of the kind of situation in which I am placed, just as Hercules was formerly with Queen Omphale??? I asked you to buy me a looking glass like yours. When you no longer require yours, which I am sending you with this note, please return it to me today, for mine is smashed. All good wishes, and don't describe me any more as "the great man"—for never have I felt so deeply as I do now the strength or the weakness of human nature. Be fond of me—[57]

The "great man" had once again been thwarted in his attempt to enter the fearful world of marriage and fatherhood. Yet, as we saw earlier, it may have been the very nature of Beethoven's creative impulse which barred the way. Indeed, it may well have been necessary that all competing outlets—Beethoven's piano virtuosity, his hearing, politics, love, and marriage—be sacrificed to his composer's career. In Schopenhauer's words: "If Petrarch's passion had been gratified, his song would have fallen silent."

Schindler tells us that Beethoven copied out three ancient Egyptian inscriptions "and kept them framed and mounted under glass, on his work table." [58] The first two of these read:

I AM THAT WHICH IS.

I AM EVERYTHING THAT IS, THAT WAS, AND THAT WILL BE. NO MORTAL MAN HAS LIFTED MY VEIL.

And the third:

HE IS OF HIMSELF ALONE, AND IT IS TO THIS ALONENESS
THAT ALL THINGS OWE THEIR BEING.

Precisely what these inscriptions, which Beethoven copied from Schiller's
essay *"Die Sendung Moses"* [The Mission of Moses], meant to him we cannot know. They seem to have a religious significance; and perhaps
they are somehow related to Beethoven's feelings of isolation from the
world. But he knew from Schiller that the first two were found on monu-
ments of the Egyptian mother goddesses. In these matriarchal inscriptions, each goddess asserts that she can conceive and give birth without
the cooperation of man. (In the full transcription by Champollion, the
second passage is followed by: "The fruit I have borne is the Sun.") The
third inscription derives from an Egyptian initiation rite current at a
later, patriarchal stage of development, and it contains precisely the
same assertion, except that it now denies the necessity of the woman
participating in the act of generation. These irreconcilable matriarchal
and patriarchal inscriptions remained under the glass of Beethoven's
work table throughout the later part of his life, poignant reminders of
the master's withdrawal to an impregnable self-sufficiency, a self-sufficiency which ultimately prevailed against his longings for love.

This conflict between a defensive narcissism and a wild, thrusting
desire to break out of a painful isolation was now to be put to the test,
in the affair with the Immortal Beloved.

Antonie Brentano. (1) Unsigned miniature on ivory (ca. 1798).
(2) Portrait in oils by Joseph Carl Stieler (1808).
(3) Unsigned miniature on ivory (ca. 1812).

15
The Immortal Beloved

THE RIDDLE

Ries was the first to observe that although Beethoven was "very often
in love," his "attachments were mostly of very brief duration." [1] Thayer
also noticed this pattern. "One all-absorbing but temporary passion, lasting until its object is married to a more favored lover, is forgotten in
another destined to end in like manner, until, at length, all faith in the
possibility of a permanent, constant attachment to one person is lost." [2]
Elliot Forbes wryly commented on the composer's frequent "decision
to plunge into work when faced with the possibility of a permanent
attachment with a woman." [3] It seems clear that there was some element
of pretense or at least self-deception in Beethoven's continual series of
flirtations which bordered upon, but never became, love affairs. The
relationship with Josephine Deym constitutes a special case, but with
other infatuations there was little possibility of their evolving into serious
relationships. Either the woman was firmly attached to another man
(e.g., Giulietta Guicciardi, Julie von Vering, Bettina Brentano, Marie

Bigot, and perhaps Elizabeth Röckel), or she exhibited little or no feeling for him (e.g., Magdalena Willmann, Therese Malfatti).

The affair with the woman known as the Immortal Beloved was of a different order. Found among Beethoven's personal effects after his death was the only unalloyed love letter of his bachelor existence—an uncontrolled outburst of passionate feeling, exalted in tone, confused in thought, and ridden with conflicting emotions. There was no tinge of amorous charade here; Beethoven, for the first and as far as we know the only time in his life, had found a woman whom he loved and who fully reciprocated his love.

July 6, in the morning.

My angel, my all, my very self— Only a few words today and at that with pencil (with yours)— Not till tomorrow will my lodgings be definitely determined upon—what a useless waste of time— Why this deep sorrow when necessity speaks—can our love endure except through sacrifices, through not demanding everything from one another; can you change the fact that you are not wholly mine, I not wholly thine— Oh God, look out into the beauties of nature and comfort your heart with that which must be—Love demands everything and that very justly—*thus it is to me with you, and to you with me.* But you forget so easily that I must live *for me and for you;* if we were wholly united you would feel the pain of it as little as I—My journey was a fearful one; I did not reach here until 4 o'clock yesterday morning. Lacking horses the postcoach chose another route, but what an awful one; at the stage before the last I was warned not to travel at night; I was made fearful of a forest, but that only made me the more eager—and I was wrong. The coach must needs break down on the wretched road, a bottomless mud road. Without such postilions as I had with me I should have remained stuck in the road. Esterhazy, traveling the usual road here, had the same fate with eight horses that I had with four—Yet I got some pleasure out of it, as I always do when I successfully overcome difficulties—Now a quick change to things internal from things external. We shall surely see each other soon; moreover, today I cannot share with you the thoughts I have had during these last few days touching my own life— If our hearts were always close together, I would have none of these. My heart is full of so many things to say to you—ah—there are moments when I feel that speech amounts to nothing at all—Cheer up—remain my true, my only treasure, my all as I am yours. The gods must send us the rest, what for us must and shall be—

Your faithful LUDWIG

Evening, Monday, July 6

You are suffering, my dearest creature—only now have I learned that letters must be posted very early in the morning on Mondays—Thursdays—the only days on which the mail-coach goes from here to K.—You are suffering— Ah, wherever I am, you are with me— I will arrange it with you and me that I can live with you. What a life!!!! thus!!!! without you—pursued by the goodness of mankind hither and thither—which I as little want to deserve as I deserve it—Humility of man towards man—it pains me—and when I consider myself in relation to the universe, what am I and what is He—whom we call the greatest—and yet—herein lies the divine in man— I weep when I reflect that you will probably not receive the first report from me until Saturday— Much as you love me—I love you more— But do not ever conceal yourself from me—good night—As I am taking the baths I must go to bed— Oh God—so near! so far! Is not our love truly a heavenly structure, and also as firm as the vault of Heaven?—

Good morning, on July 7.

Though still in bed, my thoughts go out to you, my Immortal Beloved, now and then joyfully, then sadly, waiting to learn whether or not fate will hear us—I can live only wholly with you or not at all— Yes, I am resolved to wander so long away from you until I can fly to your arms and say that I am really at home with you, and can send my soul enwrapped in you into the land of spirits— Yes, unhappily it must be so—You will be the more contained since you know my fidelity to you. No one else can ever possess my heart—never—never—Oh God, why must one be parted from one whom one so loves. And yet my life in V[ienna] is now a wretched life— Your love makes me at once the happiest and the unhappiest of men— At my age I need a steady, quiet life—can that be so in our connection? My angel, I have just been told that the mail-coach goes every day—therefore I must close at once so that you may receive the l[etter] at once.— Be calm, only by a calm consideration of our existence can we achieve our purpose to live together— Be calm—love me—today—yesterday—what tearful longings for you—you—you—my life—my all—farewell.— Oh continue to love me—never misjudge the most faithful heart of your beloved.

> ever thine
> ever mine   L.[4]
> ever ours

Missing from the letter were the year and place of its composition and the name of its intended recipient. The fact of these omissions was hidden for several decades, because on the letter's first publication in 1840, Schindler confidently identified its addressee as Countess Guicciardi and asserted that it was written in the summer of 1806 from a Hungarian spa where Beethoven had traveled "on account of his gradually increasing deafness." [5] The unsuspecting reader could know neither that Schindler had thrice inserted the date "1806" in the letter, nor that he was simply guessing the beloved's identity. By the time he completed the enlarged edition of his Beethoven biography in 1860, Schindler had doubtless learned that Giulietta married Count Gallenberg in November 1803 and immediately left for Naples, where the couple made their home. Therefore he now stated "I cannot give [the] exact date," and speculated that the letter was written in or prior to 1803.[6] In the second volume (1867) of his Beethoven biography, Ludwig Nohl continued to accept Schindler's identification of Giulietta, but he also began to subject the claim to scrutiny for the first time. He ruled out all possible years between 1800 and 1806 except 1801, and found even this date difficult because of Beethoven's presumed stay in Hetzendorf during the summer of that year.[7] There the matter rested until 1872, when Thayer shattered the entire basis for Schindler's bland assertions. The publication of the second volume of Thayer's Beethoven biography revealed the existence of a genuine riddle with respect to the identity of the Immortal Beloved for the first time. The quest for a solution thereupon commenced, and the subject became a matter of intense controversy among Beethoven scholars.

At first this debate tended to obscure more than it revealed, for most nineteenth-century biographers failed to pursue the material clues within the letter itself. Instead they first sought to demonstrate that Beethoven had been (or might have been) in love with one or another woman at some time during his life, following which they attempted to fit the affair to the letter as best they could. Even Thayer fell victim to this tendency. Not content merely to have demolished Schindler's claim for Giulietta, he proposed Therese von Brunsvik as the beloved in volume 3 of his life of Beethoven (1879). This was a strange case of biographical matchmaking, for no hard evidence of any kind existed to indicate a love affair between Beethoven and Therese. The only supporting data consisted of Therese's apparent gift to Beethoven of a copy of her portrait in oils; his retention of the portrait until his death; a letter to her brother Franz in which Beethoven wrote, "Kiss your sister Therese"[8]; his dedication of the Sonata, op. 78, to her in 1809; and Giulietta's comment to Otto Jahn: "Count Brunsvik . . . adored [Beethoven] as did his sisters, Therese and Countess Deym."[9] On the basis of this flimsy evidence, along with a predating of Beethoven's 1810 marriage project to 1807, Thayer concluded that the letter was written in 1806 to Countess Brunsvik. But 1806 was a year in which July 6 did not fall upon a Monday. As O. G. Sonneck noted, "something snapped"[10] in Thayer's reasoning—for Thayer had been the first to establish that the only years which should be considered were 1795, 1801, 1807, 1812, and 1818, because these were the only ones in which July 6 fell on a Monday. To support his thesis, however, Thayer abandoned the evidence of the letter itself and pleaded that "there is an error of one day in Beethoven's date."[11] The most scrupulously objective of all of Beethoven's biographers had fallen victim to his desire to protect Beethoven from the accusation that he might have fallen in love with a woman whose character, age, or marital status did not suit the standards of Victorian morality. He chose Therese to counter two possibilities: that the beloved was the married Giulietta, or that she might have been the then fourteen-year-old Therese Malfatti. Transparently, Thayer wrote: "Our contention has a much more serious purpose than the determination of the date of a love letter; it is to serve as the foundation for a highly necessary justification of Beethoven's character at this period in his life." [12]

Objectively, Thayer's candidate possessed fewer credentials than Giulietta as the addressee of the letter. It was, therefore, most heartening to Therese's supporters to learn that she had left a full and melodramatic account of her love affair with Beethoven, including details of their secret betrothal in 1806, which was published in 1890 by Marie Hrussoczy [Mariam Tenger] as *Beethovens unsterbliche Geliebte, Nach persönlichen Erinnerungen* [Beethoven's Immortal Beloved: from personal reminiscences].[13] The book was enthusiastically received, translations were immediately undertaken, and a second edition was called for. Although A.C. Kalischer exposed it as a fiction and a forgery in 1891,[14] it was some time before Thayer's followers could acknowledge this. In the interim, Sir George Grove had the misfortune to interpret the Fourth and Fifth Symphonies as program works precisely congruent with Tenger's narrative.[15] (The Fifth Symphony, he wrote, contains, in its main themes, "actual portraits of the two chief actors in the drama.")

It was only Thayer's extraordinary authority in Beethoven studies which permitted his hypothesis to be taken seriously for a number of years. The disintegration of the case for Therese Brunsvik was largely completed by 1909, when it was established that Beethoven had been in Vienna and Therese in Transylvania on the crucial dates in 1806. Moreover, examination of the extensive Brunsvik papers uncovered several of Therese's love affairs, but no hint of one with Beethoven. Most decisively, it turned out that in later years Therese, believing Schindler's misdating of the love letter to be correct, thought her sister Josephine to have been the Immortal Beloved. The long debate—"Therese or Giulietta?"—had come to an end, with both candidates discarded and their advocates in disarray, somewhat abashed at the shoddy scholarship that had led them astray. New books on the subject continued to repeat the old speculations, but they had lost their conviction.

Perhaps because of the high seriousness with which the debate was carried on, its comic aspects were not far from the surface. Indeed, in August 1911 a fun-loving Beethoven expert (probably Paul Bekker) persuaded the influential periodical *Die Musik* to print a "new" letter to the Immortal Beloved which he had "discovered." Several leading scholars were wholly taken in by this new forgery, which included the following delicious song fragment, supposedly written by Beethoven to his beloved:[16]

Ich lie - be Dich von gant - zem

Da capo ad infinitum

Her-zen ich lie-be ein - zig dich al-lein, Ja!

THE SUMMER OF 1812

In 1909, Wolfgang Amadeus Thomas-San-Galli published a small book entitled *Die unsterbliche Geliebte Beethovens* [Beethoven's Immortal Beloved],[17] which for the first time put the study of this question on a scientific basis. Proceeding from the evidence contained within the letter and from the accumulated knowledge of Beethoven's movements during his Vienna residence, Thomas-San-Galli eliminated from consideration as the year in which the letter could have been written every year between 1795 and 1818 with the sole exception of 1812, one of the five years on which July 6 fell on a Monday. Thayer, too, had gone over this ground, but had passed over this year in what Sonneck called a "strange oversight." [18] For Thayer mistakenly wrote that "1812 must be rejected because [Beethoven] wrote a letter to Baumeister on June 28 from Vienna and arrived in Teplitz on July 7th." [19] In fairness to Thayer, he had received an abstract from the Teplitz guest lists showing Beethoven's registration date as July 7, 1812, a correct but deceptive date, as we shall see; nor did he have access to Beethoven's letter of July 17, 1812, to Breitkopf & Härtel, which correctly gave his arrival date as July 5.[20] In any event, Thayer's unqualified rejection of the year 1812 was the foundation of two generations of pyramiding errors, until Thomas-San-Galli uncovered it—at which point a wealth of corroborative detail immediately came to the surface, to be documented in Thomas-San-Galli's brochure and, shortly thereafter, in an even keener study by Max Unger entitled *Auf Spuren von Beethovens "Unsterblicher*

Geliebten" [On the trail of Beethoven's Immortal Beloved].[21] These, together with a 1910 sister volume on the same subject by Thomas-San-Galli,[22] solved most of the substantive questions relating to the letter and laid the groundwork for the identification of its intended recipient. Later researchers have added minor supporting details to the reconstruction of the events of late June and early July 1812, which may be summarized as follows.

Each year Beethoven customarily left Vienna for some time during the summer months. Ordinarily he spent his vacations in one of the suburbs or resorts surrounding Vienna. In the years 1811 and 1812, however, he traveled to Bohemia, where the cultural eminences, the wealthy, and the ranking nobility of the German-speaking lands vacationed at such spas as Karlsbad, Teplitz, and Franzensbrunn. In 1812, Beethoven left Vienna on June 28 or June 29, on the first part of his journey. He arrived in Prague on July 1.[23] His arrival was noted in a contemporary newspaper supplement listing prominent persons entering Prague, as was his registration at the Black Horse Inn.[24] While there he discussed financial matters with Prince Kinsky and received a partial payment of 60 ducats on the amount which was due him under the 1809 annuity. On July 2, he saw Varnhagen von Ense (who reported the visit in a letter to his future wife, Rahel Levin) and made an appointment to meet him on the following evening; but the meeting did not take place, for unexplained reasons. "I was sorry, dear V[arnhagen], not to have been able to spend the last evening at Prague with you, and I found that shocking [*unanständig*], but a circumstance which I could not foresee prevented me from doing so. . . . Verbally more about it."[25] Varnhagen's memoirs are silent on this matter; apparently he never received the promised explanation.

Before noon on Saturday, July 4, Beethoven took the post coach to Teplitz.[26] Simultaneously, in a separate carriage, Prince Paul Anton Esterházy, Austrian ambassador to Dresden, left Prague, headed for the same destination.[27] It had rained continuously on July 1, and after a single day of clear weather, there was heavy rain on July 3, which continued through noon of July 4. The rain then stopped, but the skies remained overcast and the weather cold through July 5.[28] The usual post route passed through Schlan, Budin, and Lobositz and across the peak of the Mittel-Gebirge range to Teplitz. Esterházy's eight-horse coach followed the normal route, but Beethoven's driver, having only four horses, decided to avoid the mountain road: "Lacking horses, the post-coach chose another route—but what an awful one," wrote Beethoven to the Immortal Beloved. Instead they went by way of Schlan, Laun, and Bilin. "At the stage before the last [i.e., in Laun], I was warned not to travel at night—made fearful of a forest [i.e., the large forest which lay between Laun and Bilin] . . .; the coach must needs break down on the wretched

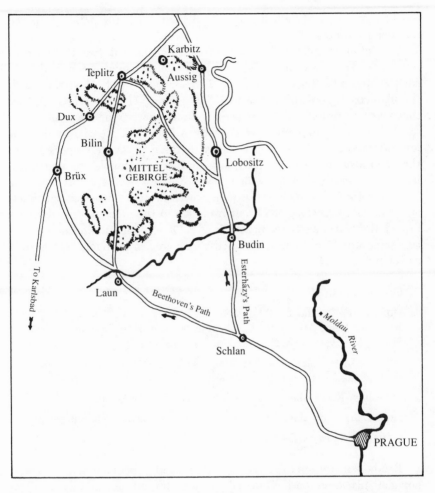

road. . . ." Beethoven arrived in Teplitz at 4:00 A.M. on July 5. There he
learned that the Esterházy coach had experienced similar difficulties.
"We say to you only that we have been here since the 5th of July," he
wrote to Breitkopf & Härtel.[29] He was given temporary quarters on that
day, no doubt on account of the lateness of his arrival ("Not till tomorrow will my lodgings be definitely determined upon"), and on July 7
he was formally registered on the Teplitz guest list: "Herr Ludwig van
Beethoven, Kompositeur, Wien, wohnt in der Eiche, Nr. 62" ("Ludwig
van Beethoven, composer, Vienna, staying at The Oak, No. 62").[30]

On the next day, "July 6, in the morning," Beethoven began the
letter, probably in response to a letter from the beloved which he may
have received in the morning mail: "Why this deep sorrow where necessity speaks," he writes, in what appears to be a reference to her letter.
Assuming that they had met in Prague, a letter mailed by her on the 4th

would have been placed on the July 5 mail-coach for delivery on the following morning.

The letter completed, Beethoven found that he had missed the morning post: "Only now have I learned that letters must be posted very early in the morning on Mondays—Thursdays—the only days on which the mail-coach goes from here to K." Therefore, "I weep when I reflect that you will probably not receive the first report from me until Saturday." It is clear from this that Beethoven knew "K" to be two days or less distance from Teplitz. The clues in these postal references led to the identification of "K" as Karlsbad, another fashionable spa one and a half days distance away, which Beethoven elsewhere abbreviated as "K".[31] Goethe, who made the trip between the two towns several times, and who often received mail sent from one to the other, repeatedly confirmed the traveling time in his diary.[32] Of striking significance was a contemporary Teplitz postal notice discovered by Unger, which read as follows:

OUTGOING MAIL:

MONDAY. Early, about 8:00 o'clock, the Reichspost goes to Saaz, Karlsbad, and Eger. After midday, about 4:00 o'clock, to Prague, Vienna, Silesia, Moravia, Italy, Hungary, Bavaria, France, etc.

TUESDAY. After midday, about 3:00 o'clock, to Dresden, Leipzig, Prussia, and the other northern countries.

THURSDAY. Early, about 8:00 o'clock, same as early Monday.

FRIDAY. After midday, about 4:00 o'clock, same as Monday afternoon.

SATURDAY. Same as Tuesday.[33]

Beethoven presumably saw this notice and concluded that he could not mail his letter until Thursday, July 9, for arrival on July 11. Evidently, however, he later learned that he had overlooked the following in small type at the bottom of the postal notice:

NOTE:

From May 15 until September 15, the mail arrives daily early in the morning from all the Austrian Imperial dominions, and also leaves daily before noon about 11:00 o'clock to the same.[34]

So in the second postscript he wrote: "My angel, I have just been told that the mail-coach goes every day—therefore, I must close at once so that you may receive the l[etter] at once."

In this way it has been proven that the letter to the Immortal Beloved was written in Teplitz, Bohemia, on July 6 and 7 in the year 1812.[35] The evidence for this was soon accepted as definitive by almost all serious Beethoven scholars. It was similarly established beyond a reasonable doubt that the place ("K") to which the letter was to be sent was Karlsbad. Ineluctably following from this is the virtual certainty that Beethoven's beloved was in (or about to arrive in) Karlsbad during the week of July 6.[36] To simplify matters, it was noted by Thomas-San-Galli that the Karlsbad police required formal registration of all arrivals.[37]

Another clue would prove useful in the identification of the intended recipient. Most Beethoven biographers believe that the following entry on the first page of Beethoven's *Tagebuch* of 1812–18, dated 1812, contains a reference to the Immortal Beloved:

> For thee there is no longer any happiness except in thyself, in thy art—
> O God, give me strength to conquer myself, since nothing must tie me
> to life. In this way with A., everything goes to ruin.[38]

Finally, another lead flows from a conversation overheard by Fanny Giannatasio in September 1816 between Beethoven and her father. She recorded the following in her diary:

> Five years ago Beethoven had made the acquaintance of a person, a
> union with whom he would have considered the greatest happiness of
> his life. It was not to be thought of, almost an impossibility, a chimera—
> "Nevertheless it is now as on the first day." [39]

The riddle was on the edge of solution early in this century. All substantive questions relating to the letter had been resolved—with the sole exception of the identity of its addressee. The quest continued. What was required was to test every woman of Beethoven's acquaintance who might be the Immortal Beloved against the requirements of the evidence.

THE SOLUTION OF THE RIDDLE

That evidence required, first, that the Immortal Beloved be a woman closely acquainted with Beethoven during the period in question, so that a love relationship could have developed, culminating in early July of 1812. It is most unlikely that the love affair was brought to its evident fever pitch via prior correspondence alone. Nor is it likely that a momentary encounter could have sparked the conflicts concerning the lovers' future plans which are so manifest in the letter of July 6–7. The Immortal Beloved, therefore, almost certainly lived in proximity to Beethoven in Vienna. Some evidence of an intimate association in Vienna during the months prior to July 1812 is an important material requirement.

Next, the letter gives rise to the powerful inference that Beethoven and his beloved had met in Prague immediately prior to July 6. He has her pencil; he does not refer to the journey from Vienna to Prague or to any events during his stay in Prague, but refers only to events from July 4 to July 7. He alludes to events of *"these last few days"*; he despairingly writes, *"Today—yesterday—*what tearful longings for you." (This last implies that they parted on July 4.) The Immortal Beloved, therefore, must be a woman whom Beethoven had seen and spoken to—almost certainly in Prague, although possibly in Vienna—during the week or two preceding July 6. Evidence that a candidate for the Immortal Beloved had been in Vienna during the last days of June 1812 would count in her favor. The demonstration that she had actually been in Prague between July 1 and July 4—when Beethoven was also there—would be the strongest possible evidence. If, in addition, it could be shown that she was actually in contact with Beethoven in either city, this would strengthen her case even more.

Finally, the *sine qua non* for identification of the Immortal Beloved is that she must be a woman who was in Karlsbad during the week of July 6, 1812. This test eliminates all but four women—Antonie Brentano, Dorothea Ertmann, Elise von der Recke, and Princess Marie Liechtenstein—all of whose names are entered on the Karlsbad police registers. Furthermore—and this eliminates three of these ladies—she must not only have been in Karlsbad during that week, but she must have *arrived* in Karlsbad very recently, en route from Vienna and/or Prague. Otherwise, she and Beethoven could not have had the meeting which necessarily preceded the letter.

(Clearly, there is no possibility of absolute certainty here, and the researcher should not exclude even the most remote possibilities. For example, it is conceivable that the letter was written to a woman in Karlsbad whose name is on the guest lists or police registers but who is wholly unknown to Beethoven researchers; or she may meet all of the requirements of time and place without our being aware of her doing so. And it is possible that the letter arose from a Prague or Vienna meeting with a woman who informed Beethoven that she was going to Karlsbad and then failed to carry out her declared intention. Despite such cautions, any inquiry into the identity of the Immortal Beloved must base itself on the most reasonable reading of the existing evidence.)

Turning now to the secondary requirements, the beloved would most probably be a woman whom Beethoven had met or become closely acquainted with approximately five years prior to 1816, when Fanny Giannatasio recorded in her diary that Beethoven remained in love with a woman whom he had met five years earlier. Ever since the date of the Immortal Beloved letter was established as 1812, it has become an overwhelming probability that the Immortal Beloved and the woman referred to by Fanny were one and the same. Fanny's diary entry should be read in conjunction with the closing lines of Beethoven's letter to Ferdinand

Ries, on May 8 of the same year, 1816: "Unfortunately I have no wife. I found *only one,* whom no doubt I shall *never possess.*" [40] (In turn, both Fanny's diary entry and the letter to Ries suggest a continuing association—in 1816—with the Immortal Beloved.) *"Only one."* The emphasis is Beethoven's. Those who have remained proponents of one or another woman as the Immortal Beloved have been forced by Fanny's reference to "five years" to assume two loved ones. For even if we take the reference to "five years" as an approximation, all previously considered candidates are eliminated by this crucial test, with the exceptions of Therese Malfatti (1809–10), Bettina Brentano (1810), Antonie Adamberger (1810), Amalie Sebald (1811), Elise von der Recke (1811), and Rahel Levin (1811). But these women do not meet any of the primary requirements.

Other possible criteria arise from veiled references by Beethoven to possibly beloved women whose names are designated by various initials. These are the "A" in the *Tagebuch* reference of late 1812, the "T" in two *Tagebuch* references of 1816, and the "M" in a note which was actually written between 1807 and 1810 but which Beethoven researchers long believed to have been written during the following decade. The Immortal Beloved need not have had the initials "A" or "T"; the opacity of Beethoven's diary entries precludes certainty in this regard. A woman having one or both of these initials would not be proven to be the Immortal Beloved unless she met the necessary requirements of time and place. However, if a woman who met all or most of these requirements also possessed one or both of these initials, it would appear to increase the probability that she was the beloved.

Another possible precondition for identification of the Immortal Beloved is that she be someone whom Beethoven believed he would shortly re-encounter. The expectation of an impending meeting arises from Beethoven's remark: "We shall surely see each other soon." The expected or actual place of the reunion is not significant. What is important is the probability that the Immortal Beloved was a woman whom Beethoven expected to see again "soon" after the letter of July 6–7.

These, then, are the requirements for the identification of the Immortal Beloved. A century of research, however, has excluded from consideration all of those—Giulietta Guicciardi, Therese Brunsvik, Magdalena Willmann, Amalie Sebald, Bettina Brentano von Arnim—who were once seriously considered. Similarly set aside were the more remote possibilities—Marie Bigot, Countess Marie Erdödy, Rahel Levin, Marie Pachler-Koschak, Antonie Adamberger. Several others remain as extremely implausible addressees of Beethoven's letter. The case for Josephine Deym —advanced by La Mara, enlarged by Siegmund Kaznelson, and recently revived by Harry Goldschmidt and others—had its day in the sun, but the disclosure in 1957 of the 1804–07 correspondence indicated an early (not chilly) end to an unconsummated romance; and although there is no certainty that the affair was not momentarily rekindled a half-decade later, neither is there any affirmative evidence that this indeed took place. Similarly, no meaningful data in favor of Therese Malfatti or Dorothea von Ertmann has been introduced, and their names have been put forward most tentatively even by their supporters. None of the above meet the necessary requirements of chronology and topography.

There is one woman, however, who meets, not just a few, but every one of the primary and secondary requirements. In her case, it is unnecessary to suggest hypothetical possibilities, to propose that "she might have" been in close contact with Beethoven in Vienna during the first half of 1812, or "could have" been in Prague between July 2 and 4, or "may have" visited Karlsbad. No speculative constructs are required; the evidence speaks for itself. Although this woman is well known in the Beethoven literature, she has, almost unaccountably, never previously been advanced as the possible addressee of Beethoven's letter to the Immortal Beloved.[41] Her name is Antonie Brentano, born Antonie von Birkenstock (1780–1869), to whom Beethoven later dedicated his Thirty-three Variations on a Waltz by Diabelli, op. 120. The weight of the evidence in her favor is so powerful that it is not presumptuous to assert that the riddle of Beethoven's Immortal Beloved has now been solved.[42]

Let us test the case for Antonie Brentano against each of the prerequisites:

•Item: *The Immortal Beloved was intimately associated with Beethoven, probably in Vienna, during the period preceding the letter.* Antonie Brentano resided continuously in Vienna from the fall of 1809 until the fall of 1812. She became acquainted with Beethoven during her sister-in-law Bettina Brentano's visit to the composer in May 1810; it is known that a close friendship developed between her and Beethoven during the next two years. Otto Jahn, who interviewed her in 1867, spoke of their "tender friendship," [43] and Schindler reported Beethoven's claim that she (and her husband, Franz) were "his best friends in the world." [44] Beethoven was a frequent visitor at the Birkenstock mansion in which the Brentanos lived; she and her family, in turn, visited him at his lodgings. He consoled Frau Brentano with improvisations on the piano when she was ill and bedridden; he acted as intermediary for her in a proposed sale to his patron, Archduke Rudolph, of rare manuscripts which she owned; and she showed him (or read to him) personal letters from Bettina. It is certain that they were in personal contact in Vienna as late as June 26, 1812, when Beethoven wrote out an affectionate dedicatory message on his easy Piano Trio in B-flat, WoO 39, to Antonie's ten-year-old daughter Maximiliane, and dated it in his own hand. Additional confirmation that Antonie was in Vienna at this time appears in an entry on the Karlsbad police register, which notes that her passport was issued in Vienna on June 26, 1812.[45] We know, therefore, that Antonie was in Vienna during the latter part of June, not only in proximity to, but in close contact with, Beethoven.

•Item: *The Immortal Beloved was in Prague between July 1 and July 4, 1812.* A list of prominent persons arriving in Prague on July 3, 1812, published in the Prague newspaper supplement which we cited above, contains the following entry:

. . .   DEN 3TEN [JULY]

. . . . H. Brentano, Kaufmann, von Wien. (woh. im rothen Haus.)

("Herr Brentano, merchant, from Vienna. Staying at the Red House Inn.")[46]

Franz Brentano, journeying from Vienna to Karlsbad with his wife, Antonie, and one of their children, stopped in Prague on July 3, 1812, and remained there for one or two nights. Here it becomes possible for the first time in the voluminous researches on Beethoven's Immortal Beloved to show that one of the women under consideration has been definitely located as having been in Prague at precisely the same time as Beethoven. There is no proof that Beethoven and Antonie met in Prague, but the presumption that they did is supported by several factors. First, since we know that they were in touch on June 26 in Vienna, it is reasonable to assume that they then discussed their respective summer vacation plans, and perhaps arranged to meet in Prague. Second, and decisively, they undoubtedly discussed a possible meeting later in the summer, for a reunion actually took place that was possible only through prearrangement. It is unlikely that these close friends—who had just parted in Vienna, and were shortly to vacation together at Karlsbad and Franzensbad—would fail to take advantage of the opportunity to meet in Prague as well.

•Item: *The Immortal Beloved was in Karlsbad during the week of July 6, 1812.* The list of departures for July 4 published in the newspaper just cited establishes that Beethoven left Prague before noon on that day.[47] The Brentanos' date of departure does not appear; we know, however, from Max Unger (who cites a guidebook of 1813) that the stage coach went daily to Karlsbad at 11:00 A.M. The Brentanos must, then, have left Prague on either the 4th or the 5th of July, because they registered at Karlsbad on July 5, 1812.

The presence of Antonie Brentano in Karlsbad has long been known in the Beethoven literature. Thomas-San-Galli was the first to examine the Karlsbad guest lists and police registers; but he failed to mention the Brentanos' registration. Unger, however, explicitly noted the arrival of Antonie Brentano on July 5. The relevant entry on the guest lists follows:

–33–

CHRONOLOGICAL NO.	NAME, POSITION, AND LODGING OF ARRIVING GUESTS	DAY OF ARRIVAL
. . .	. . .	. . .
380	Herr Franz Brentano, banker from Frankfurt, with wife and child . . .	July 5

On the following day, the Brentanos—Franz, Antonie, and their youngest child (Fanny, who had just turned six)—were entered on the Karlsbad police register (as No. 609). The entry gives their residence as Vienna and their Karlsbad address at 311 "Aug' Gottes."

The Immortal Beloved was a woman whom Beethoven knew with certainty to be in, or arriving in, Karlsbad during the week of July 6. Antonie Brentano is the only woman to meet this crucial requirement. We know that Beethoven knew her to be in Karlsbad, because he joined the Brentanos there later in the month. As for the other women who were acquainted with Beethoven and who were also on the Karlsbad guest lists around that time, it cannot be shown that Beethoven knew any of these women to have been in Karlsbad. Equally important, their arrival dates (June 7 for Frau von der Recke, June 25 for Baroness Ertmann and Princess Liechtenstein) make it highly unlikely that they could have been in personal contact with Beethoven shortly before the Immortal Beloved letter. Only Antonie Brentano arrived in Karlsbad at a time that parallels Beethoven's own movements from Vienna to Prague to the Bohemian spas.

Antonie Brentano conforms to all of the secondary requirements as well.

•Item: *The Immortal Beloved and Beethoven would soon meet again.* Beethoven left Teplitz around July 25 for Karlsbad.[48] We may safely assume that the main purpose of his journey was a reunion with Antonie and her family, and it is certain that such a reunion did take place—for Beethoven, according to the police register,[49] was lodged by July 31 in the same guesthouse, 311 "Aug' Gottes" auf der Wiese, where Antonie and her family had been living since July 5. They all remained there until August 7 or 8, at which time the Brentano family and their illustrious companion moved from Karlsbad to Franzensbad (Franzensbrunn), where they again occupied adjoining quarters, at the "Zwei goldenen Löwen." I do not know how long the Brentano family remained in Franzensbad; Beethoven's departure from that resort at the beginning of the second week of September presumably marks his separation from them as well. He arrived—alone—in Karlsbad once again on September 8 (this is confirmed by Goethe's diary); shortly thereafter (by September 16), he returned to Teplitz, where (as we shall see) the sisterly ministrations of Amalie Sebald helped to calm him during the aftermath of the turbulent affair of the Immortal Beloved.

•Item: *The Immortal Beloved was probably a woman whom Beethoven had met or become closely acquainted with approximately five years prior to 1816.* Beethoven and Antonie Brentano met in May 1810. They became intimately acquainted shortly thereafter. The Brentanos were Beethoven's closest friends in Vienna from then until their departure for Frankfurt in the fall of 1812.

•Item: *The first initial of the Immortal Beloved's name may have been "A."* There are five women to whom this initial could apply: Amalie Sebald, Bettina von Arnim, Antonie Adamberger, Anna Marie Erdödy, and Antonie Brentano. Neither Amalie nor Bettina are possibilities, because they resided in Germany rather than in Austria; and Antonie Adamberger and Marie Erdödy were not in the Bohemian spas during July 1812. Antonie Brentano, therefore, is the only woman of Beethoven's acquaintance whose initial is "A" and who could also be the Immortal Beloved.

•Item: *The initial of the Immortal Beloved's name may have been "T."* The following two notes—written in 1816—are from Beethoven's *Tagebuch*:

> Regarding T., nothing is left but to trust in God; never to go where weakness might lead to do wrong; to Him, to Him alone, the omniscient God, leave all this.

> But toward T. [be] as good as possible; her devotion deserves never to be forgotten—though, unfortunately, advantageous consequences for you could never result therefrom.[50]

The only women known to Beethoven in this period whose names begin with "T" are Therese Malfatti, "Toni" Adamberger, and Therese Brunsvik—none of whom may be seriously considered—and "Toni" Brentano. For thus was Antonie known to all of her intimate friends and relatives, including Beethoven, who on February 10, 1811, wrote to Bettina Brentano: "I see from your letter to Toni that you still remember me"[51]; and on February 15, 1817, wrote to Franz Brentano: "All my best greetings to my beloved friend Toni."[52] It may be objected that Beethoven would not designate Antonie by both "A" and "T". In fact, he alternately used both her full name and her nickname, as did many of her friends; and she herself alternated between these names in signing her letters, even to the same person.

The existence of *Tagebuch* references to the Immortal Beloved in 1816 should occasion no surprise. Beethoven's regard and affection (and, if my conclusions are accepted, his love as well) for Antonie at this very time are evident in passages from his four surviving letters to her, three of which are dated early November 1815, February 6, 1816, and September 29, 1816.[53] In addition, nine letters from 1817–18 (including one which enclosed a presentation copy of a *Lied*) to either Antonie or her husband (or both) that are mentioned in the *Tagebuch* have not been found. As an example of the depth of Beethoven's feeling for Antonie in 1816, we quote from his letter to her of February 6, 1816:

> MY MOST HONORED FRIEND:
>
> I am taking the opportunity afforded me by Herr Neate . . . to remind you and your kind husband Franz as well of my existence. At the same time I am sending you a copper engraving on which my face is stamped. Several people maintain that in this picture they can also discern my soul quite clearly; but I offer no opinion on that point— . . . I wish you and Franz the deepest joys on earth, those which gladden our souls. I kiss and embrace all your dear children in thought and should like them to know this. But to you I send my best greetings and merely add that I gladly recall to mind the hours which I have spent in the company of both of you, hours which to me are the most unforgettable—
>
>> With true and sincere regards,
>> your admirer and friend
>> LUDWIG VAN BEETHOVEN [54]

I believe that Thayer knew of the existence of a love affair between Beethoven and Antonie Brentano, although—because he was confused as to the date of the famous letter and regarded Therese Brunsvik as its addressee—he did not make the connection between this affair and the Immortal Beloved. I gather this from the following:

> Now it happens that one of Beethoven's transient but intense passions for a married woman, known to have occurred in this period of his life, has its precise date fixed by these passages in the so-called "Tagebuch" from the years 1816 and 1817. . . . As the family name of *this lady, whose husband was a man of high position and distinction though not noble by birth,* is known, it is certain that the T in the above citations is not Therese Malfatti. . .[55]

Thayer's words precisely describe Antonie and Franz Brentano, if we assume that the statement I have italicized implies that the lady was noble, though the husband was not. Antonie was born of the nobility; Franz was a prominent merchant and banker, but not a noble. No other known woman whose initial is "T" could be the woman referred to by Thayer. He specifically excludes Therese Malfatti; furthermore, she married a nobleman. Therese Brunsvik was never married. "Toni" Adamberger was not married in 1816, and her husband was an aristocrat by birth. It seems probable, therefore that "Toni" Brentano was the woman whose family Thayer attempted to shield from harmful publicity. Additional evidence for my belief lies in the fact that Thayer hints at the possibility that this "T" is connected with the "M" of the following handwritten note, first published by Schindler:

> Love—yes, love alone can make your life happy! O God, let me find someone whose love I am allowed.
> Baden, 27 July, when M. passed by and, I think, looked at me.[56]

Thayer does not say that "T" and "M" are one person, but only that they "may *indicate* the same person"; he continues: "The sight of 'M' again, for a moment, tore open a half-healed wound." This hitherto mysterious passage in Thayer becomes crystal clear if we assume "T" to be Toni and "M" to be her daughter Maximiliane, the sight of whom in 1817 (thought Thayer) revived in Beethoven the image of her mother.

Another bit of circumstantial evidence: in December 1811, Beethoven composed a song, "An die Geliebte" [To the Beloved], WoO 140, to a poem by J. L. Stoll:

> The tears of your silent eyes,
> With their love-filled splendor,
> Oh, that I might gather them from your cheek
> Before the earth drinks them in.

In the upper-right-hand corner of the first page of the autograph,[57] written in a previously unidentified handwriting, are the words:

> Den 2tn März, 1812 mir vom Author erbethen
> ("Requested by me from the author on March 2, 1812")

A comparison with a large number of Antonie Brentano's manuscript letters demonstrates that this note was written by her. She must, then, have received this love song from Beethoven shortly after its completion.* This seems to me a strong indication that Antonie Brentano, already months before the letter of July 6–7, was Beethoven's beloved.

Last among the signs which I have discovered pointing to Antonie Brentano as Beethoven's "*unsterbliche Geliebte*" is another unusual item. Found in Beethoven's personal effects were two portrait miniatures on ivory, which in 1827 came into the possession of the Breuning family.

---

* The song—with an arpeggiated triplet accompaniment—was published as a "*Lied . . .* with piano or guitar accompaniment," the only such designation in Beethoven's *Lieder* output. Since Antonie was an expert guitarist, this can be taken as additional evidence that the song was actually composed for her. A second version of the song—with a more pianistic accompaniment—was composed in December 1812.

Gerhard von Breuning succeeded in identifiying one of these as a portrait of Giulietta Guicciardi.[58] The other miniature remained unidentified by Breuning, but was later taken (probably by A. C. Kalischer) to be a portrait of Countess Erdödy and has been reprinted many times as such. However, Stephan Ley discovered in 1933, by a detailed comparison of the miniature with an authenticated portrait of the countess made available to him by her great-granddaughter in Vienna, that this identification was incorrect.[59] Returning to the subject two decades later, Ley repeated his earlier, fascinating speculation:

> Comparing this portrait with the miniature, the upshot is that the two pictures cannot be delineations of the same person; therefore the miniature is the portrait of an unknown . . . and the possibility or indeed probability arises that we may have here a portrait of the *"unsterbliche Geliebte."* [60]

A comparison of Breuning's miniature (now in the H. C. Bodmer collection of the Beethovenhaus in Bonn) with two authenticated portraits of Antonie Brentano (see p. 158 above) provides more than a strong probability that all three are portraits of the same woman. Every detail of facial construction, expression, coloring, and shape lead to this conclusion. The authenticated miniature (fig. 1) dates from ca. 1798; the portrait in oils by Joseph Carl Stieler (fig. 2) is known to have been painted in 1808; the miniature which Beethoven owned (fig. 3) seems to date from somewhat later, probably ca. 1812. The oil portrait is rather idealized, in the Romantic manner of the day. The miniature portraits, however, were executed in a realistic style; the resemblance between them is therefore especially striking, despite the age difference and the disparity of the angle at which the head is held. Frau Brentano's face became fuller with the passage of time, and her chin somewhat more prominent. But these are minor variations compared with the points of resemblance: the color and almond shape of the eyes; the curl and color of the hair; the contour of the eyebrows; the modeling and length of the nose; the long neckline; the idiosyncratic curvature of the lips; the facial outline and bone structure; the height of the forehead. All details point to Antonie Brentano as the sole model for these three portraits. (Another Stieler portrait—of Frau Brentano with her two sons in ca. 1815— is strikingly similar to the second miniature in ivory.)

Admittedly, Beethoven's possession of a miniature portrait of one of his closest friends and patrons is, by itself, no proof that she was the addressee of the letter to the Immortal Beloved. But we are no longer looking for "proof." What we do know is that the gift of such a miniature to a member of the opposite sex was often intended (and regarded) in Beethoven's time as something more than an expression of esteem.

These, then, are the threads in a powerful fabric of circumstantial evidence which, taken as a whole, makes it all but certain that Antonie Brentano was the woman to whom Ludwig van Beethoven wrote his impassioned letter of July 6–7, 1812.

ANTONIE BRENTANO AND BEETHOVEN

Antonie Brentano was born May 28, 1780, in Vienna, the only daughter of the noted Austrian statesman, scholar, and art connoisseur Johann Melchior Edler von Birkenstock and his wife, Carolina Josefa von Hay. After her mother's death in 1788, young Antonie was placed in the cloister of the Ursuline order at Pressburg, where she received a rigorous upbringing for seven years. Returning to Vienna in 1795, she led an equally sheltered existence for several years in her father's mansion until her marriage on July 23, 1798, to a sympathetic Frankfurt merchant fifteen years her senior, Franz Brentano. Brentano had visited Vienna in late 1796 and asked Birkenstock if Antonie was available; in August 1797, eight months after his return to Frankfurt, he began his courtship by correspondence and through two intermediaries in Vienna—his half-sister Sophia and his stepmother Friederike von Rottenhoff. Birkenstock gave Brentano to understand that although he approved of the match the final decision rested with Antonie; however, in later years, Antonie recalled that the marriage had been arranged without consulting her and that she had "obediently yielded" to her father's wishes.[61] She left her beloved Vienna for Frankfurt immediately after the wedding. In her reminiscences, she related that she knew "from rather certain sources" that on the day of her wedding her "true love" remained standing behind a church pillar at St. Stephen's, weeping "bitter tears" of mourning. She still recalled how she had been forced to follow her new husband to a foreign city, and she had by no means forgotten that Franz "was still so alien to her that it was only after months that she grew accustomed to the 'Du' with him."

Antonie found her new home "wholly strange," and she wept "untold hot tears" in solitude, unwilling to let her husband know her feelings. The birth of her first child in 1799 momentarily caused her to "forget all her sorrows," but the child died suddenly early in 1800. She bore four other children by 1806, all of whom survived.

She managed to present a controlled exterior to visitors during the early years. A touring Englishman described her in 1801 simply as "Mad. Brentano, a beautiful Viennese," who graciously took time from her family obligations to initiate him into German poetry.[62] Achim von Arnim was able to write in 1805 that "Toni Brentano is, as always, the well-bred hostess."[63] But the cool surface was readily shattered upon slight provocation. Franz's half-brother, the Romantic poet Clemens Brentano, wrote in July 1802 that "Toni is like a glass of water which has been left standing for a long while." [64] Others, too, noticed that all was not well. Clemens's wife, Sophie, wrote to him from Heidelberg, where Antonie was visiting in 1805, that "Toni's appearance . . . astonishes me greatly." [65] Bettina expressed her concern in a letter of June 1807 to her brother-in-law, the famous jurist Karl von Savigny, which gives one the impression that Antonie was going through a period of withdrawal and depersonalization: "Toni is in a bizarre correspondence with me: she has rouged and painted herself like a stage set, as though impersonating a haughty ruin overlooking the Rhine toward which a variety of romantic scenes advance while she remains wholly sunk in loneliness and abstraction." [66]

Antonie's malaise soon manifested itself in physical symptoms. In 1806, she wrote to Clemens: "I have a lot of headaches, and my damned irritability doesn't leave me." [67] An undated letter to Savigny refers to a nervous condition which prevents her from traveling.[68] In mid-1808 she wrote to Savigny and his wife Gunda: "The pains in my chest increased to such a degree that it almost cut my breath off. No position in bed was tolerable, until this terrible seizure dissolved in compulsive crying. . . . I have to look forward to a worsening of my condition rather than to an improvement in my health." [69] She continued, ominously, "A deathly silence (*Todesstille*) reigns within [my] soul."

Antonie's unhappiness centered on her inability to accept the separation from her native city. She longed for Vienna: "Through all difficulties—and these I was never free of—the eternal hope of my journeys to Vienna, which I made regularly every two years, held me erect." She told Reiffenstein that her father had made her promise to visit him every two years, and that for her "this was the ray of hope in a difficult life, for she indeed had a hard lot during the first years in her new home." Closely related to Antonie's yearning for her "glorious, beloved hometown" was her revulsion against Frankfurt. One gains the impression that her only moments of happiness in Germany came when she was vacationing or visiting the family estate "Winkel" on the Rhine, far removed from the Brentano house on the Sandgasse. Writing from Frankfurt to her son's teacher, Joseph Merkel, in late 1808, she described her feelings: "Here one is pressed constantly, without enjoyment. There [at Winkel] is enjoyment without stress. There is sunshine; here we follow the will o' the wisp. There truth; here deception. There frugality with little; here debauchery. There present; here past. There rest; here unrest." [70] Drawing back from the implications of this contrast, she concluded: "But these are not my words, because there means separation for me from the best of all men, and here is beautiful reunion." Nevertheless, in another letter to Merkel she summed up the heartsickness which Frankfurt inevitably engendered in her. "The shadows of the Sandgasse," she wrote, "are the gloomy backdrop to the painting of my life." [71]

In June 1809, Antonie learned that her father was dying. She wrote on June 16: "When the leaves fall in the autumn, then I will not have a father any more, and before he goes to eternal rest he shall rest in my arms and I near to his heart." [72] Antonie moved to Vienna with the children just prior to her father's death (he died on October 30), and the family took up residence in the imposing Birkenstock house—No. 98 on the Erdbeergasse in the Landstrasse.[73] Franz followed shortly thereafter and established a branch office of his firm in Vienna, leaving the Frankfurt home office in the care of his half-brother Georg.

In May 1810, Bettina Brentano (who was visiting at the Birkenstock house), accompanied by Antonie, sought out Beethoven at his lodgings at the Pasqualati house, to which he had returned on April 24, after an absence of two years. This inaugurated the friendship between Beethoven and the Brentano family. Bettina, who enchanted Beethoven, left Vienna after a few weeks, but Beethoven's friendship quickly extended to Antonie and her husband and children as well. Family tradition reported that "Beethoven often came to the Birkenstock–Brentano house, attended the quartet concerts which were given there by the best musicians of Vienna, and often gave pleasure to his friends with his glorious pianoforte playing. The Brentano children sometimes brought fruit and flowers to him in his lodgings; he in return gave them bonbons and showed the greatest friendliness toward them." [74]

What of Antonie's relationship with her husband at this time? Franz, the bourgeois paterfamilias, apparently did his best to make his aristocratic young wife happy. There are many reports in family correspondence of journeys and vacations during their first decade of marriage. His surrender to her request that they leave his paternal home and business to reside in Vienna for an extended period of time certainly shows that he was prepared to go to great lengths to please her. For her part, Antonie regarded her husband as a good man—she called him "my good Franz" and even, as we have seen, "the best of all men"—and it is clear that she respected him for his character and position and was deeply appreciative of his love for her. In her reminiscences, however, she reveals the onesidedness of the relationship: "I did not want to let my husband know how difficult it was for me, because he was always so loving and friendly toward me." One cannot help noting that she does not say "because I loved him"; nor have I found a single forthright expression of her love for Franz in Antonie's correspondence or reminiscences. Evidence of concern and affection abounds, but not of love.

And there are repeated allusions to Franz's total involvement in his business which are, perhaps, veiled complaints that she was being neglected. "Even after supper he goes to the office," she wrote to Sophia Brentano. "God, what will come of it?" [75]

Antonie compelled her husband and family to remain in Vienna for three years after the death of her father. Clearly she prolonged this stay beyond any reasonable length of time in order to postpone returning to Frankfurt, utilizing as her rationale the disposal of her father's huge collection of art objects, manuscripts, and antiquities, which she personally supervised. Her inner conflicts during this period generated a withdrawal into illness. She told Otto Jahn that, following her father's death, she "was frequently ill for weeks at a time." (She repeatedly went to Karlsbad in search of a cure, but without success.) Through this means, also, she succeeded in prolonging her residence in Vienna—where, despite her illness, she was able to find a happiness not available to her in Frankfurt: "I am kept in my hometown by sweet necessity longer than in the hometown of my children, and I enjoy the real contentment and well-being which are created through circumstances free of compulsion." [76] The bittersweet emotions aroused by her stay in Vienna are described in a letter of June 5, 1811:

> I have lived almost two years here in my father's town, in my father's house, but from which the father was carried off one and a half years ago. Oh, what a father! I have become rich in experiences of several kinds, and I believe that the home feeling which surrounds me even in sad hours I will find nowhere else. But my health is completely shattered, and that prevents me from having a pleasant life, and makes me acquainted with mortality. [77]

In light of the foregoing, I do not think it fortuitous that the letter to the Immortal Beloved was written only a few weeks after the final auction of the Birkenstock collection. In late June 1812, Antonie faced the imminent prospect of returning to Frankfurt, of being compelled to leave her childhood home and all that it represented to her. It is my assumption that she fled to Beethoven seeking salvation from that prospect—to one who represented for her a higher order of existence; to one who embodied in his music the spiritual essence of her native city. At the same time, Antonie Brentano may belatedly have been asserting her right to choose her own beloved.

We cannot say precisely when the love affair started. Following Bettina's departure—as of early June—Beethoven failed to take his accustomed summer lodgings but instead remained in Vienna, with occasional visits to Baden. He was busy with preparations for the June 15 premiere of his Incidental Music to Goethe's *Egmont*, as well as with supervising a good deal of music copying and correction of proofs, for many of his compositions were in press at this very time. In October he completed his String Quartet, op. 95 (the publication of which was delayed until 1816), but the pace of his serious compositon had slowed considerably, and this pattern was to continue into 1811, which saw the completion of but one major work, the *Archduke* Trio, op. 97, composed rapidly between March 3 and March 26 (although sketched in 1810). Nevertheless, Beethoven's mood was optimistic; he was apparently content to deal with important musical problems in fewer compositions. His thoughts turned once again to opera; he wrote to Paris "for libretti, successful melodramas, comedies, etc.," [78] and seriously considered *Les Ruines de Babylon* as an operatic subject. At this time he planned a trip to Italy; as usual, nothing came of his intended journey; instead, on the recommendation of Dr. Malfatti, he went to Teplitz, arriving, accompanied by his good friend and helper, Franz Oliva, in the first days of August 1811. There he worked on a revision of *Christ on the Mount of Olives* for publication by Breitkopf & Härtel and rapidly wrote incidental music to both *The Ruins of Athens*, op. 113, and *King Stephen*, op. 117, for performance on the emperor's name day, October 4. At first Beethoven remained secluded at Teplitz, but, through Oliva, he found warm companionship with a group of intellectuals, poets, and musicians which included Varnhagen, Rahel Levin, Christoph August Tiedge, Elise von der Recke, and Amalie Sebald. He later lamented to Tiedge that he had not made their acquaintance earlier in Teplitz. The carefree holiday was soon over, and on September 18 Beethoven left the resort, traveling via Prague to Lichnowsky's estate near Troppau in upper Silesia, where the Mass in C was at last successfully performed, and Beethoven and his patron perhaps experienced the contentment of having partially recreated the atmosphere of earlier days.

Thus far there was no sign of a romantic attachment between Beethoven and Antonie Brentano. A letter by Antonie to Clemens of January 26, 1811, however, indicates that she had already begun to revere Beethoven. Clemens had sent her a cantata text which he wanted set to music. She replied:

> I will place the original in the holy hands of Beethoven, whom I venerate deeply. He walks godlike among the mortals, his lofty attitude toward the lowly world and his sick digestion aggravate him only momentarily, because the Muse embraces him and presses him to her warm heart.[79]

At what point this worship was transformed into love is not yet known. My belief is that this took place in the fall of 1811, when Beethoven first presented Antonie with several of his compositions—the "Drei Gesänge," op. 83, and the piano transcription of *Christ on the Mount of Olives*, op. 85—with dedicatory messages. And if, as seems likely, "An die Geliebte" was composed for Antonie, it is clear enough that the love affair was underway by late 1811.

Toward the end of her life, Antonie recalled to Otto Jahn that only one person had been able to console her during her most desolate moments in Vienna. She told Jahn that during her long periods of illness, she withdrew from company and remained "in her room inaccessible to all visitors." There was one exception: Beethoven, with whom "a tender friendship" had developed, would "come regularly, seat himself at a pianoforte in her anteroom without a word, and improvise; after he had finished 'telling her everything and bringing comfort,' in his language, he would go as he had come, without taking notice of another person." [80] And in 1819, Antonie wrote to her spiritual guide, Bishop Johann Michael Sailer, describing Beethoven in terms which we can now interpret only as expressions of love. She characterized him as "this great, excellent person" who "is as a human being greater than as an artist"; she wrote of "his soft heart, his glowing soul, his faulty hearing, with his deeply fulfilling profession as an artist"; of his "warm will and hearty confidence." She concluded: "He is natural, simple, and wise, with pure intentions." [81]

If one rereads the letter to the Immortal Beloved at this juncture, its words take on new colorations. We are now confronted with a document addressed to a real person, rather than to a mysterious unknown whose character and motivations are hidden from us. The overt ethical implications of Beethoven's renunciation become apparent. His desire to accept Antonie's offer is in conflict not only with his deeply rooted inability to marry, but also with the prospect of the betrayal of a friend. Beethoven had warmed himself at the Brentanos' family hearth, partaking vicariously of their family life. He loved them both, and he could not separate them. At the critical moment of Antonie's declaration of her love, his anguish is apparent. And his answer is clear: he will continue to love both of them, as a single and inseparable unit.

There is no point in speculating on the events which occurred during Beethoven's reunion with Antonie and Franz Brentano in Karlsbad and Franzensbad during July to September 1812. It is sufficient to point out that in some way the trio managed to pass through the crisis into a new stage of their relationship. Passion had been sublimated into exalted friendship. Beethoven was visibly elated during these months, as evidenced by his correspondence and his productivity. That the close of the affair had a delayed traumatic effect on him will be seen from the events of later 1812 and 1813.

The precise date of the Brentanos' departure from Vienna is not yet fixed, but it was probably in November 1812. On October 6, Franz wrote to Clemens from Vienna about their imminent return to Frankfurt: "Toni as well as I are still not well at all [*sehr leidend*]. . . . If it had not been for my impending journey, which depends on Toni's recovery, I would have invited you to come here, so you could stay with us. But I have a strong impulse to go home, and my errant, unquiet life has lasted much too long."[82] He failed to mention that Antonie had been pregnant since June; she gave birth to her last child, Karl Josef, on 8 March 1813. Beethoven may have prolonged his stay in Linz until their departure was assured. Despite occasional revivals of his desire to see his birthplace on the Rhine, Beethoven never made the journey which might have reunited him with the Brentanos, nor, as far as I can determine, did Antonie ever again visit the city of her birth.

At the age of forty-six, Antonie Brentano began to note down the names of her friends who had died. By the end of her long life, in 1869, the yellowed sheets of paper were filled with names, each followed by the date of death. The first entry reads:

Beethoven, March 26, 1827 [83] *

THE MEANING OF THE LETTER

We saw earlier that there seemed to be an element of amorous charade in many of Beethoven's love affairs. However, there is also a somewhat sadder implication: in every single one of Beethoven's known passions for a woman, from his youth in Bonn until 1811, he had either been rejected by the woman or had withdrawn in expectation of a rebuff. Magdalena Willmann had scorned him as "ugly and half crazy"; Giulietta Guicciardi had taken the shallow Gallenberg as her lover; Marie Bigot had reported his "advances" to her husband; Julie von Vering had chosen von Breuning; the Countess Erdödy, although not his beloved, had wounded his feelings by preferring "the servant to the master"; Therese Malfatti had not responded to his attentions; Bettina Brentano had flirtatiously aroused his expectations without revealing that she was then

* Since the above was written, Martin Staehelin, director of the Beethoven-Archiv in Bonn, has kindly given me access to the following materials, formerly in the Louis Koch collection. On March 28, 1827, and in subsequent letters of April 7 and May 10, (the last wrongly marked "April 10"), a certain Moritz Trenck von Tonder (previously unknown in the Beethoven literature) wrote to Antonie Brentano: "I hesitate to bring you sorrow through the sad news concerning our friend Beethoven," he wrote, but "I know what great interest you, honored lady, take in his fate." Trenck's letters provided her with details of Beethoven's last sufferings along with a full description of the funeral and its attendant ceremonies; and he enclosed numerous materials, including a handwritten copy of Grillparzer's funeral address, a packet of poems eulogizing Beethoven, obituary notices, newspaper clippings, and announcements of concerts featuring Beethoven's music. Frau Brentano both transcribed and retained many of these, along with copies of dispatches about Beethoven that she gleaned from various European newspapers. Trenck also sent to her a report about Beethoven's last days written by his brother, Nikolaus Johann.

deeply in love with and about to marry Achim von Arnim. And a peasant girl described by Grillparzer preferred the peasant lads to the supreme composer.[84] Even Josephine Deym had first compelled Beethoven to withdraw his passionate demands and insisted upon the spiritualization of their connection, and then turned to Count Wolkenstein.

No one can be rejected so consistently without having in some way contributed to the process, without having actually assisted in bringing about an unconsciously desired result. We have already noted Beethoven's ambivalent attitudes toward women and marriage, which surely were related to lifelong inhibitions about taking his place as the head of a family. Nevertheless, the unbroken series of rejections—several of which he may have regarded as betrayals as well—must have had a devastating cumulative effect on his pride, causing painful doubts and self-questioning concerning the quality of his manhood. The pretense that he was "Hercules at the crossroads" masked the reality that—as he wrote to Zmeskall—he inwardly saw himself as Omphale's Hercules, shorn of his power.

For Beethoven, the miraculous significance of the Immortal Beloved affair, then, was that Antonie Brentano was the first (and so far as we know, the only) woman ever to wholly accept him as a man, the first to tell him that he was her beloved without reservations of any kind. "Oh continue to love me—never misjudge the most faithful heart of your beloved," he pleads, in the closing line of the Immortal Beloved letter. It was her love for him which brought to the surface his suppressed ability to express his love for a woman. At last a woman had given him her love, offered, apparently, to risk the condemnation of society in order that she might live with him.

The opportunity was at hand, therefore, to convert his conscious and professed desires for marriage and fatherhood into reality. Gratitude toward and love for Antonie, however, struggled against the ingrained patterns and habits of a lifetime. The power of the letter to the Immortal Beloved stems from the profound honesty with which it reflects this internal conflict. It is not merely a letter of renunciation, but a document in which acceptance and renunciation struggle for domination.

Perhaps, at first, Beethoven did not regard this romance as essentially different in kind from prior ones. There appeared to be only the slightest possibility of consummation: Antonie was aristocratic by birth, a married woman with four children, and Beethoven was on close terms with her husband. He consoled her during her long periods of illness and/or melancholy, and he was perhaps wont to proclaim to her the hopelessness of their situation. But if our reconstruction is correct, on July 3, 1812, in Prague, or shortly before, Antonie may well have asserted that the conditions of her existence were not an insuperable bar to their union, and advised Beethoven that she was willing to leave her husband

and remain in Vienna, rather than return to Frankfurt. Beethoven, it seems, was unprepared for this sudden turn of events; he responded in confusion, reciprocating her love, desperately attempting to respond in kind, but unable to disguise his ambivalent attitude to the prospect which had emerged so precipitously. Her reaction was one of sorrow and disappointment. Beethoven attempted to soothe her by expressing his positive feelings, and by holding out a glimmer of hope that her goal was not an unattainable one.

The first part of the letter seeks to bring Antonie comfort while avoiding the commitment she had sought. "Why this deep sorrow when necessity speaks—can our love exist except through sacrifices, through not demanding everything." Continue to love me, says Beethoven, but accept the necessity of our separation. "Can you change the fact that you are not wholly mine, I not wholly thine." Antonie had already answered this question in the affirmative, but Beethoven would not recognize the possibility of so radical a solution. He counsels stoical acceptance: "Look out into the beauties of nature and comfort your heart with that which must be." Momentarily he rises to the verge of pique against Antonie for "demanding everything"; "You forget so easily that I must live for me and for you," and in a revealing slip of the pen he continues: "If we were wholly united you would feel the pain of it as little as I." On the surface the sentence is meaningless, the "it" referring to no apparent subject. (Surely it does not refer to the pain of being wholly united!) What is perhaps meant, however, is: "Although we are not wholly united, you should feel the pain of our separation as little as I." Beethoven desperately wants to keep Antonie's love, but to do so without changing the external circumstances of their lives. He closes the letter with a repetition of his primary motif: "Cheer up—remain my true, my only treasure, my all as I am yours. The gods must send us the rest, what for us must and shall be." "Plutarch has shown me the path of resignation," Beethoven had written on another occasion; here, he is urging the lesson upon his beloved Antonie.

Having completed the letter proper, Beethoven either missed the morning mail or was unable to carry out so unqualified a rejection. When evening fell, he once again took up the pencil. With the first postscript, his determination to resist begins to disintegrate. The desire to accept Antonie's offer of herself has begun to overpower him. "You are suffering," he writes to her; and he repeats: "You are suffering." Surely the reference is to his own inner conflict and to the anguish which he himself feels. His defenses are crumbling. "I will arrange it . . . that I can live with you," he declares. With these words he has accepted the offer; thereupon his thoughts take on a wholly chaotic, free-associational quality, centering, perhaps, on the image of Christ merging with his own personality. "Humility of man toward man—it pains me—and when I consider myself in relation to the universe, what am I and what is He whom we call the greatest—and yet—herein lies the divine in man." Indistinct thoughts flow from Beethoven's mind, and then the suspicion of another possible betrayal surfaces: "Much as you love me, I love you more— but do not ever conceal yourself from me." He does not pursue the suspicion. He closes rapidly, pleading that he must arise early on the following day.

With the morning, Beethoven has reverted to Plutarch. The second postscript opens with a careful mixture of joy tempered by sadness and by the question "whether or not fate will hear us." The light of day has tempered his passion and brought him a new "solution" of the conflict: he will run away, and in his absence the problem may evaporate. "I can live only wholly with you or not at all—Yes, I am resolved to wander so long away from you until I can fly to your arms and say that I am really at home with you, and can send my soul enwrapped in you into the land of spirits." But Antonie may take heart at this sorrowful prospect ("unhappily it must be so"), for Beethoven adds that he will remain eternally faithful to her: "You will be the more contained since you know my fidelity to you—no one else can ever possess my heart— never—never—" Momentarily, anger surges through him at the uncomfortable predicament in which Antonie has placed him: "My life in V[ienna] is now a wretched life—your love makes me at once the happiest and the unhappiest of men—at my age I need a steady, quiet life— can that be so in our connection?"

Before the close of the postscript, however, Beethoven's love (and his need for a continuation of her love) once again begins to overpower his resistances. "Be calm, only by a calm consideration of our existence can we achieve our purpose to live together—" "Be calm"—again he is addressing himself, for his conflict has not been resolved. "Love me— today—yesterday—what tearful longings for you—you—you—my life—my all—farewell—Oh, continue to love me—never misjudge the most faithful heart of your beloved L." The last sentence is a plea for forgiveness— for although the letter to the Immortal Beloved contains neither an acceptance nor a rejection, Beethoven knew that he would ultimately be incapable of the breakthrough which Antonie Brentano had offered him.

We do not know if Beethoven mailed the letter to Antonie immediately after completing the second postscript. The sentence "I must close at once so that you may receive the l[etter] at once" makes it likely that he did post it. It is difficult to imagine Beethoven failing to keep his promise to write to her at once, and even more difficult to explain their reunion in the last week of July had he failed to do so. (As we now know, the opportunity to return the letter to its sender shortly arose.) Obviously there is no certainty about the matter: it is also possible that the act of writing the letter externalized the difficult decision which confronted Beethoven, and that once he had written it there was no need to mail it. And it is conceivable that he composed another, more careful and less contradictory letter in its stead, firmly closing the issue.

In our discussion of the letter, we have omitted until now the symbolism of Beethoven's account of the journey from Prague to Teplitz, which gives the letter much of its aesthetic power, for it touches on mythic and universal categories of experience:

> My journey was a fearful one . . . the post-coach chose another route, but what an awful one; at the stage before the last I was warned not to travel at night; I was made fearful of a forest, but that only made me the more eager—and I was wrong. The coach must needs break down on the wretched road, a bottomless mud road. . . . Yet I got some pleasure out of it, as I always do when I successfully overcome difficulties.

We begin to feel that Beethoven is here describing no mundane trip through the rain on a daily post-coach, but a symbolic journey portraying the danger of his own passage from a fearful isolation into manhood and fatherhood. There are resonances of a hero fantasy of grand proportions. In mythology, writes Mircea Eliade, the "road leading to the center is a 'difficult road . . .': Danger-ridden voyages of the heroic expeditions in search of the Golden Fleece, the Golden Apples, the Herb of Life; wanderings in labyrinths; difficulties of the seeker for the road to the self, to the 'center' of his being, and so on. The road is arduous, fraught with perils, because it is, in fact, a rite of the passage from the profane to the sacred, from the ephemeral and illusory to reality and eternity, from death to life, from man to the divinity. . . . "[85] Without seeking to burden Beethoven's letter with a heavier freight of interpretation than it may warrant, one surely senses that larger issues are involved than those which lie upon its surface.

The fear-inspiring forest and the bottomless mud road may be interpreted as symbolizing Beethoven's terror of Antonie's love, of an engulfing embrace to which he cannot yield because it is somehow forbidden. Conflicting emotions struggle for ascendancy in Beethoven: he is at once "fearful" and "eager." He was spurred to proceed onward, but "I was wrong" to do so. He knew that he should have remained safely at the last stage until the storm had passed over; he should have avoided the forest at night and taken the next stage in the light of day. He had not been able to resist the perilous quest, and at its close his fear is mingled with a sense of triumph. But it is a symbolic victory only: he cannot achieve it in reality.

The nature of this affair would make it impossible for Beethoven to return to his earlier pattern of amorous pretense. The meeting in Prague was a recognition scene which laid bare a previously unacknowledged aspect of his personality. While it is true that the unsuccessful outcome of his love for the Immortal Beloved was similar to the pattern of withdrawal and renunciation in his prior love affairs, there was here the essential difference that no rejection—real or imagined—had barred the way. Beethoven could no longer pretend that external circumstances or pressing creative needs were postponing his marriage project. Antonie's acceptance (and, apparently, her active pursuit) of Beethoven's love forbade any such rationalizations. The affair shattered Beethoven's own illusions that he could lead a normal sexual or family life. Accordingly, we have here the sense of a final renunciation of marriage, and an acceptance of aloneness as his fate. The first line of his *Tagebuch* reads:

Thou mayest no longer be a man, not for thyself, only for others. . . .

The italics, sad to say, are Beethoven's own.

Thereafter, we know of not a single love relationship throughout the remainder of Beethoven's life. The self-deception of Herculean heroism, the pretense of romantic masculinity, was at an end; the marriage project was abandoned, and Beethoven's attitudes toward marriage took on a cheerless character. "As far as his experience went," he told the Giannatasio family in 1817, "he did not know a single married couple who on one side or the other did not repent the step he or she took in marrying; and that, for himself, he was excessively glad that not one of the girls whom he had passionately loved in former days had become his wife." [86]

We should not, however, overlook one basic meaning of Beethoven's letter, and of the symbolism of the fearful journey. Beethoven was telling his beloved that he was scared, distraught, and alone following his separation from her in Prague. The letter is a call for a continuation of her love; it is an outcry for her assistance in assuaging his terror, a plea that she not abandon him no matter what the outcome of her desire to live with him. "Remain my true, my only treasure"; "Love me . . . Oh, continue to love me—" Beethoven understood that for one moment in his life he had within his grasp the possibility of receiving the unconditional love of a woman. His union with Antonie was barred, not by his need for a "steady, quiet life" but by unspecified terrors which overwhelmed the possibilities of a fruitful outcome. These terrors were the "fearful conditions" referred to in a *Tagebuch* entry dated May 13, 1813:

To forego a great act which might have been and remains so—O, what a difference compared with an unstudied life which often rose in my

fancy—O fearful conditions which do not suppress my feeling for domesticity—Ah, but to carry it out! O God, God, look down upon the
unhappy B., do not permit it to last thus much longer— [87]

Beethoven could not overcome the nightmarish burden of his past
and set the ghosts to rest. His only hope was that somehow he could
make Antonie understand (as he himself did not) the implacable barrier to their union without at the same time losing her love. It is to
Antonie Brentano's eternal credit that she was equal to this apparently
impossible task. In return she has earned a special sort of immortality.

Title page of the *Pastoral* Symphony, op. 68 (1809).
(Gesellschaft der Musikfreunde, Vienna)

16
The Music

At the turn of the century, Beethoven was eager to test his abilities in the larger, more popular forms and to reach wider audiences than those of the salons. *The Creatures of Prometheus*, op. 43, written in 1800–01 for a ballet by Salvatore Viganò, was his first major score for the stage; its success may have been a factor in his receipt in 1803 of a commission to write an opera for the Theater-an-der-Wien. Beethoven's ballet music—a chain of loosely connected dances and mood pieces—is a stylish and accomplished work, skillfully orchestrated and with unusual and colorful instrumental combinations. The popular overture, which was Beethoven's first essay in the genre, is Mozartian in manner, but the ballet's main influence is Haydn in his pastoral, bucolic style. There are also character-istic Beethovenian touches: the opening Allegro non troppo is virtually a first sketch of the "storm" section of the *Pastoral* Symphony, and the closing dance contains Beethoven's earliest use of the theme of the finale of the *Eroica* Symphony. But this tuneful and engaging score otherwise gives little sign of the dramatic developments to come.

Beethoven's oratorio, *Christ on the Mount of Olives*, op. 85, of early

190

1803, was his first major work on a religious subject. The choice of this subject, taken together with the composition of the six Gellert *Lieder*, op. 48, in 1801 or early 1802, and of another pious song, "Der Wachtelschlag" [The Quail], WoO 129, in 1803, gives the impression that there may have been a stirring of religious impulses in Beethoven at this time. Perhaps the deep personal, musical, and ideological crisis that he was undergoing during these years momentarily brought his religious feelings to the surface. But with the subsidence of the crisis and the consolidation of his "new path," these feelings apparently waned once again, and religious music disappeared from Beethoven's workshop for half a decade. The oratorio's secular and even operatic style, however, implies that it may have been conceived less as an expression of faith than as a non-adherent's exploration of the psychological presence of Christ.[1] Indeed, one might conclude that Beethoven—not without reason—regarded the crucifixion as a special case of the death of the hero, and that he was attracted to the subject at this time almost as a preparatory study for his most profound instrumental explorations of heroism.

But the subject of death is, by itself, an insufficient precondition for musical heroism. Beethoven wrote a number of *Lieder* and vocal works dealing with death—including "Opferlied," "Klage," "Vom Tode," "In questa tomba oscura," and the "Elegischer Gesang"—which are merely mournful, consoling, or elegiac and do not express the heroic experience. And though to Beethoven the Adagio affetuoso ed appassionato of his String Quartet in F major, op. 18 no. 1, represented the scene in the burial vault of *Romeo and Juliet*, this association leads, there, not to the heroic, but to the pathetic and the passionate. Similarly, the "Marcia funebre sulla morte d'un eroe" in the Sonata, op. 26, falls curiously within a context that neither sustains nor effectively contrasts with so weighty a subject. In *Christ on the Mount of Olives*, the absence of a counterbalancing theme—whether of heroism, resistance, or transfiguration—leads to a flawed conception; for Beethoven was temperamentally and ideologically disinclined to view Christ's crucifixion as a sorrowful but necessary submission to the Father's will.

The theme of the self-sacrificing Son has its own possibilities of profundity and, in view of the shape of his own early biography, surely touched Beethoven deeply.

O my Father, oh see, I suffer greatly; have mercy on me . . .

Father! deeply bowed and weeping, Thy son prays to Thee . . .

He is ready to die the martyr's utter death so that man, man, whom He loves, may be resurrected from death and live eternally . . .

That Beethoven set such lines to music in a perfunctory and abstract manner, avoiding the application of a personal style, perhaps indicates that he was not ready to explore certain painful areas of his own feelings and experience.[2]

The proximity of this work to the Heiligenstadt Testament raises intriguing but unanswerable questions. That it was actually sketched at Heiligenstadt is doubtful, but it clearly was created in the aftermath of the crisis, and both in its subject matter and in its size it opens—however haltingly and imperfectly—the path to the *Eroica* and to *Fidelio*. The "heroic" style seemed to be struggling for emergence, and *Christus* is a step toward that emergence, in which Beethoven returned, almost instinctively, to a form similar to that of the *Joseph* Cantata, in which he earlier treated the subjects of death and heroism. Here, as in that cantata, the discursive vocal form proved insufficient to the task.

Beethoven rewrote the oratorio extensively in 1804 and again prior to its publication in October 1811. It became extremely popular in England as well as in Vienna during the nineteenth century.

Beethoven's next composition was the *Kreutzer* Sonata for Violin and Piano, op. 47. "Written in a very concertante style, like that of a concerto," he wrote on the first edition of the Sonata, thus signaling his intention to introduce elements of dynamic conflict into one of the major Classic salon genres and to give equal weight to the two instruments. The *Kreutzer* Sonata's pianistic style looks forward to the middle-period piano sonatas, and the violin has now acquired an urgent, declamatory voice. The work is in three movements: an Adagio sostenuto—the only slow introduction in Beethoven's violin sonatas—leading to a dynamically propulsive Presto; an Andante con variazioni; and a witty Presto finale, in tarantelle rhythm, that was originally composed for the Sonata, op. 30 no. 1. In Tolstoy's novel of the same name, a performance of this sonata precipitates the crucial action: "It seemed that entirely new impulses, new possibilities, were revealed to me in myself, such as I had not dreamed of before," says Tolstoy's tragic hero. "Such works should be played only in grave, significant conditions, and only then when certain deeds corresponding to such music are to be accomplished."

With Beethoven's next work, the *Eroica* Symphony, op. 55, we know that we have crossed irrevocably a major boundary in Beethoven's development and in music history as well. The startling and unprecedented characteristics of the *Eroica*—and of many of his subsequent major compositions—were to some degree made possible by Beethoven's perception of new potentialities inherent in the flexible framework of sonata form. Because of its unique ability to release the most explosive musical concepts within binding aesthetic structures, the sonata form was eminently suited to deal with dramatic and tragic subjects. (The parallels of sonata to drama were noted even by early observers; Lacépède in 1787 compared "the three movements of a sonata or symphony to the 'noble' first act, 'more pathetic' second act, and 'more tumultuous' third act of a drama." [3]) However, their psychological outlook and the requirements of the forms of patronage under which they worked apparently did not predispose Haydn and Mozart (not to speak of their lesser contemporaries) to fully develop those possibilities. In terms of the admittedly imperfect analogy between drama and sonata, we may say, with Tovey, that the sonata cycles of Mozart and Haydn were musical analogues of the comedy of manners—rational, unsentimental, objective, witty, satirical treatments of the conventions, customs, and mores of society. In the comedy of manners, disruptions of the social fabric are momentary; the loss of love or status is provisional and temporary; undercurrents of sadness and melancholy are almost invariably dissolved in a reaffirmation of social norms and in a return to sanity and wholeness. As Einstein observed, the symphonies of Haydn and Mozart "always remained within the social frame"; and in their sonata-form works they "limited themselves to the attainment of noble mirth, to a purification of the feelings." [4] Hence, however well it mirrored the rich variety of emotional states and strivings of its composers, its patrons, its audience, and the larger collectivity of which these were parts, the high-Classic style failed to map several inescapable and fundamental features of the emotional landscape in so tumultuous an era. In particular, it rarely plumbed either the heroic or the tragic levels of experience.

And yet, there were currents developing in Austrian musical life which would repair these omissions. Viennese music responded slowly but inevitably to the reverberations of the Napoleonic Wars. In 1794, the Viennese composer Maria Theresia Paradis wrote a grand funeral cantata on the death of Louis XVI, which was performed for the widows and orphans of the Austrian soldiers; in 1796, Mozart's student Süssmayer composed a patriotic opera (*Der Retter in der Noth*), and other composers began to place their works—as they said—"on the altar of the Fatherland." Even the music of Haydn began to take on a new character: he wrote one symphony (1794) titled *Military*, another (1795) called *Drum Roll*, and in 1796 he wrote the classic national anthem, "God Save Emperor Franz," which became the rallying cry of Austrian patriotism. Also in 1796, Haydn composed incidental music to *Alfred oder der patriotische König*, followed several years later by an aria, "Lines from the Battle of the Nile," inspired by Nelson's victory at Aboukir Bay. But it was in two full-scale masses with trumpets and kettledrums, the *Mass in Time of War* (1796) and the *Nelson Mass* (1798), that Haydn approached most closely what would later become Beethoven's heroic style. Another of Beethoven's teachers, Imperial *Kapellmeister* Salieri, composed a patriotic cantata in 1799 entitled *Der tyroler Landsturm,* which contains quotations from *La Mar-seillaise* and Haydn's "Kaiser" hymn, and in which Erich Schenk has found numerous foreshadowings of Beethoven's *Creatures of Prometheus* and *Fidelio,* and even of his Seventh Symphony.[5]

The concept of a heroic music responding to the stormy currents of contemporary history was, therefore, already beginning to take shape. Despite these foreshadowings, however, Beethoven was the first fully to fuse the tempestuous, conflict-ridden subject matter of the emerging heroic style with the sonata principle, thus inaugurating a revolution in the history of music. Beethoven took music beyond what we may describe as the pleasure principle of Viennese Classicism; he permitted aggressive and disintegrative forces to enter musical form: he placed the tragic experience at the core of his heroic style. He now introduced elements into instrumental music that had previously been neglected or unwelcome. A unique characteristic of the *Eroica* Symphony—and of its heroic successors—is the incorporation into musical form of death, destructiveness, anxiety, and aggression, as terrors to be transcended within the work of art itself. And it will be this intrusion of hostile energy, raising the possibility of loss, that will also make affirmations worthwhile.

It is for reasons such as these that Beethoven's has been called a "tragic" music. But Beethoven's heroic music is not primarily a conventionally tragic, let alone a death-haunted music, for most of his works in this vein close on a note of joy, triumph, or transcendence. The Funeral March of the *Eroica* yields to an animated, explosive Scherzo and a broad, swinging finale; Florestan and his anonymous fellow prisoners ascend into the light; the precipitating "Fate" theme of the Fifth Symphony is supplanted by the rising march theme of its closing movement; Egmont's death is followed by a *Siegessymphonie* (Symphony of Victory). In this respect Beethoven remained true to the spirit of Classicism and to the Kantian vision of Schiller, who wrote: "The first law of the tragic art was to represent suffering nature. The second law is to represent the resistance of morality to suffering."[6] Furthermore, Beethoven's music does not merely express man's capacity to endure or even to resist suffering— the conventional qualities of tragic art. His sonata cycles continue to project—on a vastly magnified scale—the essential features of high comedy: happy endings, joyful reconciliations, victories won and tragedy effaced. If, as Susanne Langer has observed, tragedy is the image of Fate and comedy the image of Fortune,[7] then Beethoven's music presents the collision of these images—a clash from which Fortune emerges triumphant, so that the hero may continue his quest.

Beethoven's heroism defines itself in conflict with mortality, and mortality is, in turn, superseded by renewed and transfigured life. The components of Beethoven's concept of heroism, then, are more extensive than appear at first glance, encompassing the full range of human experience—birth, struggle, death, and resurrection; and these universals are expressed formally through a fusion of comic and tragic visions of life.

Apart from its extramusical associations, its heroic stance, and its "grand manner," the *Eroica* Symphony marks Beethoven's turning to compositions of unprecedented ambition. He has now chosen to work on a vastly expanded scale, twice the size of the symphonic model that he had inherited from Haydn and Mozart. The first movement alone spans almost 700 measures. The 250-measure development section, which in earlier Classic sonatas had usually served as a transitional pathway from the exposition to the recapitulation, now exceeds the exposition's length by more than 100 measures; it becomes the central battleground on which the issues will be fought out. The solution of the harmonic and thematic issues must, of course, await the recapitulation, which is here most suspensefully delayed by a prolonged transition section, and the lengthy coda, which provides greater rhetorical weight than ever before. The process of formal expansion that was already manifest in the opus 1 Trios and the opus 2 Sonatas here finds fulfillment.

But enlargement of forces and extension of time span do not lead here to a loosening of design and a dilution of content. The *Eroica's* temporal expansion accompanies—indeed results from—extreme thematic condensation. Early Classic melodies, based as they were on dance rhythms and forms, and normally organized around regular eight-measure periods, were typically symmetrical and balanced, suitable for orderly elaboration, ornamentation, development, and restatement. The thematic materials of the high-Classic masters were increasingly instilled with a new turbulence and assymetry through the use of a number of contrasting motifs within a more complex periodic structure. Intensifying this procedure in the *Eroica's* first movement, Beethoven works with motif cells of great compression. Describing this process of "the manipulative extension of a basic or central musical idea," Lang observes: "These sonata subjects are…motif cells that in themselves are usually altogether insignificant, but they become cogs in the machinery of design; they are twisted and turned, fragmented and tossed about with infinite inventiveness, only to be reassembled after the battle."[8] Owing to this extreme thematic condensation, critics are on occasion unable to specify what Beethoven's "themes" are. Indeed, in the first movement of the *Eroica*, Riezler believes that what is usually regarded as the main theme or principal motif may actually be "the melodic 'unfolding' of the notes already heard simultaneously in the form of chords."[9] By extension, the "motif" or thematic "cell" may consist of the two "curtain-raising" chords in measures 1 and 2:

It is even possible that here Beethoven did consciously attempt to "write without themes," to exploit the energy locked within the basic harmonic unit—the chord. The dissonant C sharp (or D flat) in measure 7 acts as a fulcrum compelling a departure from the common chord, thus creating a dynamic disequilibrium that provides the driving impetus of the movement, an impetus that continues almost unbroken until the restatement of the tonic chord in the final cadence. The result is music which appears to be self-creating, which must strive for its existence, which pursues a goal with unflagging energy and resoluteness—rather than music whose essence is already largely present in its opening thematic statement.[10]

Overlapping with this process is Beethoven's innovative procedure of developing a movement, and even an entire work, out of a single rhythmic motif. These motifs are so powerfully treated that, as Tovey has suggested, many of Beethoven's works "can be recognized by their bare rhythm without quoting any melody at all." [11] Scherchen writes that the "almost incomprehensible uniformity of the C-minor Symphony springs from the inexhaustible opportunities for development offered by the implications of its rhythmic motive, just as the massive inner compactness of the A-major Symphony is due to the basic rhythm which carries along all its four movements." [12]

Beethoven's unprecedented harmonic procedures were also decisive in shaping his "grand manner" structures. As Leonard Ratner has observed, Beethoven's unorthodox modulatory techniques, his shifts of cadential emphases, and his overdetermined harmonic meanings—which were often perceived as bizarre and whimsical by his contemporaries—served to create a "more powerful harmonic leverage than was customary in the music of Beethoven's predecessors and contemporaries . . . a leverage that creates intense harmonic thrusts and broad trajectories." [13]

Innovative features of the *Eroica* (some anticipated by Haydn and Mozart) are often cited, including the use of a new theme in the development section of the first movement, the employment of the winds for expressive rather than coloristic purposes, the introduction of a set of variations in the finale and of a funeral march in the slow movement, and the use of three French horns for the first time in symphonic orchestration. More fundamentally, Beethoven's style is now informed with an organicity both of motion and structure which gives the symphony its sense of unfolding continuity and wholeness within a constant interplay of moods.

With the *Waldstein* and *Appassionata* Sonatas, opp. 53 and 57, composed mainly in 1804 and 1805, Beethoven moved irrevocably beyond the boundaries of the high-Classic piano style, creating sonorities and textures never previously achieved. He no longer limited the technical difficulties of his sonatas to permit performance by competent amateurs, but instead stretched the potentialities of both instrument and technique to their outer limits. The dynamics are greatly extended; the colors are fantastic and luxuriant, approaching quasi-orchestral sonorities. For this reason, Lenz called the *Waldstein* "a heroic symphony for piano." The *Appassionata*—which, along with opus 78, was Beethoven's favorite sonata until his opus 106 [14]—has evoked comparison with Dante's *Inferno* (Leichtentritt), with *King Lear* (Tovey), with *Macbeth* (Schering), and with Corneille's tragedies (Rolland). Each of the sonatas is in three movements, but in both cases—especially in opus 53—the slow movements are organically connected with the finales so as to give the impression of magnified two-movement works. While the *Waldstein* closes on Beethoven's typical note of joyous transcendence, the *Appassionata* maintains an unusual tragic mood throughout. Tovey wrote: "All his other pathetic finales show either an epilogue in some legendary or later world far away from the tragic scene . . . or a temper, fighting, humorous, or resigned, that does not carry with it a sense of tragic doom." Here, however, "there is not a moment's doubt that the tragic passion is rushing deathwards." [15]

For almost a quarter of a century, beginning in 1803, Beethoven read countless librettos and considered numerous literary texts in an endless search for a suitable opera subject.[16] *Vestas Feuer, Macbeth, Melusina, The Return of Ulysses, The Ruins of Babylon, Bacchus, Drahomira, Romulus and Remus*—these were only a few of those which interested him seriously, but not sufficiently. He found fault with Mozart's librettos (*Don Giovanni* being too "scandalous" a subject) and gave high marks only to the moralistic texts of Cherubini's *Les deux journées* and Spontini's *La Vestale*. It could not have been the literary quality of the libretto of *Fidelio*—the only opera that Beethoven ever completed—which attracted him, for it is an artless text, stagnant in its action, cumbersome in its dramatic development, and awkward in its blending of styles. Clearly, the subject matter had some special appeal for him.

Fidelio, whose characters include an imprisoned noble, a faithful wife, a tyrant/usurper, and a savior/prince, was an ideal vehicle for the expression of Beethoven's Enlightened beliefs. The opera's themes of brotherhood, conjugal devotion, and triumph over injustice are basic to his ideology, but they do not signal his devotion to a Jacobin outlook. On the contrary, the 1798 French libretto by Bouilly that was adapted for Beethoven's use, based on an episode that occurred under the Terror, can be seen as a critique of the Jacobin persecutions of the French aristocracy. Perhaps this is why the "rescue opera" or "horror opera" [17]— of which Bouilly's *Léonore* was an example—became so wildly popular in France beginning in the 1790s in works by Dalayrac, Catel, Méhul, Berton, Lesueur, and, especially, Cherubini. For the rescue opera appeared to symbolize the reparation for, or even denial of, the persecution or murder of kings and nobles. Audiences may have found cathartic release in the notion that victims of the Terror had been rescued or resurrected, and that in any event all evildoing was attributable to the reprehensible machinations of a villainous and atypical tyrant. Moreover, violent death and arbitrary injustice had become commonplaces of life during the years of revolution and war; these terrors were assuaged by the happy endings typical of operas of this genre.

In the rescue opera, and in another rescue form, the Gothic novel of Mrs. Radcliffe and M. G. Lewis, which suddenly gained widespread popularity in the 1790s, there are powerful echoes of the dramas of the German *Sturm und Drang*, and especially of Schiller's works, which were then banned in Imperial Vienna. Through the rescue opera Beethoven could now deal with a theme which expressed the ideology that he shared with his adored Schiller and which at the same time touched on unresolved areas of his own psychological experience.

With Schikaneder's successful production of Cherubini's *Lodoïska* at the Theater-an-der-Wien in March 1802, the rescue opera reached and conquered Vienna—including Beethoven, who came to regard Cherubini as a composer equal to the Viennese masters and who quickly acquired, in Thayer's words, an "ambition to rival Cherubini in his own field." [18] It was not mere rivalry, however, that drew Beethoven to the rescue theme of *Léonore*. *Fidelio* is a seething compound of contradictory and ambivalent psychological themes and fantasies, lightly disguised by an ethical content and a *Singspiel* surface. It opens in a Mozartian Eden, a sunlit Arcadia in which a good father (Rocco) seeks to bring about the marriage of his daughter (Marcelline) to the young man she loves (Fidelio). But things are not what they seem. The Eden surface gives way to a darker substratum; the good father is a jailor; Fidelio is Leonore in disguise seeking her husband, Florestan, who lies imprisoned for an unspecified "crime" in a dungeon beneath the ground they walk upon. Thus light masks darkness. Marcelline's innocent love unconsciously conceals a forbidden attraction. The good Rocco, protesting, agrees to co-operate in the murder of Florestan by Pizarro as the price of the latter's approval of his daughter's marriage. And Leonore's conjugal fidelity leads her to two conjugal betrayals: of Marcelline, to whom she pledges her love, and of Florestan, whose wife now embraces another. Rocco and Leonore descend into the tomb to prepare Florestan's grave; in a sense, Leonore is cooperating in the murder of her husband. The rescue fantasy is only apparently an inversion of the Oedipus myth: the impulses behind myths of killing and saving are ultimately identical; but in the rescue fantasy the murder (and guilt) is averted by a *deus ex machina*, here the minister of state, Don Fernando. Florestan's place in the dungeon is now taken by the evil "father"—Pizarro—and the prisoners (sons) who planned the patricidal crime ascend into the light of freedom while Leonore resumes her sexual identity and receives the plaudits of the multitude for her heroism and fidelity.

Freud notes that the child conceives the wish to repay his parents for the gift of life; and often he "weaves a phantasy of saving his father's life on some dangerous occasion, by which he becomes quits with him." [19] With Beethoven, the fantasy of father rescue had been put to the test of reality during the later 1780s, and he had been forced to carry out this role for several years until, finally, his own needs for fulfillment gained ascendancy. As a matter of fact, in actual life Beethoven would often seem to be driven by a desire to rescue: he attempted to "save" both of his brothers from their wives and to "save" his nephew from imagined maternal dangers; he even, as Grillparzer observed,[20] interceded with the police on one occasion to save a drunken peasant, Flohberger, from the law. (Was he once again standing between his father and the night watch in Bonn?)

It is also worth noting Beethoven's attraction to *Fidelio*'s theme of sexual masquerade. He was drawn to this same subject in two other stage works—in *Leonore Prohaska*, WoO 96, where a maiden/heroine, disguised as a soldier, fights in a war of liberation; and in his Incidental Music to Goethe's *Egmont*, op. 84, where Klärchen wishes that she might dress herself in soldier's uniform and boldly march to join her beloved: "What a joy it would be to be changed into a man!" she sings. In such works, feelings of feminine identification could be freely expressed, while the nobility of these maidens' actions assuaged whatever anxiety might otherwise attach to such feelings. But Beethoven's emotional attachment to other figures in the opera may well be equally operative: Tyson argues the possibility of a powerful identification with Florestan, imprisoned in the soundless recesses of his cell as Beethoven was increasingly locked within the prison of his deafness.[21]

A psychoanalyst would not fail to note that the descent into the bowels of the prison, where Florestan lies in a dark cistern—"a ruined well"—carries resonances of birth and rebirth. Viewed on this level, Leonore/Fidelio has gone in search of her/his own mysterious origins; and the freeing of Florestan and his fellow prisoners becomes not only a liberation of the father/husband and brothers but a cleansing repetition of the birth process, a penetration of the ultimate creative mystery.

In this sense, *Fidelio* can be seen as an opera about resurrection as well as rescue. Florestan is not only imprisoned but entombed; Leonore and Rocco descend with their spades not to dig his grave but to exhume him from his sepulcher. A mythic pattern intrudes here: the dying vegetation god (the meaning of Florestan's name becomes clearer) lies awaiting the arrival of the bisexual goddess (Leonore/Fidelio) and the princely hero (Fernando) to restore him to life and to youth, to mark his passage from the dark ground into the sunlight. The winter god (Pizarro) is slain, replacing Florestan in the tomb, and mankind celebrates the arrival of the New Year with hymns to marriage.

A word about the overtures. *Leonore* no. 2 was written for the November 1805 premiere and revised as *Leonore* no. 3 for the revival in May 1806. In preparation for a Prague performance in 1807 which never materialized, Beethoven composed the shorter overture now known inaptly as *Leonore* no. 1, op. 138.[22] Where his only previous overture, *Prometheus,* had been composed wholly in the Viennese style, the *Leonore* overtures continue the amalgamation of Viennese and French influences which is characteristic of Beethoven's heroic style. (In a sense this synthesis is more successful in the overtures than in the opera itself, in which *Singspiel* and *Rettungsoper* characteristics are combined but not wholly fused.) Beethoven's problem with these overtures was that he summarized and anticipated in them the dramatic action—especially that of the last act—to such an extent that the listener is unprepared for the idyllic character of the first scenes. (Tovey says of *Leonore* no. 3 that it "annihilates the first act.") In 1814, Beethoven abandoned any further attempts at reworking these materials in favor of a festive curtain raiser, the *Fidelio* Overture.

Beethoven's preoccupation with *Fidelio* from late 1804 until the spring of 1806 had dammed up work on other projects. A month after the last performance of the second version of *Fidelio,* Beethoven turned to the composition of three string quartets, later known as the *Razumovsky* Quartets, op. 59. He completed them toward the end of 1806.

There is one sense in which the *Razumovsky* Quartets represent a continuation of the heroic impulse: an application of the principles of composition elaborated in the *Eroica* Symphony to another genre, an expansion of the quartet form beyond its eighteenth-century traditional boundaries to a point where one may legitimately speak of these quartets as "symphonic quartets." But there is another sense in which these works represent a withdrawal from the heroic impulse, with its insistence upon strength and virtue, its "public" style and affirmative outlook. If the heroic symphonies are in Bekker's phrase "speeches to the nation," then the quartets are interior monologues addressed to a private self whose emotional states comprise a variegated tapestry of probing moods and feelings. Sullivan glimpsed this when he wrote that in the middle-period orchestral works "the hero marches forth . . . performing his feats before the whole of an applauding world. What is he like in his loneliness? We find the answer in the Razumovsky quartets." [23] It was on a leaf of sketches for these works that Beethoven wrote a phrase which we have already cited in another context: "Let your deafness no longer be a secret—even in art." [24] Here, in these quartets, he will reveal his deepest feelings, his sense of loss, his pain and his strivings.

Although they were conceived of and published as a set, the *Razumovsky* Quartets resemble each other far less than do the six quartets of opus 18, or even the last five quartets. They constitute, Kerman writes, "a trio of sharply characterized, consciously differentiated individuals." [25] A unifying element is the use of Russian themes in the finale of no. 1 and in the Trio of the Scherzo of no. 2, along with the inclusion of a slow movement in Russian style in no. 3. Some analysts have regarded the quartets as a cycle, seeing the finale of no. 3 (a synthesis of fugue and sonata form) as the climactic counterpart of the opening Allegro of no. 1; and others have stressed the three works' common preoccupation with triumphal finales. Perhaps, however, we can find the unity of the *Razumovskys* in their very striving for diversity of mood and structure as well as in Beethoven's experimentation with many new (and even bizarre) effects and procedures. Among these are the startling use of *pizzicato* for expressive purposes in the slow movements of nos. 1 and 3; the brilliant string writing and voicing, which refashions the characteristic Classic style; the rich harmonic patterns and the extraordinary rhythmic drive; and the creation of "flowing and continuous melodies that are capable of being divided at a later stage into smaller, separable units" (Radcliffe),[26] which marks a break with the epigrammatic symphonic style and foreshadows Beethoven's (and then Brahms's) melodic practice in a number of his later works. If there are excesses and wayward moments, they are the excesses of sudden discovery and the waywardness of the explorer's vision upon reaching a prospect that stretches in all directions. Where Beethoven's creative laboratory had at first been the piano and then was the symphony orchestra, the focus of his experimental efforts was now transferred to the string quartet. In his enthusiasm for the potentialities of this genre, Beethoven wrote to Breitkopf & Härtel that "I am thinking of devoting myself almost entirely to this type of composition," [27] a wish that he actually carried out twenty years later. But in 1806 Beethoven had not gained the financial independence to permit him to disregard what he once disdainfully called "the economics of music." Furthermore, the fact is that the *Razumovsky* Quartets did not please; they were found difficult to understand. Thayer writes that "perhaps no work of Beethoven's met a more discouraging reception" from musicians and connoisseurs.[28]

At the very time that the quartets were being composed, Beethoven was also writing his Fourth Concerto for Piano and Orchestra, op. 58 (completed in the summer of 1806); the Fourth Symphony, op. 60 (completed at Lichnowsky's estate in Silesia in the fall); the Thirty-two Variations for Piano in C minor, WoO 80 (written in the fall); and the Violin Concerto, op. 61 (written shortly before its first performance by Franz Clement in December). If Beethoven's "grand manner" symphonic style had partly shaped the Piano Sonatas, opp. 53 and 57, and the *Razumovsky* Quartets, his latest orchestral works, with their temporary retreat from exalted rhetoric into a more lyrical, reflective, and serene style, appear to have taken on certain qualities of a magnified chamber music. What Bekker wrote of the Fourth Piano Concerto holds in some measure for the Violin Concerto and the Fourth Symphony as well: viz., that they are "characterized by quiet, reflective gravity, by a latent energy, capable from time to time of expressing intense vitality, but usually preserving the mood of tranquillity." [29] Although these works return in some measure to high-Classic models—Haydn in the Fourth Symphony, Mozart in the concertos—Beethoven had now arrived at a new Classic style of a more personal and individual cast.

As has often been observed, each of Beethoven's works from ca. 1802 onward has a strikingly individual character. Although his predecessors may not have stamped sets of their works from a single die, they often, to borrow an image from Rolland, tended to bake many cakes from the same batch of dough. With Beethoven, there is an apparent refusal (or at least an inability) to return to a problem that he considered to be successfully solved. Rather, there is a sense of striving for diverse solutions to each problem. Thus, for example, the Fourth Piano Concerto opens with a sonorous statement of the theme in the solo instrument followed by the *tutti*, whereas in the Violin Concerto the entry of the soloist is deferred for as long as possible, the violin's statement of the *cantabile* first theme is withheld even longer, and it is not permitted to play the full second theme—a lyric theme designed for G-string performance—until the coda. In the one, the *tutti* rises from the solo; in the other the solo emerges from the orchestral fabric and establishes its presence only after an extended process of differentiation. The slow movements are both conceived as dialogues, but that in the piano concerto is a recitative dialogue of disputants, whereas in the violin concerto we have a lyrical discussion between agreeable conversationalists. The ebullient rondo-finales are equally differentiated: Beethoven finds a pastoral solution in the violin concerto, but gives a more urgent, "military" character to the piano concerto, with its snare-drum rhythms and "bayonet motif" opening theme.

The set of C-minor Piano Variations on an original theme, WoO 80, was seriously underrated by Beethoven, who assigned it no opus number and scoffed at himself ("Oh Beethoven, what an ass you were!" [30]) for having composed it. It probably was written in response to the continuing demand for such works by his publishers: like his earlier variations, it was almost immediately printed, appearing in March 1807. But this dynamic and economical work, written in Beethoven's heroic/*pathétique* key, has significant structural features, including his first use of passacaglia form in a set of variations and the grouping of the variations into larger sections, foreshadowing the Diabelli Variations. Rounding out the year is one *Lied*, "When the Beloved Wishes to Part; or, Feelings about Lydia's Unfaithfulness," WoO 132, which Harry Goldschmidt connects, reasonably enough, with Josephine Deym's withdrawal from Beethoven and her then current affair with Count Wolkenstein.

Through some obscure dialectic of Beethoven's creative process, it was characteristic of his heroic impulse that it went into a shorter or longer state of quiescence following each of its major manifestations. It emerged with renewed energy in 1807, with the Overture to Heinrich von Collin's *Coriolan*, op. 62, the *Leonore* Overture no. 1, the Mass in C, op. 86, and the Fifth Symphony, op. 67.

Beethoven needed a new overture to open concert programs, to augment his well-worn *Prometheus*. And he evidently wished to demonstrate anew his theatrical abilities to the princely directors of the Royal Imperial Theater, to whom he had made application for a permanent position. The dramatic *Coriolan* Overture—influenced by but transcending Cherubini's overture style—was the result. It was performed in March 1807 at the Lobkowitz palace, along with the premiere performances of the Fourth Symphony and the Fourth Piano Concerto. The closing, disintegrating passage—reminiscent of the end of the *Eroica* Funeral March—symbolizes the death of the hero. Unlike Plutarch's or Shakespeare's hero, Collin's Coriolan chooses death—an action that had more than ordinary resonance to Beethoven in view of his documented suicidal impulses. Like the Sonata, op. 57, *Coriolan* demonstrates that Beethoven did not always insist on joyful conclusions, but was able to locate transcendence in the acceptance of death itself.

Beethoven was less successful with the affirmative stance of his first religious work in a traditional liturgical style, the Mass in C, op. 86. The Mass was begun early in the year and completed at Baden and Heiligenstadt during the summer so that it could be performed at the name day celebration of Princess Maria von Liechtenstein Esterházy on September 13, at Eisenstadt, under Beethoven's direction. As we have seen, it was poorly received by its intended patron; nor did it find a better reception when sections of it were performed at Beethoven's December 22, 1808, *Akademie*. It was published, after much urging by the composer and much hesitation by Breitkopf & Härtel, only in October 1812. In this work, Beethoven relies heavily on his symphonic instincts and on the precepts of Haydn to carry him through an unfamiliar form.

Beethoven now took up the C-minor Symphony, for which he had jotted down some fragmentary ideas as early as 1804 and which was fully sketched in the winter of 1806–07 or somewhat later. It was written out in the latter half of 1807 and during the first months of 1808 and was completed by the spring of that year, receiving its first performance at Beethoven's *Akademie* on December 22. The Fifth Symphony, because of its concentrated energy, its heroic stance, and, especially, the triumphal—even military—character of all of its movements save the scherzo, may have carried overtones of patriotic sentiment to Beethoven's contemporaries. It was completed precisely during the period which saw the upsurge of German patriotism—stimulated by the Treaty of Tilsit of July 7–9, 1807, which signaled the collapse of Prussia and the cession of all lands between the Rhine and the Elbe to France. The historian Roy Pascal noted that "the philosopher Fichte, the theologian Schleiermacher, poets and writers of all types, Kleist, Arndt, Görres, called on the Germans not to despair, to recall their great past, to hate the oppressor, to prepare for liberation." [31] Beethoven and many of his friends and associates in Vienna echoed and contributed to this new patriotism. Both Prince Lobkowitz and Count Razumovsky, to whom the symphony was jointly dedicated, were ardent and active enemies of France. Beethoven's own patriotic and anti-French sentiments reached their height at this time. On April 26, 1807, he wrote to Camille Pleyel: "My dear Camillus— If I am not mistaken, that was the name of the Roman who drove the wicked Gauls out of Rome. At that rate I too would like to bear that name, provided I could drive them away from where they have no right to be—" [32] Not long thereafter, Beethoven began to sketch two patriotic songs, "Oesterreich über Alles" and "Jubelgesang auf die Schlacht," the former to a text by Collin. [33] (He did not complete either song.)

Beethoven himself, however, left no programmatic references that would link his Fifth Symphony to contemporary events. Indeed, his only such reported comment indicates that he may have connected the work with antique tragedy. Schindler claimed that Beethoven, in his presence, explained the opening bars of the first movement with the words: "Thus Fate knocks at the door!" [34] Schenker doubted the story; he pointed to the same motif in the G-major Piano Concerto and asked: "Was this another door on which Fate knocked or was someone else knocking at the same door?" [35] Of course this is wide of the mark, for though the four-note motif became one of Beethoven's "musical fingerprints" for a decade or more, it is never used twice for the same purpose and never in contexts remotely similar to those employed in the Fifth Symphony.

After some initial resistance to its unheralded rhythmic concentration, economy of thematic material, startling innovations—the little oboe cadenza in the first movement, the addition of piccolo and double bassoon to the winds, the "spectral" effects of the double basses in the scherzo and trio, the trombones in the finale, the return of the scherzo in the finale—the Fifth Symphony came to be regarded as the quintessential Beethoven symphony, revealing new layers of meaning to each successive generation. Resistance to the symphony has stemmed from its monumental exterior (Goethe said, "It is merely astonishing and grandiose" [36]) and from the C-major "yea-saying" of the finale. Spohr found the last movement to be "unmeaning babel," and Berlioz acutely noted that the effect of the transition from the scherzo to the Allegro is so stunning that it would be impossible to surpass it in what follows. "To *sustain* such a height of effect is, in fact, already a prodigious effort." [37] E. T. A. Hoffmann claimed the Symphony for Romanticism in 1810, but twentieth-century criticism has tended to see the Fifth as "the consummate example of symphonic logic," [38] as the ultimate expression of Classic rationality refusing to yield to the violent tremors of impending Romanticism. Audiences have learned to identify the work with public virtues (the opening motif was a symbol of resistance to fascism during World War II), perhaps as a means of allaying the untranslatable and inexpressible terrors which this symphony arouses in every listener, despite Beethoven's C-major cathartic effects. Hoffmann and Goethe already sensed these terrors.

The Sixth Symphony (*Pastoral*) followed rapidly, for Beethoven had been working almost simultaneously on these widely disparate symphonies. Despite the sketching of one of its themes (the 2/4 theme for the trio of the third movement) in 1803, and a few jottings in 1807, [39] it was composed almost wholly in 1808, and was completed by late summer of that year. Like the Fifth Symphony, it was jointly dedicated to Lobkowitz and Razumovsky.

With the *Pastoral* Symphony, the working out of Beethoven's post-

Heiligenstadt projects seemed to be coming to a close. It was especially fitting that this cycle terminate in idyllic repose, in an Arcadian conclusion to the heroic quest of the preceding half-decade. Beethoven's struggles with Fate—which is to say, with the embodiment of the paternal principle—were not yet at an end, but were temporarily set aside while Beethoven rejoiced in a richly deserved return to Nature and to childhood, which are the twin realms of the bountiful mother. The return to Nature is on the surface of this "characteristic" or genre symphony, which is entitled "Pastoral Symphony, or Recollections of Country Life" on the autograph score, and which carries the following headings to its movements: "Pleasant, cheerful feelings aroused on approaching the countryside"; "Scene by the brook"; "Jolly gathering of villagers"; "Thunderstorm"; and "Shepherd's song. Grateful thanks to the Almighty after the storm." A return to Bonn is suggested by the fact that Beethoven adapted these movement titles from a notice of a symphony, *Le Portrait musical de la nature,* by an eighteenth-century Swabian composer, Justin Heinrich Knecht, which was advertised in about 1784 on the same page of Bossler's music journal that advertised Beethoven's three *Electoral* Sonatas, WoO 47.[40]

This innocent work is exceptional in Beethoven's output, although pastoral qualities turn up in several of his piano sonatas, in his *Prometheus,* in his Variations on a Swiss Air, WoO 64, in the Violin Sonata, op. 96, in the Eighth Symphony, and in several of his last works, including the second finale to the Quartet in B-flat, op. 130. As many have observed, in composing the *Pastoral* Symphony Beethoven was not anticipating Romantic program music but rather was continuing in the Baroque pastoral tradition, as manifested in many works by Bach, Handel, Vivaldi, and more particularly in Haydn's two oratorios.[41] Unable to compete with Haydn in the oratorio of which Haydn was the master, Beethoven had transmuted his pastoral style into a symphonic essence. Riezler writes that "it is remarkable how consistently Beethoven avoids all possibility of 'conflict' in the Symphony"; [42] but conflict is not really absent. In the fourth movement, "Fate" intrudes as the thunderous voice of the God of wrath, but withdraws without a serious struggle, leaving his children their moment of innocent rejoicing, for which he earns Beethoven's heartfelt gratitude. He wrote, on a leaf of sketches for the last movement: *"Herr, wir danken dir."*[43]

With the completion of the *Pastoral* Symphony, Beethoven turned mainly to chamber music and to the sonata for the remainder of 1808 and 1809. There are but two major exceptions, the first of which was the "Choral Fantasia," op. 80, of late 1808. Scored for solo piano, orchestra, and chorus, it consists of a fantasy for piano (improvised by Beethoven at

the first performance) followed by a set of free variations on a theme—
the "Gegenliebe," WoO 118—that Beethoven had composed in 1794 or
1795 but never published; it significantly forecasts the melodic shape
and harmony of the first phrase of the "Ode to Joy" theme. The alternation
of instrumental and choral variations also confirms the impression that
Beethoven was groping here toward issues that would occupy him in
his last symphony. Stylistically, however, there is nothing advanced or
even contemporary in opus 80. The British critic, E. J. Dent, argues
persuasively that the text expressed "the mystical spirit of eighteenth-
century Freemasonry, the new religion of liberty, equality and frater-
nity." [44] (Karl Holz maintained that Beethoven had once been a Freemason; it is certain that he was well disposed toward Freemasonry,
especially in his early years, when so many of his closest friends and
teachers belonged to the Illuminati or the Masonic Order.[45]) On a simpler
level, the "Choral Fantasia" is a latter-day ode to Saint Cecelia, in praise
of music:

> When music's enchantment reigns
> And the poet's words take flight
> Then marvellous forms arise
> And night and storm turn to light.

The Fifth Piano Concerto, op. 73 (later inaptly dubbed *Emperor*)
belongs to the invasion year, 1809, although it may have been begun in
the closing days of the previous year. Along with a March in F for Military Band, WoO 18, it may well embody Beethoven's response to the
tide of Napoleonic conquest. (Of course, its grandeur and its unparalleled solutions of strictly musical problems far transcend such considera-
tions.) Einstein called this concerto, with its warlike rhythms, victory
motifs, thrusting melodies, and affirmative character, the "apotheosis of
the military concept" in Beethoven's music.[46] According to Einstein, the
"military style," which had roots in the Viennese tradition as well as in
contemporary French music, was readily understood by Beethoven's
audiences: "They expected a first movement in four–four time of a 'military' character; and they reacted with unmixed pleasure when Beethoven
not only fulfilled but surpassed their expectations." [47] At its first confirmed public performance—in Leipzig in 1810—the majestic concerto
was greeted with ovations. It was published in February 1811 with a
dedication to Archduke Rudolph.

The leading tendency of Beethoven's work from late 1808 through
1809, however, was represented by the Piano Trios, op. 70; the String
Quartet, op. 74; the three Piano Sonatas, opp. 78, 79, and 81a; and the
Cello Sonata, op. 69, which last had been written a bit earlier and was

completed by mid-1808. For the first time in almost a decade, Beethoven had no major symphonic projects in progress or in the sketching stage. And though he considered numerous librettos for an opera during this period, he rejected all, it being doubtful that he seriously wanted to write another opera after the travail of *Fidelio.* Beethoven's productivity slackened in 1810 and 1811, the only significant works completed being the String Quartet, op. 95; the Trio, op. 97 (*Archduke*); and the Incidental Music to Goethe's *Egmont,* op. 84. The latter was Beethoven's only serious nonchamber music composition of these years. It was not until the later months of 1811, when he began to sketch two new symphonies, that his turn toward chamber music was reversed for a time.

Beethoven was no longer at pains to apply symphonic ideas to the genres of chamber music, nor was he seeking to create heaven-storming compositions. In a deepening of the trend which began in 1806 with the Fourth Symphony, the Fourth Piano Concerto, and the Violin Concerto, he now seemed to imbue many of his works with a sense of inner repose that no longer required turbulent responses to grand challenges. A new, lyrical strain enters his music, along with a pre-Romantic freedom of harmonic motion and of structural design which appears to take up where the fantasy sonatas had left off in 1802.

On the dedication copy of the broad and melodious Cello Sonata, op. 69, Beethoven wrote "Inter lacrymas et luctus" ["amid tears and sorrow"], which may be a reference to his emotional state, for it is inappropriate as a description of a work of such quiet solemnity and moderation of emotional expression. Lockwood observes that it is one of the central works in the cello and piano literature, and he writes that "the solutions found in op. 69 for the problems of range, relative sonority, and matching of importance of the two instruments . . . emerge as an achievement equal to that inherent in the originality and quality of its purely musical ideas. . . ."[48]

The Cello Sonata may have been written for Ignaz Gleichenstein; Beethoven dedicated it to him in April 1809, probably out of gratitude for his friend's role in negotiating the princes' annuity. Similarly, Beethoven dedicated the two Trios for Piano, Violin, and Cello, op. 70, to Countess Erdödy, who was equally helpful in the negotiations; it was at her home that they were first performed—during the Christmas season of 1808, with Beethoven at the piano. The Trios were Beethoven's first serious works in this form since his opus 1 of 1795. The Trio no. 1, in D major (*Ghost*), has two unproblematic and relaxed movements flanking a powerful pre-Romantic Largo, whose atmospheric tremolo effects and sudden dynamic contrasts gave rise to the work's nickname. The second trio, in E-flat, one of the masterpieces of the middle period, is so delicately balanced between the traditional Viennese style and Beethoven's own most mature style that a performance given from either of these vantage points can cast a radically different light upon the work. In an illuminating passage, Tovey observed that in works such as this trio Beethoven had at last achieved an "integration of Mozart's and Haydn's resources, with results that transcend all possibility of resemblance to the style of their origins. . . ." [49] The closing Allegro exemplifies an important tendency—Beethoven's simplification of the exposition to a point that not only its harmonic but its thematic meaning is not really elaborated until the recapitulation. (In a different context, the Overtura to the *Grosse Fuge*, op. 133, similarly will abruptly disclose several themes in rapid succession and will postpone the establishing of interconnections between these themes until later in the movement.)

Beethoven's last trio, and by general agreement his masterpiece in this form, was the Trio, op. 97, called *Archduke* because of its dedication. It is an expansive work both in size (four movements totaling 1,200 measures) and in sound. Whereas in his heroic symphonies Beethoven had generated the architecture of his compositions from the release (and control) of energy stored within condensed, explosive germinal motifs and rhythms, he generated the architectural monumentality of the *Archduke* Trio from the development of broad, moderately paced, and flowing melodies. This practice results in a sense of calm, spaciousness, and measured nobility of rhetoric which we have already encountered in the Cello Sonata, op. 69, the Violin Concerto, and the Fourth and Fifth Piano Concertos. Audacious touches in the Scherzo and moments of brusque wit in the finale contrast effectively with the spaciously lyrical and sublime quality of the opening Allegro moderato. The *Archduke* represents Beethoven's summation of the impulses toward a new type of Classicism which had characterized his chamber music with piano between mid–1808 and 1811.

In late 1809, after an absence of four years, Beethoven returned to the piano sonata and wrote three sonatas in a short space of time. In none of them is there the slightest indication that their immediate predecessors in this genre had been such works as the *Waldstein* and *Appassionata* sonatas: rather, there is in them an extension of tendencies in pre-*Eroica* sonatas such as opus 28 and opus 31 no. 1, as well as glimpses of Beethoven's last-period style. The two-movement Sonata in F-sharp, op. 78, dedicated to Therese Brunsvik, was a special favorite of Beethoven's, perhaps because of its serenity, economy of form, and songful expressiveness. The "Sonate facile ou sonatine," op. 79, which bore no dedication upon its publication in November 1810, may have originated as a gift to Therese Malfatti. It has pastoral elements, one authority hearing in it reminiscences of Beethoven's bucolic *Ritterballett* of 1790–91. The beautiful fantasy sonata, op. 81a, was composed for Archduke

Rudolph following his departure from Vienna during the French bombardment of 1809, and its expressive movement titles—"Farewell," "Absence," "The Return"—tell much about the depth of Beethoven's feeling for his young student. The sonata's second movement, Andante espressivo, with its touching chromaticisms, serves as an eloquent introduction to the finale, Vivacissimamente. On the sketches, Beethoven wrote: "The Farewell—on May 4th—dedicated to, and written from the heart for, H[is] I[mperial] H[ighness]." [50] A decade later, on the autograph score of the *Missa Solemnis,* Beethoven wrote a similar dedicatory message to Rudolph, for whom the Mass was composed: "From the heart—may it go to the heart!" [51]

On June 2, 1805, Beethoven had written, despairingly: "God knows why my piano music still makes the poorest impression on me. . . ." [52] Now, however—with these sonatas, the Cello Sonata, and the Trios, op. 70 (as well as the "Choral Fantasia" and the two piano concertos)— Beethoven was once again using the piano as his main creative vehicle. Perhaps this is why a feeling of "homecoming" and repose pervades so many of these works. But the questing side of Beethoven's nature—the sense of discontinuity and disequilibrium, of striving and restlessness— would also have to find a medium of expression. It did so in the second of the string quartets that he composed in 1809–10. The first, the E-flat Quartet, op. 74, called *Harp* because of the striking *pizzicato* arpeggios in the opening Allegro, is a lyrical, contemplative, and expressive work which—despite its unusual and climactic Scherzo—retreats from the innovative thrust of the *Razumovsky* Quartets and returns to the central vocabulary of the Viennese high-Classic style. Here, as in most of the other chamber and sonata works of this period, one senses that Beethoven was attempting to reestablish contact with styles from which he had largely held aloof after 1802. Kerman writes that whereas opus 74 is "an open, unproblematic, lucid work of consolidation," the Quartet in F minor, op. 95, written in the summer of 1810 and withheld from publication for six years, is "an involved, impassioned, highly idiosyncratic piece, problematic in every one of its movements, advanced in a hundred ways." [53] Titled "Quartetto serioso"—the only time Beethoven used this odd designation—opus 95 is an experimental work which compresses many complex ideas into a compass smaller than that of opus 74 or any of the Quartets, op. 59. Beethoven may have been groping here toward his last-period style; and he was presumably dissatisfied with his efforts, for he turned away from the genre for more than a dozen years. Perhaps what he overlooked in opus 95 was the possibility of combining its probing rhetoric and elliptical condensation with the lyricism and open communicativeness of opus 74. Such a fusion would be central to the style of the last quartets. Although opus 74 was dedicated to Prince Lobkowitz, the dedication of opus 95 to Zmeskall is another indication that Beethoven was now frequently using dedications as expressions of affection for and gratitude to his friends rather than to discharge patronage obligations.

Beethoven wrote incidental music to three stage works in 1810 and 1811—to Goethe's *Egmont,* op. 84 (composed between October 1809 and June 1810), to Kotzebue's *The Ruins of Athens,* op. 113, and to the same author's *King Stephen,* op. 117, both of which (in all, 19 separate pieces) were written in the short space of three weeks at Teplitz in late summer 1811. Opus 113 and opus 117 were composed for the opening of an imperial theater in Pesth, a patriotic occasion that called for flattery and adulation. In *The Ruins of Athens,* Minerva awakens from a two-thousand-year sleep to find Athens occupied, the Parthenon in ruins, and culture and reason banished from the Mediterranean, but, happily, still alive in Pesth under the enlightened rule of Emperor Franz. Similarly, *King Stephen,* which is subtitled "Hungary's First Benefactor," is a transparent homage to the Austro–Hungarian Kaiser. It contains several women's choruses patently derived from Haydn's *Seasons.* These works have not remained in the repertoire, although the potpourri overtures (which deeply upset the Philharmonic Society of London when it received them in 1816) are occasionally performed. The "Chorus of the Dervishes" and the "Marcia alla Turca" of opus 113 are brilliantly orchestrated and effective popular music in the exotic, "Turkish" style.

Beethoven did not have his heart in these compositions, which clearly were done as hackwork to please a royal patron. It was otherwise with the music for *Egmont,* which tells of a Flemish aristocrat arrested and condemned by the Spaniards. Klärchen, a burgher's daughter, failing in her effort to rescue Egmont, poisons herself, and Egmont goes proudly to his death, predicting the insurrection that will free his country from Spanish tyranny. The subject had great meaning for Beethoven as an expression of his belief in the *bon prince* and in the ideals of national liberation and human freedom, and, perhaps, because it touched on his own Flemish ancestry. On the surface, the story is the obverse of *Fidelio,* although retaining its linkage of love and freedom, of sacrifice and heroism. Here, however, victory is achieved not through a *deus ex machina,* but through the sacrifice of the protagonists' lives and the perpetuation of their ideals in the communal entity with which they are identified. The theme of national liberation is neatly congruent with the occupation of Vienna in 1809 by the French. Evidently the directors of the Court Theater, who commissioned the work, had contemporary events in mind, for the other possible assignment was also a story of liberation from foreign occupation—Schiller's *Wilhelm Tell.* This theme of liberation inspired Beethoven to produce his most dramatic theater music, including several songs with orchestra which did not fail to leave their mark on the young Mahler. The concentrated overture and closing *Siegessymphonie* (Symphony of Victory) are high points of the heroic style.

That the meanings of music are not translatable into language is a philosopher's truism. Kierkegaard wrote that music "always expresses the immediate in its immediacy" and that it was therefore "impossible to express the musical in language." [54] And Nietzsche, in *The Birth of Tragedy*, noted that "language, the organ and symbol of appearance, can never succeed in bringing the innermost core of music to the surface. Whenever it engages in the imitation of music, language remains in purely superficial contact with it." [55] Such warnings, however, have never stopped commentators (including, I fear, this one) from putting forth unprovable speculations as to the "meaning" of one or another of Beethoven's masterpieces. Nowhere has this tendency been more manifest than in nineteenth-century interpretations of Beethoven's Seventh Symphony. Berlioz heard a "Ronde des Paysans" in the first movement; Wagner called the symphony the "Apotheosis of the Dance"; Lenz saw it as a second *Pastoral* Symphony, complete with village wedding and peasant dances; Nohl visualized a Knight's Festival and Oulibicheff the masquerade or diversion of a multitude drunk with joy and wine. For A. B. Marx it was the wedding or festival celebration of a warrior people.[56] More recently, Bekker called it a "bacchic orgy," and Ernest Newman described it as "the upsurge of a powerful dionysiac impulse, a divine intoxication of the spirit." [57]

Quaint as these interpretations now seem, it may be worthwhile to seek some underlying common denominator in the opinions of so eminent a group of critics. Clearly, a work that so powerfully symbolizes the act of transcendence, with its attendant joyous and liberating feelings, can be represented in language by an infinity of specific transcendent images—which may tell us as much about the free associations of their authors as about Beethoven and his music. But the apparently diverse free-associational imagery of these critics—images of masses of people, of powerful rhythmic energy discharged in action or in dance, of celebrations, weddings, and revelry—comprises, at bottom, variations upon a single image: that of the carnival or festival, which, from time immemorial, has temporarily lifted the burden of perpetual subjugation to the prevailing social and natural order by periodically suspending all customary privileges, norms, and imperatives. Examples of such festivals can be found in the Greek Cronia, the Roman Kalends and Saturnalia, the French "Feast of Fools," the English "Lords of Misrule," the medieval folk carnivals and feasts, and those primitive rituals and ceremonies which annually turned society inside out.[58] Freud offered a psychological explanation of these events: "In all renunciations and limitations imposed upon the ego, a periodical infringement of the prohibition is the rule; this indeed is shown by the institution of festivals, which in origin are nothing less nor more than excesses provided by law and which owe their cheerful character to the release which they bring." [59] Of course, much more is involved here than the "cheerful." In the festival there is a joyous lifting of all restraints; a licensed eruption of the profane and the scatological; and an outpouring of mockery, ridicule, and satire expressing a comic vision of life untinged by tragic modalities.

It was apparently a festal quality which the nineteenth-century critics sensed in the Seventh Symphony and which is present as well in the Eighth, for the latter is an offshoot from the same creative impulse. In Ernest Newman's words, it "takes the overspill of the mighty Seventh," voicing, like its companion, "a mood of joyous acceptance of life and the world." [60] Wagner, too, saw the psychological similarity—and the festal character—of the two symphonies: "Their effect upon the listener is precisely that of emancipation from all guilt, just as the aftereffect is the feeling of Paradise forfeited, with which we return to the phenomenal world." [61]

Both symphonies omit the traditional slow movement—i.e., the movement of sorrow and contemplation, of mourning and tragedy—present in all other Beethoven symphonies. Indeed, the Eighth, with its Minuet and its Allegretto scherzando, goes further in this respect than the Seventh, for the Seventh has a long slow introduction to the first movement and a dreamlike Allegretto which at least appears slow by contrast with its neighboring Vivace and Presto movements. Riezler touched on the essence of their similarity when he wrote that their professions of faith were "not called upon to fight and conquer a hostile power." [62] They exist in a festive Paradise, outside of time and history, untouched by mortality. They transport us into a sphere of laughter, play, and the exuberant release of bound energy. Here, as Bakhtin writes of the medieval festival, "for a short time life came out of its usual, legalized and consecrated furrows and entered the sphere of utopian freedom." [63]

The Seventh and Eighth Symphonies were sketched successively, starting in the closing months of 1811, and were completed the following year—the Seventh by April and the Eighth by October. The main work on the Eighth was done during Beethoven's Bohemian sojourn in the aftermath of the Immortal Beloved letter. To those Viennese who heard the first performances of the Seventh on the same programs as *Wellington's Victory* in 1813 (December 8) and 1814 (January 2 and February 27), it was patently connected with the victory over Napoleon and the joyous inauguration of a long-awaited peace. The Symphony, and especially its Allegretto, became enormously popular and appeared in numerous transcriptions, including arrangements for winds, septet, string quintet, piano quartet, piano trio, piano four-hands, piano, and two pianos, the last of which was dedicated to the empress of Russia. The Symphony was published in orchestral parts and in score by Steiner in November 1816, with a dedication to one of Beethoven's most devoted patrons, the banker Count Moritz Fries, who, according to Karl Holz, paid Beethoven "a regular subsidy" for some years until his bankruptcy in 1825.[64] The Eighth Symphony was first performed at Beethoven's *Akademie* of February 27, 1814, and was published by Steiner in 1817. Not very surprisingly, it was overshadowed by both the Seventh Symphony and by *Wellington's Victory*. The critic of the *Allgemeine musikalische Zeitung* wrote that "the applause which it received was not accompanied by that enthusiasm which distinguishes a work which gives universal delight; in short—as the Italians say—it did not create a furor." [65] According to Czerny, Beethoven was angered at this reception, because he considered the Eighth "much better" than the Seventh.[66]

The Violin Sonata, op. 96, the tenth and last of Beethoven's sonatas for piano and violin, was sketched and composed in 1812, following the Seventh and Eighth Symphonies, to which it contrasts as a delicate pen-and-ink drawing to a set of major frescos. Brandenburg argues that the Sonata was probably copied out in about May 1815—and may have been changed quite a bit before publication.[67] Where the piano and violin duo had been a vehicle for the inauguration of Beethoven's "new path"· in the stormy *Kreutzer* Sonata of a decade earlier, the G-major Sonata abandons the "stile brillante molto concertante" of opus 47 in favor of a heartfelt and exquisite communicativeness, thus providing a quietly imaginative coda to the middle period. As one annotator wrote: "Instead of urgent dramatic expostulation, here the mood is one of gentle lyricism, with but glimpses of the profound depths of experience and conquest of pain that had made possible the achievement of this serenity." [68]

IV
THE FINAL PHASE

Beethoven. Engraving by Blasius
Höfel after a drawing by Louis
Letronne (1814).

17
The Dissolution of the Heroic Style

W hen Beethoven returned to Teplitz, in mid-September 1812, the sustained tension of the previous weeks had passed, and a feeling of despondency came over him. Perhaps as a result of his malaise, he apparently spent much of the remainder of his vacation in bed. On September 17 he wrote to Breitkopf & Härtel: "I am writing to you from my bed," adding, in an expression of self-questioning, "I must tell you frankly that people in Austria no longer trust me completely; and no doubt they are right, too." [1] Most of his eight notes [2] to Amalie Sebald, whom he found in Teplitz upon his return, are apologies for his inability to visit her and contain mild complaints about his physical condition, as though he was hoping to evoke a sympathetic response: "Since yesterday I have not been feeling very well, and this morning my indisposition became more serious"; or, "I really feel a little better, dear A[malie]. If you think it proper to visit me alone, you could indeed give me great pleasure." She visited him once or twice, bringing him consolation and chicken soup—for which he insisted on having a bill. He left his bed to see her on at least one occasion, but, he wrote, "After I left you yesterday my condition again

217

deteriorated." It is possible that Amalie felt something more for Beethoven than the platonic, teasing tone of his letters indicates. In the final letter, Beethoven wrote: "What on earth are you dreaming of when you say that you cannot be anything to me? When we meet again, Dear A, we must discuss this point. It was my constant wish that my presence would fill you with calm and peace. . . ." Essentially, however, it was Amalie's undemanding tenderness toward the stricken composer which endeared her to him, and it was Beethoven who drew comfort and respite from her presence as a welcome relief from the frenzy and pain of the Immortal Beloved relationship. The correspondence with Amalie ended on this note, never to be resumed.

Beethoven did not go directly from Teplitz to Vienna.[3] Instead he traveled to Linz, where his brother Nikolaus Johann was tending his apothecary and where he had been living with Therese Obermayer, who was, as Thayer says, "his housekeeper and—something more." [4] Beethoven insisted that his brother break off this affair; his brother refused, whereupon Beethoven, enraged, visited the bishop and the civil authorities, finally obtaining a police order compelling Therese to leave Linz should the illicit relationship continue. Nikolaus Johann's response was to marry Therese on November 8.

Some of the psychological determinants of Beethoven's action are fairly evident. If the eldest brother was unable to have his own woman, why should this be permitted to the youngest? Beethoven had probably known of Nikolaus Johann's liaison with Therese for some time, and it is probably significant that only in the wake of the Immortal Beloved events was he suddenly motivated to go to Linz, acting under a compulsion so strong that it led to physical violence against his brother. But the matter may be even more complex. Perhaps Beethoven needed to share in the family life of his brother, Therese, and her daughter from an earlier liaison; possibly he needed the comfort which closeness to a family member might bring following the harrowing events of the preceding months. Nor is it precluded that Beethoven unwittingly brought about the marriage as a substitute for another union—one which had not taken place.

According to Thayer, Beethoven left Linz after the marriage and "immediately hastened away to Vienna." [5] However, Beethoven's whereabouts between early November and the end of the year have not yet been firmly established. No correspondence survives for the period from late September at Teplitz until shortly before December 29, 1812, in Vienna. Ludwig Spohr could not find Beethoven at his lodgings during December.

What of Beethoven's productivity during this period? The Seventh Symphony was completed in April 1812; it was followed by the one-movement Trio in B-flat major, WoO 39, composed for Maximiliane Brentano. The Eighth Symphony was written out during the summer months and essentially completed by late August, for the *Allgemeine musikalische Zeitung* of September 2 announced that Beethoven had "composed two new symphonies." [6] The autograph, however, reads "Linz in the month of October." In Linz, Beethoven is also known to have composed Three Equale for Four Trombones, WoO 30, by November 2. Upon his return to Vienna, Beethoven took up and completed his Sonata for Violin and Piano in G, op. 96, which was first performed, by Pierre Rode and Archduke Rudolph, on December 29. As we shall see in a moment, Beethoven's creativity thereafter came to a full stop.

Evidence of emotional stress appears in Beethoven's letters of this time to Archduke Rudolph. In December 1812 he wrote: "Since Sunday I have been ailing, although mentally, it is true, more than physically." [7] And in January: "As for my health, it is pretty much the same, the more so as moral causes are affecting it and these apparently are not very speedily removed." [8] And on May 27, 1813: "A number of unfortunate incidents occurring one after the other have really driven me into a state bordering on mental confusion." [9] The severe illness of his brother Caspar Carl during the late winter caused Beethoven great concern: Caspar Carl appeared to be in the last stages of consumption (the disease from which their mother had died). His symptoms soon remitted, but not before Beethoven had persuaded him to issue a legal declaration that after his death he desired his brother Ludwig to undertake the guardianship of his son Karl, a declaration which was to have fateful consequences a few years later.

It was at approximately this time that Beethoven may have made an attempt to take his own life. Suicidal thoughts were not uncommon to Beethoven; he expressed them in the Heiligenstadt Testament ("I was on the point of putting an end to my life. . . ."), in letters to Nikolaus Johann, to his nephew Karl, to Marie Erdödy, to Zmeskall, and to Wegeler, and, obliquely, in his letter of early November 1815 to Antonie Brentano. Most often, he used the threat of suicide as a means of compelling obedience from members of his family or concern from his friends. It was quite another matter, however, to write of suicide in his private ruminations, in his *Tagebuch*.[10] As for the reported suicide attempt, Schindler related that it took place in the aftermath of the Immortal Beloved affair:

In his despair he sought comfort with his approved and particularly respected friend Countess Marie Erdödy—at her country seat in Jedlersee. . . . Thence, however, he disappeared and the Countess thought he had returned to Vienna, when, three days later, her music master, Brauchle, discovered him in a distant part of the palace gardens. This incident was long kept a close secret, and only after several years did those familiar with it confide it to the more intimate friends of Beethoven, long after the love affair had been forgotten. It was associated with a suspicion that it had been the purpose of the unhappy man to starve himself to death.[11]

Thayer wished to dispose of the story on the grounds that it could not have taken place either in 1803 or in relation to Giulietta Guicciardi, as Schindler had thought. This in no way refutes the report itself, however, or its connection with the Immortal Beloved. Schindler's account—which he claims was current among Beethoven's friends during his last decade— is sufficiently detailed to warrant serious consideration. Indeed, one of Beethoven's close friends, the tenor Joseph August Röckel, when interviewed by Nohl in 1867, confirmed the suicide attempt.[12] Unfortunately Nohl could not obtain the date, except that it was "several years" after 1806. I speculate that it took place during the spring or summer of 1813, when Beethoven's feelings of impotence and despair had brought him to (or beyond) the edge of an emotional breakdown.

It was also about this time that the first in a series of lightly disguised references to prostitutes surfaced in Beethoven's correspondence with Zmeskall. Their code word for prostitutes was "fortresses." On February 28, 1813, Beethoven wrote: "Be zealous in defending the fortresses of the empire, which, as you know, lost their virginity a long time ago and have already received several assaults." [13] Similarly: "Enjoy life, but not voluptuously—Proprietor, Governor, Pasha of various rotten fortresses! ! ! ! !"; "I need not warn you any more to take care not to be wounded near certain fortresses"; "Keep away from rotten fortresses, for an attack from them is more deadly than one from well-preserved ones." [14] Evidently Zmeskall had frequent intercourse with prostitutes, and it appears likely that he was now providing them to Beethoven as well. This seems to be the meaning of several ambiguous lines in other letters to Zmeskall: "I thank you most heartily, my dear Z, for the information you have given me concerning the fortresses, for I thought you had the idea that I did not wish to stop in swampy places"; "*Yes!* and include me too, even if it's at night"; and, most transparently: "I have seen nothing—I have heard nothing—Meanwhile I am always ready for it. The time I prefer most of all is at about half-past three or four o'clock in the afternoon." [15] Whether experiences with prostitutes deepened the crisis that followed Antonie Brentano's departure is difficult to say, but it was from this period that Beethoven's diary entries began to express his sense of guilt and even revulsion concerning sexual activity. "Sensual union without a union of souls is bestial and will always remain so," [16] he wrote. And he was undoubtedly pained by his inability to adhere to his own high standard of moral behavior; some years earlier he had written: "Oh God, let me finally find the one who will strengthen me in virtue, who will lawfully be mine." [17] One *Tagebuch* entry, however, has a somewhat stoical quality, implying an acceptance of the demands of the flesh: "The weaknesses of nature," he wrote, "are given by nature herself." [18]

Beethoven went to Baden on May 27, 1813, and remained there—except for several weeks in July—until mid-September. It was in Baden that his old friends Nanette and Andreas Streicher found him, as they told Schindler, "in the most deplorable condition with reference to his personal and domestic comforts. He had neither a decent coat nor a whole shirt, and I must forebear to describe his condition as it really was." [19] They related that "Beethoven's state of mind was at the lowest ebb it had been" in many years. This report is corroborated by another observer, the artist Blasius Höfel, who recalled that at this time he often saw Beethoven at an inn, sitting "in a distant corner, at a table which, though large, was avoided by the other guests owing to the very uninviting habits into which he had fallen. . . . Not infrequently he departed without paying his bill, or with the remark that his brother would settle it. . . . He had grown so negligent of his person as to appear there sometimes positively *'schmutzig'* [dirty]." [20] Gradually, the Streichers "induced him again to mingle in society . . . after he had almost completely withdrawn himself from it." [21]

The process of mourning for his beloved was not yet completed. By mid-1813 Beethoven had fallen into a state of mental and physical disorder which brought his musical productivity to a halt. Beethoven wrote no work of the slightest significance during 1813: essentially, he abandoned composition during the first seven months of this year, for only a few trifling works date from this period—the March and Introduction to Kuffner's *Tarpeja*, WoO 2, written in March, and "Der Gesang der Nachtigall," WoO 141, composed on May 3, 1813. For the first time since his adolescence no new projects were being sketched or seriously considered.

It was, therefore, a fortunate day late in that summer when the inventor and entrepreneur Johann Nepomuk Mälzel enthusiastically brought to Beethoven the idea and a partial draft for a new composition celebrating a British victory over Napoleon in the Peninsular War—*Wellington's Victory; or, The Battle of Vittoria*—which Beethoven orchestrated [22] and which was performed to sensational acclaim on December 8 and 12 and repeatedly thereafter.

Mälzel and Beethoven had chosen a most propitious moment for a composition of this kind. The Napoleonic tide had crested with the occupation of Moscow in September 1812; thereafter, Napoleon began to suffer the series of major defeats that eventually led to the termination of the wars which had decimated Europe for almost two decades. The retreat from Moscow, culminating in Napoleon's abandonment of his army and his return to Paris in December 1812, signaled the decline of his fortunes. Wellington's triumph of June 21, 1813, on the Iberian peninsula confirmed the irreversibility of that decline. In June, Austria, which had remained officially neutral since the occupation of Vienna in 1809, became a partner in the Quadruple Alliance, and in August it declared war against France. In October, the Allies scored a decisive victory at the battle of Leipzig. Patriotic feelings, heightened by the anticipation of imminent victory, were given free rein at the December concerts, which were given for the benefit of the Austrian and Bavarian soldiers wounded at the battle of Hanau. The leading musicians of Vienna participated in the performances of *Wellington's Victory*: Hummel and *Kapellmeister* Salieri played the drums and the cannonades; Schuppanzigh led the violins; and Spohr, Mayseder, and scores of others joined in the festivities—which, in Thayer's words, the musicians viewed "as a stupendous musical joke, and engaged in . . . *con amore* as in a gigantic professional frolic." [23] Beethoven, who had no illusions as to the quality of the work, took the occasion to present the debut of his Seventh Symphony, which was also received enthusiastically, the Allegretto being repeated at both concerts. A contemporary newspaper noted that the "applause rose to the point of ecstasy." [24] Beethoven abruptly attained a level of national popularity which he had never previously experienced, a level equal to that achieved by Haydn following the premieres of his oratorios, *The Creation* and *The Seasons*.

Buoyed and elated by this reception, Beethoven emerged from silence and resumed composition at a high level of productivity, which lasted through the early months of 1815. His output, however, though it broadened Beethoven's popularity, did little to enhance his reputation as a composer. He composed a series of vocal and choral "occasional works" in celebration of the Allied cause and its princely leaders: among these were such works as "Germania," WoO 94, composed in celebration of the capitulation of Paris on March 31, 1814; a chorus entitled "Ihr weisen Gründer glücklicher Staaten," WoO 95, composed for the European monarchs who assembled at the Congress of Vienna; and, in fawning tribute to the Congress, a full-scale cantata, *Der glorreiche Augenblick* [The glorious moment], op. 136, composed in the fall of 1814 and repeatedly performed to great acclaim.

These works, filled with bombastic rhetoric and "patriotic" excesses, mark the nadir of Beethoven's artistic career. In them his heroic style is revived, but as parody and farce. Rather than moving forward to his late style, he here regressed to a pastiche of his heroic manner. The heroic style, forged in doubt, rebellion, and defiance, had ended in conformity.

This was, of course, not the occasion for deep thinking about history; hence one can scarcely blame Beethoven for portraying the historical events of 1812–15 in unmediated terms and raw primary colors—and still less for his inability to presage the shadows of the oncoming Holy Alliance. With the exception of *Wellington's Victory*, which is a monument of trivialities [25] and a forerunner of Tschaikowsky's *1812 Overture* as a noisemaker, these works have disappeared from the repertory. Beethoven has no use for the various sonata forms in these works; he returns to the forms of the French Revolution's composers, such as the cantata and the hymn.

The "ideological/heroic" manner of these works was not a wholly new development in Beethoven's music. Indeed, one might trace the birth of this style to the *Joseph* and *Leopold* cantatas of 1790, and even to the two little Friedelberg war songs of 1796 and 1797. Thereafter, one does not find his style again for some years or, rather, until it was sublimated into a subtle and profound form of expression, exemplified by the Third and Fifth Symphonies, *Fidelio*, and the Incidental Music to Goethe's *Egmont*. As we have seen, however, Beethoven had in 1811 hastily composed incidental music for *The Ruins of Athens*, op. 113, and *King Stephen*, op. 117, in honor of Kaiser Franz, and these were clear heralds of the mock-heroic topical works of the Congress period.

"I had long cherished," wrote Beethoven with reference to *Wellington's Victory*, "the desire to be able to place some important work of mine on the altar of our Fatherland." [26] There is no reason to question the genuineness of Beethoven's patriotic feelings or the reality of his desire to celebrate the impending conclusion of the Napoleonic Wars. There is little doubt, however, that the unaccustomed popular acclaim and financial reward reaped by *Wellington's Victory* tempted him to mine this vein for all it was worth. It was worth a good deal. The pecuniary benefits were large: together with the arrears paid on his annuity, they soon sufficed to enable him to invest more than 4,000 florins in silver—first by loaning this sum at interest to Steiner and several years later by purchasing eight bank shares. Performances of his music had never taken place with such frequency. In his entire lifetime, Beethoven was able to give only eleven public concerts in Vienna for his own benefit; and nearly half of these took place during the one year of 1814. Of great significance was the revival of *Fidelio* in 1814, which, Thayer notes, was a direct consequence "of this sudden and boundless popularity of Beethoven's music." [27] Working with a new librettist, Georg Friedrich Treitschke, Beethoven made his final revision ("newly written and improved," he noted [28]) of his twice-failed and apparently forsaken opera between February and mid-May, 1814. *Fidelio* was performed on May 23, with such success that many performances were staged throughout the balance of the year. It achieved its sixteenth performance on October 9. At the May 23 performance, Beethoven "was stormily called out already after the first act, and enthusiastically greeted." [29] If in 1805–06 *Fidelio* could be understood as a rescue opera expressive of Enlightened belief in the triumph of nobility over evil, in 1814 the work unfolded fresh meanings which accelerated its popular acceptance. The new version could readily be perceived as a celebration of victory over the Napoleonic forces by the Allies, and as an allegory of the liberation of Europe from the aggressions of the tyrant/usurper.

The widespread and thunderous applause for his music was extremely gratifying to a composer who had been stung by the criticism that he was a connoisseur's composer. On July 13 an extraordinary notice was inserted in the *Friedensblätter*:

A Word to His Admirers

How often, in your chagrin that his depth was not sufficiently appreciated, have you said that van Beethoven composes only for posterity! You have, no doubt, now been convinced of your error, even if only since the general enthusiasm aroused by his immortal opera *Fidelio*; and also that the present finds kindred souls and sympathetic hearts for that which is great and beautiful without withholding its just privileges from the future.[30]

This from the composer who in 1806 angrily withdrew *Fidelio* from Baron Braun with the words "I don't write for the galleries!" Now he noted in his *Tagebuch*: "It is certain that one writes most prettily when one writes for the public. . . ."[31]

To put it gently, Beethoven was not immune to the seductions of success and was even willing to suffer charges of opportunism at the hands of his fellow musicians. Tomaschek wrote of *Wellington's Victory* that he was "very painfully affected to see a Beethoven . . . among the rudest materialists."[32] In response, Beethoven admitted the meretriciousness of the work. Similarly, Schindler claimed that Beethoven "attached no value" to *Der glorreiche Augenblick*,[33] (although one wonders, in that case, why Beethoven contemplated writing an overture for it a decade later[34]). But he surely placed great store by the emoluments and praise that such works brought him during the glittering and exhausting festivities which accompanied the convening of the Congress of Vienna from September 1814 to June 1815. All of the crowned heads of Europe were present, along with their entourages and thousands of less exalted visitors. While the serious work of the Congress—the drafting of a peace treaty and the establishment of mechanisms for the maintenance of European order and stability—went on backstage, a vast program of entertainment intended to divert the throngs of idle notables wholly occupied the foreground. Kaiser Franz appointed a festivals committee, whose members "were driven to distraction by the task of inventing new forms of amusement."[35] There was a multitude of balls, banquets, and gala performances and an endless variety of tournaments, hunts, theatricals, sleighing expeditions, ballets, operas, balloon ascents, and torchlight parades. Byron called the Congress a "base pageant." Barea writes: "For the time being, Vienna, the Kaiserstadt, the Imperial City, was the capital of Europe. They, the people of Vienna, strutted the stage as if they had been extras in a vast baroque State gala, acting as the foreigners expected them to act and as they felt like acting in their relief and release." [36]

Beethoven was one such Viennese; and his music was but a single element in the huge pattern of diversion and amusement. He was presented by Razumovsky and Archduke Rudolph to the assembled monarchs and received both their compliments and their monetary gifts; distinguished foreign visitors paid him homage; and he obtained an audience with the empress of Russia, to whom he presented a Polonaise for piano, op. 89, receiving in return a present of 50 ducats plus a belated bonus of double that sum for his 1802 dedication to Czar Alexander of the Violin Sonatas, op. 30. Schindler writes: "He used afterwards to relate, jocosely, how he had suffered the crowned heads to pay court to him, and what an air of importance he had at such times assumed." [37] It may well be true that on one level Beethoven was acting a part, playing the haughty, faintly obsequious genius in order to restore his rather depleted finances. There seems to be little doubt, however, that he enjoyed the adulation of the monarchs and princes. Elsewhere, Schindler relates that "in later days, the great master would recall not without emotion those days . . . and would say with a tinge of pride that he had allowed himself to be courted by the highest rulers of Europe and had comported himself admirably." [38] Doubtless Beethoven had mixed feelings about the various signs of his new eminence. We know that he was proud to be granted honorary citizenship of Vienna in 1815—and that he joked about this distinction too from time to time.

Nothing could be more evanescent than such excessive adulation, especially as it was largely founded upon an artificial and atypical aspect of Beethoven's music. It was not surprising, therefore, that the rapidity of Beethoven's rise to popularity was matched by a correspondingly rapid decline, beginning at the end of 1814. Ironically, the first intimations of Beethoven's fall from grace coincided with the peak moment of his popularity—the concert of November 29 in the Redoutensaal, at which *Der glorreiche Augenblick* was heard for the first time, along with *Wellington's Victory* and the Seventh Symphony, before a large audience which included two empresses, the king of Prussia, and other eminences along with the foremost virtuosos of Vienna. The hall was filled, the concert was enthusiastically received, and two repeat concerts were scheduled. But at the repetition of the same program on December 2, nearly half of the seats were empty. The third proposed concert was abandoned, and Beethoven gave no public concert for his own benefit from then until May 1824.

A November 30 report to Hager, head of the secret police, revealed the unstable basis of Beethoven's popularity: "The recital given yesterday did not serve to increase enthusiasm for the talent of this composer, who has his partisans and his adversaries. In opposition to his admirers, the first rank of which is represented by Razumovsky, Apponyi, Kraft, etc., . . . who adore Beethoven, is formed an overwhelming majority of connoisseurs who refuse absolutely to listen to his works hereafter." [39]

In a letter of this period Beethoven poetically summarizes his consciousness of the fragility of eminence: "So all is illusion, friendship, kingdom, empire, all is just a mist which a breath of wind can disperse and shape again in a different way!!" [40] During 1815 he tried to rekindle the fading embers of his popularity by pursuing the musical formulas which had worked so well during the preceding years. In the spring he completed an overture in honor of the kaiser's birthday—*Namensfeier,* op. 115—which, despite its subject matter had no appreciable impact upon his fortunes. Early in the year he composed incidental music to a drama, *Leonore Prohaska,* containing a war song and a funeral march (an orchestration of the third movement of the Sonata, op. 26), but no performances materialized, owing to difficulties with the censor. He had greater success with "Es ist vollbracht" [It is finished], a work for bass, chorus, and orchestra inspired by the Battle of Waterloo and the second occupation of Paris. It was performed several times in July, but like all of Beethoven's occasional works from the Congress period, it disappeared with the waning of the occasion which brought it forth.

Beethoven's only major concert of the year was a benefit for the Hospital Fund on Christmas Day. At this concert, he presented a revival of *Christ on the Mount of Olives,* the *Namensfeier* Overture, and "Calm Seas and Prosperous Voyage," op. 112, a brief choral setting of two poems by Goethe, with orchestral accompaniment. Opus 112, a small masterpiece of tone painting, which treats one of Beethoven's favorite subjects—tranquility penetrated by agitation, dissolving into joyful triumph—and which is reminiscent in its timbres and moods of the finale of the Ninth Symphony, is sufficient demonstration that the topical works of the Congress period had not affected the core of Beethoven's musical integrity. Indeed, setting aside the political compositions, 1814 may be regarded more favorably as the year of the final revision of *Fidelio* (including the *Fidelio* Overture), the touching "Elegischer Gesang," op. 118, and the Piano Sonata, op. 90; and 1815 as the year of "Calm Seas and Prosperous Voyage" and the two Cello Sonatas, op. 102.

It was not altogether apparent even from these significant works that Beethoven had begun to formulate, let alone explore, a new set of structural and stylistic problems whose solutions would ultimately result in his last-period compositions. It was unmistakably clear, however, that the heroic period had ended, even though its reverberations would continue to be heard from time to time in Beethoven's final decade. As Sullivan noted, the music of Beethoven's heroic period was concerned with the "posing and solution of a problem." Now, Beethoven "was beginning to realize that the experience was not, for him, a permanent possession." [41] Rosen, approaching the issue from a different perspective, reaches similar conclusions: "It was as if the classical sense of form appeared bankrupt to him, spurring him to search for a new system of expression. [The works of 1807–13] may well have seemed to exhaust beyond renewal the style and the tradition he worked in." [42] The heroic style had in substance ended in 1811–12 with the completion of the Seventh and Eighth Symphonies, the Violin Sonata, op. 96, and the *Archduke* Trio, op. 97. The long-standing problems of Beethoven's heroic opera, *Fidelio*, had been solved at last in 1814. True, the crowning work of the heroic style—the Ninth Symphony—remained to be written, but it was a work that could only be written retrospectively and in a sense even anachronistically, from the vantage point of another world and another style.

The dissolution of the heroic style did not occur suddenly or even dramatically, nor is it altogether certain that Beethoven was conscious of the process that was taking place. Rather, as he developed the implications of the Classic sonata form and sonata cycle and applied the principles of dramatic conflict, symphonic expansion, long tonal trajectories, and condensed motivic development to a succession of genres, each of these genres in turn reached what appeared to him to be its maximum fruition and was set aside. Beethoven composed no symphonies between 1812 and the completion of the Ninth in 1824; he completed no concerto after 1809 and no piano trio after 1811; and he abandoned the duo sonata after 1815. Five years elapsed between the Piano Sonata, op. 81a, of 1809, and the Sonata, op. 90, of 1814. He wrote no sets of variations for piano between 1809 and 1822–23. He now tried to return to the standard genres, sketching extensively a Piano Concerto in D and a Piano Trio in F minor, but these were permanently set aside.[43]

We are, then, at one of the turning points of music history. The frenetic activity and meretricious productivity of the Congress period may temporarily have diverted Beethoven from the consciousness that he had no major creative projects in progress, no challenging musical issues at hand. Now, with the departure of the Congress, he faced the necessity of finding new avenues and new forms for his creative energies.

Historical circumstances play their role here. From our vantage point in a later age, we can easily see that the mock-heroic style had outlived its—at best temporary—utility. The heroic, exhortatory style had itself lost its historical *raison d'être* with the close of the Napoleonic Wars, the disintegration of the old connoisseur nobility, and the beginning of a new phase in Austrian national existence. After twenty years of war, many Viennese, returning to a torpid life of peace, stability, and conservatism, began to utilize music not as a stimulant to consciousness, but as a narcotic, perhaps to mask the diminutive reality of post-Napoleonic and post-Enlightenment society. The historian Geoffrey Bruun writes: "A spirit of disillusionment, febrile and confused, succeeded the high certainties of the Age of Reason and the expectations voiced in the revolutionary creed. The philosophy of the Restoration was for many a thing of shreds and patches after the stark and glittering mirror-world the *philosophes* had held before the gaze of humanity, and the reversion to traditional pretensions, petty policies, checks and balances and compromises, though it might mark a return to sanity and repose, still left behind a despairing conviction that humanity had failed itself." [44] The Viennese had always danced; for the moment they apparently wished to do little else. They had added new delicacies to their diet of brown beer and sausages and were increasingly cultivating the Biedermeier comforts which hid the inadequacies, frustrations, and suppressed violence of Viennese life from the consciousness of its citizens. Emerging hedonist trends in Viennese society, along with a turn to both sensuous Italian music and idealized dance forms, resulted in a massive defection of Beethoven's audience from music which expressed categorical imperatives, which was of an essentially serious, ascetic, conflict-ridden character.

In rapid succession, almost all of Beethoven's most unswerving patrons were lost to him through death, emigration, or personal estrangement. Kinsky died suddenly in late 1812. Lichnowsky, who for more than twenty years had helped to strengthen Beethoven's sense of mission through his affectionate and steadfast support, died in 1814. Lobkowitz's palace, where so many of Beethoven's works were performed for two decades, was closed to Viennese musical life with the prince's death in 1816. Razumovsky's magnificent, art-laden palace was destroyed by fire on December 31, 1814, whereupon the count—now elevated to prince—returned to Russia, taking Schuppanzigh with him. Other patrons whom we encountered earlier had drifted away or were turning elsewhere—especially to Italian opera—for their musical needs. (The significance to Beethoven of the faithful—and influential—Archduke Rudolph became increasingly magnified during these years.) Still others were now becoming declassed or impoverished. The era of the connoisseur aristocracy which had nurtured Gluck, Mozart, Haydn, and Beethoven had come to an end. The nobility's private orchestras and ensembles, its salons and palaces, now belonged to the history of the *ancien régime*.

It was Beethoven's fortune that his career encompassed both the emergence and the completion of several fundamental styles which arose successively in the musical centers of Europe. It was part of his greatness that he rapidly and instinctively grasped the inherent and latent possibilities of each such stage in European musical development. Seen from this viewpoint, his four major phases as a composer reveal a progression from Classic (1782–93), to Viennese high-Classic (1794–ca. 1802), to what may be called late-Classic (1803–14), to, finally, post-Classic styles and forms. Each of these phases necessitated a partial rupture with a received tradition at the point at which it was reaching its apogee of development. Until 1815, each of Beethoven's emerging styles had already been prefigured to some extent in the work of his contemporaries. Thus, in his early Vienna works, he rapidly overtook and closed his accounts with the high-Classic sonata styles and forms of Mozart and Haydn. And the "heroic" late-Classic style had been incubating in Haydn's late works as well as in the music of the French Revolution's composers. In each of these transitions, the exhaustion of the prior style was an opportunity and a liberation for Beethoven, although it subjected him to painful reformulations of his musical ideas and vocabulary.

In 1815, however, Beethoven faced a situation new in quality. Although there were new musical trends developing, Beethoven was unwilling to explore any of them. He did not choose to work in the bourgeois–Biedermeier mixture of high-Classic and pre-Romantic styles (as in the music of Spohr, Schubert, Moscheles, etc.); he disparaged the new Italian style exemplified by the meteorically popular Rossini as suitable only to "the frivolous and sensuous spirit of the times." [45] He was then—and remained—unwilling to treat supernatural and "Gothic" subjects, which, in the operas of Spohr, Conradin Kreutzer, Marschner, and Weber, were opening the door to one of the most fruitful tendencies of German Romantic music. Beethoven had glimpsed these possibilities well before Spohr wrote his *Faust* (1818) and Weber his *Der Freischütz* (1821); he was perhaps taking the first steps toward Romanticism of this type in *Fidelio*, and in Klärchen's songs and the *Melodram* of the Incidental Music to *Egmont*. He continued to be drawn to stage projects dealing with the mythical and the magical, the sombre and the supernatural; but he set aside each of these, perhaps because he was too much a child of the Age of Reason to wholeheartedly enter the house of Romanticism. (He remarked to Collin that such subjects have "a soporific effect on feeling and reason." [46])

Above all, although Beethoven was to become a master of the evanescent mood in his last style, he resisted the impending Romantic fragmentation of the architecturally concentrated and controlled cyclic forms of the Classic era into small forms and lyric mood pieces; for this was a kind of music in which fantasy images were given free play but were essentially rendered harmless through an avoidance of conflict. The breadth of his ideas remained undiminished. Despite the exhaustion of his heroic style, Beethoven was not yet done with the problems of heroism, tragedy, and transcendence. The task he would set himself in his late music would be the portrayal of heroism without heroics, without heroes.

Beethoven could no longer find inspiration among his contemporaries, among the successors to the Neefes, Haydns, and Cherubinis. He would have to turn elsewhere, to the past—to Bach, Handel, and Palestrina. For the most part, however, his late music, to an extent never previously seen in the history of music, would be created out of the composer himself rather than through a combination and extension of existent musical elements. In the formation of his late style we have, then, an instance of the coming into being of an apparently "unprecedented" style, one whose tendencies and formative materials are not readily identifiable in the music of his contemporaries or immediate predecessors.

The emergence of the new style was to be a slow and trying process. In the years 1816–19, Beethoven's productivity declined to the lowest level of his adult life. In retrospect, of course, it may seem only natural, in view of the immensity of the task before him, that Beethoven would have to forge his way slowly, almost blindly, one masterpiece at a time, into the world of the last period.[47] But while it was taking place, the process was one of considerable anguish. The exhaustion of the middle-period styles, even more than the loss of favor and patronage, had painful consequences for Beethoven, for he required constant creative challenges and activity to maintain his psychological equilibrium, to protect himself against powerful regressive tendencies in his personality.

Heightening his vulnerability was a qualitative deterioration in Beethoven's hearing. Where he had formerly been hard of hearing, Beethoven was now fast becoming clinically deaf. His last public performance as a pianist took place on January 25, 1815, when he accompanied the singer Franz Wild in a performance of "Adelaide" for the Russian empress. In April of the previous year, he had participated in performances of the *Archduke* Trio. But Ludwig Spohr, who was present, wrote: "On account of his deafness there was scarcely anything left of the virtuosity of the artist which had formerly been so greatly admired. In *forte* passages the poor deaf man pounded on the keys till the strings jangled, and in *piano* he played so softly that whole groups of tones were omitted, so that the music was unintelligible. . . ."[48]

The grievous effect of these cumulative events upon Beethoven's self-esteem and pride cannot be overstated. For now, in a sense, it was not merely his hearing but his music which had "failed" him. The heroic style had served him well; it had helped to ward off anxieties and to defend against internal dangers; indeed, the style, the birth of which coincided so closely with the onset of Beethoven's hearing difficulties, may have helped for a time to compensate for his deafness and even to ease the pain of his sexual isolation. But now the sense of failure extended beyond Beethoven's deafness and his sexuality. It threatened to derail his creativity.

Beethoven's nephew, Karl van Beethoven. Unsigned portrait. Beethoven. Portrait in oils by Joseph Willibrord Mähler (1815).

18
Beethoven and His Nephew

On November 15, 1815, Beethoven's brother Caspar Carl died of tuberculosis, leaving a widow, Johanna, and a nine-year-old son, Karl. Beethoven thereupon moved to assume the exclusive guardianship of the boy. A protracted conflict ensued in which Beethoven and the boy's mother contested the guardianship, with Beethoven ultimately emerging as the Pyrrhic victor in 1820. Six years later, in late July 1826, Karl attempted suicide in a successful effort to break away from the domination of his uncle, whose suffocating embrace had at last become unbearable.

The narrative of Beethoven's life between the end of 1815 and early 1820 is the complex, and occasionally arcane, story of his attempt to surmount—indeed to survive—a personal and creative crisis that threatened to overwhelm his personality. We may be able better to understand this story if we view the appropriation of his nephew as not merely one manifestation of this crisis but as the primary means by which Beethoven struggled toward a new psychological and creative equilibrium.[1] That he succeeded in his efforts is attested both by the facts of his biography after 1820 and by the crystallization of the late style, inaugurated toward the end of 1817 by the commencement of the *Hammerklavier* Sonata, op. 106.

The unwitting but essential ingredients in Beethoven's salvation were, paradoxically, his nephew Karl and his sister-in-law Johanna. His obsessive entanglement with them was the means by which he forcibly wrenched his emotional energies from their attachment to the outer world and focused them upon the still unresolved issues of his family constellation. Beethoven was now in the process of converting into a strange form of quasi-reality some of the fantasies which had both veiled and motored his existence, bringing into consciousness the delusions of a lifetime so that they could be faced and ultimately neutralized.

Caspar Carl van Beethoven married Johanna Reiss on May 25, 1806. In a Conversation Book of 1823, Beethoven wrote, "My brother's marriage was as much an indication of his immorality as of his folly," [2] apparently referring to Johanna's premature pregnancy, for their only child, Karl, was born on September 4, 1806. It is probable that Beethoven opposed the marriage, just as he did Nikolaus Johann's in 1812, and as the elder Ludwig had opposed another marriage in 1767. And he probably tried to influence his brother against Johanna: a *Tagebuch* entry of 1816 suggested that Caspar Carl "would still be alive and would surely not have died so miserably" had he turned away from his wife "and come wholly to me." [3] But there was no lasting estrangement between the brothers. Caspar Carl continued to perform small duties for his brother from time to time, although important matters were handled by more capable advisers, such as Gleichenstein, Countess Erdödy, Franz Oliva, and Stephan von Breuning. As we have seen, during the French bombardment of Vienna in 1809 Beethoven turned to his brother and sister-in-law for shelter. After 1812 the brothers were in close contact, which, for them, consisted of furious quarrels alternating with passionate reconciliations. One report of violence between the brothers dates from 1813, and it is said that Johanna then played the role of peacemaker. [4]

Johanna was the daughter of Anton and Theresia Reiss. Her father was a well-to-do Viennese upholsterer; her mother was the daughter of a wine dealer and burgomaster in Retz, lower Austria. Nothing is known of her early life, not even the precise date of her birth (which was somewhere between 1784 and 1786). A sole, curious anecdote of her childhood survives: her son recalled that "she often told me that every time she wanted money her father said: 'I won't give you any, but if you can take money without my knowledge it belongs to you!' " [5] Curious, because theft—including the robbery by Beethoven of her own child—was to become the leitmotif of her existence. Rightly or not, her husband was suspected of wrongdoing in his post and was thought to have accepted bribes from Beethoven's publishers. More dramatically, she was actually convicted in 1811 for stealing an expensive pearl necklace that she had on consignment and she was sentenced on December 30, 1811, to one year's penal servitude; her husband appealed the sentence and it was reduced to one month in jail and then remitted altogether in July 1812. Beethoven later fastened upon the conviction as proof of Johanna's immorality, referring to it as a "horrible crime," and making it the basis for his legal claim that she was unfit to raise her son.[6] A more reasonable observer would take it simply as evidence that Johanna had on one proven occasion given way to a compulsion to steal for which she had been appropriately punished by the law.

Johanna had brought a large dowry to her marriage with Caspar Carl, and she had inherited from her father the large house in the Alservorstadt in which they lived and which brought them a substantial rental income. It was a strife-torn marriage, perhaps inevitably so, for none of the brothers Beethoven were well-suited to the married state. Beethoven reported that Caspar Carl had threatened his wife with divorce. Also according to Beethoven (who did not disapprove of the practice), Caspar Carl repeatedly beat his son in order to render him more tractable. Nor was Johanna spared: on one occasion he "stabbed her through the hand with a table knife; she still bore the scar as an old lady."[7]

Much of what we know about Johanna's personality has been filtered through the prejudiced writings of Beethoven and his associates. Only one of her letters has been published; it was written to Franz Liszt in the early 1840s concerning the proposed sale of Beethoven's Heiligenstadt Testament, and it shows her to be a lucid correspondent, capable of dealing diplomatically with a complex situation.[8] This letter may have been written by a scribe, however. Four unpublished letters of April 1827 to J.B. Bach, in Johanna's own hand, demonstrate her capability and intelligence. Her daughter-in-law, Caroline, described her as a forceful, emotional person: "By her letters she moved heaven and earth, and [she] understood how to present her poverty and despair in burning colors and with dramatic effect."[9] But this refers to later years, as does an 1830 report that her mode of life was "less than praiseworthy."[10]

Beethoven's attitude toward Johanna prior to Caspar Carl's death was by no means consistently hostile. Later, Beethoven even claimed that he had acted as her protector during her marriage: "Although I could never defend, still less approve, *her actions,* yet I warded off my brother's anger from her." [11] Despite his posture of outrage at her 1811 "embezzlement," Beethoven was sufficiently persuaded of her financial probity that on October 22, 1813, he arranged for his publisher, Steiner, to lend 1,500 florins to her (rather than to his brother), and agreed to personally repay the loan in the event of default.

There was no hint of his intention of appropriating his nephew, Karl, until the last minute. On November 14, 1815, the dying Caspar Carl wrote in his testament: "Along with my wife I appoint my brother Ludwig van Beethoven coguardian." Beethoven, learning of this, compelled his brother to alter the sentence to: "I appoint my brother Ludwig van Beethoven guardian." [12] Suddenly, to their dismay, Caspar Carl and Johanna realized that Beethoven wanted to exclude the mother from a joint guardianship. Caspar Carl thereupon composed a codicil to his will which he signed later on the same day:

> Having learned that my brother, Hr. Ludwig van Beethoven, desires after my death to take wholly to himself my son Karl, and wholly to withdraw him from the supervision and training of his mother, and inasmuch as the best of harmony does not exist between my brother and my wife, I have found it necessary to add to my will that I by no means desire that my son be taken away from his mother, but that he shall always and so long as his future career permits remain with his mother, to which end the guardianship of him is to be exercised by her as well as my brother. [13]

The next day, November 15, Caspar Carl died. In direct contravention of his brother's last request, Beethoven laid exclusive claim to the guardianship of Karl, the only child of the three Beethoven brothers. On November 28 he wrote to the Imperial Landrecht, the tribunal having jurisdiction over legal matters affecting the nobility, "I now have the chief claim to this guardianship," [14] and on December 15 he inquired of the Civil Court: "In order to prevent the establishment of an illegal joint guardianship which would be detrimental to the interests of the ward, I . . . require proof of the sentence passed on his mother, Johanna v. Beethoven, who has been tried for embezzlement." [15] A few days later, on December 20, he again petitioned the Landrecht, asking that it set aside those provisions of Caspar Carl's will which provided for joint guardianship and claiming that Johanna lacked "moral and intellectual qualities" sufficient to permit her to serve in that capacity. [16] On January 9, 1816, the Landrecht ruled in Beethoven's favor, and ten days later Beethoven was legally appointed guardian, empowered to take possession of the boy. On February 2, Karl was taken from his mother and placed in Cajetan Giannatasio del Rio's private school for boys. Shortly thereafter, Beethoven and Giannatasio petitioned the court to wholly exclude the widow from direct communication with the boy; the Landrecht compromised by permitting her to visit the boy "in his leisure hours," but only if she were accompanied by Beethoven's representative.

On February 6 Beethoven wrote triumphantly to Antonie Brentano:

"I have fought a battle for the purpose of wresting a poor, unhappy child from the clutches of his unworthy mother, and I have won the day—Te Deum laudamus." [17] This was only the opening round, however, in a struggle that would increasingly take its toll upon all the protagonists.

Beethoven's conscious view was that he was merely a good uncle striving to rescue an ungrateful child from an unfit mother. It is clear, however, that from the outset, deeper currents were shaping this series of events. Suddenly, and in rapid succession, a number of delusions emerged which suggest that Beethoven was beginning to have trouble distinguishing fantasy from reality. He suspected, without any basis, that Johanna had poisoned her husband, and this fantasy would be laid to rest only after he received Dr. Bertolini's assurance that it had no foundation.[18] He soon began to fear that she was monitoring his movements; early in February he wrote that she had bribed his servant for some unstated purpose unrelated to her son.[19] Later in February he came to believe that Johanna might be a prostitute: "Last night that *Queen of Night* was at the Artists' Ball until three A.M. exposing not only her mental but also *her bodily nakedness*—it was whispered that she—was willing to hire herself—for 20 gulden! Oh horrible!" [20] These persecutory and sexual fantasies were subsidiary to a complex rescue fantasy: Beethoven believed that he was carrying out a sacred task of an unspecified nature. "Ignore all gossip, all pettiness for the sake of this holy cause," he wrote in his *Tagebuch;* "Now these circumstances are very hard for you, but He who is above exists; without Him there is nothing. In any case, the token has been accepted." [21] Beethoven had come to regard his "rescue" of Karl as a heroic, divinely authorized mission. By 1816, he had exhausted his symbolic exploration of heroism; now he was enacting a bizarre "heroic" drama in an apparent effort to become the conquistador of his innermost fantasies.

But Beethoven's central delusion in this pathological sequence was even more extraordinary: he began to imagine that he had become a father in reality. On May 13, 1816, he wrote to Countess Erdödy: "I now regard myself as [Karl's] father." [22] "You will regard K as your own child," he noted in his *Tagebuch.*[23] The full import of this was revealed in September, when he wrote to Kanka: "I am now the real physical father [*wirklicher leiblicher Vater*] of my deceased brother's child." [24] A few weeks later he wrote to Wegeler: "You are a husband and a father. So am I, but without a wife." [25]

But was he without a wife? Beethoven's fantasy that he was the real physical father of Karl indicates that in some mystifying way he may have been participating in an illusory marriage to the "Queen of Night" herself.

To pursue the implications of this somewhat further: the death of Caspar Carl may have opened up for Beethoven the road to a surrogate wife. Johanna became "available" to Beethoven, perhaps activating in him impulses toward union with a mother figure and mobilizing the terror of paternal retribution which often follows from fantasies of such a union. From the start, then, Beethoven's aggression against Johanna can be seen as a denial of his desire for her. This may be why he chose to regard her as a prostitute; for such fantasied degradation of a woman often has its source in the wish to make her sexually available to one who dreads union with a feminine ideal.

In this light, Beethoven's "capture" of his nephew takes on the aspect of a complex ruse which he unconsciously employed in order to remain entangled with his brother's widow. At the same time, it is possible that Beethoven's manifest fear of Johanna, especially of being alone with her, and his attribution to her of destructive and corrupting powers clearly far beyond her capabilities arose out of a perception of the implications of taking his brother's place in his own family. In the codicil to his last will and testament, Caspar Carl had in effect urged the union of his wife and his brother: "Only by unity can the object which I had in view in appointing my brother guardian of my son be attained, wherefore, for the welfare of my child, I recommend *compliance* to my wife and more *moderation* to my brother. God permit them to be harmonious for the sake of my child's welfare. This is the last wish of the dying husband and brother." [26] Perhaps Beethoven could avoid the anxieties which this directive implied only by forcefully rejecting Johanna as coguardian.

The negative side of Beethoven's attitude toward Johanna is quite manifest. His letters and Conversation Books are filled with vitriolic and unfounded accusations against her; he reviled her with epithets and applauded Karl when the boy repudiated her. Not surprisingly, the sheer quantity of Beethoven's negative references to Johanna—and his actions in depriving her of her son—has led to the general conclusion that he was implacably hostile toward her; and this has been the unqualified view of previous biographies, from those of Schindler and Thayer—who explain Beethoven's actions in terms of Johanna's supposed unfitness and Beethoven's lofty (if misguided) motivations—to the Sterbas' hostile psychoanalytic study, which portrays the composer as consumed by unalloyed hatred ("blind," "bitter," "relentless") toward his sister-in-law. Several of Johanna's contemporary defenders shared this view. For example, Father Frölich and Jacob Hotschevar stated to the Landrecht that "there is great dislike between Ludwig van Beethoven and the mother" and spoke of "the enmity which for years, and indeed from the very beginning, prevailed between Herr Ludwig and Frau Johanna v. Beethoven." [27]

Such uncontrolled and passionate feelings of hostility, however, are in themselves a form of denial, an attempt to stave off powerful positive impulses. Unchecked emotions such as Beethoven's toward Johanna are compounded of a broad range of contrary feelings: the more powerful the manifest emotion, the greater may be the opposite feeling which it strives to keep in check. "In such circumstances," Freud writes, "the conscious love attains as a rule, by way of reaction, an especially high degree of intensity, so as to be strong enough for the perpetual task of keeping its opponent under repression." [28] This holds as well for consciously expressed hatred, which often serves to mask powerful positive emotions: "Feelings of love that have not yet become manifest express themselves to begin with by hostility and aggressive tendencies; for it may be that the destructive component in the object cathexis has hurried on ahead and is only later on joined by the erotic one." [29]

With the death of Caspar Carl and the onset of the guardianship, signs of volatile ambivalence toward Johanna emerged with full force, characterized by alternations between aggressive and conciliatory behavior. Beethoven repeatedly barred Johanna from access to Karl; but each time he relented, suggesting (and even insisting) that she visit the child in his presence. Throughout 1816 he remained in frequent contact with her, having apparently succeeded in assuring her that his actions were beneficial to her son. On December 28 he asked Kanka to act as curator for the estate of Johanna's cousin for the benefit of Karl, adding that "the mother, too, will probably derive some benefit from the arrangement." [30] In early 1817 he drew closer to her, had her meet the child at his house, took Karl to visit her ("His mother wants to place herself on a better footing with her neighbors, and so I am doing her the favor of taking her son to her tomorrow in the company of a third person" [31]), and persuaded her without protest to assign half of her widow's pension "for the education and maintenance" of Karl. [32] Beethoven carefully kept his positive relationship with Johanna well hidden from most of his associates and especially from headmaster Giannatasio. He was somewhat more forthright about his friendly actions toward Johanna in a letter to Zmeskall: "After all," he wrote to him, " it might hurt Karl's mother to have to visit her child at the house of a stranger; and in any case it is a less charitable arrangement than I like." [33]

In August 1817, however, Johanna mortified Beethoven by repeating certain criticisms of Karl's schoolmaster which he had confided to her. Regarding this as a betrayal as well as an embarrassment, Beethoven turned against her: "This time I wanted to see whether she could perhaps be reformed by a tolerant and more gentle attitude. . . . But it came to nothing." [34] He thereupon reverted to his "original, strictly severe attitude" and barred her from Karl. Yet in March of 1818 he again moved cautiously toward reconciliation, offering Johanna financial assistance and once again apparently permitting her limited access to her son, whom she had not seen for many months. Then in June, at Mödling, where he had brought his nephew, he discovered that she had persuaded his servants to provide her with information; at the same time he learned that Karl had secretly been meeting with his mother. Beethoven took these events as constituting a "horrible treachery," was thrown into an ominous condition of mental confusion, and reacted with the rage of one who feels utterly betrayed by all concerned. As he wrote to Nanette Streicher:

> I had been noticing signs of treachery for a very long time; and then on the eve of my departure I received an anonymous letter, the contents of which filled me with terror; but they were little more than suppositions. Karl, whom I pounced on that very evening, immediately disclosed a little, but not all. As I often give him a good shaking, but not without valid reason, he was far too frightened to confess absolutely everything. We arrived here in the middle of this struggle. As I frequently reprimanded him, the servants noticed it; and the old traitress [the housekeeper], in particular, tried to prevent *him from confessing the truth.* But . . . everything came to light. . . . K[arl] has done wrong, but—a mother—a mother—even a bad mother is still a mother. . . . I am not inviting you out here yet, since everything is in confusion. *Still it won't be necessary to take me to the madhouse.*[35]

Despite his fury, Beethoven could not wholly condemn Johanna. But she, now convinced that no further reconciliation was possible and alarmed at the harmful effects upon Karl of Beethoven's guardianship, began a lawsuit to recover custody of Karl. This inaugurated a period of total confrontation during which Beethoven, now unable to control his actions, described her in the worst possible terms and called for her complete rejection. He had hoped to have it otherwise. "If the mother could have repressed her wicked tendencies and allowed my plans to develop peacefully," he lamented, "then an entirely favorable result would have been the outcome." [36]

Beethoven's attitude toward his young nephew was similarly riddled with contradictions. Here, too, Beethoven's conscious feelings served to mask opposite ones. His repeated protestations of love were not matched by consistent benevolence in his behavior toward the boy. At first he would fetch Karl from school and take him to lunch, to see a carnival, or to hear a concert; but this solicitousness did not last long. In the summer of 1816 Karl underwent a hernia operation, performed by Dr. Carl von Smetana, but Beethoven did not make the short trip from Baden to Vienna to be at the bedside of his deeply beloved "son." On September 22 he wrote to Giannatasio, asking for news: "You will understand that I long to hear how my beloved K[arl] is now progressing. . . . I am beginning to think that you must look upon me as a rather thoughtless barbarian."[37] But a letter to Antonie Brentano, written on September 29, shows that he was genuinely elated by Karl's recovery; Beethoven felt that he had come through a personal trial and described to her "how burdened I am with a father's very real cares...."[38] Throughout, he exhibited a "torturing tenderness" toward his nephew, with intense anxiety and constant watchfulness readily alternating with complaints and reproaches. In November, he took the ten-year-old to task for laxness in his studies and punished him by a deliberate show of coldness: "We walked along together more seriously than usual. Timidly he pressed my hand but found no response" [39]—this on the day preceding the first anniversary of the death of the boy's father. In 1817 he authorized, indeed encouraged, Giannatasio to beat Karl "to enforce the strictest obedience." He wrote to the headmaster: "I have already told you how during his father's lifetime he would obey only when he was beaten. Of course that was very wrong, but that was how things were done, and we must not forget it." [40] To make sure that his nephew was fully aware of his attitude, Beethoven added a postscript: *"Please read this letter with Karl."* As we will see, in subsequent years, when it became apparent to Beethoven that he had not succeeded in breaking the bond between mother and son, his treatment of Karl took the form of physical violence on more than one occasion, and extremely negative feelings toward the boy repeatedly rose to the surface.

The depth of Beethoven's hostility toward Karl, however, cannot be gauged by his occasional violence or coldness, or even by his endless reproaches. More extremely, Beethoven deprived the fatherless child of his sole remaining parent—which is to say, he made him an orphan. And from the beginning, Beethoven actually referred to Karl as "a poor orphan." [41] Furthermore, for years it remained Beethoven's hope that he could obtain permission from the courts to send the boy away from Vienna. It became his goal as early as January 1816, when he wrote to Giannatasio: "It will certainly be best to remove him later on from Vienna and send him to Mölk or somewhere else. There he will neither see nor hear anything more of his beastly mother; and where everything about him is strange he will have fewer people to lean upon and will be able solely by his own efforts to win for himself love and respect." [42] Apparently, one motivation of Beethoven's "rescue" of his nephew was the drive to separate Karl from his mother so that he might not have what Beethoven desired—access to Johanna. At first this meant no more than a mother's love, but in later years, especially after the boy reached the age of puberty, Beethoven seems to have suffered from fantasies of incestuous union between Karl and Johanna. He urgently pressed on his nephew the twin imperatives of abstinence and obedience: "You must not hate your mother," wrote Beethoven in a Conversation Book, "but you must not regard her like another good m[other]. . . . If you become *guilty* of further offenses against *me*, you cannot become a good man, that is the same as if you rebelled against your father." [43] Beethoven was able to control Karl by means of such appeals to the boy's guilt concerning his Oedipal strivings.

These hostile—and even sacrificial—impulses were at war with, and repeatedly yielded to, Beethoven's loving and possessive tendencies. For despite his protestations that he was rescuing Karl and that his motives were altruistic ("I do not *need my nephew*, but *he needs me*," he wrote,[44]) Beethoven became increasingly dependent upon his nephew. In later years he overvalued him to such an extent that he "would sometimes sing or play him a theme he had thought of for a projected work, in order to get his opinion and preference."[45] Karl was Beethoven's savior, not the reverse. Beethoven received from the boy the protective warmth of family feeling, relief from loneliness, the pride of (delusory) parenthood, and even a sense of immortality ("I want *by means of my nephew* to establish a fresh memorial to my name"[46]), at a time when numerous leavetakings and losses had left him in a forlorn and lonely state.

And so, Beethoven's conflict-ridden attitudes toward Karl and Johanna resulted in a contradictory set of relationships, taking the form of a "marriage" in which no member of the "family" was living with any other. He had created the basic family triad—father, mother, son—but was unable to take the step that would have united the three as a cooperative and protective family unit.

If Beethoven's desires for a harmonious relationship with a woman to complete this family triad could not find fulfillment in Johanna, they nevertheless found another object in his strange and intense relationship with Frau Nanette Streicher (née Stein) between early 1817 and the summer of 1818. Born in 1769, Anna Maria Stein rapidly showed signs of becoming a musical prodigy; when she was eight, Mozart wrote of her, "She may succeed, for she has great talent for music."[47] Her talents were to be expended elsewhere, however, as the owner of a piano factory in which she was joined by Johann Andreas Streicher after their marriage in January 1794. Beethoven and the Streichers, whose salon was for decades one of the musical centers of Vienna, became fast friends beginning in the 1790s, and as we saw earlier, it was they who, in 1813, nursed him back to health from his post–Immortal Beloved depression. Beginning in the early months of 1817, Beethoven called on Frau Streicher once more for assistance, in a series of over sixty letters (more than he ever wrote to any other person in a comparable period of time) in which he bares his innermost feelings and repeatedly asks her for help in coping with the minutiae of his daily life. Frau Streicher became, in the Sterbas' phrase, his "motherly protectress and counselor,"[48] to whom he turned for advice about all his domestic matters—cooking, laundry, the hiring and conduct of servants, the care and purchase of household articles, changes of lodging, and the education and upbringing of nephew Karl. To Frau Streicher Beethoven poured out his deep fears that his servants were in league with Johanna, or were deceiving him, or stealing from him. In the course of the correspondence, which began in good humor and with friendly reserve, Beethoven increasingly drifted into expressions of deep dependency and feelings of helplessness:

The day before yesterday my splendid *servants* took three hours, from seven until ten in the evening, to get a fire going in the stove. The bitter cold, particularly in this house, gave me a bad chill; and almost the whole day yesterday I could scarcely move a limb. Coughing and the most terrible headaches I have ever had plagued me the whole day. As early as six o'clock in the evening I had to go to bed, where I still am. But I am feeling better. . . . I am in so many respects your debtor that when I think of it I am frequently overcome by a feeling of shame.[49]

The housekeeper's departure terrified me so that I was already awake at three o'clock—My lonely condition demands the assistance of the police—

If by chance you are returning home today, do come to me quickly. You will find me at home after five o'clock. What a dreadful existence? ! [50]

Frau Streicher's involvement in Beethoven's domestic affairs and their constant visits to each other inevitably gave rise to suspicions—not, however, on the part of her husband—that they were lovers. At some point in late 1817 they decided that it would be best if he did not see her at her home: "I am glad that you *yourself* realize that it is impossible for me ever to set foot in your house again—" [51] Beethoven wished to keep this a secret from his servants: "It would be well *for you, as it certainly would be for me, not to let my two servants notice that unfortunately I can no longer have the pleasure of going to see you.* For, if this arrangement were not observed, there might be *very disastrous consequences* for me, because it might seem as if in this respect you wished to detach yourself altogether." [52] Beethoven's servants also had their suspicions: "They always have their revenge on me whenever they deliver our letters or notice that something is going on between you and me—" [53] By late January Beethoven was again visiting Frau Streicher at her home. The most intense period of their relationship had now passed, however, and the correspondence itself tapered off, coming to an end in the late spring or early summer of 1818. In one of his last letters, Beethoven tried to revive the feeling of ease which her ministrations had brought him: "Please send us soon a comforting letter about the arts of cooking, laundering, and sewing." [54] He had received from her the mothering and comfort which he needed, and had been able through her to freely regress to the status of a son at the very time that he was affirming his fitness to be a father.

Just as he needed this motherly protectress, so Beethoven needed to feel the warmth of real family experiences. During the two years that Karl was at the Giannatasio Institute, Beethoven made himself at home with the Giannatasios and their two grown daughters, the elder of whom, Fanny, kept a touching diary filled with keen observations.[55] She recalled that Beethoven "seemed to want to consecrate body and soul" to Karl, and that in April 1817 he took lodgings in the neighborhood of the Institute so that he could be closer to him. (Frau Streicher also lived nearby.) She remembered, too, how Johanna would disguise herself as a man and come to the school playground so that she could see her son during the gymnastic exercises. She described Beethoven's tears when Karl ran away to his mother and she wrote down his pathetic outcry: "He is ashamed of me!" Fanny, who had recently had a tragic love affair, fell in love with Beethoven, but in accordance with his usual pattern of being attracted to unavailable women, Beethoven claimed to prefer the younger sister, Anna, who was engaged to another. "She does not want me," he would lament, "she has her lover!" He called Fanny "Madam Abbess," which, she wrote, "pleased me not at all," and he occasionally indulged in "small sarcasms" which hurt her deeply. ("He seemed sometimes so hostile and cold," she wrote.) During some months he was an almost nightly visitor, and a morose one. "Unhappily, interesting evenings were rare. . . . Throughout the evening, he would remain seated at the round table near us, plunged, it seemed, in his thoughts, sometimes throwing us a smiling word, spitting incessantly into his handkerchief and then looking into the handkerchief as though expecting to find blood there." (This might have been worse: others reported that Beethoven "sometimes spat into his hand." [56]) He was not always so unpleasant: one day he brought violets and said to the delighted Fanny: "I bring you spring!" He accompanied the young women at the piano and gave them concert tickets and newly published editions of his *Lieder*. He became friendly with Anna's suitor, Leopold Schmerling, who was also hard of hearing, and jestingly advised him of what to expect: "Schmerling, take it easy, things go from bad to worse!" He composed a "Wedding Song," WoO 105, for Anna upon her marriage in 1819. He spoke freely to them of his family matters, and expressed to them his negative views on marriage and his newfound notions of free love. That he also told them idealized stories about his youth, his parents, and his revered grandfather certainly suggests that he regarded them as a surrogate family during these trying years, and that the events concerning the guardianship had revived his yearning for the past without bringing the actualities of his childhood into consciousness.

Beethoven's suspicions concerning the adequacy of Giannatasio's care for and education of Karl finally overcame his better judgment, and on January 24, 1818, he withdrew Karl from the Institute and brought him home to a household that included a new housekeeper, a new housemaid, and a private tutor. Beethoven had fulfilled a long-held desire. As early as May 1816 he had written to Ferdinand Ries: "I shall have to start a proper household, where I can have him to live with me," adding later in the same letter, "Unfortunately I have no wife. . . ."; [57] and again: "What is a boarding school compared with the immediate sympathetic care of a father for his child?" [58] In a diary entry of 1817 Beethoven expressed his preference that Karl be raised within the bosom of a warm family: "A thousand beautiful moments vanish when children are in wooden institutions, whereas, at home with good parents, they could be receiving impressions full of deep feeling, which endure into the most extreme old age." [59] Characteristically, Beethoven was simultaneously hoping at this time to send the boy to a foreign city.

Until early 1818 neither Beethoven nor Johanna had been in possession of Karl, who remained on neutral ground at the Giannatasio Institute. This arrangement had been tolerable to Johanna, who, despite her difficulties in obtaining access to her son, apparently felt that he was being properly educated and cared for. And it had neutralized the most severe effects of Beethoven's influence over his nephew. When Beethoven took Karl into his own disordered home, however, thereby transforming part of the "marriage" into reality, the armed truce was shattered: Johanna now resumed her efforts to contest the guardianship. It had, indeed, been a strange form of mock marriage, and so fantastic and unstable a set of relationships could hardly endure for very long. Karl was torn between obedience toward his uncle and the desire to return to his mother; Johanna and Beethoven oscillated between mutual rejection and cooperation. Inexorably the arrangement collapsed, inaugurating a period of explosive conflict.

In September Johanna petitioned the Landrecht to remove from Beethoven the authority to direct Karl's future education. Although her petition was denied on September 18, she persisted, applying to the court for permission to place Karl in a state school, the Royal Imperial Konvikt. This too was rejected, for the Landrecht consistently—partly through the intervention of Beethoven's influential friends—upheld the composer's viewpoint, despite the injustice of his actions. Karl was placed in a public school in November, but on December 3 he ran away to his mother and had to be removed from her home by the police and taken back to the Giannatasio Institute. Fortified by her son's love, appalled by new evidence of Beethoven's mistreatment of the child, and fearful that he was about to send Karl out of the country, Johanna made yet another application to the court, returnable on December 11. Her case was ably argued by Jacob Hotschevar, a distant relative, who presented evidence that she had been barred from access to her son, that the boy's moral, educational, and physical condition left much to be desired, and that Beethoven's eccentricity and deafness were sufficiently marked that he should be removed from the guardianship. Moreover, Hotschevar now introduced a draft letter from Caspar Carl which confirmed that he had not wanted his brother to be the sole guardian and that his will had been entered into under compulsion, and in exchange for the 1,500-florin loan of 1813:

> *Never* would I have drawn up an instrument of this kind if my long illness had not caused me great expenses; it is only in consideration of these that I could, *under compulsion*, sign this instrument; but at the time I was determined to demand the return of same at an opportune moment or to invalidate it by another instrument, for my brother is too much a composer and hence can *never*, according to my idea, and with my consent, become my son's guardian.[60]

Nephew Karl was called as a witness; he testified that he had resisted his mother's attempt to restore him to Beethoven "because he feared maltreatment," and he told the court that Beethoven had "threatened to throttle him" upon his return.[61] Beethoven himself then took the stand. An outcome favorable to him was a foregone conclusion, but Beethoven, probably ridden with guilt and reeling from the impact and the implications of Karl's flight to his mother, proved to be his own worst witness. The court asked him about his plans for Karl's education, and he responded: "After half a year he would send him to the Mölker Konvikt, which he had heard highly commended, or if he were but of noble birth, give him to the Theresianum," a school for sons of the aristocracy. The court, hearing the negative reference to Karl's nobility, pursued the question: "Were he and his brother of the nobility, and did he have documents to prove it?" Beethoven admitted that he had no proof, though he tried to imply that he was, indeed noble: "'Van' was a Dutch predicate which was not exclusively applied to the nobility; he had neither a diploma nor any other proof of his nobility." Johanna was then questioned: "Was her husband of noble birth?" "So the brothers had said," she responded; "the documentary proof of nobility was said to be in the possession of the oldest brother, the composer. At the legal hearing on the death of her husband, proofs of nobility had been demanded; she herself had no document bearing on the subject."

On learning of Beethoven's deception in the matter of his nobility, the Landrecht dismissed the case from its jurisdiction in a declaration of December 18: "It . . . appears from the statement of Ludwig van Beethoven, as the accompanying copy of the court minutes of December 11 of this year shows, that he is unable to prove nobility; hence the matter of guardianship is transferred to the Magistrat," [62] that being the civil court which had jurisdiction over cases involving common citizens. If we can credit Schindler—and the Conversation Books appear to support him in this instance—this had a devastating effect on the composer. Schindler wrote that it "drove Beethoven beside himself; for he considered it the grossest insult that he had ever received and . . . an unjustifiable depreciation and humiliation of the artist—an impression too deep to be ever erased from his mind." He was so "deeply mortified" that he "would have quitted the country." [63]

With Beethoven's confession the nobility pretense was shattered, but the Family Romance on which it was based continued its tenacious hold on the composer. It was precisely during the next years that Beethoven refused to permit any action to refute the proliferating reports of his royal ancestry. For Beethoven had not been "pretending" to nobility: he felt that he was, indeed, of noble origin but was unable to demonstrate it because of the mysterious (as he thought) circumstances of his birth. His adoption of Karl had been the adoption of a commoner by a noble: "I have raised my nephew into a higher category," he wrote in 1819; [64] and Schindler observed that Beethoven's intent was to bring Karl up "like the child of a nobleman. . . ." [65] In some unfathomable way, Beethoven's seizure of his nephew was his delusory way of repairing his own presumed illegitimacy, of fulfilling the prophecy of the Family Romance, of becoming the noble father of a commoner's child. Unable to locate the noble father of his daydreams, he had created him in his own person.

The Magistrat did not look favorably upon Beethoven's position in the litigation. Karl was returned to his mother for several weeks early in 1819, and a hearing was held on January 11 which evidently went badly for the composer, for it inspired an excited letter to the Magistrat on February 1, in which Beethoven attacked Johanna and defended his own qualifications as guardian. Johanna, he wrote, induced Karl "to dissimulate . . . , to bribe my servants, *to tell lies* . ., even *gives him money* in order to arouse lusts and desires which are harmful to him. . . . [He] has spent several years under her care and been completely *perverted* and *even* made to help her *deceive* his own father. . . ." Affirming his own fitness, he wrote, unabashedly: "I confess that I myself feel that I am better fitted than anyone else to inspire my nephew *by my own example* with a desire for *virtue and zealous activity*." [66] Unmoved by this appeal, the Magistrat compelled Beethoven to surrender the guardianship, and on March 26 Councillor Matthias von Tuscher replaced him upon the composer's own recommendation. Through Tuscher, Beethoven attempted to persuade the Magistrat to send Karl out of the country to Landshut University in Bavaria; Bishop Sailer, who headed the University, had agreed to accept the boy after a heartfelt letter of February 22, 1819, from Antonie Brentano. The Magistrat rejected the plan, however, and Karl, who had temporarily been placed under the tutorship of a certain Johann Kudlich during the spring, was entered in late June at Joseph Blöchlinger's school for boys, where he remained for more than four years.

"I have now taken the necessary steps for the most careful higher education of my ward and nephew," wrote Beethoven to the Magistrat, asking that instructions be forwarded to Blöchlinger empowering him "to repel with due severity the mother's untimely and disturbing interruptions." [67] Beethoven was now obsessed with the desire to prevent meetings between mother and son: he wrote to Bernard, "It is desirable to make Karl realize that he is no longer to see such a vicious mother, who by means of God knows what Circean spells or curses or vows bewitches him and turns him against me." [68] He continued to hope that Karl could be sent abroad, a move which would have minimized Johanna's influence and at the same time would have had the beneficial effect of relieving Beethoven's own anxieties at his proximity to his nephew, against whom he had turned during this period, furiously referring to him as unloving, ungrateful, and callous. "He is an utter scamp and is most fit for the company of his own mother and my *pseudo*-brother," he wrote.[69] And again: "He is a monster"; "My love for him is gone. *He needed my love.* I do not need his." Yet, his feelings toward Karl were undergoing a series of ambivalent reversals, for he quickly added: "You understand, of course, that this is not what I *really* think (I still love him as I used to, but without weakness or undue partiality, nay more, I may say in truth that I often weep for him)." [70]

Johanna and Nikolaus Johann now entered into an alliance to try to protect Karl from Beethoven's patently pathological behavior, and in the summer Johanna proposed Karl's "other" uncle to the Magistrat as a fit guardian. Beethoven's rage was now aroused against every possible object—Johanna, Karl, his brother, the Magistrat (which he accused of corruption), Councillor Tuscher, and even his loyal friend, the journalist Karl Bernard, to whom he now wrote, "I must say that I have a suspicion that to me you are just as much an enemy as a bit of a friend— . . . Oh, may the whole miserable rabble of humanity be cursed and damned—" [71]

His worst fears were realized on September 17, when the Magistrat rendered its decision, accepting Tuscher's resignation and awarding the guardianship to Johanna van Beethoven, with Leopold Nussböck, a municipal official, as co-guardian. Beethoven momentarily considered kidnapping Karl and taking him to Weissenbach in Salzburg; under the steadying influence of his attorney, Johann Baptist Bach, he instead addressed a carefully considered petition to the Magistrat on October 30, asking that he be reinstated as guardian and discreetly suggesting for the first time that he would not be opposed to a joint guardianship with his sister-in-law: "[Karl's] whole future depends upon this education, which cannot be left to a woman or to his mother alone," he wrote.[72] But the Magistrat was in no mood for compromise; on November 4 and December 20 it twice rejected Beethoven's protest, whereupon, on January 7, 1820, Beethoven petitioned the Imperial and Royal Court of Appeal of Lower Austria for a reversal of the lower court decision. Here again he took a conciliatory position, suggesting a three-way guardianship on the part of himself, his friend Karl Peters, and Johanna: "Since my sole object is the welfare of the boy, I am not opposed to some kind of co-guardianship being granted to his mother. . . . But henceforth to entrust the guardianship to her alone, without appointing an efficient guardian to assist her, such a step would assuredly be tantamount to bringing about the ruin of the boy." [73]

Despite the stream of assaults by Beethoven upon Johanna's character and morality, which lasted until the final appeal in 1820, it was at this time that the extraordinary rumor began to circulate that Beethoven was in love with his sister-in-law. This rumor is central to the meaning of their relationship, because it was initiated by Johanna herself, and therefore presumably constituted her own understanding and explanation of Beethoven's attitude toward her. In November 1819, Bernard wrote in a Conversation Book: "I saw too that the Magistrat believes everything that it hears, for example that she said that you were in love with her." [74] Shortly thereafter, Beethoven himself twice noted the story—in a letter to Bernard and in his draft memorandum to the Court of Appeal, where he wrote that Herr Piuk "retailed the *well-worn complaints of Fr. B about me*, even adding '*that I was supposed to be in love with her, etc.*' and more rubbish of that kind." [75] If anything, these reports may have fortified Beethoven in what was to be his most extreme rejection of Johanna.

On January 10, the Appellate Court requested a comprehensive report from the Magistrat. This was forthcoming on February 5. The Magistrat wrote, in part:

a. that the appellant, because of his physical defect and because of the enmity which, as the codicil to the will [shows], he entertains toward the mother of the ward, is held unfit to undertake the guardianship.

b. that the guardianship by law belongs to the natural mother.

c. that her having committed an embezzlement of which she was guilty against her husband in the year 1811 and for which she was punished by a police house arrest of one month, is now no longer an impediment. . . . [76]

In a supplementary report the Magistrat was even more forceful, pointing out that the only evidence adduced by Beethoven in support of depriving Johanna of Karl was her misdemeanor of 1811, and adding:

everything else which appears in appellant's statement . . . is unproven gossip to which the R. I. Landrecht could give no consideration, but which is eloquent testimony to how passionately and hostilely appellant has long since treated the mother and still treats her, how easily he falls to reopening her healed wounds, now when, after undergoing punishment, she is reinstated in her previous rights, reproaching her with a misdemeanor which she expiated many years ago, a misdemeanor which her wronged husband himself forgave her, inasmuch as he not only petitioned for leniency in the punishment meted out to her but also, in his testamentary dispositions, recognized her as fit and worthy to act as guardian of his son. . . .

In a reflection of the passions which this case aroused, the Magistrat gratuitously overstepped the bounds of judicial restraint and stated that Beethoven's sole aim was "to mortify the mother and tear the heart from her bosom." [77]

Beethoven now set about composing a draft memorandum marshaling all of the facts in the case from his point of view. By February 18 he had completed a forty-eight-page document and forwarded it to Bernard to use as "raw material" [78] in preparing a statement of Beethoven's position. In this chaotic memorandum,[79] Beethoven agitatedly listed Johanna's transgressions—which reduced themselves to the 1811 embezzlement of household funds, having allegedly had "intimate relations with a lover" after Caspar Carl's death, having shown negligence in caring for her son, and, especially, having turned Karl against Beethoven while scheming to take him for herself. "She did her best by means of the most horrible intrigues, plots, and defamatory statements to disparage me, his bene-factor, mainstay, and support, in short, his father in the true sense of the word." (That Beethoven was not Karl's father "in the true sense of the word" seems as yet not to have occurred to him.) At the same time, he sanctimoniously set forth his own qualifications, although he confessed to occasional errors or weaknesses in his treatment of Karl—including a violent scene in which he had caused the boy some injury in the genital region: "And if, *being human, I have erred now and then or if my poor hearing must be taken into account, yet surely* a child is not taken away *from his father for those two reasons.*" Brief sections of the memorandum are given over to discussions of the state of Karl's education, the cost of maintaining him, and other financial matters. A supplement contains a lurid attack on the moral character of Father Frölich, who had given evidence in support of Johanna during the earlier proceedings. The cen-tral thrust of the memorandum is, however, Beethoven's obsessive rejec-tion of Johanna, whom he has now come to regard as the embodiment of feminine evil and as his persecutor. He saw himself as beset by schemes, intrigues, and plots, woven by Johanna not out of love for her son, but out of a desire for revenge. He wrote: "I too am a man, harried on all sides like a wild beast, misunderstood, often treated in the basest way by this vulgar authority; with so many cares, with the constant battle against this monster of a mother, who always attempted to stifle any good brought forth. . . ." [80]

There is no sign that the memorandum was formally presented to the Court of Appeal. But that, apparently, was not its real purpose. On March 6, Beethoven wrote to Karl Winter, one of the appellate judges, informing him that he would soon receive from Beethoven "a memorandum consisting of information about Frau van Beethoven, about the Magistrat, about my nephew, about myself, and so forth," and grandiosely suggesting that if he were to be denied the guardianship, "such a contingency would certainly provoke the disapproval of our civilized world." [81] In a clear effort to influence the court, Beethoven sent the memorandum to Winter by a messenger who was in the employ of Archduke Rudolph—crude notice to the judge that a member of the imperial family took an active interest in an outcome favorable to Beethoven. Indeed, as soon as he decided to appeal, Beethoven secured a testimonial from Archduke Rudolph for presentation to the Court, and he almost certainly asked him to obtain Archduke Ludwig's intercession as well. Johanna was virtually defenseless against political influence of such power. Judge Winter, fearful of giving the appearance that he had been bribed or unduly influenced, told Rudolph's messenger that he would give him no verbal or written response. [82] Meanwhile, a copy of the memorandum was also forwarded to another of the appellate judges, Joseph von Schmerling (the brother of Anna Giannatasio del Rio's husband), whom Beethoven was attempting to influence through Bernard and Matthias von Tuscher. [83] Schmerling, a member of the Landrecht, had assisted Beethoven in 1816 in limiting Johanna's access to Karl at the Giannatasio Institute. [84] Beethoven's attorney, Bach, advised him to personally visit both Schmerling and Winter, and a few days before the appellate decision Beethoven brought Karl to see one of them, to demonstrate the boy's desire to remain with his uncle.

A hearing before the Magistrat took place on March 29, at the suggestion of the Appellate Court. The magistrates, aware that political influence had been brought to bear ("Schmerling helped a great deal," wrote Bernard in a Conversation Book [85]), were propitiatory, but refused to reverse themselves. Beethoven, now persuaded that a favorable decision from the Court of Appeal was assured, abandoned his earlier conciliatory position and again insisted on the total exclusion of Johanna from the guardianship. On April 8, the Court of Appeal ruled for Beethoven and appointed him and Peters as joint guardians. Johanna appealed the decision to the emperor, but to no avail. On July 24 the Magistrat notified the parties that the case was closed.

Griefstricken and weary from her long struggle, eager to build a new life and, perhaps, to replace her stolen child, Johanna became pregnant in the spring of 1820 by finance councillor Johann Hofbauer, a "noted, very well-to-do" [86] person, who later freely acknowledged his responsibility. In June, Blöchlinger wrote in the Conversation Book: "It seems to me recently that Frau Beethoven might be in the family way." [87] Perhaps in response to this traumatic news, Karl, who had during the preceding period assured his uncle that he had no use for his mother ("She promised me so many things that I could not resist her; I am sorry that I was so weak at the time and beg your forgiveness" [88]) again ran away to her. He was quickly returned to Beethoven. Later in the year, Johanna gave her newborn daughter the name Ludovica, the female form of Ludwig—an uncanny testimony to the strength of the bond between the antagonists in this drama, the first act of which had now come to an end.

It is usually taken for granted that Beethoven's creativity was brought almost to a full stop by his total absorption in these events. But the relationship between the guardianship struggle and the graph of Beethoven's productivity is a more complicated one and will not yield to simple assertions of cause and effect. During 1816 and 1817, when his conflicts with Karl and Johanna were relatively minimal, his productivity was extremely low; indeed, following the completion of *An die ferne Geliebte*, op. 98, in April 1816, and the Piano Sonata, op. 101, in November, Beethoven wrote nothing of substance for almost a year. Toward the end of 1817 he began work on the *Hammerklavier* Sonata, op. 106; he completed its first two movements by April 1818. The years 1817–18 also saw the emergence of fragmentary ideas for the Ninth Symphony. But the raging litigation, which lasted from the summer of 1818 until early 1820, seems not to have had an adverse effect on Beethoven's productivity; on the contrary, in this period he completed the *Hammerklavier* Sonata, began to sketch the Diabelli Variations and made very substantial progress on the *Missa Solemnis*, completing the Kyrie, the Gloria, and part of the Credo before the end of 1819. Thus the formulation of Beethoven's late style, along with the completion of substantial work on several of its central masterpieces, took place in the midst of an emotional firestorm.

Nor was Beethoven's involvement in music making seriously impaired by his domestic and legal preoccupations. Although he no longer performed in public as a pianist, he continued to perform annually as a conductor, a role for which he had never been well suited. He conducted the Seventh Symphony at a concert for the Hospital of St. Mark on December 26, 1816, the Eighth Symphony at a Christmas concert for the Hospital Fund in 1817, and the Seventh once again on January 17,

1819, at a charity concert. Two other charity concerts, of March 30 and 31, 1817, featured the Seventh Symphony and *Christus am Oelberge*.

Beethoven's music no longer aroused popular enthusiasm, however. At the 1816 concert the Seventh Symphony was faintly applauded and the beloved Allegretto failed to receive its customary encore, facts which Beethoven's friends at the *Wiener Musik-Zeitung* quaintly attributed to the "dense crowding of the audience [which] hindered the free use of their hands." [89] Only one other large-scale work by Beethoven was given a public performance in Vienna during these years—the "Choral Fantasia", which was performed at a benefit concert on November 15, 1817. Beethoven complained to Karl Bursy, a visitor in 1816: "Art no longer stands so high above the ordinary, is no longer so respected, and above all is no longer valued in terms of recompense." [90]

But if public performances were not as frequent and if influential segments of the Viennese populace were no longer interested in Beethoven's music, there nevertheless remained significant numbers of connoisseurs and music lovers whose appreciation counterbalanced these losses. They gathered at musicales given at the homes of Carl Czerny, the Ertmanns, the Streichers, and elsewhere, to perform and to hear his piano and chamber music. Beethoven himself sometimes participated in these private concerts. Czerny remembered that "in the years from 1818 to 1820 I organized concerts by my pupils every Sunday in my lodgings; they played to quite a select audience, and Beethoven was usually present; he still improvised even then, and did so several times for us; everyone was deeply stirred and moved." [91] The musician Friedrich Starke recalled that during the years 1816–18 Beethoven was "seldom absent" from the weekly musicales at the Streicher house, which had a private concert hall, and that on occasion he brought along his nephew, Karl, to hear his music.[92] Furthermore, Beethoven was at this time commissioned by Johann Wolfmayer—a wealthy cloth merchant—to write a *Requiem*, and by the *Gesellschaft der Musikfreunde* (Society of the Friends of Music) to compose an oratorio on a "heroic" subject. His popularity in England, of course, continued unabated, and in 1817 he was invited by the Philharmonic Society to visit London the following winter. Beethoven accepted the offer, which called for him to compose two new symphonies for performance at several concerts for his own benefit. The planned journey never came to fruition, but the offer was the impetus leading to the first serious consideration of the Ninth Symphony and even of plans for a Tenth.

Beethoven's main biographers did not approve of his actions in the guardianship struggle, on either pragmatic or ethical grounds, nor was the eccentricity of his behavior lost upon them. Two recent commentators, Editha and Richard Sterba, have not only condemned Beethoven's actions, but have attributed them to "a breakdown of the ethical structure of his personality." [93] The facts of the matter, however, do not compel so extreme an interpretation, one which would force us to believe that the masterpieces of Beethoven's last years were composed by a cruel and unethical human being. For Beethoven's feelings of guilt at separating Karl from his mother were a constant source of concern and pain to him. As early as 1816, Fanny Giannatasio reported that he cried out: "What will people say, they will take me for a tyrant!" [94] And in his *Tagebuch* of 1817 he quoted these lines from Schiller: "This one thing I feel and deeply comprehend: life is not the greatest of blessings, but guilt is the greatest evil." [95] In early 1818, Beethoven revealed in full the agony which his obsessive actions against Johanna were causing him:

I have done my part, O Lord! It might have been possible without offending the widow, but it was not. Only Thou, Almighty God, canst see into my heart, knowest that I have sacrificed my very best for the sake of my dear Karl: bless my work, bless the widow! Why cannot I obey all the prompting of my heart and help the widow? Thou seest my inmost heart and knowest how it pains me to be obliged to compel another to suffer by my good labors for my precious Karl!!! [96]

His diary then noted the debts with which his sister-in-law was burdened, and Beethoven now addressed Johanna directly, lamenting: "Woeful fate! Why can I not help thee?" [97]

In his most private musings, then, Beethoven acknowledged the unethical nature of his actions, showing that his ability to make moral judgments had not been impaired. He yielded to impulses which his conscience rejected, but he yielded with considerable anguish, and he ultimately sought to atone for his actions. We may condemn his aggressive actions against Karl and Johanna, but we should balance this by understanding that he was in the grip of forces which he could not control, and, as we shall see, that he attempted to atone for his wrongs.

One cannot hope, amidst the multitude of inextricably blended motivational impulses behind Beethoven's behavior, to isolate any one as the single, unmediated determinant of his actions. On one level, the Sterbas are surely correct in stressing that Beethoven regarded Karl as a continuation of his brother, in that he appropriated Caspar Carl's son and became entangled with his wife. Perhaps—to extend their thesis somewhat—Beethoven sought thereby to resurrect (or to take the place of) the brother to whom he was still ambivalently connected by powerful ties no doubt dating from their very earliest days as children in Bonn. For quasi-psychotic symptoms such as those manifested by Beethoven are invariably a continuation of, and are modeled on, archaic conflicts dating from infantile and childhood experiences. On another level, Beethoven's actions can be understood as a series of violent alternations between incestuous and matricidal drives, these having their ultimate source in his attitude toward his own mother, an attitude in which love and desire apparently warred with feelings of neglect and even abandonment. One senses in reading Beethoven's distraught listings of Johanna's alleged "crimes" (which objectively amount to so little) that he was unconsciously accusing her of another set of offenses that he was unable to formulate, for they stemmed from what the Sterbas rightly term "disillusionments in the first exemplary love-object." [98] What were those offenses? It is difficult to say, but they may have included his mother's sexuality itself, or perhaps her (presumed) preference for another child (Caspar Carl? Ludwig Maria?), or her denigration of Beethoven's father, or her negligence in caring for her oldest son, or her failure to protect him from Johann's harsh pedagogy, or even her insistence that he conform to an ethical standard of such rigor that it prevented him from leading a fulfilled, normal existence.

Johann van Beethoven is not absent in the nephew struggle: Beethoven may well have been attempting in his fashion to take upon himself the role of the righteous, "good" father (modeled, perhaps, on his image of his grandfather), which his own father had not been able to fulfill. Paradoxically, his crude behavior toward Karl reveals his unwitting emulation of his father's pattern: he was simultaneously repairing and repeating his father's ill-treatment of himself. But on the simplest level, Beethoven had here finally put himself in the place of the father: he had gotten himself a son. His rage against Johanna arose, perhaps, from the fact that her motherhood irrefutably contradicted his claim of fatherhood.[99]

There is abundant evidence that Beethoven's strivings were of a paternal nature. The death of his brother presented Beethoven, perpetually thwarted in his plans for marriage, with an opportunity to become the head of a family. So deep was his desire to accomplish this, so great his need to find a mode of substitute creativity at this difficult moment of his musical evolution, that his perception of reality blurred and he (perhaps unconsciously) persuaded himself that he had become a father in fact. We may recall that Beethoven had once before assumed the role of head of the family, following the deaths of his mother and eighteen-month-old sister in 1787 and the descent of his father into terminal alcoholism. It is not impossible that Beethoven's appropriation of his nephew had its root in a compulsion to repeat the experiences of the last, tragic years in Bonn, when he had cared for his helpless father and young brothers; perhaps Beethoven was attempting now to make reparation for his abandonment of his family in late 1792, and even to assuage his guilt at the death of his father, which followed so poignantly upon his departure for Vienna.

There are many ghosts at the party; indeed, all of the primal figures of Beethoven's life appear to have gathered here in reunion. In his frenzied, almost hallucinatory state, the leading characters in this domestic tragedy successively and even simultaneously took on the images of the members of Beethoven's original family. His sister-in-law was "split" into fragments of the mother image, alternately perceived as the neglectful, poisoning wife and as the valiant defender of her offspring, as prostitute and as unattainable love object. Sometimes, even, he seems to have identified her with his father—as an embezzler and pursuer of the pleasure principle, unfit to rear a child; and sometimes with an "ideal" father or grandfather—the omnipotent and wrathful superego who aroused his terror and awe to such an extent that he variously referred to her as Minerva, as Circe, as Medea, and, repeatedly, as the "Queen of Night" of Mozart's *Magic Flute*. (In one letter of 1819, following the exposure of his own nobility pretense, Beethoven even granted her the aristocratic honorific "von," twice writing her name as "Frau *von* Beethoven." [100]) Beethoven's perception of his nephew was equally fluid: Karl was Beethoven himself, rescued from his false and unworthy parents by the good prince, royal father, and nourishing mother; he was Beethoven's child, narcissistically (divinely) conceived; he embodied the wish which Karl Abraham described, "to have begotten oneself, that is to say, to be one's own father"; [101] he was a passive surrogate for and continuation of Caspar Carl, whose rebirth was reenacted in Beethoven's "rescue" of his son; he was at once Beethoven's infantilistic father and his partly orphaned younger brothers with whose care the adolescent Beethoven had been charged in 1787; and—even more speculatively—he may also have been a revenant of the first-born Ludwig Maria, subject, therefore, to alternations of Beethoven's fratricidal and loving impulses as well as to a high degree of overvaluation.

There is a dizzying series of splittings and substitutions here, in which Caspar Carl, Karl, and Beethoven are alternately perceived in the roles of father, brother, and son. As for Beethoven himself, he had quite simply united father, mother, brother, and son in a single body—his own. Beethoven had returned to the houses on the Bonngasse, the Wenzelgasse, the Dreieckplatz, and the Rheingasse, there to wrestle with ancient events and relationships in a dreamlike attempt to rewrite the history of his childhood, to create an ideal family in accordance with the strange logic of his desires.

In the course of the formation and dissolution of this fantasy family, Ludwig van Beethoven learned something of the nature of parenthood and touched regions of experience from which he had hitherto been excluded. The appropriation of his nephew represented the distorted form through which Beethoven shattered the frozen patterns of a bachelor existence and experienced the passions and tragedies of deep human relations. The abstract, spiritualized aspects of conjugal love had been celebrated in *Fidelio*; the *"ferne Geliebte"* had been the ideal beloved precisely because of her unattainability; now Beethoven had penetrated to the tragic substratum which underlies relationships between real human beings.

To what extent these experiences were necessary in shaping the special qualities of Beethoven's last works is difficult to tell. Certainly he emerged from this ordeal a changed person. Beethoven's psychological regression in the years from 1815 to 1820 involved the dissolution of his weakened and malfunctioning defenses, the smashing of his nobility pretense, and the partial emergence of the Family Romance and its attendant fantasies of illegitimacy so that they could be examined in the light of reason. Karl and Johanna had served as catalysts to bring Beethoven's deepest conflicts and desires to the surface, perhaps thereby laying the groundwork for a breakthrough of his creativity into hitherto unimagined territories.

The road to Beethoven's last works was a dangerous one, fraught with anxieties and touching realms of traumatic significance sufficient to undermine—and almost overwhelm—the composer's personality. In the course of this titanic struggle, Beethoven approached the borderline of an irreversible pathology. He turned back both by tapping the resources of his ego and through the assistance—however unwitting—of Johanna van Beethoven, who held up to him the mirror of reality and insisted that his actions be measured against the standards of law and morality. Ultimately it was Johanna's heroic and passionate struggle for her son and for the preservation of her motherhood which prevented Beethoven from losing contact with the inner core of his own humanity.

Beethoven. Chalk drawing by August
von Klöber (1818).

19
Portrait of an Aging Composer

That Beethoven was a man of considerable eccentricity had been known
to his contemporaries since Bonn days. After his appropriation of nephew
Karl, however, the belief that he was something more than eccentric became common currency in Vienna. In 1816, for example, Charlotte Brunsvik wrote: "I learned yesterday that Beethoven had become crazy." [1]
The German composer Zelter wrote to Goethe in 1819: "Some say he is
a lunatic." [2] During these years, Beethoven railed openly against the
nobility, the courts, and the emperor himself, seemingly oblivious of the
possible consequences in Metternich's police state. "He defies everything
and is dissatisfied with everything and blasphemes against Austria and
especially against Vienna," reported Karl Bursy;[3] and young Peter Joseph
Simrock heard Beethoven, still smarting from the devaluation of the
Austrian currency, say of Kaiser Franz, "Such a rascal ought to be
hanged." [4] The police did not disturb Beethoven, in part because he was
Beethoven and because he had several friends in imperial circles, but also
because he was thought to be a little touched. When Rossini in 1822
implored the Austrian court aristocracy to mitigate Beethoven's financial

distress, the universal reply was that there was no point in offering aid; they considered Beethoven not merely deaf, but a misanthrope, a recluse, and an eccentric.

Beethoven was well aware of this reputation. In 1820 he warned his admirer Dr. W. C. Müller "not to be misled by the Viennese, who regard [me] as crazy." And he told Müller "If a sincere, independent opinion escapes me, as it often does, they think me mad." [5]

Signs of neurotic eccentricity—sudden rages, uncontrolled emotional states, an increasing obsession with money, feelings of persecution, ungrounded suspicions—persisted until Beethoven's death, reinforcing Vienna's belief that its greatest composer was a sublime madman. Grillparzer, who became closely acquainted with Beethoven in 1823 during a fruitless collaboration on an opera, told Thayer that Beethoven was "half crazy," and on another occasion reported that when Beethoven was irritated "he became like a wild animal." [6] Beethoven's manner and appearance during his later years did nothing to retard the spread of these impressions. Schindler wrote: "His head, which was unusually large, was covered with long, bushy gray hair, which, being always in a state of disorder, gave a certain wildness to his appearance. This wildness was not a little heightened when he suffered his beard to grow to a great length, as he frequently did." [7] The story of his arrest by the Wiener Neustadt police in 1821 or 1822 on the grounds that he had been peering into windows and looked like a tramp was surely widely circulated. In the taverns and restaurants he would dicker with waiters about the price of each roll, or would ask for his bill without having eaten. On the street, his broad gestures, loud voice, and ringing laugh made Karl ashamed to walk with him, and caused passersby to take him for a madman. Street urchins mocked the stumpy and muscular figure, with his low top hat of uncertain shape, who walked Vienna's streets dressed in a long, dark-colored overcoat which reached nearly to his ankles, carrying a double lorgnette or a monocle and pausing repeatedly to make hieroglyphic entries in his notebook as he hummed and howled in an off-key voice.

Beethoven's health also began to deteriorate after around 1815. By 1820–21 the first symptoms of jaundice, an ominous sign of liver disease, made their appearance. Beethoven ultimately developed cirrhosis of the liver, which was no doubt accelerated by a substantial intake of alcoholic beverages. Thayer, scrupulously following every lead, extracted the cost of Beethoven's wine purchases from his daily housekeeping records, and found that his consumption of wine was far from moderate. [8] But there is no reason to conclude from this that Beethoven had now begun to follow in his father's footsteps. "He drank a great deal of wine at table," said Holz to Jahn, "but could stand a great deal, and in merry company he sometimes became tipsy." [9] But he rarely exceeded his one bottle of wine per meal, and when he and Holz once tried to drink Sir George Smart under the table ("We will try how much the Englishman can drink," Smart overheard him say to Holz), it was Beethoven who had the worst of the trial.[10]

It is a measure of Beethoven's character that those who knew him during this diffcult period withheld neither their love nor their sympathy from him. The music critic J. F. Rochlitz, who visited Vienna in 1822, wrote that Beethoven's "talk and his actions all formed a chain of eccentricities, in part most peculiar. Yet they all radiated a truly childlike amiability, carelessness, and confidence in everyone who approached him."[11] The journalist, Friedrich Wähner, also spoke of Beethoven's "childlike naivete" and likened him to "an amiable boy."[12] Grillparzer, who was no sentimentalist, told of "the sad condition of the master during the latter years of his life, which prevented him from always distinguishing clearly between what had actually happened and what had been merely imagined"; but this recognition did not lessen his compassion: "And yet," he wrote on another occasion, "for all his odd ways, which . . . often bordered on being offensive, there was something so inexpressibly touching and noble in him that one could not but esteem him and feel drawn to him."[13] Many who had been warned of Beethoven's peculiarities feared to visit him, but met instead with a warm and friendly reception, and even received a fond embrace upon their departure.

Beethoven had gradually formed a new circle of friends. These men were for the most part devoted but faintly sycophantic, always ready to serve his needs, whether these were for companionship, for advice, for small services, or for endless small talk. His friends of this sort were quite numerous, and only the leading ones can be mentioned here. They fall into several groups. The first was centered in the Viennese music publishing world, and included such men as Antonio Diabelli, Sigmund Anton Steiner, and Tobias Haslinger. Beethoven regularly visited Steiner's music shop in the narrow Paternoster–Gassel at the north-east end of the Graben, where many musicians, writers, and admirers—including Schuppanzigh, Czerny, Holz, Böhm, Linke, and Mayseder—gathered to speak with him or, like Franz Schubert, worship him from a distance. Beethoven's association with Steiner's firm, which began in 1813 and lasted a full decade, was, despite several business quarrels for which Beethoven bore the entire blame, the most amiable and enjoyable of his associations with publishers. He enlisted its members in his private army, dubbing himself the Generalissimo, Steiner the Lieutenant General, Haslinger the Little Adjutant, and Diabelli the Provost Marshal. Beethoven was fondest of young Haslinger—an associate of Steiner's who ultimately became sole owner of the firm—and engaged in a merry correspondence with him during his last decade; occasional strains in their relationship were readily dissolved in jest.

Another group of friends loosely formed what we may term Beethoven's Conversation Book circle. These gathered with him at favorite taverns and restaurants and discussed everything under the sun—music, politics, gossip, the news of the day, Beethoven's family affairs and career decisions—in the rambling, free-associational fashion one would expect in such situations. Rochlitz—a keen observer—left a vivid description of Beethoven holding court with his entourage at an inn:

> I found a seat from which I could see him and, since he spoke loud enough, also could hear nearly all that he said. It could not actually be called a conversation, for he spoke in monologue, usually at some length, and more as though by hapchance and at random. Those about him contributed little, merely laughing or nodding their approval. He philosophized, or one might even say politicized, after his own fashion. He spoke of England and the English, and of how both were associated in his thoughts with a splendor incomparable—which, in part, sounded tolerably fantastic. Then he told all sorts of stories of the French, from the days of the second occupation of Vienna. For them he had no kind words. His remarks all were made with the greatest unconcern and without the least reserve, and whatever he said was spiced with highly original, naive judgments or comical fancies. He impressed me as being a man with a rich, aggressive intellect, an unlimited, never resting imagination.[14]

The members of this retinue included a number of Vienna's leading journalists and editors, such as Karl Bernard, editor of the *Wiener Zeitung*, Friedrich August Kanne, editor of the *Wiener Allgemeine musikalische Zeitung* from 1820 to 1824 (succeeding Beethoven's close friend Ignaz von Seyfried in that post), Johann Schickh, editor of the *Wiener Zeitschrift für Kunst, Literatur, Theater und Mode*, and Friedrich Wähner, who edited *Janus* from 1818 until it was suspended in June 1819. Kanne, a prolific (but unsuccessful) composer as well as a theologian, physician, and poet, was the most interesting—and most eccentric—of this group. He counseled Beethoven on literary and aesthetic matters and evidently, as Kirkendale argues, guided him through the abstruse literature on Catholic liturgy and ecclesiastical music during the composition of the *Missa Solemnis*. Wähner, who originally had been a Protestant preacher, was evidently the most radical (or least discreet) of this group, for he was expelled from Vienna by the police in the mid-1820s.

Other members of the circle were, at various times, Karl Peters, tutor of the younger Lobkowitz children; Franz Oliva, who, after a long absence from Vienna between 1813 and 1818, became Beethoven's frequent associate from then until late 1820, when he took up permanent residence in Russia; Beethoven's lawyer and friend, Johann Baptist Bach, who headed the law faculty at the University of Vienna; Joseph Blöchlinger, the director of the institute attended by nephew Karl, who occasionally could be seen engaged in a game of chess with Beethoven; and Anton Schindler, a competent musician (formerly a law student), who had briefly met Beethoven in 1814 and who became, sometime after Oliva's departure in December 1820, Beethoven's factotum, amanuensis, and scapegoat for a period of several years. He detested Beethoven's relatives and was jealous of many of the composer's close associates. His attitude toward Beethoven himself was compounded of servility, worship, and hatred in more or less equal parts, all of which alternate freely in his unreliable biographical studies of the composer.

The German-speaking countries had entered what historians call the "quiet years," which Taylor describes as "the dead period when the Napoleonic storm had blown over and when the new forces which were to disrupt Germany had not established themselves." [15] Although most of Beethoven's friends had secure and even important positions in Viennese life, the Conversation Books reveal that they were disenchanted and dismayed by the regressive aspects of imperial rule, which could no longer be disguised as patriotic necessities. They felt cheated by currency devaluations, certain that they were getting less than their fair share of social and economic prerogatives. "The aristocrats are again receiving charity in Austria," the musician F. X. Gebauer wrote in a Conversation Book, "and the republican spirit smolders only faintly in the ashes."[16] Many members of Beethoven's circle—including Oliva, Blöchlinger, nephew Karl, Schindler, Bernard, and Grillparzer—often inveighed against the censorship. Grillparzer bitterly noted: "The censor has broken me down.—One must emigrate to North America in order to give his ideas free expression." [17] Holz observed: "The poets are worse off than the composers with the censor, which works for obscurantism and the introduction of stupidity." [18]

To Beethoven, whose intellectual development took place within the context of the German striving for *Gedankenfreiheit* (freedom of thought), there could be no greater evil than the suppression of ideas and of rational inquiry. Accordingly, he despised the Austrian government, with its network of police agents and its rigid censorship, and, as we have seen, he was not fearful of voicing his sentiments. He summed up his feelings about the government in a succinct phrase: "A paralytic regime." [19] At least one of his friends regarded him (perhaps in jest) as a firebrand; Peters wrote: "You are a revolutionary, a Carbonaro." [20] Nephew Karl, however, feared reprisals, and repeatedly urged caution upon Beethoven: "Silence! The walls have ears," [21] he wrote; and he warned: "The Baron is a chamberlain of the Emperor. I think that you should not speak against the regime with him." [22]

Nevertheless, these men led quiet, orderly, and productive lives, and they did not envisage or advocate any radical restructuring of society. In the main they expressed little but helpless regret and impotent resentment at what they viewed as the decline of a rationalist Europe. "It seems to me that we Europeans are going backwards, and America is raising itself in culture," wrote Bernard.[23] The group was momentarily stirred by the news of the murder in 1819 of Beethoven's former librettist, August Kotzebue, by a member of one of the groups of frustrated, highly nationalistic, anti-Semitic students, the *Burschenschaften*. The subsequent heightened repression and censorship embodied in Metternich's Karlsbad Decrees only deepened the sense of political futility.

Beethoven and his friends hoped in some vague and undefined way for a return of the Josephinian reform period, which they remembered as having been opposed to entrenched interest. (Bernard wrote: "Before the French Revolution there was great freedom of thought and political liberty here." [24]) They had no clear social program, and they appeared to pin their tenuous hopes for change on a powerful redeemer who could restore the assumed glories of an earlier time. "The whole of Europe is going to the dogs," wrote Bernard; "N[apoleon] should have been let out for ten years" [25] to set things straight. But no such redeemers were readily at hand. In the meanwhile, Beethoven and his associates grumbled and complained, and gazed with envy at the British political system, with its constitutional monarchy and reputed freedom of expression. Above all, these men cherished the past, and looked back to the pre-Napoleonic period as Vienna's Periclean or Augustan Age.

But politics and social issues were not the only—or even the central—concerns of the Conversation Book circle.[26] Kanne and Beethoven, until they ultimately tired of endless disputation, engaged in heated debates about musical keys, with the former insisting that no one key had a special psychological quality, while Beethoven urged that each had unique emotional characteristics, which were destroyed by transposition. The conversations occassionally turned bawdy: Beethoven remarked, on seeing a passing woman, "What a magnificent behind, from the side!" [27] and Franz Janschickh (or Janitschek) slyly asked Beethoven whether it was true that Jesus' male organ was exhibited as a relic in a certain woman's cloister in Bonn.[28]

Women were totally absent from the list of Beethoven's close friends during his last years. The extent of this withdrawal is thrown into high relief by a single statistic: of 293 Beethoven letters written between 1787 and 1809, 25 were to women; of 639 between 1810 and 1818, 109 were addressed to women; but of 637 letters from the last eight years and three months of Beethoven's life, only four were to women—one to Countess Erdödy in 1819, one to Maximiliane Brentano in 1821, and, in 1824, one each to Johanna van Beethoven and Henriette Sontag. His voluminous

correspondence with Nanette Streicher ended in 1818, never to be resumed. Antonie Brentano and her daughter were remembered through
dedications of the Sonata, op. 109, the Diabelli Variations, op. 120, and
the English edition of the Sonata, op. 111, but they were the only women
to receive dedications of Beethoven's works during the 1820s.[29] Beethoven no longer indulged in his love pretenses, as he had with Anna Giannatasio and, perhaps, with Marie Pachler-Koschak, during the latter's
Viennese visit in 1817. Nor did he attach himself to any surrogate families after his separation from the Giannatasios in 1819.

This is not to say that Beethoven now avoided women. He was still
capable of teasing the singers Henriette Sontag and Karoline Unger when
they visited him in 1822. From a distance, Beethoven repeatedly warned
Ries that he would shortly be arriving in London to kiss Ries's wife.
"Take care," he wrote, "You think that I am *old,* but I am a *youthful
old man."* [30] Beethoven's sexual activity continued during this period.
"Where were you going today on the street near the Haarmarkt?" a
visitor asked Beethoven, who replied frankly (and in bad Latin): "*Culpam
transferre in alium* [Blame it on the flesh]."[31] In a Conversation
Book of 1819 Beethoven noted down the name of a book, *On the Art of
Recognizing and Curing All Forms of Venereal Disease,* indicating, perhaps that this was a subject in which he took a more than theoretical
interest. (It is thought that he may once have suffered from a minor
venereal disease which responded successfully to treatment.) He was now
no longer sleeping only with prostitutes, however. "Would you like to
sleep with my wife?" asked Karl Peters in a Conversation Book of January 1820.[32] Rolland thinks this was said "for the fun of it," [33] but though it
may have had its comical aspects there is no reason to treat it as though
it did not happen. Peters was about to leave on a trip and generously
offered his wife—whom Fanny Giannatasio described as "very promiscu-
ous" [34]—to Beethoven for a night. Beethoven's reply has not been preserved, but it was apparently affirmative, for Peters wrote that he would
go and "fetch his wife." The next day, or a few days later, Janitschek
greeted Beethoven with the words: "I salute you, O Adonis!" and a few
lines later Peters chimed in: "You appear to be very adventurous today.
Therefore, why don't you protest against the sole visit to my wife." [35] On
several other occasions documented in the Conversation Books, Peters
offered a girl to Beethoven. And it appears that Janitschek's wife (from
whom he had separated the previous year) was also available. Bernard
wrote: "Peters tells us that Frau Janitschek pulled off his mantle as Poti-
phar did that of Joseph. You also should sleep with Frau von Janitschek."[36]
We need not here explore the full implications of this free exchange of
sexual favors among members of Beethoven's Conversation Book circle:
the latent homosexual aspects of this *ménage* are quite on the surface.
What it tells about Beethoven is that he had limited his sexual activity

to a succession of loveless relationships which served to discharge his sexual tension but did not touch his emotions.

At every point in his life up to 1820, Beethoven had maintained contact with and leaned upon one or more mother figures, who helped to maintain his ethical integrity and encouraged or inspired his creativity. This line began with the widows von Breuning and Koch in Bonn, and continued with Princess Lichnowsky (and perhaps Countess Thun) in the early Vienna years and with Countess Erdödy and the women of the Brunsvik–Guicciardi families up to approximately 1810. Antonie Brentano combined this role with that of the saintly, understanding, and beloved woman for a number of years after 1810, even at a distance from Vienna. The gifted Nanette Streicher served as Beethoven's archetypal self-sacrificing mother substitute in 1817 and 1818. And Johanna van Beethoven's steadfast defense of her rights as a woman and a mother had prevented him from altogether giving way to pathological tendencies. In this sense she, too, assumes an honored place in this line of nourishing women who sensed Beethoven's deepest needs and helped him to maintain his commitments, both to art and to the categorical imperative.

These commitments were now embedded in Beethoven's nature. The voices of authority and conscience had been wholly internalized. Beethoven now had no Neefe or Lichnowsky to teach and encourage him, and no surrogate mothers to nurture him. But his inner need for an external source of strength was now being met in another way. Earlier, we saw the signs of a brief religious awakening in Beethoven during the critical years in which he first felt the serious symptoms of his deafness. Those religious impulses largely disappeared from view for a decade thereafter; apparently, Beethoven's deep worship of nature along with his devotion to Reason managed to serve him as substitutes for theology. However, the long crisis which inaugurated Beethoven's late style, coinciding as it did with the close of the Age of Reason, and accompanied as it was by the undermining of Beethoven's rationality in the course of the guardianship struggle, also saw Beethoven begin a broad and complex search for a religious faith.[37] He embarked upon a spiritual journey through numerous world religions—Eastern, Egyptian, Mediterranean, and various Christian forms as well—the details of which may be read in his *Tagebuch*. For it was in his intimate diary that he communed with a wide variety of deities and freely gave expression both to his yearnings for solace and to his feelings of dependency upon a supernatural being. This is not to say that Beethoven became a religious observer in any formal sense: apart, perhaps, from his enfeebled acceptance of the last rites upon the urging of his friends and relatives, he never tempered his disdain for hierarchical religion or for the ikons of revealed faith. Nor did he abandon his stalwart adherence to Reason. Rather, he now sought to unite Enlightened precepts with a conception of an omniscient, omnipotent, ubiquitous, and benevolent father principle reigning in a futuristic peaceable kingdom.

In a letter to Archduke Rudolph, Beethoven wrote: "God . . . sees into my innermost heart and knows that as a man I perform most conscientiously and on all occasions the duties which Humanity, God, and Nature enjoin upon me. . . ." [38] "Humanity, God, and Nature"—these were Beethoven's spiritual trinity, which stood as the foundation of an ever-ascending superstructure of faith and expectation, and which would not fail to leave its impress upon his last works.

In order to compose those works, Beethoven now needed conditions of tranquility which had been absent from his life for too long. "Plea for inner and outer peace," he wrote on sketches of the *Missa Solemnis*,[39] in a phrase of personal as well as of religious significance. Fragile, sickly, rapidly aging, wounded by the events of the previous years, and, perhaps, stunned by the implications of his own compulsive actions in the guardianship struggle, Beethoven entered the 1820s.

Beethoven. Portrait in oils by Joseph
Carl Stieler (1819–20).

20
Reconstruction

The longest crisis of Beethoven's life came to an end with his "victory" in the Court of Appeal in early 1820. In the broadest sense, this crisis—which reached its climax in 1818–20—had begun as early as 1812, in the painful aftermath of the Immortal Beloved affair. Now, battered and torn from the stresses of the intervening experiences, Beethoven set about reconstructing his life and completing his life's work.

Beethoven's output in his remaining years can be rapidly outlined. He was apparently in no hurry to demonstrate his genius, despite the proliferating rumors that he was written out.[1] In 1820 he completed only one work, the Piano Sonata in E major, op. 109. The Sonata in A-flat major, op. 110, was finished on Christmas Day 1821, and was soon followed by Beethoven's last Sonata, in C minor, op. 111, the manuscript of which is dated January 13, 1822. Beethoven achieved a prodigious productivity, however, in 1822: he completed the *Missa Solemnis* (save for minor finishing touches), the Sonata, op. 111, and the Overture to *The Consecration of the House*, op. 124; he also composed most of the Thirty-three Variations on a Waltz by Diabelli, op. 120, rewrote the last movement of the Sonata, op. 110, and for the first time made substantial progress on the Ninth Symphony. In addition, he wrote a number of less significant works, such as his last setting of Matthisson's "Opferlied," op, 121b, for soprano, chorus, and orchestra; "Bundeslied," op. 122; and six of the Bagatelles, op. 119; and he began planning the String Quartet, op. 127. Johann Sporschil, a historian and publicist who was then studying in Vienna, described the Beethoven of 1822 and 1823 as "one of the most active men who ever lived" and recalled that "deepest midnight found him still working." [2] He often failed to appear for meals and gatherings, to the dismay of his housekeeper and friends. His absent-mindedness increased: he would forget his hat and be seen bareheaded in inclement weather, his long gray hair dripping in the rain.

Everything was subordinated to his work. He no longer strove for the heights of personal gratification; the small pleasures of life—walking, eating, drinking, conversation, an occasional pipe—were sufficient. He had reached a stage where he had become wholly possessed by his art. Karl is scarcely mentioned in his correspondence at this time. Beethoven's close Bonn friend, Bernhard Romberg, gave a cello recital in February 1822, but Beethoven did not appear, at first pleading an earache as the cause, but then giving the real reason—his preoccupation with his work: "If I have not called on you, just bear in mind the distance of my rooms and my almost ceaseless occupations, the more so as for a whole year I have been constantly ill and thus prevented from finishing many compositions which I had begun." [3]

In 1822, the *Allgemeine musikalische Zeitung* reported the news that he was improvising at the piano for a small circle of friends, and could still "handle his instrument with power, spirit, and tenderness." [4] But he received few visitors. Rossini sought him out in the spring of the year, was praised for his *Barber,* and received Beethoven's blunt opinion that he should not attempt *opera seria* ("ill suited to the Italians. You do not possess sufficient musical knowledge to deal with real drama. . . ." [5]). Schubert reportedly delivered a set of variations inscribed to Beethoven from "his Worshipper and Admirer Franz Schubert" but did not find Beethoven at home. Rochlitz arrived from Leipzig bearing a proposal from Breitkopf & Härtel that Beethoven write incidental music for Goethe's *Faust,* but Beethoven, although he had long entertained the fancy of setting Goethe's masterpiece to music, was deeply involved in other projects: "For some time past I have been carrying about with me the idea of three other great works. . . . These I must first get rid of: two great symphonies each different from the other, and each also different from all my other ones, and an oratorio. . . . I dread beginning works of such magnitude. Once I have begun, then, all goes well." [6]

The major projects which had originated during Beethoven's conflcts with Johanna were now coming to fruition. The autograph score of the

Missa Solemnis was wholly finished by mid-1823; and the Diabelli Variations by March or April of the same year; the Ninth Symphony then
occupied him for the balance of 1823 and the first two months of 1824.

The remainder of Beethoven's life was devoted to the String Quartets,
opp. 127, 130, 131, 132, and 135. Never before had Beethoven concentrated so exclusively and for so long upon a single genre. The Quartet
in E-flat major, op. 127, was largely composed during the second half of
1824, and was completed early in the following year. From February to
midsummer of 1825 he composed the A-minor Quartet, op. 132. He wrote
most of the first version of the Quartet in B-flat, op. 130—including the
Grosse Fuge, which was later published separately as opus 133—in July and
August, and completed it in November. In the following year he wrote
the quartets in C-sharp minor, op. 131, and in F major, op. 135, ending
his creative career in November 1826 with a new finale for opus 130. A
few trifles, a fragment of a string quintet, and an arrangement for piano
four-hands of the *Grosse Fuge* aside, the quartets were Beethoven's sole
preoccupation from February 1824 onwards. This is not to say that he
had forsaken all future projects: briefly, in 1826, when his cycle of quartets was drawing to a close, he began to discuss new ideas for operas,
oratorios, concertos, and other works; [7] a sketchbook of 1825 seems to hint
at a Tenth Symphony and at an overture on the letters of Bach's name
(B-flat–A–C–B); and on his deathbed Beethoven spoke regretfully of his
plans for a *Requiem* and for *Faust*, and of his ambition to have written
a piano method.

This productivity took place against a background of reviving popularity. Beethoven's works were taken up again in Vienna during the years
beginning with the season of 1819–20. In 1820, three concerts of the
Society of the Friends of Music featured the *Eroica*, Fifth, and Eighth
Symphonies, as well as a chorus from *Christ on the Mount of Olives;* a
benefit concert for widows and orphans, held on April 16, 1820, included
one of his overtures, probably *Namensfeier*, op. 115; and a new concert
series, *Concerts spirituels*—founded by Beethoven's friend F. X. Gebauer—
featured, in its twenty-eight concerts of 1819–21, eight performances of
Beethoven's symphonies, plus the Mass in C, his oratorio, and two performances of "Calm Seas and Prosperous Voyage." In 1822, Beethoven
was asked to provide music for the opening of the Josephstadt Theater,
to take place on October 3, the eve of the Kaiser's name day. The music
consisted of a revision of *The Ruins of Athens* to a modified text, with
a new chorus, along with a new overture, *The Consecration of the House*,
which, however, was not ready for the premiere. Beethoven co-conducted
at the opening to an enthusiastic reception, and the work was repeated
on three succeeding nights.

Only a few months earlier, Beethoven had complained to Rochlitz:
"*Fidelio?* They cannot give it, nor do they want to listen to it. The sym-

phonies? They have no time for them. My concertos? Everyone grinds out only the stuff he himself has made. The solo pieces? They went out of fashion here long ago, and here fashion is everything." [8] Accelerating Beethoven's newfound popularity was the revival of *Fidelio* at the Kärnthnerthor Theater in a benefit performance for Wilhelmine Schröder on November 3, 1822, which enjoyed six repeat performances in the succeeding months. Buoyed by his Josephstadt Theatre success, Beethoven tried to conduct the dress rehearsal. Schröder (later Madame Schröder–Devrient) subsequently described the scene:

> The last rehearsals were set, when I learned before the dress rehearsal that *Beethoven* had asked for the honor of conducting the work himself in celebration of the day. . . . With a bewildered face and unearthly inspired eyes, waving his baton back and forth with violent motions, he stood in the midst of the performing musicians and *didn't hear a note!* . . . The inevitable happened: the deaf master threw the singers and orchestra completely off the beat and into the greatest confusion, and no one knew any longer where they were.[9]

Schindler was given the painful task of informing Beethoven of his failure. The latter fled the theater in despair; "he never wholly recovered from the effect of this blow," wrote Schindler.[10] (He briefly sought treatment for his deafness, first with Dr. Smetana and then with the priest, Pater Weiss, who had treated him in vain two decades earlier.)

As we have seen, however, Beethoven's productivity was unaffected by the knowledge that, just as he could no longer play the piano in public, so he could no longer conduct. He wrote to Ries in London on December 20, 1822: "Thank God, Beethoven can compose—but, I admit, that is all he is able to do in this world. If God will only restore my health, which has improved at any rate, then I shall be able to comply with all the offers from all the countries of Europe, nay, even of North America; and in that case I might yet make a success of my life." [11]

New proposals came his way. In 1823, the Philharmonic Society of London offered 50 pounds for a manuscript symphony. The management of the Kärnthnerthor Theater—encouraged by the success of the *Fidelio* revival—asked Beethoven for a new opera, and he began to examine librettos in search of a fruitful subject. Prince Nikolas Galitzin wrote from St. Petersburg commissioning Beethoven, for a generous fee, to compose one or more string quartets. On January 25, 1823, Beethoven accepted the offer, promising (optimistically) to complete the first quartet by mid-March at the latest. Visitors now found Beethoven in good spirits, despite eye trouble and other ailments. Carl Maria von Weber wrote in astonishment that "this rough, repellent man actually paid court to me, served me at table as if I had been his lady." [12] Beethoven met several times with Grillparzer, planning their phantom opera, *Melusine*. Although he despised infant prodigies, he suffered Czerny's student, Franz Liszt, to play for him, and is said to have made appropriate remarks for posterity about the young genius. The musician, Louis Schlösser, found Beethoven, "usually so careless about his attire, dressed with unwonted elegance." [13]

In the winter of 1823–24 Beethoven received an open letter from his most devoted Viennese followers which laid the groundwork for the greatest public event of this period of his career—the concert of May 7, 1824, at the Kärnthnerthor Theater. His friends, who knew well his dissatisfaction with present Viennese patronage of serious art, hoped to preserve for their city the premieres of the *Missa Solemnis* and the Ninth Symphony. They wrote, in part:

Out of the wide circle of reverent admirers surrounding your genius in this your second native city, there approach you today a small number of the disciples and lovers of art to give expression to long-felt wishes, timidly to prefer a long-suppressed request. . . .

Do not withhold longer from the popular enjoyment, do not keep longer from the oppressed sense of that which is great and perfect, a performance of the latest masterworks of your hand. We know that a grand sacred composition has been associated with that first one in which you have immortalized the emotions of a soul, penetrated and transfigured by the power of faith and superterrestrial light. We know that a new flower glows in the garland of your glorious, still unequaled symphonies. For years, ever since the thunders of the victory at Vittoria ceased to reverberate, we have waited and hoped to see you distribute new gifts from the fulness of your riches to the circle of your friends. Do not longer disappoint the general expectations! . . .

Need we tell you with what regret your retirement from public life has filled us? Need we assure you that at a time when all glances were hopefully turned towards you, all perceived with sorrow that *the one* man whom all of us are compelled to acknowledge as foremost among living men in his domain, looked on in silence as foreign art took possession of German soil. . . .[14]

The letter was signed by thirty of the leading musicians, publishers, and music lovers of Vienna. Beethoven was deeply moved by the appeal: "That was very nice of them. It pleases me very much," he reportedly said to Schindler.[15] He and his friends gathered to discuss the proposed concert and its program and performers, and after much indecision on Beethoven's part, the date and theater were confirmed. Special permission was obtained from the censor to allow the public performance of a sacred work. The size of the orchestra was increased to 24 violins, 10 violas, and 12 basses and cellos, with doubled winds.

The concert included the Overture, op. 124; the Kyrie, Credo, and

Agnus Dei of the *Missa Solemnis;* and the Ninth Symphony. The theater was filled. Zmeskall, crippled by arthritis, was borne to his seat in a sedan chair. Schuppanzigh—who had returned from Russia the previous year—shared the conducting duties with *Kapellmeister* Umlauf. Beethoven stood turning the pages of his score, beating time. Umlauf warned the choir and orchestra to pay no attention to the composer, who was so deaf that he could not hear the thunderous applause.

Beethoven had high hopes that the concert would be a financial success. (Eager for a large profit, he had, indeed, sought to raise the prices, but was refused permission.) His brother had estimated that with the proceeds Beethoven could pay his long-standing debt to Steiner and "still have 2,000 florins in paper money left over for the summer." [16] His share actually amounted to only a few hundred florins, however. Disappointed, and perhaps overcome by the stresses of the occasion, Beethoven partly spoiled his triumph by charging that the management and Schindler had cheated him. Although Beethoven subsequently withdrew the accusation against Schindler, his anger was unappeased, and Schindler disappeared from the foreground of Beethoven's activities until late in 1826. His place was soon taken by the convivial violinist Karl Holz, the last in the long succession of Beethoven's unpaid and worshipful assistants. ("When I think of the music of Beethoven," he wrote in a Conversation Book, "I am happy to be alive." [17])

A repetition of the concert on May 23, with a slightly different program, was a failure: partly because it was given at midday on a beautiful Sunday, the house was less than half full, and the receipts were 800 florins short of actual expenses. Beethoven had to be persuaded to accept the fee of 500 florins which had been guaranteed to him.

Although these were the last public concerts held for Beethoven's benefit during his lifetime, performances of his works remained frequent. In 1825 alone, in addition to the first performances of the Quartets, opp. 127 and 132, there were concerts featuring the Fourth and Seventh Symphonies and the *Archduke* Trio, op. 97. In May, the Ninth Symphony, conducted by Ferdinand Ries, was performed in Aix-la-Chapelle. Many concerts at this time also opened with one or another Beethoven overture.

The frequency of performances increased toward the end of the year, with performances of the Mass in C at the Karlskirche, of both of the Trios, op. 70, and of the *Eroica* Symphony, the "Choral Fantasia," and the Septet. On November 29, Beethoven was belatedly elected to honorary membership in the Society of the Friends of Music. The Society was apparently reconciled to the fact that it would never receive its promised oratorio, although Beethoven continued to hint to Bernard, author of the libretto, that it was still forthcoming.

Beethoven's greatness had long since become an article of faith in several leading European countries, and his fame was beginning to extend to more distant lands as well. Programs of the Philharmonic Society of London during the 1820s featured sixty performances of his symphonies and twenty-nine of his overtures. In Vienna, encomiums to his genius in the press were, if anything, excessively flattering. As for Germany, a contemporary traveler reported in 1825 that "the Germans esteem him the most distinguished musical genius of Europe, except Mozart." [18] The German Romantic writers—led by Clemens Brentano and E. T. A. Hoffmann—admired him to the point of adulation. Schopenhauer regarded his symphonies as expressing the essential nature of music. Only Hegel, an admirer of Rossini, maintained his reserve, and his sole comment on Beethoven's music (in which, interestingly, he avoids mention of the composer's name) decries its "powerful contrasts," holding that the "characteristic features of such music readily incur the risk of overstepping the finely drawn boundaries of musical beauty, more especially when the intention is to express force, selfishness, evil, impetuosity, and other extremes of exclusive passion." [19]

During the early 1820s, Beethoven earned little money from publications, dedications, or concerts. His main income was the princes' annuity, along with the interest on his eight bank shares (worth 4,000 florins in silver; 10,000 in depreciated currency). These were not sufficient, however, to meet Beethoven's rather high expenses. He maintained two servants at virtually all times, took a summer residence each year, and had a taste for simple but well-prepared foods and good wines. Furthermore, he had to pay for Karl's board and schooling—2,000 florins per year, he claimed; Johanna's contribution from her pension had long since fallen into arrears. And legal fees, although we do not know their size, must have substantially eroded Beethoven's finances. Like most older people on a fixed income, he feared to touch his capital and insisted that the bank shares had been set aside as Karl's inheritance. It is not surprising, then, that Beethoven began to slip into debt. Over the preceding years, he had borrowed almost 2,500 florins from Steiner. Furthermore, Wolfmayer had apparently paid Beethoven 1,000 florins for his *Requiem*. And in 1820, Artaria loaned him 750 florins, with repayment guaranteed by Archduke Rudolph. The previous year, he had also obtained an advance of 400 florins from the Society of the Friends of Music as partial payment for its oratorio. In December 1820, Steiner wrote a restrained but firm letter to Beethoven requesting his money, and repeatedly reminding the composer of his moral obligations: "It is doubly painful to me now to be embarrassed because of my good will and my trust in your word of honor . . . wherefore I conjure you again not to leave me in the lurch and to find means to liquidate my account as soon as possible." [20] Beethoven and Steiner agreed on an extended repayment schedule, and the composer managed to forestall other creditors' demands for several more years; but the pyramiding debts would ultimately lead Beethoven into a complex series of machinations concerning the sale of his *Missa Solemnis* and, more poignantly, to a rupture in his relationship with several close friends and associates.

In 1820 he offered the publishing rights to the Mass to Simrock in Bonn, settled on terms, and promised to send it upon completion via Franz Brentano. Simrock was instructed to place 900 gulden in escrow with Brentano, the sum to be released upon delivery of the manuscript; but in 1821, Beethoven persuaded Brentano to advance to him out of his own pocket the full amount of Simrock's escrow payment. Despite this, he now entered into negotiations concerning the Mass with the Leipzig firm of C. F. Peters, from whom he accepted a payment of 1,000 gulden. The full import of Beethoven's dubious conduct became clear with his letters of September 13, 1822, to Brentano and to Simrock, in which he insisted upon an increase in the fee, failing which he would "dispatch the Mass to another quarter." [21] Brentano thereupon insisted that Beethoven either fulfill the contract or immediately return the advance. The composer sold off one of his bank shares to meet this and other obligations (even his tailor, Lind, was threatening a lawsuit) and made a partial payment to Brentano in an attempt to renew their friendship: "Command me to undertake whatever task you choose, provided it be within my power to perform it, and I will make every effort to prove to you my regard, my affection, and my gratitude." [22] Brentano, however, apparently demanded full payment, which was not forthcoming; and the friendship ended with Beethoven's words: "I only wish that I were in a position to express my thanks to you in the manner you would most desire." [23]

The vexatious publication history of the Mass was far from ended. Unknown to Peters, Beethoven was also negotiating with Artaria and Schlesinger for its publication. It was not until the first days of 1825, after further negotiations with Diabelli, Probst, Schlesinger, Peters, and Schott's Sons, that Beethoven settled upon the last of these as worthy of publishing his prize composition. In the interim, Beethoven formed a grandiose plan according to which he would withhold the Mass from publication altogether for a time, and instead offer manuscript copies by subscription to the sovereigns of Europe at 50 gold ducats per copy. Identical letters were sent out in February 1823, along with additional letters to Goethe, Cherubini, and Bernadotte, who was now king of Sweden. Ultimately ten copies were sold, which took more than a year to copy and deliver. This was not solely or even primarily undertaken as a commercial enterprise, although Beethoven's profit, after deducting the cost of copying, was more than 1,600 florins. Beethoven had always treasured medals and honors; now he was able to freely acknowledge his need for recognition and appreciation, and he reached out to the elevated and royal figures of Europe for tangible signs of their regard. This may be why he decided, after seven years, to remind King George IV of England that he had never acknowledged by sign or honorarium Beethoven's dedication to him of *Wellington's Victory*. His letters to Goethe and Cherubini contain unaccustomed expressions of adoration for these giants of contemporary culture. "The admiration, love, and esteem which I have cherished since my youth for the one and only immortal Goethe have persisted . . . I feel constantly prompted by a strange desire to say all this to you, seeing that I live in your writings."[24] And to Cherubini: "I honor and love you—"[25] So great was Beethoven's yearning for recognition that when the Swedish Royal Academy of Music elected him to honorary membership he wrote in 1823 to several editors, asking them to spread the news: "I should consider it an honor if you would be kind enough to mention in your so generally esteemed paper my election as foreign member of the Royal Swedish Academy of Music."[26]

Also at this time, the opportunity arose to fulfill Beethoven's old wish to become associated with the imperial court. The court composer, Anton Teyber, died, and Beethoven applied for the position in a letter to Count Moritz Dietrichstein of ca. January 1, 1823: "I hear that the post of Imperial and Royal Chamber Music Composer, which Teyber held, is again to be filled, and I gladly apply for it, particularly if, as I fancy, one of the requirements is that I should occasionally provide a composition for the Imperial Court."[27] Beethoven's friends at court—Dietrichstein, Moritz Lichnowsky, and Archduke Rudolph—paved the way for the appointment, evidently obtaining a verbal commitment that the position would be his if Beethoven would write a Mass for the emperor to show his homage (to place him, as Thayer wrote, "into the Emperor's good books"[28]). At first, Beethoven welcomed the challenge; he wrote to Simrock and to Peters that he was writing two more masses ("I intend to compose three at least"), with which he could satisfy the court as well as his irate publishers.[29] But writing another Mass was no minor task, and Beethoven had other creative projects in progress. Moreover, Beethoven's brother persuaded him that Teyber's position would not be filled. Although Nikolaus Johann was surely not privy to the plans of the imperial court, his prediction turned out to be accurate. In any event, the Mass for the emperor was not written—although it was still talked about as late as 1826.

That Beethoven's attitude toward honors was occasionally ambivalent is shown by Schindler's well-known—but questionable—story that in 1823 Beethoven had been offered the choice of a royal decoration or 50 ducats for the Prussian court's subscription to the *Missa Solemnis*; Beethoven unhesitatingly answered "50 ducats," preferring the cash to the ribbon.[30] Schindler took this as "striking proof how lightly he prized insignia of honor or distinctions in general." [31] Nevertheless, he himself also related that Beethoven's receipt in 1824 of a gold medal weighing 21 louis d'or and inscribed by the king of France was "the greatest distinction conferred upon the master during his lifetime." [32] Beethoven wrote to Bernard that Louis XVIII's gift showed "that he is a generous King and a man of refined feeling," and asked him to print the news of the royal distinction in Bernard's *Wiener Zeitung*.[33] He sent an impression of the medal to Prince Galitzin and wrote proudly to him: "The medal weighs a half pound in gold and [has] Italian verses about me." [34] Soon, indeed, Beethoven was even able to bring himself to ask for a Royal Order from the king of Prussia.

That Beethoven's desire for recognition may somehow have been connected with his Family Romance is suggested by the circumstances surrounding the dedication of his Ninth Symphony. Not since the Mass in C had Beethoven vacillated to such an extent about a dedication. He first promised the dedication to Ries (perhaps only for England) and then considered in turn the Philharmonic Society of London, Kaiser Franz, Czar Alexander (who died late in 1825), and the king of France. He was determined that the symphony "be dedicated," as he wrote, "to a great lord." [35] Finally he settled upon Friedrich Wilhelm III, the king of Prussia, and on March 28, 1826, he was happy to learn from the Prussian embassy that "His Royal Majesty graciously permits me to dedicate to His Supreme Person the D-minor symphony with choruses." [36] One wonders if it is altogether accidental that Beethoven chose to dedicate his symphony on the brotherhood of man to the son of the man rumored to be his own father.

Beethoven. Engraving after a drawing by Martin Tejček (ca. 1823). Beethoven's funeral. In the background is the Schwarzspanierhaus.

21
The "Return" to Bonn

Beneath the simple, even prosaic, "surface" events which we sketched in the preceding chapter, a profound shift in Beethoven's psychological makeup was taking place. In his last years we are able to glimpse traces of the course by which he stripped away the fantasies and delusions of a lifetime. His attempt to create a fantasy family through the appropriation of his nephew had been accompanied by an unleashing of powerful emotional forces. Although these forces were eventually brought under control—the first years of the 1820s are relatively free of aggressive actions and pathological signs—they had set in motion an irreversible process of self-analysis which affected the deepest layers of the composer's personality.

The shattering of his nobility pretense in December 1818 may well have been a decisive stage in this process. As we have, seen, Beethoven himself confessed his lack of a patent of nobility, and this surely indicated not only that the weight of the long deception had become insupportable but that he was at last beginning to comprehend that he was not "noble" in a literal sense. True, it was precisely during the next several years that Beethoven refused to refute the proliferating reports of his royal ancestry. He would tenaciously attempt to hold on to this fantasy until almost the very end. Nevertheless, the Family Romance had begun to weaken, and it was probably inevitable that the entire structure, once seriously thrown into question, would ultimately give way.

The importance of this may be stated simply: Beethoven's birth fantasies barred him from fully acknowledging, accepting, and loving his own family. And they therefore stood in the way of Beethoven's own self-acceptance, self-love, and self-knowledge. To be rid of these fantasies was not merely to pass from illusion to reality in some abstract sense, but to take his place as a member of a family, to "belong" to his own flesh and blood. A sense of kinship and a sense of personal identity were simultaneously at stake. Is it not possible that Beethoven's capture of Nephew Karl was in some way a desperate attempt to hold fast to the slender threads of kinship, a kinship which his own delusions had led him to deny? In becoming Karl's "father," in forging this false connection, was not Beethoven in a sense giving the lie to his own Family Romance and affirming that he was indeed a Beethoven rather than the illegitimate son of a king? Surely the war for possession of Karl proved that the concept of "family"—more than any other—could stir Beethoven's passions to their depths.

Immediately after the close of the guardianship litigation, Beethoven suddenly expressed the desire to return to his birthplace. He wrote to Simrock, in Bonn: "I cherish the hope of being able perhaps to set foot next year on my native soil and to visit my parents' graves." [1] It is a noteworthy fact that this is the first reference to Beethoven's mother in his correspondence since shortly after her death in 1787, and the first such reference to his father since the petition of 1793 to the elector. Beethoven wrote again to Simrock in March 1821: "I am still hoping to visit Bonn this summer." [2] Events had somehow unearthed this desire, but Beethoven could not make the journey that would have "reunited" him with his parents, perhaps because he did not wish to shatter a consciously idealized image of his childhood home, perhaps because this would have meant returning to the site of early, painful experiences. More: to return to Bonn—to go home—would have been to undermine the Family Romance, for it seems doubtful that this fantasy could have withstood the reality of walking through the Bonngasse and the Rhinegasse and standing in the courtyard of the Fischer house, reviving the memories of early years.

It was also at this critical juncture of Beethoven's life that his birth-year fantasy began to weaken somewhat. Around 1820, his admirer Wilhelm Christian Müller asked him about his birthday so that he could give him a present. Beethoven replied that he "didn't know precisely either the day or the year." [3] Müller's daughter thereupon wrote to Bonn and obtained from the church register a copy of Beethoven's baptismal certificate, which, as usual, designated the date as December 17, 1770. Müller eagerly brought this news to the composer, who, instead of rejecting it out of hand, as was his earlier pattern, "jestingly said that he would not have believed that he was such an old bloke." It is nice to learn that Beethoven had reached a point at which he could joke about his age, but Müller's evidence did not settle the question. For a Conversation Book of February 1820 shows Beethoven still speculating about the identity of his godmother: "Bongard must have been the name of the woman who was my godmother—or Baumgarten." [4] He still could not accept the validity of the certificate, on which his godmother's name— Frau Baum—was clearly set forth.

Apparently, the Family Romance persisted despite the evidence of the baptismal certificate. But the yearning for familial reconciliation continued. In May 1822, shortly after Nikolaus Johann took a winter residence with his wife's Viennese relatives, Beethoven renewed his intimacy with his surviving brother, with whom he had had only minimal contact after 1812, the year of Nikolaus Johann's marriage. Beethoven expressed his hope "that all life's wretched trivialities need not cause any disturbances between us," and he prayed that "God grant that the most natural bond, the bond between brothers, may not again be broken in an unnatural way." [5] He hastened to assure his brother: "I repeat that I have nothing against your wife." Nikolaus Johann thereafter began to take a role in Beethoven's personal and business affairs, and he appeared frequently in the Conversation Books. Rejoicing in this reconciliation, Beethoven wrote twelve letters to his brother during 1822, and he borrowed money from him during the summer, in return for which Nikolaus Johann was formally given ownership of several compositions as security. Of course, it was not long before close proximity to his brother's family revived Beethoven's attempt to undermine the marriage. By 1823 he was strenuously objecting to Therese's less than commendable associations, and he apparently brought these, as he wrote to Schindler, to "the notice of the worthy police authorities." [6] "Am I to become so degraded as to mix in such low company?" he asked his brother, and he soon abandoned his lodgings, which adjoined those of Nikolaus Johann's family. But he assured him: "I hover over you unseen and influence you through others, so that the scum of the earth may not strangle you." [7] The newly formed tie was not broken, however, and the brothers remained closely associated for the rest of Beethoven's life.

Beethoven also needed to be reconciled with Johanna van Beethoven. Following the decision of the Court of Appeal, she had let it be known that she did not wish to see her brother-in-law under any circumstances, and there is no indication of any contact between them for a year or two. But in 1822 Beethoven advised his brother that he had taken over a portion of her debt to Steiner, and he wrote: "I want to do everything I can for her insofar as it isn't against Karl's interest." [8] Early in the following year he was disturbed to learn through Bernard that Johanna was ill and unable to pay for her medicines.[9] He determined to assist her, at first with small cash gifts made anonymously through her doctor, and then— much more handsomely—by restoring the half of her pension which she had yielded to Karl in May 1817. Surprisingly, Karl protested vigorously against this proposed generosity toward his mother and maligned her in an attempt to forestall a rapprochement between her and his uncle. Evidently there had been an estrangement between Karl and his mother following the birth of her daughter. He may have felt that he had been supplanted as the sole object of her love; doubtless he was wounded by her belated "confirmation" of Beethoven's charges of her immorality. Despite Karl's opposition, however, Beethoven would not be dissuaded. He wrote to Bernard: "I am sending her herewith 11 gulden. . . . Please have it delivered to her through the *doctor* and, what is more, in such a way that she may not know where it has come from. . . . If we could be fully informed about all the circumstances, then we might see what could still be done for her; and I am prepared to help in every way." [10] Shortly thereafter, Beethoven, no longer hesitant to let Johanna know of his intentions, wrote to Bernard:

> Please do make inquiries today about Frau van Beethoven and, if possible, assure her at once through her doctor that from this month onwards she can enjoy her full pension *as long as I live*. . . . As she is so ill and in such straitened circumstances, she must be helped at once. . . . I shall make a point of persuading my pigheaded brother also to contribute something to help her.[11]

The following year, 1824, opened on a significant note of reconciliation, which coincided precisely with the time during which Beethoven was composing the "Ode to Joy" choral finale of his Ninth Symphony. On January 8, 1824, in response to Johanna's friendly New Year's greeting, he wrote: "I assure you now in writing that henceforth and for good you may draw Karl's half of your pension. . . . Should I be comfortably off later on and in a position to provide you from my income with a sum large enough to improve your circumstances, I will certainly do so." [12] He then offered her his assistance in various matters, wished her "all possible happiness," and assured her that he was "most willing to help you." Clearly Beethoven no longer consciously regarded Johanna as the incarnation of evil, but had come to see her as an individual, as a member of the family who needed his help. And, as we shall see, his most dramatic gesture toward Johanna was yet to come.

The ingrained patterns of a lifetime could not be altered easily, however, let alone all at once. Beethoven had invested too much in his fantasies of illegitimacy to abandon them without one last struggle. Inevitably, the issue turned on nephew Karl's entry into manhood and his attempt to achieve a separation from his uncle.

Fittingly enough, Karl had drifted somewhat out of the focus of Beethoven's attention during the early 1820s. Even when he ran away to his mother in mid-1820, it did not arouse his uncle's fury in the old way. In that year, Karl visited Beethoven at Mödling during his summer vacation and then returned to the Blöchlinger Institute, where he was to remain as a boarder until August 1823. Karl's presence is scarcely noted in Beethoven's correspondence of the next few years, and the relationship between the two was at its most harmonious during this period: Karl functioned as Beethoven's secretary in certain matters and apparently spent a good many weekends, as well as several of his summers, with him. After his transfer from the Blöchlinger Insitute to the university, however, Karl once more came to live with Beethoven, and quarrels between the aging composer and the tearful adolescent are recorded in the Conversation Books of this period. In the summer of 1824 he did not accompany Beethoven on his summer holiday, and so became a source of great concern. On October 6 Beethoven wrote urgently to Haslinger asking that he discover where the "missing" Karl had slept on recent nights. Beethoven feared that the boy, now eighteen, might be having sexual relationships, with all their attendant "dangers": "It is not surprising when one thinks of these wretched institutions that one is anxious about a young fellow who is growing up," he wrote; "And in addition there is that poisonous breath coming from dragons!"[13] Karl turned up at Baden with his close friend Niemetz, to whom Beethoven strenuously objected: "He is a burdensome guest, lacking completely in decency and manners. . . . Besides, I suspect that his interests are more with the housekeeper than with me—Besides, I love quiet; also the space here is too limited for several people." Karl steadfastly defended his friend and the right to choose his friends: "For my part I will not stop loving him as I would my brother, if I had one."[14] Upon his return to Vienna in early November, Beethoven continued his quarrels with Karl, to such an extent that his landlady served notice.

In January 1825, Beethoven received and accepted a new invitation from the Philharmonic Society to travel to London and supervise a series of concerts of his music. But a grave illness soon made these travel plans academic. For on April 18 he wrote to Dr. Anton Braunhofer: "I am not feeling well and I hope that you will not refuse to come to my help, for I am in great pain."[15] Beethoven was suffering from an intestinal inflammation, a condition which aroused the alarm of the doctor as well as the patient. Braunhofer warned Beethoven to control his diet: "No wine, no coffee; no spices of any kind. . . . I'll wager that if you take a drink of spirits, you'll be lying weak and exhausted on your back in a few hours." [16] He also recommended an early departure to the country for "fresh air" and "natural milk." Beethoven moved to Baden on May 7 and remained there—with occasional visits to Vienna—until October 15. His condition remained serious; he wrote to Braunhofer: "I spit a good deal of blood, but probably only from my windpipe. . . . Judging by what I know of my own constitution, my strength will hardly be restored unaided." [17] He closed with a canon: "Doctor close the door to Death! Music will also help in my hour of need." Perhaps it did help. Beethoven was then composing the A-minor String Quartet, op. 132, and in a Conversation Book of this time he wrote: "Hymn of Thanksgiving to God of an Invalid on his Convalescence. Feeling of new strength and reawakened feeling"[18]—words which, in slightly altered form, are now found on the Molto Adagio of opus 132.

Beethoven's ill health and his premonitions of death apparently overwhelmed his resistances at this time, unloosing a flood of terrors and pathological reactions, which centered on Karl. Beethoven suspected (perhaps rightly) that Karl had again been meeting with his mother. He wrote on May 22: "So far only suppositions, though indeed someone assures me that you and your mother have again been associating in secret—Am I to experience once more the most horrible ingratitude?" [19] And on May 31 he burst out: "God is my witness that my sole dream is to get away completely from you and from that wretched brother and that horrible family who have been thrust upon me. May God grant my wishes." [20] It was a harrowing time, reminiscent of the bleak days of 1818 and 1819. He poured out his feelings to Bernard: "I had to face a behavior on [Karl's] part such as I have only experienced in the case of his deceased father, an uncouth fellow. . . . I suspect that that monster of a mother is again involved in this little game and that it is partly an intrigue of that gentleman, my brainless and heartless brother . . . with his overfed whore and bastard." Beethoven's suppressed longings for a woman's love surfaced briefly in an anguished sentence: "That awful fourth floor, O God, *without a wife,* and what an existence; one is a prey to every stranger—" [21]

Karl—who received a torrent of letters from Baden—was beaten into temporary submission by these outbursts, whereupon Beethoven once again became the loving, protective, and heavy-handed father: "I embrace you. Be my good, hardworking, noble son as I am always your faithful father." [22] But it was to be a precarious truce, for Beethoven had now become obsessed with Karl's sexuality. He exerted every effort to block his nephew from sexual opportunities of any sort; he spied upon the boy and continued to attempt to separate him from his friend Niemetz. He alternately berated and pleaded with him, rejected and forgave him. In early October he wrote to Matthias Schlemmer, a Viennese official with whose family Karl was boarding (close by the Polytechnic Institute, to which he had transferred in the spring of the year):

> One might be led to suspect that perhaps he really is enjoying himself in the evening or even at night in some company which is certainly not so desirable—I request you to pay attention to this and not to let Karl leave your house at night under any pretext whatever, unless you have received something in writing from me through Karl.[23]

Beethoven had now gone too far. Karl evidently wrote to his uncle threatening some drastic action (suicide, Cooper thinks). Beethoven responded: "My beloved Son! Stop, no further—Only come to my arms, you won't hear a single hard word. For God's sake, do not abandon yourself to misery. . . . On my word of honor you will hear no reproaches, since in any case they would no longer do any good. All that you may expect from me is the most loving care and help." [24] But Beethoven could not keep his resolve long enough even to complete his letter. For the postscript reads: "If you do not come you will surely kill me."

Beethoven's health was now somewhat restored and he was freely disregarding his doctor's injunction against alcoholic intake; he received a number of visitors, who found him in excellent spirits—in part, perhaps, by reason of the great surge of creativity which was seeing the Quartet in B-flat, op. 130, to completion, and perhaps also because of the renewal of his friendship with Stephan von Breuning. In October, Beethoven took up his final lodgings—in the Schwarzspanierhaus—hard by Breuning's residence, and, for the first time in a decade and the last time in his life, he once more tried to become a member of a warm and loving family. He took many of his meals at the Breunings, sometimes sending over a favorite fish to be prepared by Breuning's wife, and he attended on Frau von Breuning to such an extent that it became a source of embarrassment to her. And once again he expressed his longing "for domestic happiness and much regretted that he had never married." [25]

Nevertheless, by the winter of 1825–26, Beethoven's conflicts with his nephew were moving toward their unavoidable climax. Beethoven had continued his close watch on the young man's social activities, restricting these to the barest minimum by means of threats, through Holz's and Schlemmer's supervision, and by withholding expense money, thereby forcing Karl into borrowing and debt. When Karl attended a carnival ball, Beethoven wanted to accompany him and was apparently dissuaded only by Holz's promise that he would serve as chaperon. Beethoven received regular reports (presumably from Schlemmer) about Karl's whereabouts ("One night in the Prater. Two nights did not sleep at home" [26]). Karl attempted to withdraw from Beethoven, but this only increased Beethoven's reproaches and suspicions. He waited at the Polytechnic Institute at noon, "waiting to escort his nephew home arm in arm." [27] Beset by these pressures, Karl alternated between depression and defiance. To Beethoven's attempt to compel him to move back in with him, Karl responded diplomatically: "But it is the *last* year [of my schooling]; then we need never be separated any more." Privately, in letters to Niemetz, he referred to his uncle as "the old fool." [28] His attempts to reason with Beethoven were of no avail, because the aged composer was once again in the grip of forces which he could not understand or acknowledge, let alone control. (In a June letter to Karl, he wrote: "Do not think that I have anything else in mind but your welfare; and judge my actions by this." [29]) He was frantically trying to bar his nephew from sexual experience, a pathological effort which, though it carried implications of homoerotic domination, centered around the warped paternal desires as well as the incest fear which together had barred Beethoven from normal family existence for a lifetime. Beethoven's reawakened desire for his brother's widow appears to have been projected onto his nephew, where it could be stifled, if not annihilated. Meanwhile, Karl was now regularly visiting his mother, feeding Beethoven's worst fears. Inevitably, violence would prove to be the only means by which this tangled thread could be cut. Towards the summer of 1826 Karl struck Beethoven and fled the house, apparently in terror of his own passions. His only hope for temporary surcease was Beethoven's customary departure for the country in the summer. He repeatedly mentions Beethoven's vacation in the Conversation Books: "In the summer we will not feel the distance as much." [30] But this year, for the first time since the 1790s, Beethoven did not go to the country, even for a short stay; he delayed, vacillated, offered numerous pretexts. Clearly, he remained in Vienna so that he could stand guard over Karl.

At the end of July, Karl escaped from his virtual imprisonment at Schlemmer's house. Schlemmer reported to Beethoven and Holz that he had discovered a loaded pistol in Karl's room and had appropriated it. He begged Beethoven: "Be lenient with him or he will despair." [31] Holz found Karl at the Polytechnic Institute, but the youth said: "What good will it do you to detain me? If I do not escape today, I will at another time." Fleeing from Holz, he now pawned his watch, purchased two new pistols, and on July 30 repaired to Baden, where, after writing suicide notes to Beethoven and Niemetz, he climbed up a neighboring mountain and shot himself. Wounded, with a bullet in his scalp, he was taken to his mother's house.

The police, who had jurisdiction over attempted suicides, removed Karl to the general hospital on August 7, and he remained there until September 25. Beethoven's friends urged him to relinquish the guardianship and to permit Karl to enter the army. "Once with the military," Holz wrote, "he will be under the strictest discipline." Breuning agreed: "A military life will be the best discipline for one who cannot endure freedom; and it will teach him how to live on little." [32] Dr. Bach suggested that he be dispatched to a business establishment in another country. As for Karl, his preference now lay with military service: "If my wish concerning a military career can be fulfilled, I will be very happy."[33] Breuning, who now became Karl's guardian, arranged with his friend Field Marshal von Stutterheim to accept the boy as a cadet in Stutterheim's regiment. Before Karl could present himself for service, however, it was thought necessary that his hair be allowed to grow in to conceal the scars: "I cannot go to the Field Marshal," he wrote in a Conversation Book, "until I am able to appear without any visible sign left of what happened to me." [34] And so it was decided that Beethoven and Karl spend some time at Nikolaus Johann's country estate in Gneixendorf. Beethoven and his nephew left Vienna on September 28, and all of the members of the Beethoven family, save Johanna, were united on the following day. It was planned that Beethoven and Karl would stay for a week or two, but they remained in Gneixendorf ("the name resembles to a certain extent a breaking axle," Beethoven wrote to Haslinger [35]) until the first day of December. Neither of the participants in this drama could bring himself to make the move that would result in their final separation. Even Karl postponed his departure from week to week, until Nikolaus Johann and Breuning insisted that he hasten to his new calling.

Despite inescapable quarrels and reproaches, the reunion was not without its nostalgic and idyllic overtones. Beethoven wrote to Schott: "The district where I am now staying reminds me to a certain extent of the Rhine country which I so ardently desire to revisit. For I left it long ago when I was young." [36] Nikolaus Johann and his wife did their best to make Beethoven comfortable, offering him a permanent home with them, providing him with a young servant, Michael Krenn, to whom he became exceedingly attached (perhaps as a substitute for Karl), and attempting to smooth his relations with Karl. Therese, who was able to forgive Beethoven his ill will toward her, wrote consolingly in a Conversation Book: "It seems that [Karl] has some of your rash blood. I have not found him angry. It is you that he loves, to the point of veneration." [37] Beethoven spent much of each day rambling through the open fields; at dawn and in the evenings he worked on his last compositions. Here he completed the F-major Quartet, op. 135, and the new finale for the B-flat-major Quartet, op. 130. These works may themselves attest that the process of psychological separation from Karl was removing a great burden from Beethoven, for they reflect a tranquil and confident return to a happier, Haydnesque play world.

When asked why he had tried to commit suicide, Karl said he was "tired of life" and "weary of imprisonment." He told the police magistrate that Beethoven "tormented him too much" and that "I grew worse because my uncle wanted me to be better." [38] There is much truth in these explanations, but they are by no means the whole story, nor is it to be expected that Karl would wholly understand his own action. Classically, there are a number of interlocking motives in a suicide attempt. First, and this is clearly present here, there is an assertion of independence from a set of intolerable constraints. Closely linked to this is the process (described by the Sterbas) of "turning upon oneself" as a substitute for a desired aggression against another. Hence, Karl's suicide effort may have been a deflection of his violent impulses against Beethoven; the Sterbas observe that the act "discharged enough aggression to allow him to free himself from the intolerable pressure which his uncle's personality had exercised on him." [39] Karl needed to free himself from his uncle, and it is apparent that he instinctively chose the correct course to accomplish this, for Beethoven was now suddenly resigned to the necessity of their separation. There may have been another set of motives at work here, however. The suicide often seeks reunion in death with a lost or departed love object; he may want to die in order to join one from whom he has been forcibly separated. Here Karl's desire to be reunited with his mother is on the surface. On being discovered by a passing drover, he asked to be taken to his mother in Vienna; later, in the hospital, he at last firmly asserted his rights as a mother's son:

> I want to hear nothing about her that is derogatory to her, and it is absolutely not my place to pass judgment on her. If I should spend the little time I shall be here with her, it would be no more than a small compensation for all that she has suffered on my account. There can be no question of any harmful influence on me, even if it could occur, simply by reason of the shortness of the time. But in no case will I treat her more coldly than has hitherto been the case, no matter what anyone may say.[40]

The suicide attempt liberated Karl from his own extreme rejection of his mother—which had taken place, as he thought, on the instructions of Beethoven, and which for several years exceeded Beethoven's own negative attitude in intensity. The pistol shots were a child's cry for help, a way of telling Johanna that her son still needed her and wanted her forgiveness and love. Karl's tragedy, however, lay not only in his long, forcible separation from his mother. As we saw earlier, Beethoven's appropriation of his nephew embodied his desire to be the boy's "real, physical father" and thereby to take Caspar Carl's place. For more than a decade he had tried to train the boy to accept him as his true father, setting up a sequence of intolerable conflicts centering around the denial of the boy's real male parent. In this, Karl seems to have been the means by which Beethoven irrationally translated his own Family Romance into reality: he had replaced Karl's real father by a more noble surrogate—himself—and thereby elevated the boy to a noble rank. In a sense, he had created an artificial Family Romance for Karl to match his own fantasies of illegitimacy and royal birth. In so doing, he had deprived Karl of his father and substituted himself as his begetter and sole parent.

Karl, although ambivalently and painfully acceding to the rejection of his mother, and although he on occasion addressed Beethoven as "My dearest Father," had never accepted the replacement of his father. Beethoven had tried unsuccessfully to mold the boy in his own image: he engaged Carl Czerny, and later Joseph Czerny, to train him as a pianist, but was forced to abandon the effort. He then hoped to persuade Karl to enter a career in the humanities, encouraging him to matriculate at the university as a student of philology. But Karl resisted this path also, at first expressing the desire to be a soldier and then, in 1825, insisting on enrolling in the Polytechnic Institute to pursue a commercial career—which may well have been an expression of Karl's desire to follow in the footsteps of his father, who had pursued a career as cashier in the state tax apparatus. Ultimately, after his discharge from army service, Karl became, like his father, a minor official in the Austrian bureaucracy and lived a useful, bourgeois, and apparently contented existence.

Karl's suicide attempt thus bespoke his shattering rejection of Beethoven's presumed fatherhood. "All my hopes have vanished," Beethoven wrote to Holz, "all my hopes of having near me someone who would resemble me at least in my better qualities!" [41] The structure of Beethoven's Family Romance was fast disintegrating under the pressure of these events. The separation from Karl would now permit Beethoven himself to come to terms with the facts of his ancestry.

Beethoven's health began to fail at Gneixendorf. Nikolaus Johann wrote: "He would eat nothing at lunch except soft-boiled eggs, but then he would drink more wine so that he often suffered diarrhea; thereby his belly became bigger and bigger, and he wore a bandage over it for a long time." [42] He complained of thirst, loss of appetite, and pains in his abdomen. His feet became filled with fluids. On December 1, he and Karl set out for Vienna. Dr. Wawruch, who was soon to become his attending physician, wrote: "He was compelled to spend a night in a village tavern where, besides wretched shelter, he found an unwarmed room without winter shutters. Toward midnight he experienced his first fever chill, a dry, hacking cough accompanied by violent thirst and cutting pains in the sides." [43] On the following day he arrived at his lodgings in the Schwarzspanierhaus. Dr. Wawruch, who was called on December 5 (Braunhofer and Staudenheim would not come), described his condition thus: "I found Beethoven afflicted with serious symptoms of inflammation of the lungs. His face glowed, he spat blood, his respiration threatened suffocation, and a painful stitch in the side made lying on the back a torment. A severe countertreatment for inflammation soon brought the desired relief; his constitution triumphed and by a lucky crisis he was freed from apparent mortal danger, so that on the fifth day he was able, in a sitting posture, to tell me, amid profound emotion, of the discomforts which he had suffered." It was on that day, December 7, 1826, that Beethoven belatedly replied to Wegeler's letter of December 28, 1825. A brief passage from Beethoven's letter was cited at the beginning of this book. Now the letter can be given in full:

MY BELOVED OLD FRIEND!

Words fail me to express the pleasure which your letter and Lorchen's have afforded me. And indeed an answer should have been sent off to you as swiftly as an arrow. But on the whole I am rather slack about writing letters, for I believe that the best people know me well in any case. Often I think out a reply in my head; but when it comes to writing it down, I usually throw away my pen, simply because I am unable to write as I feel. I remember all the love which you have always shown me, for instance, how you had my room whitewashed and thus gave me such a pleasant surprise, and likewise all the kindnesses I have received from the Breuning family. Our drifting apart was due to changes in our circumstances. Each of us had to pursue the purpose for which he was intended and endeavor to attain it. Yet the eternally unshakable and firm foundations of good principles continued to bind us strongly together. Unfortunately I cannot write to you today as much as I should like to, for I have to stay in bed. So I shall confine myself to answering a few points in your letter. You say that I have been mentioned somewhere as being the natural son of the late King of Prussia. Well, the same thing was said to me a long time ago. But I have adopted the principle of neither writing anything about myself nor replying to anything that has been written about me. Hence I gladly leave it to you to make known to the world the integrity of my parents, and especially of my mother. You mention your son. Why, of course, if he comes to Vienna, I will be a friend and a father to him; and if I can be of use to him or help him in any way, I shall be delighted to do so.

I still possess Lorchen's silhouette. So you see how precious to me even now are all the dear, beloved memories of my youth.

As for my diplomas, I merely mention that I am an honorary member of the Royal Scientific Society of Sweden and likewise of Amsterdam, and also an honorary citizen of Vienna. A short time ago a certain Dr. Spiker took with him to Berlin my latest grand symphony with choruses; it is dedicated to the king, and I had to write the dedication with my own hand. I had previously applied to the legation for permission to dedicate this work to the king, which His Majesty then granted. At Dr. Spiker's instigation, I myself had to give him the corrected manuscript with the alterations in my own handwriting to be delivered to the king, because the work is to be kept in the Royal Library. On that occasion something was said to me about the Order of the Red Eagle, Second Class. Whether anything will come of this, I don't know, for I have never striven after honors of that kind. Yet at the present time, for many other reasons, such an award would be rather welcome. In any case, my motto is always: *Nulla dies sine linea* [No day without a line]; and if I let my Muse go to sleep, it is only that she may be all the more active when she awakes. I still hope to create a few great works and then, like an old child to finish my earthly course somewhere among kind people. You will soon receive some music from the Gebrüder Schott at Mainz. The portrait I am sending with this letter is certainly an artistic masterpiece, but it is not the latest one which has been done of me. Speaking about my honors, which I know you are pleased to hear of, I must add that the late king of France sent me a medal with the inscription: *Donné par le Roi à Monsieur Beethoven*. It was accompanied by a very courteous letter from the Duc de Chartres, Premier Gentilhomme du Roi.

My beloved friend! You must be content with this letter for today. I need hardly tell you that I have been overcome by the remembrance of things past and that many tears have been shed while the letter was being written. Still we have now begun to correspond, and you will soon have another letter from me. And the more often you write to me, the greater will be the pleasure you afford me. Our friendship is too intimate to need inquiries from either of us. And now I send you all good wishes. Please embrace and kiss your dear Lorchen and your children for me, and when doing so think of me. God be with you all!

Ever your true and faithful friend who honors you,

BEETHOVEN [44]

Dying, momentarily given respite from a mortal crisis, Beethoven at last renounced the legend of his noble birth. Perhaps he could begin to take leave of his Family Romance only after his creative career had run its course. He was, however, not yet wholly rid of his birth delusions. As we noted in our first chapter, having written the letter to Wegeler authorizing the refutation of the Family Romance, Beethoven neglected to mail it until the latter half of February 1827—a few weeks before his death, and only after the receipt of a reproachful letter from his Bonn friend. And in the letter itself, Beethoven unconsciously restated his lingering adherence to the Family Romance by means of a long recital of his medals and honors, and especially by stressing his dedication of the Ninth Symphony to Friedrich Wilhelm III, the scion of his supposed father.

As we have seen, Beethoven had obtained permission earlier in the year to dedicate the Ninth Symphony to the Prussian king. In September, Haslinger had been delegated to have the presentation copy of the score luxuriously bound ("If you would be so kind as to have the score . . . as beautifully bound as befits *a king*, you would do me a great favor" [45]), and Beethoven wrote an appropriate dedicatory message: "Your Majesty is not only the supreme father of your subjects but also the patron of arts and sciences. . . . I too, since I am a native of Bonn, am fortunate enough to regard myself as one of your subjects." [46] Beethoven delayed his departure for Gneixendorf for three days to be certain that all details had been attended to. As he informed Wegeler, it was his hope and expectation that a Royal Order would be forthcoming as a token of appreciation. Approaches were made through the Prussian ambassador, Prince Hatzfeld, and through Dr. Spiker, the king's librarian. The Berlin publisher Adolph Martin Schlesinger reported to Beethoven in Vienna that he need have no fear of a slipup: "You will certainly receive it." [47] Holz advised that the path was well paved, and he, too, reassured the composer: "[Spiker] says that the decoration will be very easy; the king is very inclined in your favor. . . . The decoration will come sooner than you think." [48] Nephew Karl saw the matter in its proper perspective: "I believe that a decoration could not make you greater than you are without it," he said, and he told of a certain doctor who had ten decorations but about whom no one gave a second thought. [49]

In any case, this trivial honor, which meant so much to Beethoven and which would have given him so much pleasure, was denied him. The decoration was not forthcoming, and in its stead Beethoven was sent a ring. "I thank you for this gift," wrote the king to Beethoven in December, "and send you the accompanying diamond ring [*Brillant-ring*] as a token of my sincere appreciation." [50] Beethoven's disappointment was temporarily assuaged by the expectation of a costly present: he and his friends fluttered with excitement as they awaited its delivery. Beethoven drafted a letter to Prince Hatzfeld at the embassy: "I must ask you to be so kind as to send me the ring which H. M. the King of Prussia has decided to give me—I am very sorry that an indisposition prevents me from receiving in person this token (which is so precious to me) of H. M.'s love of art." [51] The ring turned out to contain, however, not a diamond, but a cheap, "reddish"-looking stone which Holz took to the court jeweler for appraisal. When he returned with the news that the ring was worth only 160 florins, Beethoven insisted that it be sold. "Holz tried to prevent this with the remark: 'Master, keep the ring, it is from a King.' Beethoven rose up before Holz and with indescribable dignity and self-consciousness he called out: 'I too am a King!' "[52] In this pronouncement we may have the final and poignant efflorescence of Beethoven's Family Romance fantasy before it yielded to the importunities of reality and to the gathering harbingers of mortality.

Karl remained at Beethoven's bedside throughout December, tending to his uncle's needs. Their conflicts were at an end: there were no further quarrels, suspicions, or reproaches, and Karl, at last, could now freely and unreservedly express his love for his uncle. On January 2 he left for Iglau to join his regiment; the next day Beethoven wrote a will, declaring that "Karl van Beethoven, my beloved nephew, is the sole heir to all my property" and appointing his attorney, Dr. Bach, as trustee of the estate.[53] On January 13, Karl wrote to Beethoven: "My dear father . . . I am living in contentment, and regret only that I am separated from you." [54] Two other letters from Karl to Beethoven have been preserved—the last written on March 4, asking for news and signed, "Your loving son"—but not a single further letter from Beethoven to his nephew.

Following the temporary remission during the second week of December, Beethoven's condition rapidly deteriorated. Wawruch wrote: "Trembling and shivering, he bent double because of the pains which raged in his liver and intestines, and his feet, thitherto moderately inflated, were tremendously swollen. From this time on dropsy developed, the segregation of urine became less, the liver showed plain indication of hard nodules, [and] there was an increase of jaundice." [55] The abdominal fluids were tapped on December 20, following a consultation between Wawruch and Staudenheim. The fluids amounted to 25 pounds, and the afterflow to five times as much. A second operation took place on January 8, and on January 11 a council of physicians—including Beethoven's long-estranged old friend, Dr. Malfatti—was held. (According to Gerhard von Breuning, Beethoven "awaited Malfatti's visits as eagerly as those of a Messiah." [56]) There being no medical treatment which stood any chance of success, Malfatti recommended that Beethoven be given a frozen alcoholic beverage to relieve his discomfort and his frequent periods of melancholy. At first, attempts were made to limit his intake to one glass per day; following two further abdominal tappings on February 2 and 27, however, all restrictions as to quantity were lifted.

As the news of Beethoven's mortal illness circulated, old friends gathered at the Schwarzspanierhaus to wish him well, and to bid him farewell. Schindler, Holz, the Breunings, Nikolaus Johann, and Beethoven's housekeeper, Sali, were in regular attendance. Visitors included Haslinger, Diabelli, Clement, Piringer, Schickh, Andreas Streicher (but, apparently, not his wife), Bernard, Doležalek, Schuppanzigh, and Moritz Lichnowsky. Gleichenstein made several appearances, bringing his wife and son. Beethoven's old friend and rival, Hummel, arrived with his young student, Ferdinand Hiller, and with his wife Elizabeth. She took her handkerchief and wiped the perspiration from Beethoven's face several times. "Never," Hiller wrote, "shall I forget the grateful glance with which his broken eye looked upon her."[57] (Contrary to legend, Schubert did not visit the death bed but he and his friends followed the progress of Beethoven's illness with deep concern.) Zmeskall, confined to his house, sent greetings to his old comrade, and Beethoven responded:

> A thousand thanks for your sympathy. I do not despair. But what is most painful to me is the complete cessation of my activities. Yet there is no evil which has not something good in it as well. May Heaven grant you, too, an alleviation of your painful condition. Perhaps we shall both be restored to health and then we shall meet and see one another again as friendly neighbors.[58]

Beethoven's friendly former landlord, Baron Pasqualati, cheered the patient with gifts of Viennese desserts. The Philharmonic Society of London, learning of Beethoven's illness and being informed by him in letters to Smart, Stumpff, and Moscheles that he was in financial distress, unanimously passed a motion to lend him 100 pounds "to be applied to his comforts and necessities during his illness." [59] (Later, learning that he had left a fairly sizable estate, the society felt that it had been deceived, but it decided to take no action to recover its loan.) Beethoven gratefully promised that he would compose a new symphony or overture for the society.

In mid-February, Diabelli brought to Beethoven a lithograph of Haydn's birthplace in Rohrau which he had just published. Gerhard von Breuning writes: "The picture caused him great pleasure; when I came at noon, he showed it to me at once: 'Look, I got this today. Just see the little house, and such a great man was born in it. Your father must have a frame made for me; I'm going to hang it up.'" Gerhard brought the lithograph to his piano teacher, who made the frame and added in the lower margin: "Joseph Hayden's [sic] Birthplace in Rohrau." Beethoven became furious at the misspelling of Haydn's name; his "face turned red with rage and he asked me angrily: 'Who wrote that, anyway? . . . What's that donkey's name? An ignoramus like that calls himself a piano teacher, calls himself a musician, and can't even spell the name of a master like *Haydn*.'"[60]

He delighted, though, in showing the lithograph to visitors. Hiller related that Beethoven showed it to him and to others with the words: "It gave me a childish pleasure—the cradle of a great man." [61] Can we understand a note of puzzlement in Beethoven's comment: "See the little house, and such a great man was born in it"? Is there here an intimation that Beethoven marveled that greatness was not incompatible with lowly origins?

In any event, Beethoven had become fully reconciled with Haydn, had transformed him into his good "Papa" once again. Feelings of love had surfaced during these months of Beethoven's final illness and of his long-awaited reconciliations. The lithograph of Haydn stood next to his deathbed; on the wall was the oil painting of Ludwig van Beethoven, the elder. The images of two *Kapellmeister* gave Beethoven solace at the end.

Two young singers, Ludwig Cramolini and his fiancée Nanette Schechtner, paid their respects to the composer whom they worshiped. Beethoven asked Cramolini to sing for him, but the young man was so overcome by the occasion that he could not produce any sounds. When Schindler told Beethoven what had happened, Beethoven burst out laughing and said: "Go ahead and sing, my dear Louis! I can hear nothing, alas! I only want to see you sing." [62]

The end was fast approaching. The last sacraments were rendered, with Beethoven's consent. "Here I have been lying for four months!" he cried out; "One must at last lose patience!" [63] Seeking comfort in tasty foods, he wrote to Pasqualati: "I thank you for the dish of food which you sent me yesterday. An invalid craves like a child for something of that kind. So I am asking you today for the stewed peaches. . . ." [64] And again: "Please send me some more stewed cherries today, but cooked quite simply, without any lemon. Further, a light pudding, almost like gruel, would give me great pleasure." [65] His thoughts turned to the Rhine, and he wrote to Schott in Mainz, on March 10, asking that he send him some Rhine wines: "They will certainly bring me refreshment, invigoration, and good health." [66]

Beethoven still needed to achieve one more—perhaps the most important—reconciliation. On March 23, he picked up his pen for perhaps the last time in his life and began to copy a codicil to his will which Breuning had prepared. According to the original draft, the capital of Beethoven's legacy would be held in trust, with his nephew to "draw the interest, and the principal to pass to the nephew's legitimate offspring after his death." [67] Nikolaus Johann, Schindler, Breuning, and Breuning's son all watched as Beethoven painfully transcribed the codicil in a faltering hand. His pen trembled and he was unable to form the words clearly, adding extra letters to several words and omitting others from his signature:

> My nephew Karl shall be my sole legatee, but the capital of my estate shall fall to his natural or testamentary heirs.
>
> LUWIG VAN BEETHOEN [68]

He set down the pen with the words: "There! I won't write another word." Despite the protests of the astonished observers, Beethoven refused to change this altered provision, by which the entire capital of his estate would pass to Johanna van Beethoven—the "Queen of Night"— in the event of the death of her son, who was unmarried and who had just entered military service.[69] For she was then the only "natural or testamentary heir" of nephew Karl. By this action, Beethoven at last made his peace with the woman who, more than any other, had shaped the biographical, and perhaps the creative, currents of his last decade.

On the following day, March 24, Schindler wrote to Moscheles: "He feels the end coming, for yesterday he said to me and H. v. Breuning, 'Plaudite, amici, comoedia finita est.' (Applaud, friends, the comedy is ended.)" [70] On the same day the wines arrived from Mainz, and Schindler brought the bottles to the bedside table. Beethoven whispered, "Pity, pity—too late!" and spoke no more. He fell into a coma that evening, which lasted until his death on the 26th. Late in the afternoon of the final day, during a snowfall and thunderstorm, Beethoven momentarily opened his eyes, lifted his right hand, and clenched it into a fist. When his hand fell back from this effort, Beethoven was dead.

According to the testimony of Anselm Hüttenbrenner, who witnessed Beethoven's moment of death, Johanna van Beethoven was the only other person present at the end.[71] This was startling information when Thayer received it in 1860, for Schindler had suppressed the identity of the woman in the room. Thayer could not believe that Johanna and Beethoven had been reconciled, and he apparently urged Hüttenbrenner to reconsider his testimony, whereupon Hüttenbrenner substituted Therese van Beethoven's name for that of Johanna.[72] Although there can no longer be any certainty in this matter, Hüttenbrenner's first recollection remains the best evidence, and it is therefore probable that Johanna was the Frau van Beethoven who cut a lock of hair from Beethoven's head and handed it to Hüttenbrenner "as a sacred souvenir of Beethoven's last hour." [73]

Shortly after Beethoven's death, his brother, Breuning, Schindler, and Holz searched his lodgings for the composer's seven remaining bank shares, eventually finding them in a concealed drawer of an old cabinet. Also found were two miniature ivory portraits, of Giulietta Guicciardi and Antonie Brentano. As we noted in our introduction, Schindler surreptitiously gathered up and removed many items of memorabilia: included were 400 Conversation Books; many manuscripts; Beethoven's eyeglasses and ear trumpets; numerous statuettes of male figures, including a bust of Brutus; the clock carved in alabaster, which the Princess Lichnowsky had given to Beethoven many years before; and the letter to the Immortal Beloved. Beethoven's remaining manuscripts and scores were taken for appraisal by Jacob Hotschevar, Johanna's former advocate, who became guardian of nephew Karl upon the death of Stephan von Breuning in mid-1827. Among these papers was found the Heiligenstadt Testament, which was published in the *Allgemeine musikalische Zeitung* on October 17. Beethoven's belongings were auctioned on November 5, 1827, and brought 1,140 florins. Included were all of his sketchbooks, autographs of his published works, fragments of unpublished works, original manuscripts, parts, scores, printed music, and books. The original autograph of the *Missa Solemnis* sold for 7 florins, while that of the Septet brought 18. The entire estate, including the bank shares, brought just over 10,000 florins.

The Viennese, who, in addition to having an affection for Beethoven, always enjoyed *"eine schöne Leich"* (a lovely funeral), turned out en masse to bid farewell to their greatest composer. Ten thousand or more (some estimated the throng at double and even triple that number) crowded the streets on March 29 to witness the great procession, which wound through the streets from the courtyard of the Schwarzspanierhaus to the church in the Alsergasse and thence to the suburb of Währing, where Grillparzer's eloquent funeral oration was rendered by the actor Anschütz and Beethoven was buried in the parish cemetery. The pallbearers were eight *Kapellmeister;* the torchbearers included many of Beethoven's closest friends as well as Vienna's leading musicians. A choir sang a solemn *Miserere* to the somber accompaniment of trombones. Close behind the coffin followed numerous friends and admirers, led by Stephan and Gerhard von Breuning, Nikolaus Johann, and Johanna van Beethoven.

Title page of the *Grosse Fuge*,
op. 133 (1827).

22
The Music

Beethoven continued to uphold the ideals of the Enlightenment, of Classicism, and of aristocratic excellence even after historical conditions had rendered these anachronistic. Nor did he abandon—rather, he expanded—his search for a multiplicity of musical syntheses. In the late works, his archetypal patterns retain their impress: struggle is sublimated into ecstasy, as in the Arietta of the Sonata, op. 111; chaos strives for lucid formation, as in the transition to the fugue of the *Hammerklavier* Sonata and in the opening of the finale of the Ninth Symphony; victorious conclusions are incessantly sought after and discovered, as in the *Grosse Fuge,* the Sonata, op. 110, and the finale of the Quartet in C-sharp minor, op. 131. Beethoven could no longer confront such issues, however, with his previous musical vocabulary or procedures. As Parry observed, Beethoven had by now found "the accepted scheme of organization which he himself had brought to perfection too constraining and restrictive to the impulse of his thought, and therefore endeavored to find new types of form and to revive sundry earlier types of organization and combine them in various ways which departed from the essential principles upon which composers had been working for generations." [1]

As we shall see, Parry's implication that Beethoven was to create "new" forms in his late works may well be overstated, for Beethoven never relinquished his reliance upon the Classic structures; rather he imbued them with greater freedom and fantasy. Nevertheless, Beethoven's achievement of an unprecedented "modernism" was made possible by his recognition that in certain respects the received Classical style had become an impediment to further development, and his realization that there remained unexplored avenues in earlier stages of musical development which had been bypassed by the composers of the post-Baroque generations. The Classical style had, in the music of Haydn, Mozart, and Beethoven, created an extensive and unique body of masterpieces and revolutionized musical forms and vocabulary. In a certain sense, however, the Classical style can also be thought of as constituting a great regression in music history—setting aside as it did the entire superstructure of Baroque style, with its advanced harmonic language, its rich polyphonic procedures, its highly organized and complex forms, and its simultaneous dedication to both spirituality and splendor. This took place in accordance with the prevailing hedonism of the eighteenth-century aristocratic courts and salons, and with the sanction of the Enlightenment's best theoreticians. It was a regression cloaked in the authority of Reason, opposed to theological contrivances and devoted to rationality and simplicity. Typically, in his *Lettre sur la musique française* (1753), Rousseau wrote: "With regard to counterfugues, double fugues, inverted fugues, ground basses, and other difficult sillinesses that the ear cannot abide and which reason cannot justify, these are obviously remnants of barbarism and bad taste that only persist, like the portals of our Gothic cathedrals, to the shame of those who had the endurance to build them." [2]

With the passing of the Enlightenment and its aesthetic dogmas, Beethoven was free to seek and to find new influences within the very heritage which it had superseded, to create more flexible musical structures and new tonal trajectories by means of a partial restoration of some of the Baroque and pre-Baroque techniques, forms, and procedures which had been thrown overboard by Classicism. It is this trend—one which should not be overstated—which provides the retrospective current in Beethoven's late works, and which paradoxically gives to them a simultaneously archaic and prospective cast of thought. And so, late Beethoven is characterized by a highly concentrated exploration of counterpoint and polyphonic textures, by a serious interest in Bach and Handel, by a new awareness of the church modes, by the utilization of Baroque-style "theme types" with specific symbolic meanings, by a turn toward instrumental recitative, by a pre-Classic richness of ornamentation employed for expressive purposes, by a heightened preoccupation with monothematic development and variation procedures. These constitute not a return to an idealized past in the manner of many German Romantics, nor a set of antiquarian researches, but rather the expression of Beethoven's search for germinating influences and modes of expression which could aid him in the symbolization of new spheres of psychic and social experience, spheres which were inaccessible to the dramatic and overtly dialectical procedures of sonata form and obbligato style.

So deeply are these influences embedded within Beethoven's personal style that it has taken scholars a century and a half to make a small start on unearthing them. Of course, one cannot dissolve Beethoven's late style into its sources, as some have recently attempted to do, because many of its characteristics, as well as its "sound," are unprecedented in the history of music. One can only hint here at the extraordinary and unique characteristics of the late style (the reader is referred to the excellent discussions in Kerman, Cooper, Riezler, and Tovey)—the organic use of the trill for the intensification of emotion; the use of simple, even prosaic musical materials both to contrast with a sublime rhetoric and to reveal the sublimity hidden within the commonplace; the aggressive, dotted-rhythmic polyphonic textures which create a simultaneous sense of irresistible motion and unbearable strain; the turn toward thematic material that is ever more terse and pregnant; the attempt to capture the expressiveness of the human body by a magnified use of dance and march forms (this is part of what Cooper calls a "transfigured 'play' element" [3] in Beethoven's last compositions); and, as Kerman has written, a profound yielding to the "vocal impulse" in both his vocal and instrumental music, which makes the late works Beethoven's "crowning monument to lyricism." [4] And not only lyricism, but rhetoric, declamation, and recitative as well: speech and song together press to fulfill Beethoven's drive toward immediacy of communication.

We last mentioned Beethoven's *Lieder*—apart from brief references to the Gellert *Lieder* and to the orchestral *Egmont* songs—in our discussion of his music of the Bonn period. During the intervening years, he continued to show an intermittent interest in this genre, composing more than fifty *Lieder* between 1793 and 1815 and sketching numerous others which he never completed. His main *Lieder* publications were the Six Gellert Songs, op. 48 (1801–02), which included at least two distinguished songs, "Bitten" and "Vom Tode," the latter with pungent chromaticisms and a Schumannesque quality; Six Songs, op. 75 (published in 1810, although composed at various earlier dates) to texts by Goethe and Reissig; and three Goethe Songs, op. 83 (1811), including the touching "Wonne der Wehmut." Several individual *Lieder* are of interest, such as "An die Hoffnung," op. 32, and "Gedenke mein," WoO 130, both of which were presented to (and subsequently taken back from) Josephine Deym in early 1805; "An die Geliebte," WoO 140, written for Antonie Brentano in 1811; and, especially, a second, through-composed setting of "An die Hoffnung" c. 1815, cast in the form of a recitative and aria, a form he had used less persuasively in several early Vienna songs, the "Seufzer eines Ungeliebten und Gegenliebe," WoO 118, and the popular "Adelaide," op. 46.

Between late 1809 and 1818 Beethoven also composed about 180 arrangements of Scottish, Irish, and Welsh songs for one or more voices with piano, violin, and cello accompaniment. They were commissioned by the Edinburgh publisher, George Thomson, who obtained similar work from Pleyel, Koželuch, Haydn, Hummel, Weber, and others in a multivolume project. Thomson published 126 of Beethoven's arrangements and paid Beethoven well for his work (over 550 pounds), but the results are of little value: Beethoven was not provided with the texts and he failed to treat the underlying modal harmonic structure and irregular time in the pentatonic and hexatonic traditional songs. The settings of composed songs (with contemporary texts by Scott, Burns, Campbell, and others) are more successful, and several of these, such as that of Scott's "On the Massacre of Glencoe," WoO 152 no. 5, are extremely beautiful.

The theme of yearning for the unattainable pervades many of Beethoven's best *Lieder*. Indeed, he composed six songs entitled "Yearning" ("Sehnsucht")—five set to two poems by Goethe (WoO 134; op. 83 no. 2) and one in the winter of 1815–16, to a poem by Reissig, WoO 146. Yearning was, of course, the subject of Beethoven's song cycle, *An die ferne Geliebte* [To the distant beloved], op. 98, composed in April 1816 to a Romantic pastoral text by Alois Jeitteles, a young poet and medical student then closely associated with many of Vienna's theatrical and musical personalities. Jeitteles apparently wrote the poems especially for Beethoven, perhaps to his order. Rolland and others have speculated that the cycle may have been written as a love offering to the Immortal Beloved;[5] and it is true that Beethoven was wont to use *Lieder* as love offerings—to Josephine Deym, to Therese Malfatti ("Sehnsucht," op. 83 no 2), to Antonie Brentano. Or was it resistance to his desire for Johanna shortly after the death of her husband which brought this counterbalancing, Platonic *Liederkreis* into existence? Or is the cycle's yearning quality more generalized, its sense of loss flowing from the numerous leavetakings and deaths of so many of Beethoven's close friends and patrons during the preceding years? (Does this bear upon the dedication of the work to the dying Prince Lobkowitz in October 1816?) A psychoanalyst might object that the "distant beloved" is unfailingly and fundamentally the imago of the idealized mother and that the yearning, renunciatory tone of the *Liederkreis* therefore represents the symbolic fulfillment or sublimation of Oedipal desires. It is impossible to tell which, if any, of these factors were operative here, especially since the impulse which gives rise to a work of art may be years or decades old by the time its working-out begins.

Still, *An die ferne Geliebte,* which Kerman calls "a quiet herald of the third-period style," [6] occupies a special place in Beethoven's life and work. It bids farewell to his marriage project, to romantic pretense, to heroic grandiosity, to youth itself. It is a work which accepts loss without piteous outcry, for it preserves intact the memory of the past and refuses to acknowledge the finality of bereavement:

> For song effaces
> all space and all time,
> and a loving heart attains
> that to which a loving heart consecrates itself.[7]

The musical significance of *An die ferne Geliebte* is that, primitive anticipations by such composers as Himmel and Reichardt aside, it was the first through-composed song cycle and became the point of departure for the cycles of Schumann and many others (though not of Schubert, who maintained a deliberate independence). Beethoven actually carried the process of unification of his material further than the Romantics, for he wove the six songs together so tightly, by means of interconnecting piano passages, that they cannot be sung separately. Rolland therefore calls the cycle "one *Lied,* with varied episodes," and Boettcher dubs it "a single, prodigiously extended *Lied.*" [8] In the forms and keys of the songs, Beethoven established a symmetrical architectonic plan. With a view to still further symmetry, the tune of the first song was originally intended for the sixth one as well, but Beethoven eventually settled on a variant, related melody and then introduced the opening melody as a conscious reminiscence (a touch derived from instrumental practice) just prior to the close of the cycle, with heartbreaking effect.

Kerman, in his illuminating study of this work, stresses the ways in which it opens the way to Beethoven's last style: the cyclic form of the *Liederkreis* is the prototype of similar structures in the last works, such as the Quartet, op. 131, and the *Grosse Fuge,* op. 133 (and, he might have added, the Bagatelles, op. 126). And he sees the song cycle as inaugurating the "vocal impulse" which will reach fruition in songful movements of the late sonatas and late quartets, and in the Adagio and "Ode to Joy" of the Ninth Symphony.

Two further songs close out Beethoven's significant *Lieder* production: the melancholy "Resignation," WoO 149, of 1817, and "Abendlied unterm gestirnten Himmel," WoO 150, a deeply felt dramatic ode to the deity, composed on March 4, 1820, while Beethoven was awaiting the decision of the Court of Appeal.

Beethoven often complained about the limitations of the piano, and he continued to do so up until his last year, when he told Holz: "It is and remains an inadequate instrument." [9] Nevertheless, it was perhaps inevitable that the piano, the earliest vehicle of Beethoven's fantasy, invention, and virtuosity, should now take the lead in the forging of his late style. His song cycle completed, Beethoven turned once again to the piano sonata and composed his last five piano sonatas between mid-1816 and the beginning of 1822. These sonatas, along with the Diabelli Variations and the Bagatelles, op. 126, form one of the pillars of Beethoven's creative achievement in his last years. It was in them that he first worked out the fusion of fugue, variation form, and sonata form which is fundamental to the formulation of his new musical thought. The Sonata, op. 101, was completed in November 1816 and published the following February by Steiner with a dedication to Dorothea Ertmann. The work is similar in design to the fantasy sonatas of earlier years, with its climax reserved for the finale and an expressive "Langsam und sehnsuchtsvoll" introduction leading to a dramatic, contrapuntally conceived sonata-form movement, the development section of which is a four-part fugue. With the Sonata, op. 101, it became clear that the fugue of the finale of the Cello Sonata, op. 102 no. 2, of 1815, was not an isolated musical event but rather the first expression of a veritable contrapuntal obsession during Beethoven's last decade.

Beethoven received from Albrechtsberger a solid grounding in counterpoint, but, as Nottebohm observed, he did not acquire from him "a thorough training in fugue." [10] During his first two decades in Vienna Beethoven utilized fugal elements and procedures in many works, including the opus 18 quartets and the first Mass, and occasionally composed fugatos (as in the Funeral March of the *Eroica* Symphony, the Allegretto of the Seventh Symphony, and several choruses of *Christ on the Mount of Olives*); but his only really large fugal movements were the finales of the Quartet, op. 59 no. 3, and of the Variations and Fugue, op. 35. Nottebohm would not grant that even these were proper fugues, and, according to Schindler, neither would many of Beethoven's more pedantic contemporaries, who spread the word: "Beethoven is incapable of writing a fugue." [11] Schindler, in his simplicity, believed that Beethoven's preoccupation with the fugue in his last period was his response to this criticism. But what Misch calls "the rebirth of fugue from the spirit of the sonata" [12] arose out of Beethoven's need to create musical movement of a different type than was permitted by the obbligato style, and at the same time expressed his search to expand the possibilities of sonata form itself. More than half of Beethoven's major works would henceforth contain a full-scale fugue, and many others would contain fughettas, fugatos, canons, and other brief contrapuntal passages.[13] In his last decade, Beethoven, who had come to maturity in an antipolyphonic age, reinstated the polyphonic principle as a rival of (and perhaps as the completion of) the sonata principle. The years 1816–17 were a turning point. In 1817 he wrote a string quintet movement in D minor as an introduction to a fugue which was not composed; he began an arrangement for string quartet of the B-minor fugue from Bach's *Well-Tempered Clavier*, Book One; and he completed a Fugue in D major for String Quintet, later published as op. 137.[14]

The first climax of this preoccupation with polyphony occurs in the *Hammerklavier* Sonata, op. 106, of 1817–18. Beethoven's longest sonata (it is almost 1,200 bars), the *Hammerklavier* is in Classic four-movement form. Even more than Beethoven's other late sonatas, it presents technical difficulties which place it far beyond the reach of amateur pianists. (One tradition has it that Beethoven composed the work in competition with Hummel's "unplayable" Sonata in F-sharp minor.[15]) The sonata apparently received several private performances (reportedly by Czerny, Ries, Cipriani Potter) in Beethoven's lifetime; eventually, through the efforts of Liszt and Moscheles in particular, it came to be considered one of the greatest and most challenging works of the piano repertory. Beethoven is said to have told Artaria, who published the work in September 1819: "Now there you have a sonata that will keep the pianists busy when it is played fifty years hence." [16]

The fugue in three voices constitutes the entire finale, save for the 15-bar transitional Largo. It is filled with learned contrapuntal devices— Riezler even describes it as "overladen to the point of artificiality with all the arts of the fugue" [17]—which serve to intensify the aggressive and rebellious thrust of the movement, with its defiant and relentless striving (*Allegro risoluto*) to surmount immense obstacles. Never had Beethoven attempted so difficult an affirmation, and it is this effort which dictates the special nature of the contrapuntal writing. In his earlier years, Beethoven had utilized counterpoint to convey urbane humor (the Scherzo of opus 18 no. 4) or to introduce a measured and heroic solemnity (the Funeral March of the *Eroica* Symphony), to momentarily disrupt periodicity (the first movement of opus 18 no. 1) or to create a seamless, powerful rhythmic impulse (the Finale of opus 59 no. 3; the Cum sancto spiritu and the Et vitam venturi of the Mass in C). Here the textures are harsh and angular and the counterpoint rough-hewn and granulated, bursting outward with explosive force, the fugue's jagged qualities accentuated by the occasional lyrical passages which interrupt its unremitting advance. Cooper writes: "There is in this finale, as in the Grosse Fuge, an element of excessiveness . . . an instinct to push every component part of the music . . . not just to its logical conclusion but beyond," and he feels that in a sense Beethoven was thereby "doing violence to his listener." [18] The violence is not in Beethoven's intent, however, but in his subject matter, for here, as in the *Grosse Fuge*, the fugue's closest analogue is the process of birth, the pain-ridden, exultant struggle for emergence—and the passage through the labyrinth, from darkness to light, from doubt to belief, from suffering to joy, cannot be without its special torments. By the same token, such an emergence is not without its manic raptures, and it is this aspect which led Rolland to stress the mood of turbulent caprice, the laughing spirit which erupts from the fugal texture.[19]

Rosen has demonstrated the organic unity of the *Hammerklavier* Sonata in a detailed analysis which shows that all of its movements are built up from a "central idea"—a relentless use of chains of descending thirds.[20] It is not altogether clear, however, that Beethoven felt he had succeeded in forging an aesthetically whole four-movement Classic work from materials which were disruptive of Classical form. Perhaps he momentarily questioned his own effort, for in late March 1819, he authorized Ries to publish the sonata in England in any one of three forms:

1. The first two movements alone.
2. The Allegro risoluto by itself, without the Largo.
3. The first three movements, with the order of the Scherzo and Adagio reversed.

"I leave it to you to do as you think best," [21] Beethoven wrote, whereupon Ries arranged to publish the English edition as two separate though connected works: a "Grand Sonata for the Piano Forte," consisting of the first three movements in the order I, III, II; and an "Introduction & Fugue for the Piano Forte," consisting of the Largo and Allegro risoluto.[22] Many scholars believe that Beethoven, knowing that the sonata was being published correctly in Vienna, did not mind what was done with it in London.[23]

In summary, Rosen observed that opus 106 "is not typical of Beethoven, and does not sound it; it is not even typical of his last period. It is an extreme point of his style. He never again wrote so obsessively concentrated a work. In part, it must have been an attempt to break out of the impasse in which he found himself." [24]

Beethoven wrote the three last sonatas following the close of the guardianship litigation and during the composition of the *Missa Solemnis*. The Sonata in E, op. 109, was completed by late summer of 1820; opus 110, in A-flat, by the end of 1821; and opus 111, in C minor, by the beginning of 1822. They were published by Schlesinger in November 1821, ca. August 1822, and ca. April 1823, respectively.[25] Here Beethoven no longer attempted to impart a symphonic breadth to his sonata style, but returned to the smaller dimensions of the Sonatas, op. 90 and op. 101, which were now infused alternately with a variety of rigorous polyphonic textures and an etherealized improvisatory tone. In all three, the climax of the cycle has again been shifted to the finale: in opus 110 this is a long and complex fugue which, however, has none of the cross-grained quality of opus 106. It is the smoothest of Beethoven's fugal finales and surely also one of the most moving, with its introductory recitative and "sorrowful song" (Arioso dolente), which returns to alternate with the fugue and thus to prepare for the sonata's harmonious conclusion. In the two other sonatas, however, the concluding movements are sets of variations—the first time that Beethoven had utilized variation form in the finale of a piano sonata, although he had done so earlier in the closing movements of the *Eroica* Symphony, the Quartet, op. 74, and the Violin Sonatas, op. 30 no. 1 and op. 96.

By 1820, Beethoven had written more than sixty sets of variations, either as separate works or as movements of larger cycles; but with opus 109 and opus 111 he imbued the form for the first time with a "transfigured," almost ecstatic content and a profundity of expression which indicated that he had found in this basic musical form a new vehicle for his most imaginative musical thought. Thereby, variation form joins fugue as one of the leading characteristics of the late style, and variation movements appear in many of his last masterpieces, including the Adagio and finale of the Ninth Symphony and crucial movements of the Quartets, opp. 127, 131, 132, and 135. The crowning work of this new preoccupation is the Thirty-three Variations on a Waltz by Diabelli, op. 120.

In his middle period, the model for Beethoven's sonata cycle was drama—comedy, tragedy, and the combined forms of these which touch upon mythic and collective levels of experience. This model retained its resiliency and power in the last "public" works: the *Missa Solemnis* and the Ninth Symphony. Perhaps the *Hammerklavier* Sonata embodied Beethoven's powerful desire to hold on, not only to Classicism and the received sonata style, but to the dramatic model as well. Beethoven's aggressive and disruptive contrapuntal procedures had already undermined this model, while retaining the dialectic and synthesizing functions which are as characteristic of fugue as of sonata. But with the "grand variation" or "chorale with variations" (as d'Indy alternately names Beethoven's late variation works), we are at a loss to specify the new model which Beethoven is drawing on. Blom recognized this problem when he asked, after outlining Beethoven's alternating use of the two standard procedures of variation—melodic and harmonic—in the Diabelli Variations: "Wherein consists the startling novelty, the greatness and originality that has been so often claimed for them? How, in other words, did Beethoven advance the variation form?" [26]

From a technical point of view, Blom found the most important advance to lie in Beethoven's "recognition of the fact that a theme may be modified almost without limit in detail, so long as the structure of any variation keeps closely to the structure of the theme itself at the critical [i.e., harmonic, modulatory] points." But he acknowledged that neither this structural approach nor Beethoven's unusually extended development

of the coda were true innovations, and he concluded that technical novelty by itself is unable to account for the advance:

> The answer to our question must be completed by the assertion that
> Beethoven added a spiritual quality to his greatest variation sets . . .
> which is the personal secret of his genius. It may be said that whereas
> earlier composers—and later ones, too, if it comes to that—*transformed*
> their themes more or less ingeniously, he *transfigured* his in his best
> variation works.

This statement may appear to avoid issues rather than to illuminate them,
but it is this elusive quality of transfiguration—with its overtones of sublimated and ecstatic states—that most listeners have sensed in Beethoven's late variations. These qualities are not abstractions, however; they
too must have their prototypes in psychological processes and mental
phenomena.

Variation is potentially the most "open" of musical procedures, one
which gives the greatest freedom to the composer's fantasy. It mirrors
the unpredictability and chance nature of human experience and keeps
alive the openness of human expectation. Fate cannot knock at the door
in the variation form: such concepts as necessity and inevitability need
a dialectical musical pattern within which to express their message,
whereas the variation form is discursive and peripatetic, in flight from all
messages and ideologies. Its subject is the adventurer, the picaro, the
quick-change artist, the impostor, the phoenix who ever rises from the
ashes, the rebel who, defeated, continues his quest, the thinker who
doubts perception, who shapes and reshapes reality in search of its inner
significance, the omnipotent child who plays with matter as God plays
with the universe. Variation is the form of shifting moods, alternations
of feeling, shades of meaning, dislocations of perspective. It shatters appearance into splinters of previously unperceived reality and, by an act
of will, reassembles the fragments at the close. The sense of time is effaced—expanded, contracted—by changes in tempo; space and mass dissolve into the barest outline of the harmonic progressions and build up
once again into baroque structures laden with richly ornamented patterns.
The theme remains throughout as an anchor to prevent fantasy from losing
contact with the outer world, but it too dissolves into the memories,
images, and feelings which underlie its simple reality. In this the theme
is like the manifest dream—a simple, condensed sequence of images
masking an infinity of latent dream thoughts. The manifest dream is
deceptively simple, wrapped in disguises of distortion, censorship, condensation, and displacement. Analysis (variation) pierces these veils;
recollection fills the dream (the theme) with a significance that illuminates
the past and points toward future possibilities of transcendence and
fulfillment.

We cannot really press the analogy further. The most that can be said is that Beethoven himself was conscious of composing his music in accordance with internalized visual images of an unspecified nature. "I have always a picture in my mind, when I am composing," he told Neate, "and work up to it." [27] And to Louis Schlösser he described how he carried his thoughts with him for a long time before setting to work: "Then the working-out in breadth, length, height, and depth begins in my head, and since I am conscious of what I want, the basic idea never leaves me. It rises, grows upward, and I hear and see the picture as a whole take shape and stand forth before me as though cast in a single piece. . . ." [28] And though we have only an unverified statement to rely upon, we cannot refrain from noting Schindler's claim that Beethoven called two of the movements of his Sonata, op. 101, "Träumerische Empfindungen"— "Dreamlike Sensations." [29]

The Diabelli Variations were begun in 1819, completed in 1823, and published in June 1823 by Cappi and Diabelli, who perceptively announced it as "a great and important masterpiece worthy to be ranked with the imperishable creations of the old Classics," entitled "to a place beside Sebastian Bach's famous masterpiece in the same form." [30] Bachian tendencies are much in evidence here, especially in the many contrapuntal variations and in the extended double fugue of variation 32. Beethoven combines melodic and harmonic variation techniques, both as Mozart had done before him and in accordance with his own practice in the Variations, op. 35, and in the finale of the *Eroica* Symphony.

In a number of the Diabelli variations, the melodic tie is tenuous, or even absent. Beethoven had become increasingly attached to the harmonic (analytic, structural) variation style during his middle period. The melodic variation was, perhaps, perceived by some as a superficial procedure; and indeed, in the typical ornamental, melodic variation, few risks are taken: the composer strays no farther than the garden gate, fearing to leave the comforts of home. By his last years, Beethoven was nothing but a risk taker; hence, far from abandoning the melodic variation procedure, he turned to it for the expression of his deepest meditations, as in several of the present variations and in the Sonatas, opp. 109 and 111, the Adagio ma non troppo of the Quartet, op. 127, and the Adagio of the Ninth Symphony; in these, increasingly elaborate ornamentation of the theme creates the sense of strophic song whose accompaniment comments on an implied text and magnifies its meaning.

Tovey breaks down Diabelli's theme into its components to show the wealth of implicit ideas ("rich in solid musical facts") in its simple, even banal progression of notes—the opening turn, descending fourths and fifths, rising sequences, and simply articulated harmonic and rhythmic framework. He argues that these variations "need no analysis beyond comparison with the theme; their grouping and contrasting explain themselves with dazzling effect. . . ." [31] Others have sought to uncover a larger, homogeneous architecture in the set, some finding a four-movement sonata hidden in it, Halm analyzing it as a work in seven sections, and Geiringer finding an archlike construction in five sections with an epilogue, creating "a strictly symmetrical organization. . . such as the Bach period loved to employ." [32] It is, perhaps, preferable to regard the Diabelli Variations as a gigantic cycle of bagatelles,[33] covering the full range of Beethoven's fantasy and invention; what Ernest Walker wrote of late Beethoven as a whole serves well as a description of this *Pilgrim's Progress* on a Biedermeier waltz: "We find side by side grim uncouthness and unearthly serenity, wild passion and noble majesty, inconsequential antics and delicate charm, tortuous involutions and limpid simplicity." [34] The Variations is a work in which extremes meet to an extent previously unknown even in Beethoven's music: here the tawdry and the sublime rub shoulders; Leporello materializes amidst music of the spheres; the miniature and the fresco merge into one; the perpetual motion of variation 19 collides with the virtual motionlessness of variation 20; variation 32's constructive synthesis dissolves in a coda in which "the material seems to be gradually broken up and scattered into dust" (Blom).[35]

The Diabelli Variations was Beethoven's last extended work for piano. His only other keyboard compositions of the 1820s—apart from two Waltzes and an Ecossaise of 1824–25—were the Bagatelles, op. 119, completed in 1820–22, and op. 126, composed during the winter of 1823–24. With the Bagatelles, op. 126, and the Diabelli Variations, Beethoven became a master miniaturist, capable of sketching a variety of emotional states in a few quick tone strokes. The opus 126 Bagatelles were conceived as a cycle ("Ciclus von Kleinigkeiten," he wrote on the sketches [36]) and perhaps even as a first sketch of the multi-movement form of several of the late quartets. It would not be the first time that the piano, with all its inadequacies ("clavicembalo miserabile" [37]), had opened the way toward new creative possibilities.

In his last years, according to Schindler, Beethoven's playing at times "was more painful than agreeable. . . . The outpourings of his fancy became scarcely intelligible." Sometimes he would place his left hand flat upon the keyboard "and thus drown, in discordant noise, the music to which his right was feelingly giving utterance." [38] He did not wish his musical thoughts to be overheard. Thus, even at the end, the piano remained Beethoven's most intimate means of self-communion.

Like Beethoven's first Mass, the *Missa Solemnis*, op. 123, was written for a specific occasion; it was intended to celebrate the installation of Archduke Rudolph (1788–1831) as Archbishop of Olmütz (in Moravia) on March 9, 1820. Rudolph, the son of Emperor Leopold II and brother of

Emperor Franz, was the most important of Beethoven's patrons from around 1809 onward and was the recipient of fifteen dedications, including those of the Fourth and Fifth Piano Concertos, the Trio, op. 97 (*Archduke*), the Sonatas, opp. 106 and 111, and the *Grosse Fuge*, op. 133. For many years he was Beethoven's only regular piano student in Vienna, as well as his only long-term composition student. Rudolph seems to have worshiped Beethoven, carefully preserving more than 100 letters and collecting first editions, autographs, and fair copies of his compositions. Beethoven, in turn, became deeply attached to him, perhaps in part because Rudolph was the nephew of the revered Joseph II; it was reported that he spoke Rudolph's name "with childlike reverence, as he does no other," [39] and his letters to him are filled with expressions of adoration. Numerous negative or ambivalent statements about Rudolph to third persons serve only to preserve the privacy of Beethoven's deep feelings for this orphaned and epileptic aristocrat.

Rudolph was also important as Beethoven's protector, as his personal passport to the imperial court. And for many years it was apparently Beethoven's expectation that when Rudolph assumed his bishopric, Beethoven would become his *Kapellmeister*. This, at least, is what Reichardt reported in a letter of March 27, 1809,[40] and in later years, several of Beethoven's letters seem to confirm this impression.[41] Rudolph perhaps kept Beethoven's hopes on this score alive for an unreasonably long time, and it still remains unclear why this expectation—which may have provided one of the motivations behind the composition of the *Missa Solemnis*—was never fulfilled.

The Mass became Beethoven's absorbing passion for four years, replacing *Fidelio* as the great "problem work" of his career. Indeed, there is a sense in which the *Missa Solemnis* came to be regarded by Beethoven as a talismanic composition, whose value to him was so great that—as we saw earlier—he embarked on a unique series of financial negotiations and manipulations in respect of its publication which cost him several friendships and gave him an unpleasant reputation for sharp business practice.

None of this, however, speaks to the religious meaning of the work for Beethoven, for it might well have been the purely musical substance of the Mass which led him to prize it so highly. Beethoven's creativity required repeated musical challenges: in his earlier Vienna years he had methodically set about demonstrating his command of the main genres of the Classical tradition. In the late period, a similar determination is once more evident: in the encyclopedic essays in fugue and in variation technique of the *Hammerklavier* Sonata and the Diabelli Variations, and in the *Missa Solemnis*, which establishes Beethoven's mastery of the highest form of liturgical music.

Although we may be certain that Beethoven poured his deepest religious feelings into the *Missa Solemnis*, we may be equally sure that it was not obeisance to Catholicism that prompted the work. As has often been noted, the piece has never been fully at home in either concert hall or church. On several occasions Beethoven suggested that it could be performed as "a grand oratorio" (adding, parenthetically, "for the benefit of the poor"),[42] and he was not disturbed to learn that in its first performance, in St. Petersburg, it was indeed presented as an oratorio.[43] He himself did not hesitate to retitle the Kyrie, Credo, and Agnus Dei of the Mass "Three Grand Hymns with Solo and Chorus Voices," in order to obtain permission from the censor for their performance at his concert of May 7, 1824.[44] But the clearest evidence of Beethoven's nonsectarian attitude toward his Mass is his offer to provide Simrock with a German-language version to facilitate performances in Protestant communities.[45] As Rolland wrote, Beethoven had "a great need to commune with the Lamb, with the God of love and compassion," but the *Missa Solemnis* "overflows the church by its spirit and its dimensions." [46]

This is not to diminish the religious significance of, or religious intention behind, the Mass. "My chief aim," he wrote to Andreas Streicher, "was to awaken and permanently instill religious feelings not only into the singers but also into the listeners." [47] And to Archduke Rudolph: "There is nothing higher than to approach the Godhead more nearly than other mortals and by means of that contact to spread the rays of the Godhead through the human race." [48]

Beethoven had written one Mass in the Viennese style, with an admixture of grand-manner symphonism. It seems clear that he now felt the Classic tradition to be insufficient for the composition of a major work in this form, or for the expression of feelings of highly sublimated spirituality. Apparently he had felt this lack as early as 1809, when he observed that "in the old church modes the devotion is divine. . . and God permit me to express it someday." [49] Now he systematically and painstakingly set about mastering the musical vocabularies of religious music of earlier periods. Just prior to the commencement of the Mass he wrote in his *Tagebuch*: "In order to write true church music . . . look through all the monastic church chorales and also the strophes in the most correct translations and perfect prosody in all Christian–Catholic psalms and hymns generally." [50] He and his friends combed the libraries of Lobkowitz and Archduke Rudolph in search of old music and treatises on liturgical procedures, and Beethoven immersed himself in the music of Palestrina and his Renaissance contemporaries and in the music of Handel, Bach, and C. P. E. Bach. ("Do not forget [C. P. E.] Bach's Litanies," he wrote in the *Tagebuch*.[51]) It is not surprising, then, that the resulting work is an amalgam of archaic and modern styles, more deeply rooted in older traditions than any other work of Beethoven's but retaining the grandeur and dynamic thrust of a symphonism growing out of the sonata style. In a brilliant essay which removes the *Missa Solemnis* from the historical vacuum in which it is ordinarily studied, Warren Kirkendale writes: "Today we see that he not only retained traditional thought to an unexpected degree, but even uncovered much older, buried traditions, and formed musical 'ideas' in the plain and concrete sense of the century in which he was born—naturally with an incomparably freer, personal vocabulary." [52] And he demonstrates that Beethoven's Mass achieves its immense power partly through the complex use of conventional images and traditional patterns of musical rhetoric whose associational meanings had been built up through centuries of usage and development.

The productive imagination must be given its due as well, however, and though there are many "new roads to old ideas" in the *Missa Solemnis*, its historic importance lies largely in the way in which it reshaped rather than reproduced the traditions of liturgical music. It did this by very much the same method which created the great religious music of Beethoven's predecessors, from Dufay and Josquin to Handel and Bach: viz, a refusal to accept the received forms and languages as eternal models, and an infusion of "secular" elements derived from nonliturgical musical styles which expanded the expressive possibilities of the form, giving rise to new associational meanings which in turn became embedded in the matrix of later musical grammar. Beethoven knew that he was not writing his *Missa Solemnis* in the traditional church style; he wrote to Zelter that he regarded the *a capella* style as "the only true church style," [53] but he chose to avoid this model, perhaps because he did not wish the work to serve its normal pacifying function as an idealization of the eternality and unchangeability of belief. In bypassing the Palestrina style (though utilizing it to achieve a specific mystical quality in the Et incarnatus est), Beethoven was rejecting its beatification of hierarchical and, by implication, feudal forms. Beethoven introduced a restless, questioning element into the received forms of the Mass. Lang writes: "To the Christian whose supreme law is obedience, the Beethovenian attitude seems repellent, for submission is preceded in him by a struggle with doubts; faith is gained through a Faustian trial." [54]

Beethoven's consciously employed archaisms and reminiscences—the use of Dorian and Mixolydian modes, the Gregorian "fossils," the quotations from Handel's *Messiah* in the Gloria and Agnus Dei—and his employment of procedures and musical imagery derived from older liturgical styles are, in context, modernistic devices which also serve to stretch the expressiveness of his music beyond the boundaries set by the style of high-Classic and late-Classic liturgical music. These devices, as well as the theatrical use of "military" and "pastoral" motifs in the Dona nobis pacem, are also shortcuts in the communication process, rapidly assimilable musical ideographs to ease the process of understanding the grand design of the Mass, which Beethoven called "the *greatest* work which I have composed so far." [55]

Bekker called the *Missa Solemnis* a "Divine Heroic Symphony," and he wrote: "In the *Eroica* the hero wins culture for humanity as the fruit of his life and death; but here the prize is life everlasting." [56] Contrary to Beethoven's usual practice, however, the *Missa Solemnis* does not strive for a heroic, transcendent, or even necessarily affirmative conclusion. As Ernest Newman observed: "The conclusion of it all is enigmatic. . . . Does Beethoven really believe that the prayer will be answered, or does he leave it all as a kind of question mark projected upon the remote, indifferent sky?" [57] One need not go quite this far—and William Mann has pointed out that one does not ordinarily end a prayer with heroic peroration, but with an "Amen." [58] Nevertheless, one wonders whether Beethoven indeed felt that he, or mankind, would win the prize of life everlasting. There was in him a deep yearning for immortality. In 1803 he had written to the painter Alexander Macco: "Continue to paint—and I shall continue to write down notes; and thus we shall live—for ever?— yes, perhaps, for ever." [59] In the *Tagebuch* he asked: "What more can be given to man than fame and praise and immortality?" [60] Each of these references to immortality includes a question mark, as does the *Missa Solemnis*. Beethoven hoped for, indeed he yielded to none in his yearning for, resurrection, but this was a desired consummation which came into conflict with his materialism and rationalism. In April 1823, his friend Karl Peters wrote in the Conversation Book: "Granted that you don't believe in it you will be glorified, because your music [is] religion." [61] Clearly Beethoven had expressed his doubts to Peters, who sought to reassure him: "You will arise with me from the dead—because you must. Religion remains constant, only Man is changeable." [62] And so Beethoven's ongoing conflict between faith and doubt is revealed in the *Missa Solemnis*. As Riezler knew, in the Dona nobis pacem, with its sounds of strife and warfare and its anguished cries for peace, both inner and outer, Beethoven had "dared to allow the confusion of the world outside to invade the sacred domain of church music." [63] In this sense, the *Missa Solemnis* forecasts the theological questions and doubts—along with the warfare between science and religion—that were to dominate the intellectual battleground of the nineteenth century.

"Utopias are often only premature truths," Lamartine wrote; and Hugo called utopia "the truth of tomorrow." Both quotations express the anticipatory nature of visionary art, its expectation of fulfillment, its capacity for hovering upon the horizon of possibility, its principle of hope. At the same time, utopian art arises out of the disharmony that the artist feels with the conditions of his present existence. Thus Buber: "The vision of 'what should be'—independent though it may sometimes appear of personal will—is yet inseparable from a critical and fundamental relationship to the existing condition of humanity. All suffering under a social order that is senseless prepares the soul for vision." [64] Finally, if the trajectory of utopian art leads toward a transcendent future, and its origins are in a diseased present, its dreamed-of alternatives are modeled on memories or fantasies of an Edenic state.

We have already encountered utopian elements in Beethoven's music—in his evocations of a pastoral Arcadia, in his idealization of the *bon prince*, in the triumphal *Siegessymphonie* of his *Egmont* music, and in the emergence of Pizarro's prisoners into the light. In a sense, all of Beethoven's best music is utopian, in that it holds out images of beauty, joy, and renewal as models of future possibility. It is only with the Ninth Symphony, however, that the utopian model is avowedly predictive, clearly in the future tense (with, perhaps, a hint of the imperative): "All men *shall be* brothers," and *shall* dwell in harmony with the "loving father" under the protection of that female "*Freude*, daughter of Elysium," who had eluded Beethoven's grasp during his lifetime. With the Ninth Symphony, the anachronistic Enlightenment model has returned to the stage long after the exhaustion of the social and intellectual impulses born of the *philosophes*. Perhaps it could only return—as pure hope—after the apparent historical failure of the dream which Rousseau had shared with Schiller and with the young Beethoven, and after Beethoven's separation from the aristocratic and national collectivities which had nourished his sense of communality. Beethoven's Ninth is his refusal to accept the finality of that failure and of that separation.

Although there is a sense in which much of late Beethoven embodies a return to the unrealized projects of his youth, that return is in the Ninth Symphony a quite literal one. According to Fischenich, who may have introduced Beethoven to Schiller's works at Bonn University or at the *Lese–Gesellschaft*, and who also evidently regarded the young composer as his protégé, Beethoven had planned to set Schiller's "An die Freude" (written in 1785, published in 1786) before he left Bonn for Vienna.[65] Indeed, a brief passage from Schiller's Ode already appeared in the *Leopold* Cantata of 1790. One wonders whether the censorship which Schiller's works encountered in Vienna during Beethoven's early years there had anything to do with the long postponement of this project. In 1793, the censor banned *Die Räuber* as "immoral" and "dangerous," and it was only beginning in 1808 that Schiller's works were again staged and his books reappeared in the stalls. His popularity thereafter became such that in the years from 1813 to 1825 there were 320 performances of his plays at the Theater-an-der-Wien alone.[66]

Beethoven himself told Czerny that Schiller was a difficult poet to set because no musician could surpass his poetry.[67] (Besides the "Ode to

Joy," Beethoven set only the "Song of the Monks," WoO 104, from *Wilhelm Tell*, in 1817, and one stanza of the Ballade "Das Mädchen aus der Fremde," in 1810.[68]) It is also possible that Beethoven actually completed a now lost setting of the Ode, for in a sketchbook of 1798–99 appears music for the Ode's "Muss ein lieber Vater wohnen" [There surely dwells a dear father], and in 1803 Ries offered the "Ode to Joy" to Simrock as one of eight *Lieder* which Beethoven had written within the past "four years." [69]

In 1812, Beethoven momentarily interrupted the sketching of his Seventh and Eighth Symphonies to jot down some ideas on "Freude schöner Götterfunken," perhaps intended for a D-minor symphony, more likely as a choral overture; [70] in 1814–15, this thematic material was utilized in the *Namensfeier* Overture, op. 115. In 1818, Beethoven had the idea of using voices in a symphony on mythical themes, but not until 1822–23 did it occur to him that his Schiller project could here be fulfilled. He continued to explore alternative instrumental solutions to the finale, however, as late as the summer of 1823.

The "Ode to Joy" melody itself was also long in the fashioning. A lilting tune which foreshadows its opening phrase appeared in "Gegenliebe," WoO 118, of 1794 or 1795, and again in the vocal finale of the "Choral Fantasia," op. 80, in 1808. Two years later, it is heard once again in the song "Kleine Blumen, kleine Blätter," op. 83 no. 3, set to a text by Goethe. Numerous other anticipations of one or another element of the Ninth Symphony have been traced, including in the *Leopold* and *Joseph* Cantatas of 1790, the Second Symphony, *Fidelio* (which incorporates a couplet from Schiller's Ode), the "Choral Fantasia," and the closing bars of the Overture to *King Stephen* (which anticipates the Turkish variation of the Ninth's finale). Sketches of what later became the theme of the scherzo date from 1815.[71]

It is in other, perhaps more crucial, ways that the Ninth Symphony stems from a retrospective impulse. For in it, Beethoven returned unreservedly to the heroic style which he had effectively completed by 1812–14. Actually, he retraced his steps still further: the festal Paradise of the Seventh and Eighth Symphonies was now beyond reach, so he turned once again to the *Eroica* Symphony model of 1803–04, with its archetypal patterns and its grand-manner "Empire" style, creating what Cooper terms "a cross between *sinfonia eroica* and *hymne de la république*." [72] It is extraordinary that an apparently superseded style still retained such vitality, and such technical and expressive possibilities. Clearly, the intervening experiences—both biographical and musical—had enriched Beethoven's perception of the potentialities of the conventional sonata-form four-movement symphonic cycle, and as in the four-movement *Hammerklavier* Sonata, which was conceived almost simultaneously, he felt the impulse to test his powers against the restraints of the Classic model—to bring the model to its dynamic and expressive outer limits in one final, perfecting (and destroying) essay.

Yet, the seeming conventionality of the Ninth Symphony's harmonic language and of its forms—sonata form in the first movement, a traditional scherzo (albeit with a fugato and a double repeat), two sets of variations in the Adagio and finale—is belied by the fundamental novelty of the Symphony, which became the prototype of one branch of nineteenth-century Romantic symphonism, extending from Liszt to Mahler. This resulted from the unprecedented spaciousness and grandeur of the work, from its humanist message—which blends mystical, theological, and utopian/revolutionary strands of thought—and from an organic unity of design reminiscent of the Fifth Symphony, but which here repudiates epigrammatic and dynamic condensation in favor of rhetorical sublimity. There has long existed a school of Beethoven analysts—among them Hans Mersmann, Walter Engelsmann, Fritz Cassirer, and Rudolph Reti—seeking to establish that each of his multimovement works derives from a single motif or theme, as though this would unlock the deepest secrets of his creative process. In the Ninth Symphony, and especially in its first three movements, they have one of their strongest cases. As d'Indy noticed, "*all* the typical themes of the symphony present the arpeggio of the chords of D or B flat, the two tonal bases of the work; one might, therefore, consider this arpeggio as the real cyclic theme of the Ninth Symphony." [73] Reti also demonstrates the thematic unity of much of the work, and even urges convincingly that the "Seid umschlungen Millionen" theme of the finale is an inversion of the second subject of the Allegro. [74]

Despite such demonstrations, however, there is a sense in which Beethoven himself claimed to explicitly reject the unity of the four movements. Indeed, this is the point of departure of the finale, in which each of the previous movements is recalled only to be dismissed, whereupon the bass recites Beethoven's words: "O friends, not these sounds; rather let us intone pleasanter and more joyful ones," thus inaugurating the main theme of the "Ode to Joy." Of course, this is essentially a ruse, a means by which Beethoven achieves a supremely integrated structure through the use of more powerful and individual contrasts than is customary in a sonata finale. And, more precisely, Beethoven is here setting aside the past, with its memories of strife, tragedy, and loss; he is not repudiating his own music, but rather the states which it symbolizes: "tragedy," "satiric drama," "beauty of an order too sublime for a world of action"—Tovey's shorthand will serve as well as any to describe the first three movements of the symphony. [75] In place of these he sets his joyous affimation, with its discovery (again Tovey) of "a theme on which the mind could rest as a final solution of typical human doubts and difficulties." [76] In the sketches for the bass recitative, Beethoven made even more explicit this underlying meaning of his rejection of the prior movements; he wrote: "No, this chaos reminds us of our despair. Today is a day of celebration, let it be celebrated with song and dance." [77]

The war between faith and skepticism, which we encountered in the *Eroica* and in the *Missa Solemnis*, is far from ended: Beethoven has probed the issues, failed to find a permanent solution, and settled upon pure wish as the closest approximation to a provisionally satisfactory outcome. Doubtless this is an "ideological" solution—one which brooks no opposition and admits no nuances of opinion. In this sense, the finale of the Ninth belongs in the line of compositions which extends from the *Joseph* Cantata of 1790 to *Der glorreiche Augenblick* of 1814. However, it succeeds here where all his other avowedly ideological music failed, by compelling its message to emerge from powerful opposing forces— from the tragic, frenzied, and probing modalities of its earlier movements—and by grafting the cantata form into the sonata cycle. It succeeds, primarily, because of the rich ambiguity of a message which manages to transcend the particularities of its origin and to arrive at a set of universal paradigms.

From a certain point of view, we may say that Beethoven wrote his own text to the Ninth Symphony's "Ode to Joy." He utilized only half of the eighteen sections of Schiller's version of 1803 and freely rearranged it in accordance with his own poetic vision. He omitted all of the verses which made "An die Freude" an elevated drinking song—such as

> Brethren, thus in rapture meeting,
> Send ye round the brimming cup.—
> Yonder kindly spirit greeting,
> While the foam to heaven mounts up!

Clearly Beethoven did not see this as an occasion to express literal Dionysian notions. And despite his hatred of despotism, Beethoven chose to ignore Schiller's antityrannical sentiments:

> Safety from the tyrant's power!
> Mercy e'en to traitors base!

Also omitted (from the 1785 version) is Schiller's "Beggars shall be brothers of princes," which Beethoven, in a sketchbook of 1812, had marked for setting.[78] In Beethoven's rearrangement of the poem, we are first introduced to Joy, the embodiment of the nurturing mother ("All creation drinks joy from the breasts of nature"), in whose protective embrace all mankind is reunited ("All men shall be brothers there where thy gentle wings tarry"), thereby opening the way toward reunion with the benevolent father/God ("Brothers, above the starry vault, there surely dwells a dear Father"). It is a simple scenario, which extracts a kernel from Schiller's poem and universalizes it into a condensed parable of familial reconciliation.

Whatever the psychological sources of the "Ode to Joy" may have been, there are in it larger relevancies and manifold meanings which have given it undying status as a model of human transformation. We need not reject Nietzsche's interpretation: "Now the slave emerges as a freeman; all the rigid, hostile walls which either necessity or despotism has erected between men are shattered. Now that the gospel of universal harmony is sounded, each individual becomes not only reconciled to his fellow but actually at one with him. . . ." [79] And Rolland's vision remains intact: "In the Ninth Symphony . . . is mingled a scorching mysticism, a passionate intuitive belief in God-in-Nature and in the moral conscience, a German–mythological theosophism, nourished by Schiller, by philosophical readings, perhaps by Schelling, . . . by his contacts with the Orientalists—the whole stirred by a heroic and revolutionary will to action, in the spirit of the time of his youth." [80] For Rolland, as for so many others, the "Ode to Joy" preaches "the kingdom of God on earth, established by the brotherhood of man, in reason and in joy." In the last analysis, Beethoven's private quest and his ideological thrust are identical: his was a search for an ideal, extended communal family to assuage the inevitability of personal loss, to maintain and to magnify the sanctified memory of his—and every man's—personal Eden.

A word about the vocal impulse in the Ninth Symphony. Kerman's emphasis on the drive toward songful communicativeness in Beethoven's late works has special relevance here. In the first movement, Beethoven retains the condensed "heroic" thematic technique, developing his materials from an arpeggiated common chord germ motif; and the scherzo, with its demonic dance character and rhythm-dominated thrust, is similarly far removed from song. With the two expressive and consoling themes of the Adagio, however, the speech-inflected accents of the human voice enter the Ninth Symphony, and they do so within a variation form which—as we noted earlier—takes on the character of an extended, through-composed song without words. (The lessons of *An die ferne Geliebte* are not forgotten.) The Adagio also foreshadows the finale in its conscious reminiscences of the arpeggio theme of the opening movement; and, according to Grove,[81] Beethoven in his sketches had considered the possibility of having the chorus enter (to what words?) with the statement of the movement's second theme, Andante moderato, a step-wise, *espressivo* melody which itself forecasts the Joy theme.

This confirms the link between the Ninth and its forerunner, the planned "Adagio Cantique" which Beethoven had described in 1818:

Pious song in a symphony in the ancient modes—Lord God, we praise Thee, alleluia!—either alone or as introduction to a fugue. The whole second symphony [two symphonies were conceived at this time] might be characterized in this manner, in which case the vocal parts would enter in the last movement or already in the Adagio.[82]

Even without words, song enters the Ninth Symphony as prayer and mourning, as consolation and yearning, as thanksgiving and praise.

Kerman writes of Beethoven's "determination to touch common mankind as nakedly as possible," and he marvels at "the spectacle of this composer, having reached heights of subtlety in the pure manipulation of tonal materials, battering at the communications barrier with every weapon of his knowledge." [83] In the finale, the vocal impulse overwhelms that barrier, and it does so by introducing the human voice itself into the tonal fabric. Schenker had made much of Beethoven's "inconsistency" in following the first sounding of the Joy melody by the "horrorfanfare" that repudiates everything which preceded it; [84] but there is no inconsistency here: Beethoven thereby affirms that the "Freude" melody in its merely instrumental manifestation was not sufficient to express his vision of the future. Nor, if we are correct in our hearing of this finale, was voice itself sufficient. Beethoven had written on the sketches that the celebration must take the form of "song and dance," and in the variations which follow he explores a wide variety of dance and march rhythms which unite the voice with the expressive movements of the human body. Furthermore, in accordance with his late-period practice, he adds a double fugue, with its symbolization of triumphant motion and its religious connotations, to complete the texture. Four of the pivotal characteristics of Beethoven's late style—song, dance, variation, and fugue—are merged in the "Ode to Joy."

"I want to revoke the Ninth Symphony," cried Adrian Leverkühn in Mann's *Doctor Faustus*. The Ninth has been perceived by later generations as an unsurpassable model of affirmative culture, a culture which by its beauty and idealism, some believe, anaesthetizes the anguish and the terror of modern life, thereby standing in the way of a realistic perception of society. Marcuse writes: "Today's rebels against the established culture also rebel against the beautiful in this culture, against its all too sublimated, segregated, orderly, harmonizing forms. . . . The refusal now hits the chorus which sings the "Ode to Joy," the song which is invalidated in the culture that sings it." [85] The fatal (and destructive) error behind such attitudes is this: if we lose our awareness of the transcendent realms of play, beauty, and brotherhood which are portrayed in the great affirmative works of our culture, if we lose the dream of the Ninth Symphony, there remains no counterpoise against the engulfing terrors of civilization, nothing to set against Auschwitz and Vietnam as a paradigm of humanity's potentialities. Masterpieces of art are instilled with a surplus of constantly renewable energy—an energy that provides a motive force for changes in the relations between human beings—because they contain projections of human desires_ and goals which have not yet been achieved (which indeed may be unrealizable). In Max Raphael's formulation: "The work of art holds man's creative power in a crystalline suspension from which it can again be transformed into living energies." [86] Beethoven was no stranger to such ideas, for he wrote: "Only art and science give us intimations and hopes of a higher life." [87] To the followers of Kant, Schiller, and Goethe, it was clearly the mission of art to lead humanity to an inner harmony and toward a social order which would permit the unfettered development of the universally human, the "fulfillment of beautiful possibilities" (Goethe). The discovery of the prospective and transcendent nature of art was the work of German classical aesthetics. In the *Critique of Judgment,* Kant maintained that man is "the single being upon earth that possesses . . . a capacity for setting before himself ends of his deliberate choice." [88] Schiller thereupon urged that the artist "multiply . . . the symbols of perfection, till appearance triumphs over reality, and art over nature." [89] The symbols of perfection (which Schiller called "the effigies of the ideal")—the Ninth Symphony and the late quartets, the trumpet call of *Fidelio,* the Heiliger Dankgesang, the festal Paradise of the Seventh Symphony, the Bacchus resurrection of the *Eroica*—these keep alive mankind's hope and sustain faith in the possibilities of human renewal. Hegel wrote that "it is the defects of immediate reality which drive us forward inevitably to the idea of the beauty of art"; [90] perhaps so, but Schiller expressed his own, and Beethoven's, view when he perceived the opposite process at work: "To arrive at a solution even in the political problem, the road of aesthetics must be pursued, because it is through beauty that we arrive at freedom." [91]

On November 9, 1822, Prince Nikolas Galitzin, a cellist and a connoisseur of Beethoven's music, wrote from St. Petersburg to ask Beethoven if he would consent "to compose one, two, or three quartets for which labor I will be glad to pay you what you think proper," adding, straightforwardly, "I will accept the dedication with gratitude." [92] Beethoven, deeply occupied with the final stages of the *Missa Solemnis,* delayed his reply until January 25, 1823, when he wrote: "You wish to have some quartets; since I see that you are cultivating the violoncello, I will take care to give you satisfaction in this regard." [93] He set the fee at 50 ducats per quartet, and bound himself to complete the first quartet by midMarch at the latest. But it was not Galitzin, or anyone else, who initiated this project. The previous May, Leipzig publisher C. F. Peters had written to Beethoven asking him for, among other works, some piano quartets and trios. Beethoven responded on June 5, offering the Mass along with other completed works and setting a price of 50 ducats for a string quartet "which you could also have very soon." [94] Peters thought the price rather high and, after some further correspondence in July, refused the offer, admitting frankly (and tactlessly) that he really wanted a piano quartet (and "only on the condition that it will not be too difficult") because he already had string quartets in press by Spohr, Romberg, and Rode, "which are all excellent." [95] Beethoven promised to do what he could about a piano quartet, for which—in view of Peter's eagerness and his own reluctance to write one—he raised his fee to 70 ducats. But it was not piano quartets which interested him. As Rolland says, "It is clear that he carried within him a quartet ready to be born." [96] And more than one. Apparently, as soon as he received Galitzin's commission, he wrote asking Ries to see what he could do about selling quartets in London; Ries rapidly found a customer, for on February 25, 1823, Beethoven wrote to Neate: "As Ries has written to tell me that you would like to have three quartets from me, I am writing to ask you to be so kind as to let me know when you would like to receive them. I am satisfied with the fee of 100 guineas which you offer." [97] Meanwhile, he continued negotiations with Peters and with Schott's Sons for publication rights. Galitzin's quartets were to serve double and triple duty.

The Russian prince wrote often—and impatiently—in 1823 and 1824 about his quartets, but received nothing except Beethoven's reassurances. First the Mass, the Diabelli Variations, and the Ninth Symphony had to be completed; it was only after the concerts of May 1824 that Beethoven turned to his quartets. To briefly recapitulate the chronology of the late quartets: the first, in E-flat major, op. 127, was completed in February 1825; the second in order of composition, in A minor, op. 132, was completed by July 1825; the third, in B-flat major, op. 130, with the *Grosse Fuge* as finale, was written more rapidly, between July/August and November 1825; the fourth, in C-sharp minor, op. 131, was begun toward the end of 1825 and completed by about July 1826; the last, in F major, op. 135, occupied Beethoven (with time out to compose an arrangement of the *Grosse Fuge* for piano four-hands, op. 134) from July to October; and in October and November, at Gneixendorf, Beethoven wrote the new finale for the Quartet, op. 130. Schott published opus 127 in June 1826, but the remaining quartets were published posthumously in 1827 by Matthias Artaria (opus 130 and the *Grosse Fuge*, op. 133), Schott (opus 131), and Schlesinger (opuses 132 and 135). One more quartet was apparently planned but never written.[98] The first three were dedicated to Galitzin, the C-sharp-minor Quartet to Field Marshal von Stutterheim, and the F-major to Beethoven's faithful supporter, Johann Wolfmayer, as a solace for the *Requiem* that he had commissioned a decade earlier.

It was an opportune time for Beethoven's string quartets to come into existence. In many historical eras in which the large social forms are controlled by censorship and the public is ridden with apathy or is utilizing art primarily for hedonistic gratification, serious art flees to the margins of society and to the more private forms, where it sets up beachheads in defense of its embattled position in life. The artist and his audience rise to the defense of the sanctity of art at those moments when its social function has become endangered and its aesthetic and ethical purposes called into question. Such was the case in the aftermath of the Napoleonic Wars, with the breakdown of aristocratic patronage and of Enlightened attitudes toward the arts. The entire concept of the avant-garde in art seems to have originated following the Bourbon Restoration, and Beethoven in his late sonatas and quartets may be regarded as the originator of the avant-garde in music history. In this he is quite different from Bach, who wrote his *Art of Fugue* in a spirit of solitary inquiry; different also from C. P. E. Bach, who wrote: "Among all my works, especially for the piano, there are only some trios, solos, and concertos that I wrote in all freedom, and for my own use." [99] Beethoven's late sonatas and quartets, despite their difficulties and their experimental character, were hardly written without an audience in mind. His was now a very special audience, which had tested its strength against the prevailing artistic currents in its sponsorship of Beethoven's May 1824 public concerts and found itself wanting in numbers but not in spirit; it was an audience drawn from many walks of life—artists and writers, musicians and music lovers, bankers and merchants, along with the remnants of the old connoisseur aristocracy—which worshiped Beethoven (not uncritically) as the stalwart symbol of better days past and to come.

The late sonatas had been Beethoven's first works that were composed without the expectation of performance in either aristocratic salon or public concert: we saw earlier that their audience was in the private musicale—of the Streichers, Ertmanns, and Czerny. Now, a few years later, the number of such music lovers had grown substantially. Schuppanzigh, who twenty years earlier had been the first musician in Austria to undertake public quartet concerts,[100] returned from Russia toward the end of April 1823 and resumed his concerts, which at once became major events in this rarefied sphere of Viennese musical life. For example, nephew Karl reported to Beethoven about Schuppanzigh's concert of January 25, 1824, which featured a Haydn Quartet in C major and Beethoven's Septet, that it was so crowded that "the people had to stand in front of the door." [101] Many of Beethoven's close friends, patrons, and admirers were there: Haslinger, Wolfmayer, Piringer, Schickh, Tuscher, and Kalkbrenner, along with numerous amateurs (*Dilettanten*) who bombarded brother Nikolaus Johann with questions about the forthcoming *Akademie*.

Although as many as 500 people attended such concerts, Beethoven was no longer concerned with the size of his audience, and several of the premiere performances of the last quartets were given privately or semiprivately for small groups of colleagues, disciples, and favored individuals. Nevertheless, it was a necessity to Beethoven that his works be understood and appreciated, despite his occasional claims to the contrary. In this respect the atmosphere was extremely favorable to the quartets. Schuppanzigh pleaded to be granted the premiere of the first: "If [you have] a mind to hand me the quartet for a performance," he wrote in a Conversation Book, "there may be a big difference in my present subscription." [102] The response to the first Quartet, op. 127, was excellent: after a failed performance by Schuppanzigh, due to lack of rehearsal, the Quartet was "studied industriously and rehearsed frequently under Beethoven's own eyes" [103] (he could not hear, but followed the motion of the bows), and then was played successfully four times by Böhm, again by Schuppanzigh, and twice more by Mayseder—all within two months. The Quartet, op. 132, was performed first at small private gatherings in September 1825 and twice in public concerts in November; and opus 130, after its public performance by Schuppanzigh on March 21, 1826, was eagerly sought after by Böhm and Mayseder for performance at private quartet parties.

Such private performances of the late quartets continued during the next year. The C-sharp-minor Quartet was rehearsed several times at Artaria's at the beginning of August; Holz wrote in a Conversation Book that Artaria "was enraptured, and the fugue, when he heard it for the third time, he found wholly intelligible." [104] Schlesinger reported in early September that the A-minor Quartet was given successfully in Berlin.[105] References to performances of opus 130 and opus 131 appear in the Conversation Books in December,[106] and Schuppanzigh reported to Beethoven that a recent performance of opus 127 was received "with enthusiasm." [107] The new finale of the B-flat-major Quartet was rehearsed in the latter half of December and was found "altogether heavenly" by the musicians.[108] There were private performances of the quartets in 1826 and 1827. And we know that Schubert was given a private reading of the Quartet, op. 131, in November 1828, five days before Schubert's death. ("He fell into such a state of excitement and enthusiasm," Holz reported, "that we were all frightened for him."[109]) But none of these were public performances: apparently there had been a rapid falling off of broader interest. The Conversation Books allude to planned public performances by Schuppanzigh and by Linke, but these failed to materialize. (Beethoven's friends may have given the distraught and mortally-ill composer false encouragement on this score.)

With the Quartet in B-flat, op. 130, Beethoven perhaps (almost certainly) had tried to carry his audience with him into a realm which their training and sensibility would not permit them to enter. The Leipzig review which called the *Grosse Fuge* "incomprehensible, a sort of Chinese puzzle" [110] was not atypical. Neither Schindler nor Holz appreciated the B-flat Quartet as a whole, and Holz reported that the audience at the first performance was "inspired, astonished, or questioning" and failed to find fault with it only because of their "awe" for Beethoven.[111] Perhaps a total acceptance of the late quartets would have required a rebellious-ness of spirit, a refusal to accept the given conditions of life, which was beyond the reach of even the sensitive and the disaffected in Viennese society. They still preferred the Septet, with its harmless evocation of those better days before the war.

Accordingly, neither opus 131 nor opus 135 was performed in concert during Beethoven's lifetime. Indeed, opus 131 did not receive its first public performance in Vienna until 1835, and between 1827 and 1850 the quartets were played there in concert only four times—once each for opus 130 and opus 135, twice for opus 131.[112] The quartets were kept from oblivion during their first decades by performances else-where: in Berlin, in Leipzig, and, especially, in Paris.

Beethoven at first intended to write two, perhaps three, string quar-tets. The sketches for the first two quartets overlap somewhat: while working on the finale of opus 127 he sketched several sections of opus 132. However, as Holz recalled, in the course of composing the first three quartets, "new ideas streamed from Beethoven's inexhaustible fan-tasy in such richness that he almost unwillingly had to write the C-sharp-minor and F-major Quartets." [113] "Something has again occurred to me," Beethoven told Holz as they were out walking, rejoicing in the strength of this creative surge which made it possible for him to complete five major works in rapid succession.

There is a tension in Beethoven's evolution between adherence to, and a rebellious need to dissolve—or at least to reshape—the received Classical forms. This tension is present in his work at all times after 1800, but it becomes clearest after 1815. The Classical forms remain the touchstone to which Beethoven inevitably returns after each of his (in-creasingly adventurous) forays into experimental regions. The traditional forms are tacitly undermined in the deceptively transparent song cycle and the opus 101 and opus 102 sonatas of 1815–16, quietly opening the door to Romanticism. The *Hammerklavier* Sonata of 1817–18 constitutes an overreaching attempt to hold on to the traditional structure by a magnification of time scale and an intensification of contrast. However, the three sonatas of 1820–22 and the Diabelli Variations (completed in 1823) are once more all for new departures. As Cooper observes, Beethoven's conception of sonata form moves away "from the dramatic principle of contrast with its implicit idea of struggle. In its place we find a unified vision where music borrows nothing from the theatre, which had played so important a part in late-eighteenth century musical aesthetics, and aspires to its own unique condition." [114] Thereafter, the Ninth Symphony again restores the four-movement Classic symphonic form, together with contrast, struggle, and a level of theatricality which had been absent from Beethoven's music for almost a decade.

That this alternating pattern would extend to the quartets was, therefore, wholly predictable. Seen from this point of view, the series is introduced by a quartet (opus 127) in relatively traditional four-movement form, perhaps to reestablish Beethoven's control of the medium; this is followed by three experimental works (opuses 132, 130, 131) which create a variety of new formal structures; and the set closes with the almost Haydnesque, again traditional four-movement Quartet, op. 135, indicating that the cycle has been brought to its conclusion. Throughout his career, Beethoven repeatedly bid farewell to the Classic tradition but never said a firm goodbye. Had he lived longer, there is no reason to believe that this would have been his last farewell to the eighteenth century.

Unlike many of the influential earlier commentators, who stressed the stylistic unity of the quartets as a group and drew attention to the many threads which connect each, and especially the central three quartets, to the others, Joseph Kerman holds that "each of them provides us with a separate paradigm for wholeness," a "total integrity" which arises out of its individuality of form, feeling, and procedure. In each, Kerman sees "the musical image of an underlying psychological progress," and he holds that "the sense of a particular psychological sequence is what gives the late quartets their particular individual intensities—in spite of technical threads crossing from one to the other." [115] In this view he has Beethoven's support, for when Holz asked Beethoven which quartet was the greatest, he answered: "Each in its own way!" [116] At that time he had written but three; later, he avowed the C-sharp-minor Quartet, op. 131, to be the greatest, again confirming his perception of the works as discrete entities.

Kerman sees lyricism as the guiding impulse of the Quartet, op. 127, "inspiring the intimate *aveu* of the opening movement, the popular swing of the Finale, and the great stream of melody in the Adagio variations." [117] Opus 127 can be seen as a natural outgrowth of the last piano sonatas, though it reflects a commitment to Classical structure which they were then tending to disavow. The Quartet minimizes contrast (the first movement avoids development in favor of ornamentation), with only the Scherzando vivace supplying "the intellectual, mordant note, the note of contrast." [118] Despite its unenigmatic approachability and lyricism, the Quartet is not without its "late style" characteristics—the driving dotted rhythms of the Scherzo; the contrapuntal textures; the fantastic, idealized, occasionally violent dance rhythms of the pastoral finale; and, especially, the luxuriously ornamental variations of the Adagio, in the course of which the theme itself is transformed into a new entity.

The A-minor Quartet, op. 132, expands the framework to five movements, with a scherzo and a brief, marchlike movement filling both of the usual alternative positions for the dance movement and serving as necessary and "normal" transitions into and out of the unearthly Molto Adagio in the archaic Lydian mode. They serve also to help form what appears to be a consciously wrought arch structure, which is in turn mirrored and capped by the five-sectioned arch construction of the central Heiliger Dankgesang. As all commentators, beginning with Lenz and Nottebohm, have noted, the opening theme of the first movement is strikingly similar in shape to the main theme of the *Grosse Fuge* and to the opening fugue theme of the Quartet, op. 131. Similar themes were occasionally used by Beethoven in several early vocal compositions—"Klage," "Ah Perfido!," "Vom Tode"—as well as in his last two sonatas, but in the quartets they take on an unprecedented emotional character. Erich Schenk has shown them to be similar to (or derived from) a typical thematic configuration of the Baroque period (the similarity to the "royal theme" of Bach's *Musical Offering* is especially striking), which symbolized "melancholy conceptions" such as pain, sorrow, trespass, and preparedness for death; [119] this cluster of feelings is apparently communicated by means of an upward-striving, constantly-defeated melodic shape and by insistent references to the leading tone. We do not need this analysis, however, to tell us that the subject matter of this quartet is pain and its transcendence. Just recovered from a serious illness, Beethoven headed the chorale theme of the slow movement "Holy Song of Thanksgiving by a Convalescent to the Divinity, in the Lydian Mode." (Music here appears to become an implicit agency of healing, a talisman against death.) The contrasting, dancelike (rather, *attempting* to dance) section is marked "Feeling New Strength"—a heading which may also designate the main character of the remaining movements, the Alla Marcia and the closing rondo, Allegro Appassionato, whose urgent, floating waltz melody is an etherealization and dancing fulfillment of the "Feeling New Strength" section, with its haltingly striving 3/8 time.

The B-flat-major Quartet, op. 130, is the most enigmatic of the late quartets. It was originally composed in six movements (the same structure as opus 132, but with a second slow movement—the tearful Cavatina—preceding the finale), the last of which was Beethoven's lengthiest chamber-music movement, a colossal, multisectional fugue which was later separated from the work by the publisher in favor of an unproblematic rondo-finale. For some reason, Beethoven did not attend the first performance. As soon as the concert was over, Holz rushed to a neighboring tavern, where the composer was awaiting a full report. On hearing that the Alla danza tedesca and the Cavatina had received such thunderous applause that they had to be encored, he snapped in exasperation: "Yes, these delicacies! Why not the Fugue?" [120] and then gave his opinion of the audience: "Cattle! Asses!" [121]

Kerman finds the opus 130 Quartet representative of a "drive toward dissociation" in Beethoven's late works, a drive which is the dialectical obverse of his dominant synthesizing impulses.[122] However, Bekker, who also perceived the kaleidoscopic changes of mood within the total structure, and who described the quartet as "a suite, almost a pot-pourri, of movements without any close psychological interconnection," found an organic explanation to account for this phenomenon. "Each movement," he wrote, "is merely episodic inasmuch as it prepares for the finale"; the movements "do not stand in direct sequence, nor do they represent a continuous line of development; each from a different view-point relates directly to the close." [123] Of course, Bekker is referring here to the original finale, the *Grosse Fuge;* for him, the substitute finale is but "another gem in the multi-colored ornament," which therefore wholly pushes the work into dissociation, for it fails to gather up the trails leading to the Fugue which Beethoven scattered so skillfully and deliberately throughout the earlier movements.

Why did Beethoven agree to separate the Fugue from the Quartet? Most biographers of Beethoven have marveled that this most stubborn of composers should so readily agree to alter the structure of a major composition: some have attributed it to his preoccupation with nephew Karl's suicide attempt; others to his desire for an additional 15-ducat fee; still others to his disdain for the "Cattle! Asses!" who were unable to grasp his intention. But the fact remains that the *Grosse Fuge* has struck many sensitive musicians, including its first hearers, as an unsatisfactory close to the quartet. And so it is possible that Beethoven too came to feel that the Fugue was a miscalculation. Perhaps he concluded that the Fugue was too powerful (and too strange) an experience to properly close the Quartet, that the cycle needed to emerge into the light. Beethoven must originally have believed that he had accomplished this in the enormous coda of the Fugue, with its dancelike *Siegessymphonie* and its feeling of sunshine after storm. Evidently, however, the reverberations of pain and strife had not yet sufficiently died away, let alone been fully dissipated. And so he may have decided that the work required a catharsis, a return to normality, an epilogue in full daylight, a simple descent to earth, a reversion to Classicism such as we find in the Allegro finale.

The idea of a new finale was not Beethoven's own, however. The publisher Matthias Artaria (not the well-known firm of Artaria & Co.) was doubtful about the commercial possibilities of the Quartet because of the difficulties and abstruseness of the Fugue, and it is clear that he wanted a substitute finale. He did not dare openly broach the issue, however. Instead, on April 11, 1826, he wrote—flatteringly, and no doubt falsely—in a Conversation Book: "There have been already many requests for a four-hand arrangement of the Fugue. Do you permit that I publish it in that form?—Score, the parts, the Fugue *à 4 mains* arranged by you, to be published simultaneously." [124] Beethoven authorized the four-hand arrangement, and he may well have authorized a separate publication of the Fugue in score and parts, but it is clear that he still expected the Quartet to be published with the Fugue, for Artaria thereafter sent it to the engraver in its original form. The proofs were ready in mid-August. Artaria then asked Holz to try to persuade Beethoven to compose a substitute finale. Holz related the story to Lenz in 1857:

> The publisher Artaria, to whom I had sold the rights for the edition of the Quartet in B-flat for a price of 80 ducats, had charged me with the terrible and difficult mission of convincing Beethoven to compose a new finale, which would be more accessible to the listeners as well as the instrumentalists, to substitute for the Fugue which was so difficult to understand. I maintained to Beethoven that this Fugue, which departed from the ordinary and surpassed even the last quartets in originality, should be published as a separate work and that it merited a designation as a separate opus. I communicated to him that Artaria was disposed to pay him a supplementary honorarium for the new finale. Beethoven told me he would reflect on it, but already on the next day I received a letter giving his agreement.[125]

The letter has not survived, but there is sufficient confirmation of Holz's story in the Conversation Books. "You could easily have made two [quartets] from the B-flat Quartet," he wrote to Beethoven in early September 1826; "When one thinks so highly of art as you do, it cannot be any other way; but it would be more money for you, and the publisher would have to pay the costs." [126] Shortly thereafter he indicated that the matter was settled: "Artaria is highly pleased that you have found his proposal so acceptable; he will gain much therefrom; the two separate works will be more sought after." [127] In later years, Holz told Lenz that it was the composer's wish that the Rondo follow the fading away of the Cavatina "without a long pause." [128] This last comment by Holz is of the utmost importance, because it is the only evidence that Beethoven intended the new finale as a substitute for the *Grosse Fuge* rather than as a seventh movement designed to follow the Fugue.

We need not enter here into the debate which has raged for two-thirds of a century as to which finale is the "proper" one: the failure of the debate to settle the issue indicates that Riezler may have been wrong when he avowed that "both endings are 'organic,' and both are in keeping with the 'idea' of the work." [129] There have been attempts to find more in the Allegro than meets the ear, but Kerman is surely correct in observing that the substitute finale "trivializes the journey which it means to terminate." [130] As for the fugal finale, many have felt that it overshadows—even annihilates—the earlier movements. That there will be no solution to this dilemma is illustrated by Stravinsky's vacillation: at one time he exclaimed, "How right Beethoven's friends were when they convinced him to detach it from opus 130!" [131] But he reversed himself on this issue before his death,[132] realizing not only that the Fugue was intended as the Quartet's climax, but may well have been the work's point of departure as well.

Beethoven's favorite quartet, in C-sharp minor, op. 131, is in seven movements to be performed virtually without pause, thereby giving a greater sense of deliberate unification than prevails in any other work since the song cycle of 1816. A continuity of rhythmic design adds to the feeling that this is one of the most completely integrated of Beethoven's works. But there are many pressures toward discontinuity at work in this Quartet: six distinct main keys, thirty-one changes of tempo (ten more than in opus 130), a variety of textures, and a diversity of forms within the movements—fugue, suite, recitative, variation, scherzo, aria, and sonata form—which makes the achievement of unity all the more miraculous. Beethoven is here pressing dissociation so far that it turns into its opposite—perfect coherence and profound integration. Perhaps Beethoven considered this Quartet a summary work, ending the exploration of the set of musical problems to which the late quartets (and perhaps all of the late works) were devoted; and this may explain what appear to be numerous references to other works—from the already noted similarity of the opening fugue to themes from opus 132 and the Fugue of opus 130, to what I hear as conscious recollections of the Heiliger Dankgesang in the fourth variation of the Andante (bars 1-4), and of the main theme of the opening Allegro of opus 132 in the third variation (bars 1-2, 9-10). The raging, victorious finale is surely the *Grosse Fuge* revisited—and conquered.

With the Quartet in F major, op. 135, Beethoven came "home" at last. This is not to say that it is a conservative or anachronistic work— the hallmarks of the late style are too deeply imprinted in it for such a judgment to be viable. Radcliffe notes the "astonishing variety of textures" and the "bare, spare contrapuntal writing," [133] which, despite occasional extreme passages, reflects a withdrawal from the almost baroque luxuriance, fierce drive, and passionate expressiveness of the earlier quartets into a detached, objective irony. Yet, if the F-major Quartet avoids the sentimentality of nostalgia, it does "[turn] sharply back . . . more so than any other major work in a decade" (Kerman).

Earlier in this book I related this "homecoming" to the drives toward reconciliation which controlled Beethoven's personality during his last decade (and which reached their fulfillment following Karl's suicide attempt, for it liberated Beethoven from his pathological fixations quite as much as it freed Karl from his uncle's obsessive domination). Earlier in this chapter, however, I was equally certain that the Quartet's provisional return to Classicism was part of a recurrent stylistic pattern in Beethoven's musical development. Seen from yet another standpoint, the withdrawal from the borderlines of musical exploration may well have represented a compromise with a historical milieu unprepared to accept so radical a disruption of its sensibilities. Bruers and Cooper both find in this Quartet and in the second finale of opus 130 a concession to the bourgeois taste for the unproblematic, a "touch of Biedermeier domesticity" and even "a reduction of visionary power" stemming from the mental climate of Metternich's Vienna.[134] There is no need to accept any of these views, which may appear to place too heavy a freight of interpretation upon a fragile musical composition. It does no harm, however, to be aware that every creative act arises at the intersection of a multiplicity of forces and events—the biographical, historical, intellectual, and artistic being only the leading ones. It was Max Raphael who noted the paradox that "the work of art closest to perfection is both most profoundly determined by its time and goes furthest beyond it into timelessness."[135]

And since this book has been devoted to paradoxes and origins, we may as well close with Beethoven's own words on the subject:

> Let us begin with the primary original causes of all things, how something came about, wherefore and why it came about *in that particular way* and became what it is, why something is *what it is*, why something *cannot be exactly so!!!* Here, dear friend, we have reached the ticklish point which my delicacy forbids me to reveal to you at once. *All that we can say is*: it cannot be.[136]

One does not want wholly to understand this, nor did Beethoven wish us to do so. Better to answer the eternal, Hamlet question, "Muss es sein?" [Must it be?]—which is the heading of the last movement of the last Quartet—with Beethoven's simple, ironic reply: "Es muss sein!"

Roman sarcophagus with emblems of the Muses (third century A.D.). Vatican Museum, Rome. *Photo:* Deutsches Archäologisches Institut, Rome.

Abbreviations

AMZ	*Allgemeine musikalische Zeitung.*
Anderson	Emily Anderson, ed., *The Letters of Beethoven*, 3 vols. (London, 1961).
BB	Beethovenhaus, Bonn.
BJ	*Beethoven-Jahrbuch.* 1st ser. ed. Theodor von Frimmel; 2nd ser. ed. Joseph Schmidt-Görg and Paul Mies.
B&H	Breitkopf & Härtel.
Breuning	Gerhard von Breuning, *Aus dem Schwarzspanierhause* (Vienna, 1874).
Fischer	Joseph Schmidt-Görg, ed., *Des Bonner Bäckermeisters Gottfried Fischer: Aufzeichnungen über Beethovens Jugend* (BB, 1971).
Frimmel, *Handbuch*	Theodor von Frimmel, *Beethoven-Handbuch*, 2 vols. (Leipzig 1926).
JAMS	*Journal of the American Musicological Society.*
Kastner-Kapp	Emerich Kastner and Julius Kapp, eds., *Ludwig van Beethovens sämtliche Briefe*, 2nd ed. (Leipzig, 1923).

Kerst	Friedrich Kerst, ed., *Die Erinnerungen an Beethoven*, 2 vols. (Stuttgart, 1913).
Kinsky-Halm	Georg Kinsky, *Das Werk Beethoven. Thematisch-bibliographisches Verzeichnis seiner sämtlichen vollendeten Kompositionen*, completed and ed. Hans Halm (Munich, 1955).
Köhler-Beck	*Ludwig van Beethovens Konversationshefte*, vol. II, ed. Karl-Heinz Köhler and Dagmar Beck (Leipzig, 1976).
Köhler-Herre	*Ludwig van Beethovens Konversationshefte*, ed. Karl-Heinz Köhler and Grita Herre (Leipzig, 1968–).
Leitzmann	Albert Leitzmann, ed., *Ludwig van Beethoven: Berichte der Zeitgenossen, Briefe und persönliche Aufzeichnungen*, 2 vols. (Leipzig, 1921).
MQ	*The Musical Quarterly.*
M&L	*Music & Letters.*
MR	*The Music Review.*
NBJ	*Neues Beethoven Jahrbuch*, ed. Adolf Sandberger.
N I	Gustav Nottebohm, *Beethoveniana* (Leipzig and Winterthur, 1872).
N II	Gustav Nottebohm, *Zweite Beethoveniana* (Leipzig, 1887).
Nohl	Ludwig Nohl, *Beethovens Leben*, 3 vols. in 4 (Leipzig, 1867–77).
Rolland	Romain Rolland, *Beethoven: Les grandes époques créatices*, éd. définitive (Paris, 1966).
Schiedermair	Ludwig Schiedermair, *Der junge Beethoven* (Leipzig, 1925).
Schindler-MacArdle	Anton Schindler, *Beethoven As I Knew Him*, ed. Donald W. MacArdle (London and Chapel Hill, 1966). Trans. of 3rd ed. (1860) of Schindler, *Biographie von Ludwig van Beethoven.*
Schindler-Moscheles	Schindler, *The Life of Beethoven*, ed. Ignaz Moscheles (Boston, n.d. [1841]). Trans. of 1st ed. (1840) of Schindler, *Biographie von Ludwig van Beethoven.*
Schünemann	Georg Schünemann, *Ludwig van Beethovens Konversationshefte*, 3 vols. (Berlin, 1941–43).
Sonneck	O. G. Sonneck, *Beethoven: Impressions of Contemporaries* (New York, 1926).
Thayer	Alexander Wheelock Thayer, *Ludwig van Beethovens Leben*, 3 vols. (Berlin, 1866, 1872, 1879).
Thayer-Deiters	A. W. Thayer, *Ludwig van Beethovens Leben*, vol. 1, 2nd ed., ed. Hermann Deiters (Leipzig, 1901).
Thayer-Deiters-Riemann	A. W. Thayer, *Ludwig van Beethovens Leben*, ed. and enlarged by Hermann Deiters and Hugo

Riemann, 5 vols. (Leipzig, 1907–17; reissued 1922–23).

Thayer-Forbes   *Thayer's Life of Beethoven,* ed. Elliot Forbes, 2 vols. (Princeton, 1964; rev. ed. 1967).

Thayer-Krehbiel   A. W. Thayer, *The Life of Ludwig van Beethoven,* ed. and completed by Henry E. Krehbiel, 3 vols. (New York, 1921; rpt. London, 1960).

Wegeler-Ries   Franz Wegeler and Ferdinand Ries, *Biographische Notizen über Ludwig van Beethoven* (Coblenz, 1838). *Nachtrag* (Supplement) by Wegeler (Coblenz, 1845).

WoO   Werk(e) ohne Opuszahl (work[s] without opus number). As listed in Kinsky-Halm.

Notes

PREFACE

1. Köhler-Beck, II, 24; Schünemann, II, 8.
2. Anderson, Appendix I, no. 7, III, 1451.
3. Leitzmann, II, 262 (no. 148).
4. Johann Aloys Schlosser, *Ludwig van Beethoven: Eine Biographie* (Prague: Stephani & Schlosser, 1828 [1827]).
5. Maynard Solomon, Review of Fischer, *Notes*, 30 no. 2 (December 1973), 269–72.
6. *Standard Edition of the Complete Psychological Works of Sigmund Freud* (London: Hogarth Press, 1953–74), VIII, 80.

CHAPTER 1: FAMILY BACKGROUND

1. See Thayer-Forbes, p. 305. The trans. in Anderson, Appendix A, improperly transposes the reference into the past. A diary notation written between December 1793 and early 1794 indicates that Beethoven may have then believed that he was born in December 1768 or December 1769. See

330

Dagmar von Busch-Weise, "Beethovens Jugendtagebuch," *Studien zur Musikwissenschaft*, 25 (1962), 77.

2. Anderson no. 256; trans. Thayer-Forbes, p. 490.

3. Thayer-Forbes, p. 54.

4. See Solomon, "Beethoven's Birth Year," *MQ*, 56 (1970), 702–10.

5. Köhler-Herre, I, 179, 247; for other references to this matter in the Conversation Books, see Solomon, "Beethoven: the Nobility Pretense," *MQ*, 61 (1975), 289–90, n. 73.

6. Thayer-Deiters-Riemann, V, 278–79.

7. Anderson no. 1542.

8. Anderson no. 1551.

9. Fischer, p. 25; Thayer-Deiters, I, 421.

10. Fischer, p. 27.

11. Schiedermair, p. 101.

12. Fischer, p. 24; trans. Thayer-Forbes, p. 49.

13. Fischer, p. 23.

14. See Johann Jacob Wagner, "Neues über Beethovens Grosseltern mütterlicher Seite," *Kölnische Volkszeitung*, December 8, 1919: summarized in *Zeitschrift für Musikwissenschaft*, 1 (1919), 263–64.

15. Schiedermair, pp. 101–102; trans. Walter Riezler, *Beethoven* (London: Forrester, 1938), p. 20.

16. Fischer, pp. 61–62.

17. Fischer, p. 30.

18. Frimmel *Handbuch*, II, 245.

19. Fischer, pp. 21–22.

20. Fischer, p. 25.

21. Jacques-Gabriel Prod'homme, *La Jeunesse de Beethoven* (Paris: Delagrave, 1927), p. 50.

22. Edward Glover, "The Etiology of Alcoholism," in *On the Early Development of Mind* (London: Imago, 1956), p. 83. See also Karl Abraham, *Selected Papers* (London: Hogarth Press, 1927), pp. 80–89; Nolan D. C. Lewis, "Personality Factors in Alcoholic Addiction," *Quarterly Journal of Alcohol*, 1 (1940), 21–44.

23. Decree of April 26, 1768, cit. Thayer-Forbes, p. 21. Other examples of his difficulties with musicians date from 1771 and 1773. See Joseph Schmidt-Görg, *Beethoven, die Geschichte seiner Familie* (BB, 1964), p. 220; Schiedermair, p. 93 f.

24. Fischer, p. 21; Thayer-Deiters, I, 419.

25. Thayer-Forbes, p. 55.

26. Thayer-Forbes, p. 78.

27. Schiedermair, pp. 97–98.

28. Schmidt-Görg, *Familie*, p. 224; Schiedermair, "Zur Biographie Johann van Beethovens (Vater)," *NBJ*, 3 (1927), 32–41.

29. Thayer-Forbes, p. 136.

30. Fischer, pp. 38–39.

31. Fischer, p. 61.

32. Thayer-Forbes, p. 51.

33. Fischer, p. 30.

34. Thayer-Deiters, I, 425; Thayer-Forbes, p. 51; Fischer, p. 30.

35. Fischer, pp. 62–63; Thayer-Deiters, I, 439.

36. Fischer, pp. 37–38; trans. Paul Bekker, *Beethoven* (London: Dent, 1925), p. 5, amended.

CHAPTER 2: CHILDHOOD

1. Anderson no. 51 (June 29, 1801).

2. Thayer-Forbes, p. 849.

3. Wegeler-Ries, p. 8.

4. Kerst, I, 216.

5. Anderson no. 1302; trans. Thayer-Forbes, p. 918.

6. Thayer-Forbes, p. 57.

7. Fischer, p. 32.

8. F.-J. Fétis, *Biographie universelle des musiciens,* 2nd ed. (Paris: Firmin-Didot, 1883), I, 298.

9. Thayer-Forbes, p. 57.

10. Thayer-Krehbiel, I, 61 n.

11. Kerst, I, 10.

12. See Schiedermair, p. 130; Thayer-Forbes, pp. 57–58.

13. Fischer, pp. 32–33. Trans. combined from Sonneck, p. 4 and Editha and Richard Sterba, *Beethoven and His Nephew* (New York: Pantheon, 1954), pp. 82–83.

14. Otto Erich Deutsch, *Mozart: A Documentary Biography* (London: A. & C. Black and Stanford: Stanford Univ. Press, 1965), p. 21.

15. Thayer-Forbes, p. 58, n. 8. (The remark is by Elliot Forbes.)

16. Fischer, p. 29.

17. Fischer, p. 33.

18. Thayer-Forbes p. 62.

19. Schindler-MacArdle, p. 46.

20. Schindler-Moscheles, p. 9; Wegeler-Ries, p. 122.

21. Anderson no. 1 (to J. W. von Schaden, Sept. 15, 1787). For the only other references to either of his parents in Beethoven's correspondence, see Anderson nos. 3, 1028, 1374, 1400, and 1542.

22. Fischer p. 40.

23. Breuning, p. 13.

24. Wegeler-Ries, p. 122.

25. Thayer-Krehbiel, I, 85.

26. Thayer-Forbes, p. 66.

27. Fischer, p. 51.

28. Ludwig Nohl, *Beethoven nach den Schilderungen seiner Zeitgenossen* (Stuttgart: Cotta, 1877), p. 4.

29. Kerst, I, 10.

30. Thayer-Forbes, p. 59.

31. Kerst, I, 10–11.

32. Thayer-Forbes, p. 58.

33. Thayer-Deiters, I, 448.

34. Fischer, p. 32.

35. Thayer-Forbes, p. 58.

36. Phyllis Greenacre, "The Family Romance of the Artist," in *Emotional Growth* (New York: International Univ. Press, 1971), II, 531.

37. Fischer, pp. 56–57.

38. Freud, "The Relation of the Poet to Day-Dreaming," in *Collected Papers*, IV (New York: Basic Books, 1959), 176.

39. Fischer, pp. 33–34.

40. Sigmund Freud, "Family Romances" (1909), in *Collected Papers*, V (New York: Basic Books, 1959), 74–78; Otto Rank, *The Myth of the Birth of the Hero* (1909; New York: Vintage Books, n.d.), pp. 65–96. The extensive literature is surveyed, with bibliography, in Linda Joan Kaplan, "The Concept of the Family Romance," *Psychoanalytic Review*, 61 (1974), 169–202.

41. See Phyllis Greenacre, "The Childhood of the Artist," in *Emotional Growth* (New York: International Univ. Press, 1971), II, 479–504, esp. p. 495.

42. J. J. Bachofen, *Myth, Religion, and Mother Right* (1861; Princeton: Princeton Univ. Press, 1967), p. 109.

43. Ludwig Nohl, *Beethovens Brevier* (Leipzig: Günther, 1870), p. 18. According to Otto Jahn, Beethoven also copied this passage into his notebooks (A. C. Kalischer, *Beethoven und seine Zeitgenossen* [Berlin and Leipzig: Schuster & Loeffler, 1908–10], II, 47).

44. Rank, p. 66.

45. Nohl, *Beethovens Brevier*, p. 19; trans. Schindler-MacArdle, p. 310.

CHAPTER 3: BEETHOVEN'S SECOND DECADE

1. Fischer, pp. 51–52; trans. Sonneck, p. 8.

2. Fischer, p. 43.

3. Thayer-Forbes, p. 66.

4. Anderson no. 6.

5. Beethoven was listed as a "student of Neefe" in standard music dictionaries of his time. See Emerich Kastner, *Bibliotheca Beethoveniana*, 2nd ed., rev. Theodor Frimmel (Leipzig: B&H, 1925), pp. 3–6.

6. Schiedermair, p. 141; Irmgaard Leux, *Chr. Gottlob Neefe* (Leipzig: Kistner & Siegel, 1925), pp. 14–15.

7. Trans. Paul Nettl, *Forgotten Musicians* (New York: Philosophical Library, 1951), pp. 246–64.

8. See Solomon, "Beethoven's Productivity at Bonn," *M&L*, 53 (1972), 165–72.

9. Nohl, I, pp. 371–72. Neefe is sometimes blamed for his pupil's deficiencies; but he himself was the first to criticize them. Beethoven complained to Wegeler "of the too severe criticisms made of his first efforts in composition" by Neefe (Wegeler-Ries, p. 113; Thayer-Forbes, p. 65).

10. This was of the Twenty-four Variations for Piano on Righini's "Venni amore," WoO 65. No copies have survived.

11. Thayer-Forbes, p. 79.

12. *Loc. cit.*

13. Anderson no. 1 (to J. W. von Schaden, Sept. 15, 1787).

14. Thayer-Forbes, p. 145.

15. Ernst Simmel, "Alcoholism and Addiction," in Sandor Lorand, ed., *The Yearbook of Psychoanalysis*, V (New York: International Univ. Press, 1950), 251.

16. Thayer-Forbes, p. 95.

17. Thayer-Forbes, p. 94.

18. Anderson no. 3.

19. *Loc. cit.* Trans. amended.

20. Fischer, p. 72; Schiedermair, p. 130.

21. Helene Deutsch, "Absence of Grief," in *Neuroses and Character Types* (New York: International Univ. Press, 1965), p. 235.

22. Thayer-Forbes, p. 105.

CHAPTER 4: LAST YEARS IN BONN: ENLIGHTENMENT

1. Baron Riesbeck, *Travels Through Germany in a Series of Letters* (London, 1787), III, 261.

2. *Ibid.*, III, 286.

3. *Ibid.*, I, 256.

4. A. J. P. Taylor, *The Habsburg Monarchy, 1809–1918* (London: Hamish Hamilton; rpt. New York: Harper, 1965), p. 19.

5. Schiedermair, p. 29.

6. See Alfred Einstein, *Mozart: His Character, His Work* (London, New York, Toronto: Oxford, 1945, pp. 82–83; Katherine Thomson, "Mozart and Freemasonry," *M&L*, 57 (1976), 25–46.

7. Alfred Becker, *Christian Gottlob Neefe und die bonner Illuminaten* (Bonn: Bouvier, 1969), *passim*.

8. Max Braubach, "Beethoven's Abschied von Bonn: Das rheinische Erbe," in E. Schenk, ed., *Beethoven-Symposion* (Vienna, 1970), pp. 25–41.

9. Thayer-Forbes, p. 79.

10. Wegeler-Ries, p. 13.

11. Wegeler-Ries, p. 18.

12. Schindler-MacArdle, p. 47.

13. Thayer-Forbes, p. 108.

14. Anderson no. 334 (to Varena, December 1811).

15. Anderson no. 1306 (to Nägeli, September 9, 1824).

16. Anderson no. 139 (to the Bigots, March 1807).

17. Students were excluded from membership (Schiedermair, p. 31).

18. Wegeler-Ries, *Nachtrag*, p. 9.

19. Anderson no. 228 (November 2, 1809).

20. Heine, *Religion and Philosophy in Germany*, trans. John Snodgrass (rpt. Boston: Beacon, 1959), p. 120.

21. Köhler-Herre, I, 235.

22. Herbert Marcuse, *Reason and Revolution* (New York: Oxford, 1941; rpt. Boston: Beacon, 1960), p. 15.

23. Paul Henry Lang, *Music in Western Civilization* (New York: Norton, 1941), p. 619.

24. *BJ*, 1st ser., 2 (1909), 331–32; Thayer-Forbes, pp. 120–21.

25. Hans Rosenberg, *Bureaucracy, Aristocracy and Autocracy: The Prussian Experience 1660–1815* (Cambridge, Mass: Harvard Univ. Press, 1958; rpt. Boston: Beacon, 1966), pp. 41–42.

26 This does not contradict Beethoven's alleged republicanism, which many biographers, beginning with Schindler, have emphasized. For a republic meant something quite different to Enlightenment thinkers from what it has come to mean to later observers. Rousseau wrote: "I give the name *Republic* to every state that is governed by laws, no matter what its form of administration may be" (*Social Contract*, II, chap. 6).

27. Anna Freud, "Adolescence," in *Psychoanalytic Study of the Child*, 13 (1958), 260.

28. Anderson no. 1.

29. Thayer-Forbes, p. 108.

30. Simrock, cit. Thayer-Forbes, p. 245.

31. Simrock to Junker, cit. Nohl, *Beethoven nach den Schilderungen*, p. 12; Kerst, I, 16.

32. Wegeler-Ries, p. 18.
33. See Thayer-Forbes, pp. 100–101 and 105–106; H. C. Robbins Landon, *Haydn: Chronicle and Works,* III (Bloomington: Indiana Univ. Press, 1976), 192–93.
34. Thayer-Forbes, p. 121.
35. Fischer, p. 74.
36. "According to the Brockhaus *Konversations-Lexikon* which appeared in 1809, Beethoven intended to permanently leave Vienna in 1794 or 1795, the time that coincided with the termination of the studies which were the reason for his voyage" (Prod'homme, *Jeunesse,* p. 166; see also Nohl, I, 335, 432).

CHAPTER 5: THE MUSIC (BONN)

1. For the musical inventories of the Bonn court chapel and of the electoral music library, see Adolf Sandberger, "Die Inventare der Bonner Hofkapelle," in *Ausgewählte Aufsätze zur Musikgeschichte, II* (Munich: Drei Masken, 1924), 109–30; and Sieghard Brandenburg, "Die kurfürstliche Musikbibliothek in Bonn und ihre Bestände im 18. Jahrhundert," *BJ,* second ser., 8 (1975), 7–47.
2. Thayer-Forbes, p. 101.
3. Schiedermair, p. 274.
4. J.-G. Prod'homme, *Les Sonates pour piano de Beethoven* (1937; Paris: Delagrave, 1950), p. 26.
5. Personal communication.
6. William S. Newman, *The Sonata in the Classic Era* (Chapel Hill: Univ. of North Carolina Press, 1963), p. 507.
7. Joseph Kerman, ed., *Ludwig van Beethoven: Autograph Miscellany from circa 1786 to 1799* (London: British Museum, 1970), II, 283.
8. Thayer-Forbes, p. 119.
9. Thayer-Forbes, p. 106.
10. Thayer-Forbes, p. 120.
11. Max Graf, *Die innere Werkstaat des Musikers* (Stuttgart: Enke, 1910), pp. 155–56.
12. Alfred Heuss, "Die Humanitätsmelodien im 'Fidelio,'" *Neue Zeitschrift für Musik,* 91 (1924), 545 ff. See Eduard Hanslick, *Suite: Aufsätze über Musik und Musiker* (Vienna & Teschen: Prochaska, n.d.), pp. 153–62.
13. Hans Gál, "Die Stileigentümlichkeiten des jungen Beethoven," *Studien zur Musikwissenschaft,* 4 (1916), 58–115. See esp. pp. 68 ff.
14. Jules Combarieu, *Histoire de la musique,* II (Paris: Armand Colin, 1920), 420.

15. Reminiscences of Bernhard Mäurer, in Kerst, I, 11; see also Frimmel *Handbuch,* I, 248–49.

CHAPTER 6: A PIANIST AND HIS PATRONS

1. Thayer-Forbes, p. 115.
2. Thayer-Forbes, pp. 103–104.
3. Thayer-Forbes, p. 185.
4. Anderson no. 9.
5. Anderson no. 9. Wegeler names Gelinek as one pianist whom Beethoven accused (Wegeler-Ries, pp. 59–60).
6. Czerny, "Recollections from My Life," *MQ,* 42 (1956), 304.
7. *Ibid.,* p. 309.
8. The dates of these known concerts were: March 29, 1795; March 30, 1795; March 31, 1795; December 18, 1795; January 8, 1796; late 1796; April 6, 1797; March 29, 1798; April 1, 1798; April 2, 1798; and October 27, 1798. See Thayer-Forbes, *passim;* Hermann Reuther, "Beethovens Konzerte," in *Ein wiener Beethoven Buch,* ed. Alfred Orel (Vienna: Gerlach & Wiedling, 1921), pp. 72 ff.
9. Wegeler-Ries, p. 109; Thayer-Forbes, pp. 184–85.
10. Anderson no. 16.
11. To Jahn, cit. Thayer-Forbes, p. 444.
12. Schindler-Moscheles, p. 21.
13. Otto Jahn, *Life of Mozart* (London: Novello, Ewer, 1882; rpt. New York: Kalmus, n.d.), II, 385; III, 218–19; George Grove, *A Dictionary of Music and Musicians,* 1st. ed., (London: Macmillan, 1879–90), IV, 9.
14. Schindler-MacArdle, p. 49.
15. Thayer-Forbes, p. 211; Kinsky-Halm, p. 22.
16. Holz to Jahn, cit. Thayer-Forbes, p. 258.
17. Thayer-Forbes, pp. 170–71, 187; Wegeler-Ries, p. 28.
18. Grove's *Dictionary,* 1st. ed., II, 132; Thayer-Forbes, pp. 356-57.
19. Czerny, "Recollections," p. 309.
20. Emily Anderson, ed., *The Letters of Mozart and His Family* (1938; 2nd ed. London: Macmillan, 1966), II, 717–18.
21. Röckel, cit. Thayer-Forbes, p. 389.
22. See Anderson no. 110 (to Josephine Deym, spring 1805).
23. The Lichnowskys had a son of their own, Edward Maria (1789–1845), who became a distinguished agriculturalist and historian.
24. Wegeler-Ries, p. 33.
25. Wegeler-Ries, p. 33; trans. Schindler-MacArdle, p. 61.

26. Anderson no. 51 (June 29, 1801).

27. Anderson no. 53 (July 1, 1801).

28. Schindler-MacArdle, p. 50. Trans. revised.

29. Alan Tyson, "Beethoven to the Countess Susanna Guicciardi: A New Letter," in *Beethoven Studies*, ed. Tyson, 1 (1973), 9.

30. Anderson no. 254 (to Ignaz von Gleichenstein, spring 1810).

31. Wegeler-Ries, p. 19; trans. Schindler-MacArdle, p. 45.

32. Fischhof Manuscript (Deutsche Staatsbibliothek, Berlin), fol. 4ᵛ.

33. Wegeler-Ries, p. 20; trans. Schindler-MacArdle, p. 45.

34. Nohl, *Beethoven nach den Schilderungen*, p. 20; Frimmel, *Handbuch*, II, 322.

35. Ernest Newman, *The Unconscious Beethoven* (New York: Knopf, 1927), p. 53.

36. Thayer-Forbes, p. 212.

37. Constantin von Wurzbach, *Biographisches Lexikon des Kaiserthums Oester-reich, 1750–1850* (Vienna, 1856–91), XV, 309. In one instance Wurzbach confused the present Prince Lobkowitz with a Lobkowitz of a prior genera-tion; therefore, these reports cannot be accepted as wholly conclusive.

38. Nohl, II, 461; memoirs of Lulu Thürheim, cit. George Marek, *Beethoven: Biography of a Genius* (New York: Funk & Wagnalls, 1969), p. 108.

39. Nohl, *Beethoven nach den Schilderungen*, p. 20.

40. Karl Geiringer, *Haydn: A Creative Life in Music* (New York: Norton, 1946), p. 67.

41. Geiringer, pp. 85–86.

42. Geiringer, p. 55.

43. Geiringer, p. 86.

CHAPTER 7: HAYDN AND BEETHOVEN

1. A. B. Marx, *Ludwig van Beethovens Leben* (2nd ed., Berlin: Janke, 1863), I, 22.

2. Wegeler-Ries, p. 86; Thayer-Forbes, p. 178.

3. H. C. Robbins Landon, ed., *The Collected Correspondence and London Notebooks of Joseph Haydn* (London: Barrie & Rockliff, 1959), p. 128 (to von Genzinger, Jan. 17, 1792).

4. Geiringer, *Haydn*, p. 111; Landon, p. 132 (letter of March 2, 1792).

5. Schenk's "Autobiography," cit. Thayer-Forbes, p. 140. For the complete "Autobiography," see Paul Nettl, ed., *Forgotten Musicians* (New York: Philosophical Library, 1951), pp. 265–79. Schenk claimed that his in-struction of Beethoven extended until early June 1793, when—he asserted—Beethoven left Vienna with Haydn for Eisenstadt. His claim is confirmed

by a letter to Zmeskall (now in BB). Schenk's instruction therefore lasted for at most five months.

6. Thayer-Forbes, p. 141.

7. *Ibid.*

8. Schindler-MacArdle, p. 55.

9. Gustav Nottebohm, *Beethoven's Studien. Beethoven's Unterricht bei J. Haydn, Albrechtsberger und Salieri* (Leipzig & Winterthur: Rieter-Biedermann, 1873), I, 21–43.

10. Landon, *Collected Correspondence*, p. 117 (letter of August 4, 1791).

11. Geiringer, p. 135.

12. For a cogent modern appraisal of Haydn's effectiveness as Beethoven's teacher, see Alfred Mann, "Beethoven's Contrapuntal Studies with Haydn," *MQ*, 56 (1970), 711–26; Mann, "Haydns Kontrapunktlehre und Beethovens Studien," in Carl Dahlhaus et al., eds., *Bericht über den internationalen musikwissenschaftlichen Kongress Bonn 1970* (Kassel: Bärenreiter, 1971), pp. 70–74. See also Vincent d'Indy, *Beethoven: A Critical Biography* (Boston: Boston Music Co., 1912), pp. 17–18.

13. Thayer-Forbes, p. 141.

14. Max Unger, "Kleine Beethoven-Studien," *NBJ*, 8 (1938), 80.

15. Douglas Johnson, forthcoming dissertation, Univ. of Calif. at Berkeley. See also Thayer-Forbes, p. 165; N I, 51; N II, 27–28; Kerman, *Autograph Miscellany*, II, 276.

16. Breuning p. 97.

17. Thayer-Forbes, p. 144; Landon, *Collected Correspondence*, pp. 141–43.

18. Thayer-Forbes, p. 145.

19. *Ibid.* Beethoven's letter was enclosed in the same envelope as Haydn's letter.

20. I. Moscheles, *Recent Music and Musicians* (New York: Henry Holt, 1873), p. 7.

21. Anderson no. 192 (to B&H, January 7, 1809).

22. Otto Erich Deutsch, ed., *Schubert: A Documentary Biography* (London: Dent, 1946), p. 64. Frimmel, *Handbuch*, II, 95-96.

23. Printed in *Musica divina* (Vienna), Jan.–Feb. 1921, pp. 10–11.

24. Thayer-Deiters-Riemann, II, 200.

25. Wegeler-Ries, p. 86; trans. Thayer-Forbes, p. 149.

26. Wegeler-Ries, p. 84.

27. Wegeler-Ries, p. 85; trans. Thayer-Forbes, p. 164.

28. Thayer-Forbes, pp. 237–38.

29. Reported by Aloys Fuchs, Kerst, I, 109.

30. Kerst, II, 192.

31. For a brief but extremely thorough summary of the literature dealing with Haydn's influence on Beethoven, see Georg Feder, "Stilelemente Haydns

in Beethovens Werken," in *Bericht über den internationalen musikwissen-schaftlichen Kongress Bonn 1970*, pp. 65–70.

32. Czerny, "Recollections," p. 305.

33. *AMZ*, 1 (1799), 252, cit. Jahn, *The Life of Mozart*, II, 384.

34. *AMZ*, 1 (1799), 366, 570; see Schindler-MacArdle, pp. 76–77.

35. Ignaz von Seyfried, *L. v. Beethovens Studien* (1832; trans. H. H. Pierson, Leipzig: Schuberth, 1853), Supplement, p. 17.

36. *Ibid.*

37. *Ibid.*

38. Letter of December 14, 1803, in *Haydn-Studien*, 1 no. 2 (February 1966), 99–100.

39. Letter of January 4, 1804, in *Haydn-Studien*, p. 100.

40. Thayer-Forbes, p. 430.

41. Geiringer, *Haydn*, p. 170.

42. Anderson no. 376 (to Emilie M., July 17, 1812).

43. Anderson no. 59 (July 13, 1802). Ital. omitted.

44. Kerst, II, 192; Thayer-Forbes, p. 259.

45. Giuseppe Bertini, *Dizionario, storio-critico degli scrittori di musica* (Palermo, 1814), I, 96.

46. These are the reminiscences of Louis Drouet printed in Thayer-Deiters-Riemann, II, 197–200.

47. According to Moscheles, "Haydn heard that Beethoven had spoken in a tone of depreciation of his oratorio *The Creation*. 'That is wrong of him,' said Haydn; 'What has he written then? His Septet?' " Haydn then added: "Certainly that is beautiful, nay, splendid!" (Moscheles, *Recent Music and Musicians*, p. 23).

CHAPTER 8: PORTRAIT OF A YOUNG COMPOSER

1. Nohl, *Beethoven nach den Schilderungen*, pp. 19–20. Sonneck, pp. 20–21.

2. Sonneck, p. 155.

3. Nohl, *Beethoven nach den Schilderungen*, p. 20; Sonneck, p. 21.

4. Schindler-MacArdle, p. 120.

5. Seyfried, Supplement, p. 22.

6. *Loc. cit.*

7. Thayer-Forbes, pp. 466 and 537.

8. Schindler-MacArdle, p. 120.

9. Thayer-Forbes, p. 802; Sonneck, p. 128.

10. Sonneck, p. 31.

11. Nohl, *Beethoven nach den Schilderungen*, pp. 41–42.

12. Anderson no. 296 (February 10, 1811).

13. Seyfried, Supplement, p. 16.

14. Breuning, p. 98.

15. Seyfried, cit. in Nohl, *Beethoven nach den Schilderungen*, p. 43.

16. Thayer-Forbes, p. 501.

17. Anderson no. 258 (to Therese Malfatti, May 1810).

18. Leitzmann, II, 261 (no. 140).

19. Seyfried, Supplement, p. 17.

20. Thayer-Deiters-Riemann, I, 496.

21. Thayer-Forbes, pp. 223–24.

22. Thayer-Forbes, p. 261.

23. Anderson no. 94 (July 24, 1804).

24. Anderson no. 202 (ca. March 14, 1809).

25. Anderson no. 248 (February 1810) and no. 291 (ca. 1810).

26. Anderson no. 12 (August 2, 1794).

27. Thayer-Forbes, p. 232.

28. Wegeler-Ries, p. 43.

29. Anderson no. 16 (February 19, 1796).

30. Holz to Jahn, Kerst, II, 186. It is not known when this reported incident took place.

31. Köhler-Herre, I, 211.

32. Seyfried, Supplement, p. 22.

33. Kerst, I, 123; Thayer-Forbes, p. 439.

34. Anderson no. 7 (November 2, 1793); trans. Thayer-Forbes, p. 162.

35. Dagmar von Busch-Weise, "Beethovens Jugendtagebuch," *Studien zur Musikwissenschaft*, 25 (1962), 77; Thayer-Forbes, p. 182.

36. Anderson no. 6 (before October 26, 1793).

37. Ernest Walker, *Beethoven* (New York: Brentano's, 1905), p. 141.

38. Thayer-Forbes, p. 864.

39. Anderson no. 48.

40. Anderson no. 4 (to A. Vocke, May 22, 1793). (Schiller, *Don Carlos.*)

41. Anderson no. 30.

42. Anderson no. 53 (to Amenda, July 1, 1801). Beethoven refers to his audience as "the rabble" in Anderson no. 57 (to Hoffmeister, April 8, 1802).

43. Anderson no. 12 (August 2, 1794).

44. See Solomon, "Beethoven: The Nobility Pretense," *MQ*, 61 (1975), 272–294.

45. W. A. Thomas-San-Galli, *Die unsterbliche Geliebte Beethovens* (Halle, 1909), p. 65; Martin Cooper, *Beethoven: The Last Decade* (London: Oxford, 1970), p. 16.

46. Eduard Hanslick, *Geschichte des Concertwesens in Wien* (Vienna, 1869), pp. 50 ff.

47. Köhler-Herre, I, 252.

48. Anderson no. 979 (to J. B. Bach, October 27, 1819).

49. Otto Fenichel, *Collected Papers* (London: Routledge & Kegan Paul, 1954–55), II, 158.

50. Kerst, I, 215.

51. Anderson no. 1194 (end of June 1823).

52. Schindler-Moscheles, p. 70.

53. Köhler-Herre, I, 219.

CHAPTER 9: VIENNA: CITY OF DREAMS

1. A. J. P. Taylor, *Habsburg Monarchy*, p. 38.

2. For a fuller discussion of class subdivisions in Viennese society, see my "Beethoven's Class Position and Outlook," in *Bericht über den internationalen Beethoven-Kongress in Berlin 1977*, ed. K. Niemann, et al. (forthcoming).

3. Riesbeck, *Travels through Germany*, I, 251, 244.

4. Riesbeck, II, 4.

5. John Owen, *Travels into Different Parts of Europe, in the Years 1791 and 1792* (London: Cadell & Davies, 1796), II, 473.

6. John Russell, *A Tour in Germany, and Some of the Southern Provinces of the Austrian Empire, in the Years 1820, 1821, 1822* (Boston: Wells & Lilly, 1825), p. 396.

7. Russell, p. 398.

8. Henry Reeve, *Journal of a Residence at Vienna and Berlin in the Eventful Winter of 1805–1806* (London: Longmans Green, 1877), p. 25.

9. Ilse Barea, *Vienna* (New York: Knopf, 1966), p. 151.

10. Taylor, *Habsburg Monarchy*, p. 12.

CHAPTER 10: THE MUSIC (EARLY VIENNA)

1. Anderson no. 228 (to B&H, November 2, 1809).

2. Rolland, p. 112, n. 2; *Beethoven the Creator* (New York: Harper, 1929), p. 367.

3. D. F. Tovey, *Beethoven* (1944; rpt. London: Oxford, 1965), p. 7.

4. Thayer-Forbes, p. 209.

5. Wegeler-Ries, p. 101; Thayer-Forbes, p. 348.

6. Anderson no. 18. For an illuminating study, see W. S. Newman, "Beethoven's Pianos versus his Piano Ideals," *JAMS*, 23 (1970), 484–504.

7. Anderson no. 66 (November 1802).

8. Anderson no. 67 (ca. December 18, 1802).

9. Anderson no. 72 (to B&H, April 8, 1803).

10. Thayer-Forbes, p. 164.

11. Denis Arnold and Nigel Fortune, eds., *The Beethoven Reader* (New York: Norton, 1971), p. 205.

12. Walter Riezler, *Beethoven*, p. 126.

13. Alfred Mann suggests the possibility that Beethoven studied quartet composition with Haydn (*MQ*, 61 [1970], 725, n. 10). It is also possible that Beethoven studied quartet composition with Emanuel Aloys Förster (1748–1823). See Thayer-Forbes, pp. 261–62.

14. N II, 494; *M&L*, 58 (April 1977), 127–52.

15. Joseph Kerman, *The Beethoven Quartets* (New York: Knopf, 1967), p. 55.

16. Philip Radcliffe, *Beethoven's String Quartets* (London: Hutchinson, 1965; New York: Dutton, 1968), pp. 44–45.

17. Charles Rosen, *The Classical Style* (New York: Viking, 1971), p. 381.

18. Anderson no. 48 (to B&H, April 22, 1801).

19. Kerman, *Autograph Miscellany*, II, 166–74; 190–91.

20. Hanslick, *Geschichte des Concertwesens*, pp. 34–35.

21. Tovey, *Essays in Musical Analysis*, I (London, Oxford, 1935), 21.

22. *AMZ*, 3 (1800), 49.

23. Tovey, "Beethoven," in *Encyclopaedia Britannica*, 14th ed. (1929), III, 320, col. 1.

24. Riezler, p. 115.

25. Anderson no. 44 (to Hoffmeister, ca. January 15, 1801). Trans. revised.

26. William S. Newman, *The Sonata in the Classic Era*, p. 515.

27. Paul Bekker, *Beethoven*, p. 106.

28. Eric Blom, *Beethoven's Pianoforte Sonatas Discussed* (London: Dent, 1937; rpt. New York: Da Capo, 1968), p. 123.

29. Ludwig Misch, *Beethoven Studies* (1950; Eng. trans. Norman: Univ. of Oklahoma Press, 1953), p. 53.

30. Czerny, *On the Proper Performance of All Beethoven's Works for the Piano* (Vienna: Universal, 1970), p. 13; Kerst, I, 46.

CHAPTER 11: CRISIS AND CREATIVITY

1. Anderson no. 263. This letter, usually dated July 9, 1810, may well date instead from July 1801.

2. Anderson no. 51.

3. Anderson no. 53.

4. Anderson no. 54.

5. Anderson no. 51 (letter of June 29, 1801).

6. Anderson no. 53.

7. Anderson no. 51.

8. Anderson no. 57 (to Hoffmeister).

9. Anderson no. 58 (letter of April 22, 1802).

10. It is usually assumed that Ries arrived in Vienna in September or October 1801, at the earliest, but this makes it difficult to account for several of his reminiscences of events in 1800. I follow the suggestion of Ludwig Ueberfeldt in his dissertation *Ferdinand Ries' Jugendentwicklung* (Bonn: Rost, 1915), p. 12.

11. Wegeler-Ries, pp. 98–99; Thayer-Forbes, p. 304.

12. Anderson, Appendix A, III, 1351–54; trans. Thayer-Forbes, pp. 304–306.

13. The Sterbas speculate that the Testament was directed solely to Caspar Carl, and that Beethoven was so angry with Nikolaus Johann that he could not write his name (*Beethoven and His Nephew*, p. 32). See also A. C. Kalischer, *The Letters of Beethoven*, trans. J. S. Shedlock (London: Dent, 1909), I, 62, for a wholly improbable speculation.

14. George Grove, *Beethoven and His Nine Symphonies* (3rd ed. London, 1898; rpt. New York: Dover, 1962), p. 45 n.

15. Anderson no. 16.

16. Anderson no. 1151.

17. Anderson, Appendix C (nos. 1, 5, 6, and 11).

18. Anderson no. 205 (March 28, 1809); cf. Anderson no. 148 (to Gleichenstein, after June 23, 1807).

19. Nohl, III, 812.

20. Anderson no. 3.

21. Thayer-Forbes, p. 1059.

22. See G. Bilancioni, *La Sordità di Beethoven* (Rome: Formíggini, 1921), pp. 132 ff; Waldemar Schweisheimer, *Beethovens Leiden* (Munich: Müller, 1922), pp. 62 ff; Schweisheimer, "Beethoven's Physicians," *MQ*, 31 (1945), 289; Walther Forster, *Beethovens Krankheiten und ihre Beurteilung* (Wiesbaden: B&H, 1955), *passim;* Edward Larkin, "Beethoven's Medical History," in Cooper, *Beethoven*, pp. 440–41.

23. Sonneck, p. 26; Czerny, "Recollections," p. 306.

24. Thayer-Forbes, pp. 370–71.

25. Wegeler-Ries, p. 98.

26. Wegeler-Ries, *Nachtrag*, p. 10 (letter of Nov. 13, 1804); Thayer-Forbes, p. 358. Breuning and Beethoven shared an apartment for a short time in 1804, but the stresses of such proximity led to a violent quarrel, followed by a passionate reconciliation in the fall of the same year.

27. Thayer-Forbes, p. 690.

28. Kerst, II, 186.

29. Nohl, *Beethoven, Liszt, Wagner* (Vienna: Braumüller, 1874), p. 112.

30. Thayer-Forbes, p. 373.

31. See Anderson nos. 51 and 53; Thayer-Forbes, p. 850; Thayer-Forbes, p. 252; Nohl, *Beethoven Depicted by His Contemporaries* (London: Reeves, 1880), p. 243; George Smart, *Leaves from the Journal of Sir George Smart*, ed. H. B. Cox and C. L. E. Cox (London: Longmans, Green, 1907), p. 124; Thayer-Forbes, p. 187.

32. Thayer-Krehbiel, I, 263–64.

33. Leitzmann, II, 257 (no. 100).

34. Anderson no. 53.

35. Anderson no. 60 (July 14, 1802).

36. N II, 89; Thayer-Forbes, p. 400.

CHAPTER 12: THE HEROIC DECADE (I)

1. Moscheles, *Recent Music and Musicians,* pp. 3–4. As early as 1797, Beethoven's works were second in quantity only to Mozart's on a list of music owned by the young pianist Dorothea Graumann (later Baroness Ertmann). See Hellmut Federhofer, "Ein thematischer Katalog der Dorothea Graumann," in Dagmar Weise, ed., *Festschrift Joseph Schmidt-Görg zum 60. Geburtstag* (BB, 1957), pp. 100–110. Not all young musicians were Beethoven's partisans, however. The young C. M. von Weber called Beethoven's post-1800 works "a confused chaos, an unintelligible struggle after novelty" (Letter of May 1, 1810, to Hans Georg Nägeli, cited in Nohl, ed., *Letters of Distinguished Musicians,* trans. Lady Wallace [London: Longmans, Green, 1867], p. 209).

2. Czerny, "Recollections," p. 311; AMZ, 7 (1805), 321, 501.

3. Anderson no. 132 (to B&H, July 5, 1806).

4. Arthur Loesser, *Men, Women, and Pianos: A Social History* (New York: Simon & Schuster, 1954), p. 116.

5. Thayer-Forbes, p. 445.

6. Nicholas Temperley, "Beethoven in London Concert Life, 1800–1850," *MR,* 21 (1960), 207–14.

7. Seyfried, Supplement, p. 21.

8. Newman, *Sonata in the Classic Era,* p. 528, citing Schindler *Biographie* (1860), I, 240; H. Earle Johnson, *Musical Interludes in Boston, 1795–1830* (New York: Columbia Univ. Press, 1943), p. 144; see Hanslick, *Geschichte,* p. 278.

9. See Alan Tyson, *The Authentic English Editions of Beethoven* (London: Faber, 1963), p. 39. Several of these were first editions: see Tyson, p. 19, and MacArdle, "First Editions of Beethoven Published in England," *Monthly Musical Record,* 90 (1960), 228 ff.

10. See Thayer-Forbes, pp. 309–13.

11. Anderson no. 82 (ca. September 18, 1803).

12. This and the following references are from Erich H. Müller, "Beethoven und Simrock," *Simrock Jahrbuch,* 2 (1929), pp. 24–28. I am indebted to Alan Tyson for raising the possibility that Beethoven intended to leave Vienna permanently at this time.

13. Anderson no. 90.

14. Joseph Schmidt-Görg, ed., *Dreizehn unbekannte Briefe an Josephine*

Gräfin Deym geb. v. Brunsvik (BB, 1957), pp. 15, 23; André Hevesy, *Beethoven the Man* (London: Faber & Gwyer, 1927), p. 77. See also Anderson no. 88 (to Joseph Sonnleithner).

CHAPTER 13: BONAPARTE: THE CRISIS OF BELIEF

1. Wegeler-Ries, p. 78; Thayer-Forbes, pp. 348–49.
2. Schindler claimed to have heard the same story from Moritz Lichnowsky, whom he cited as his main authority for material on Beethoven's middle years in Vienna (see Schindler-MacArdle, p. 116; Schindler-Moscheles, pp. 34–35). In view of several errors in Schindler's account of the genesis of the *Eroica* Symphony, there is no reason to accept this claim.
3. The symphony was first performed at Prince Lobkowitz's palace in the latter half of 1804. It was followed by semipublic performances in the winter of 1804–05 at Herr von Würth's, and had its first public performance on April 7, 1805. The program of the April 1805 performance announced it as a "new grand symphony in D-sharp" (Thayer-Forbes, p. 375).
4. Anderson no. 96.
5. I follow the reading of Nottebohm in *Ein Skizzenbuch von Beethoven aus dem Jahre 1803* (Leipzig: B&H, 1880), p. 76, and Prod'homme in *Les Symphonies de Beethoven* (Paris: Delagrave, 1906), pp. 83–84. See also Thayer-Forbes, p. 349; Grove, *Beethoven and His Nine Symphonies*, p. 55; Nohl, *Die Beethoven-Feier.* . .(Vienna: Braumüller, 1871), p. 33.
6. *Simrock Jahrbuch*, 2 (1929), 27; Kinsky-Halm, p. 131.
7. Emile Zola, *Les Romanciers naturalistes* (Paris, 1923), pp. 94–95; trans. George Steiner, *Tolstoy or Dostoevsky* (New York: Vintage, 1961), p. 23.
8. Barea, *Vienna*, pp. 123–24.
9. Goethe, *Conversations with Eckermann* (New York & London, 1901), p. 304; Hegel, cit. in Karl Löwith, *From Hegel to Nietzsche* (Garden City, L.I.: Anchor, 1967), p. 214.
10. Heine, *Religion and Philosophy in Germany*, p. 145.
11. J. Christopher Herold, ed., *The Mind of Napoleon* (New York: Columbia Univ. Press, 1955), p. 273.
12. *The Poetical Works of Percy Bysshe Shelley*, ed. Mary Shelley (rpt. Boston: Little, Brown, 1857), I, 137.
13. Anderson no. 57.
14. For further discussion of this proposed trip, see Max Unger, "Zur Enstehungs- und Aufführungsgeschichte von Beethovens Oper 'Leonore,'" *Neue Zeitschrift für Musik*, 105 (1938), 130 ff.
15. Anderson no. 51.
16. Anderson no. 44 (ca. January 15, 1801). Nathan Fishman informs me that the term "Magasin des Arts" (Magazin der Kunst) was current in

Saint-Simonian utopian writings of the period. The French had established an organization with this name in the later 1790s.

17. E. J. Hobsbawm, *The Age of Revolution, 1789–1848* (New York: Mentor Books, 1964), p. 109.

18. *NBJ*, 2 (1925), 104–118; see also Schmitz, *Das romantische Beethoven-bild* (Berlin & Bonn: Dümmler, 1927), pp. 163–76.

19. Boris Schwarz, "Beethoven and the French Violin School," *MQ*, 44 (1958), 431–47.

20. See Riezler, *Beethoven*, p. 89.

21. Thayer-Forbes, p. 403.

22. Sonneck, pp. 74–75; see *MQ*, 6 (1920), 378.

23. Thayer-Forbes, p. 442.

24. Anderson no. 414 (April 8, 1813).

25. Thayer-Forbes, pp. 470-71.

26. Max Unger, "Beethovens vaterländische Musik," *Musik im Kriege*, 1 (1943), 170 ff; cit. from D. W. MacArdle, *Beethoven Abstracts* (Detroit: Information Coordinators, 1973), p. 156. See *BJ*, 2nd ser., 7 (1971), 207 (no. 494).

27. Grove, *Beethoven and His Nine Symphonies*, p. 54.

28. Czerny, *Proper Performance*, p. 8.

29. Schindler-MacArdle, pp. 111–12 and 115–16.

30. Kerst, I, 55; II, 194; Czerny, *Proper Performance*, p. 13.

31. Georg Brandes, *Main Currents in Nineteenth-Century Literature*, II (New York, 1902), 27.

32. Ernst Cassirer, *The Philosophy of the Enlightenment* (Princeton: Princeton Univ. Press, 1951), p. 136.

CHAPTER 14: THE HEROIC DECADE (II)

1. Anderson no. 88 (to Joseph Sonnleithner). Previously assigned to early 1804; internal evidence compels a date between November 1804 and February 1805.

2. Thayer-Forbes, p. 388.

3. Henry Reeve, *Journal of a Residence at Vienna*, pp. 64–65.

4. Thayer-Forbes, p. 393.

5. In Arnold and Fortune, eds., *The Beethoven Reader*, p. 364.

6. Thayer-Forbes, p. 397.

7. Anderson no. 481 (ca. March 14, 1814).

8. See the letters of Caspar Carl van Beethoven to B&H of October 10, 1804, and November 24, 1804 (Thayer-Deiters-Riemann, II, 623–24).

9. Kinsky-Halm, p. 141.

10. Ernest Walker, *Beethoven,* p. 181.

11. Schindler-MacArdle, p. 60.

12. Prod'homme, *La Jeunesse de Beethoven,* p. 176.

13. Reeve, *Journal of a Residence at Vienna,* p. 79.

14. Letter of Ries to Wegeler, December 28, 1837, in Stephan Ley, ed., *Beethoven als Freund der Familie Wegeler-v. Breuning* (Bonn: Cohen, 1927), pp. 252–53.

15. Wegeler-Ries, *Nachtrag,* p. 12.

16. Anderson, Appendix I (1), III, 1444–45. Unger argues that this petition should be dated not earlier than fall 1807 (*NBJ* 2 [1925], 76–83). Although I do not find his arguments persuasive, the question remains open.

17. Anderson no. 143 (May 11, 1807); trans. amended.

18. Thayer-Forbes, p. 423; see Schindler-Moscheles, p. 50.

19. Letter of December 25, 1808, cit. Nohl, *Beethoven nach den Schilderungen,* p. 51.

20. Thayer-Forbes, p. 439.

21. Anderson no. 169 (after July 16, 1808).

22. Anderson no. 170 (summer 1808).

23. Thayer-Forbes, p. 457.

24. Thayer-Forbes, p. 456.

25. Anderson no. 202.

26. Anderson no. 220.

27. Anderson no. 228.

28. André Hevesy, *Les petites amies de Beethoven* (Paris: Champion, 1910), p. 29; Hevesy, *Beethoven: The Man,* p. 56. Hevesy misdated the letter "1800" despite its clear reference to the August 5, 1803, performance of opus 85.

29. Schünemann, II, 363–64; Köhler-Beck, II, 365–66; Thayer-Forbes, p. 290.

30. Anderson no. 54.

31. Schünemann, II, 365; Köhler-Beck, II, 367.

32. Thayer-Forbes, p. 358.

33. Schmidt-Görg, ed., *Dreizehn unbekannte Briefe,* pp. 15–16; Hevesy, *Beethoven: The Man,* pp. 75 and 77; Thayer-Forbes, pp. 359 and 377.

34. Marianne Czeke, ed., *Tagebücher und Aufzeichnungen der Gräfin Therese Brunsvik* (Budapest, 1938; rpt. n.p., n.d.), p. 71.

35. Hevesy, *Beethoven: The Man,* p. 212.

36. Thayer-Forbes, p. 379.

37. Anderson no. 110 (spring 1805).

38. *Ibid.*

39. Undated draft letter, *BJ,* 2nd ser., 6 (1969), 207.

40. Schmidt-Görg, ed., *Dreizehn unbekannte Briefe,* p. 28; trans. George Marek, *Beethoven: Biography of a Genius,* p. 244.

41. La Mara, *Beethovens Unsterbliche Geliebte*, p. 67.

42. Siegmund Kaznelson, *Beethovens ferne und unsterbliche Geliebte* (Zürich: Standard-Buch, 1954), pp. 181–82; La Mara, *Beethoven und die Brunsviks* (Leipzig: Siegel, 1920), pp. 70–72.

43. Anderson no. 151 (Sept. 20, 1807).

44. Anderson no. 153 (fall 1807).

45. Anderson no. 156.

46. Thayer-Forbes, p. 425.

47. Anderson no. 139 (shortly after March 5, 1807); the other letter of apology is Anderson no. 138a (March 5, 1807).

48. See Schmidt-Görg, "Wer war 'die M.' in einer wichtigen Aufzeichnung Beethovens?" *BJ*, 2nd ser., 5 (1966), 75–79. See p. 175 below.

49. Breuning, p. 24.

50. Prod'homme, *Beethoven, raconté par ceux qui l'ont vu* (Paris: Stock, 1927), p. 89.

51. N II, 261; Kalischer, *Beethoven und seine Zeitgenossen*, II, 229.

52. Anderson no. 208 (March 1809).

53. Anderson no. 258 (May 1810); trans. Thayer-Forbes, p. 489. The Bagatelle, WoO 59, known as "Für Elise" was probably written for Therese Malfatti (Kinsky-Halm, p. 505) although sketched in 1808.

54. Thayer-Forbes, p. 490.

55. Anderson no. 254 (spring 1810); trans. Thayer-Forbes, p. 488, amended.

56. Anderson no. 256 (May 2, 1810).

57. Anderson no. 259.

58. Schindler-MacArdle, p. 365; see Thayer-Forbes, pp. 481-82.

CHAPTER 15: THE IMMORTAL BELOVED

1. Wegeler-Ries, p. 117.

2. Thayer-Forbes, p. 293.

3. Thayer-Forbes, p. 289.

4. Anderson no. 373; trans. Thayer-Forbes, pp. 533–34, amended.

5. Schindler-Moscheles, p. 39.

6. Schindler-MacArdle, p. 105.

7. Nohl, II, 477–78.

8. Anderson no. 143 (May 11, 1807).

9. Thayer-Forbes, p. 291.

10. Sonneck, *The Riddle of the Immortal Beloved* (New York: Schirmer, 1927), p. 21.

11. Thayer-Krehbiel, I, 332.

12. Thayer-Krehbiel, I, 333.

13. Bonn, 1890. English trans. by Gertrude Russell (London, 1893), and by Caroline T. Goodloe in *Music*, 4 (Chicago, 1893).

14. A. C. Kalischer, *Die "Unsterbliche Geliebte" Beethovens. Giulietta Guicciardi oder Therese Brunswick?* (Dresden: Bertling, 1891), pp. 1–29.

15. Grove, *Beethoven and His Nine Symphonies*, pp. 112, 140, and 154–56.

16. Paul Bekker, "Beethoven an die Unsterbliche Geliebte–ein unbekannte Brief des Meisters," *Die Musik*, 10⁴ (1911), 131 ff. The tune is from the finale of the String Quintet, op. 29–"evidence" that the letter dated from 1801.

17. Halle: Hendel, 1909.

18. Sonneck, *Riddle*, p. 16.

19. Thayer-Krehbiel, I, 332.

20. Anderson no. 375 (the letter was first published in 1906; Thayer died in 1897).

21. Langensalza: Beyer, 1911.

22. Thomas-San-Galli, *Beethoven und die unsterbliche Geliebte: Amalie Sebald/Goethe/Therese Brunsvik und Anderes* (Munich: Wunderhorn, 1910).

23. A traveler leaving on the evening coach would arrive on the morning of the third day. Possibly, however, Beethoven left Vienna on the morning of June 29.

24. *Beilage zur kaiserlich-königlich-privilegirten Prager Oberpostamts-Zeitung*, No. 80, Friday, July 3, 1812, col. 1. The earliest use which I have located of this newspaper supplement to establish Beethoven's arrival in Prague is in Jan Racek, *Beethoven a České Země* (Brno, 1964), p. 31. See also Marek, *Beethoven*, pp. 302–303.

25. Anderson no. 374 (July 14, 1812); trans. amended.

26. *Beilage zur . . . Prager Oberpostamts-Zeitung*, No. 81, Monday, July 6, 1812, col. 2. See Racek, p. 31. The earliest documentation of the date of Beethoven's departure from Prague is in Unger, "The 'Immortal Beloved,'" *MQ*, 13 (1927), 253. Unger found this information in the *Prager Post-Zeitung*.

27. *Beilage zur . . . Prager Oberpostamts-Zeitung, loc. cit.* The newspaper supplement mistakenly gives Esterházy's destination as Karlsbad.

28. According to Goethe's diaries, cit. Unger, *Auf Spuren*, p. 21.

29. Anderson no. 375 (July 17, 1812); trans. Thayer-Forbes, p. 535.

30. Sonneck, *Riddle*, p. 42. For a transcription of Beethoven's entry on the Teplitz *Anzeigsprotokoll*, see Racek, p. 43, n. 64.

31. Anderson no. 380 (to B&H, August 9, 1812).

32. Unger, *Auf Spuren*, pp. 22–23.

33. *Ibid.*, p. 24.

34. *Loc cit.*

35. Schmidt-Görg (in Racek, pp. 49–50) found twenty letters written by Beethoven with similar watermarks dating from the years 1812 to 1818,

including four letters dated July 14, July 17, August 9, and August 12, 1812 (Anderson nos. 374, 375, 380, and 381).

36. Unger, *Auf Spuren*, p. 15, was the first to observe the logic of this.

37. Thomas-San-Galli, *Beethoven und die unsterbliche Geliebte*, p. 35. Harry Goldschmidt informs me that this requirement had been in effect for some years prior to 1812, and that the police registers are not necessarily exhaustive (personal communication).

38. Leitzmann, II, 242 (no. 8); trans. Sonneck, *Riddle*, p. 48.

39. Thayer-Forbes, p. 646; trans. amended.

40. Anderson no. 632. Trans. amended. For a different interpretation, by Kerman, see *Beethoven Studies*, ed. Tyson, 1 (1973), 130, n. 10.

41. Unger dismissed her as a possibility, without stating his reasons (*Auf Spuren*, p. 74), as did Rolland (p. 1488), Jean and Brigitte Massin (*Ludwig van Beethoven* [Paris: Fayard, 1967] p. 240), and Marek (*Beethoven*, 306–7). In his forthcoming book, *Um die unsterbliche Geliebte*, Harry Goldschmidt, an advocate of Josephine Deym, reviews the case for Antonie Brentano and acknowledges the strength of the evidence in her favor, but suspends judgment concerning her candidacy.

42. There is still room for a reasonable doubt. However, in order to follow the implications of my proposed identification somewhat further, I have in the later sections of this chapter acted upon the assumption that Frau Brentano has been proved to have been the Immortal Beloved.

43. [Otto Jahn], "Ein Brief Beethovens," *Die Grenzboten: Zeitschrift für Politik und Literatur*, 26/2 (1867), 100–101. Partly reprinted in Thayer-Forbes, p. 492, and Thayer-Deiters-Riemann, III, 214–15.

44. Schindler-MacArdle, p. 259. We have only Schindler's word for this, since the letter has not survived.

45. See also Wilhelm Grimm's letter to Achim von Arnim, June 21, 1812, in Reinhold Steig, *Clemens Brentano und die Brüder Grimm* (Stuttgart & Berlin, 1914), p. 174, n. 2.

46. *Beilage zur . . . Prager Oberpostamts-Zeitung*, No. 81, Monday, July 6, 1812, col. 1. The Brentanos' presence in Prague is confirmed by Franz Brentano's letter of July 15, 1812, to Clemens Brentano (Goethe Museum of the Freie Deutsche Hochstift, Frankfurt [hereinafter *GM*]).

47. *Ibid.*, col. 2.

48. The exact date of his arrival is not known. He did not register with the police until July 31. Goethe's diary for July 27, 1812, notes: "Beethoven left here several days ago for Karlsbad." (Cited in Thomas-San-Galli, *Beethoven und die unsterbliche Geliebte*, p. 37; see also Thomas-San-Galli, *Die unsterbliche Geliebte Beethovens*, p. 65.)

49. See Frimmel, *Beethoven-Forschung*, 10 (January 1925), 45.

50. Leitzmann, II, 258–59 (nos. 115 and 119); trans. Sonneck, *Riddle*, p. 60.

51. Anderson no. 296.

52. Anderson no. 758. See also Anderson no. 1064 (December 20, 1821).

53. Anderson nos. 570, 607, and 660. The fourth letter (Anderson no. 659)

is undated, but probably belongs to 1814, despite Miss Anderson's assignment of it to the fall of 1816. (See *BJ*, 1st ser., 2, 214.)

54. Anderson no. 607; trans. amended.

55. Thayer-Deiters-Riemann, IV, 62–63; Thayer-Forbes, p. 686; italics added.

56. Schindler-MacArdle, pp. 102–4. See above, chap. 14, n. 48.

57. The manuscript is in the Bibliothèque Nationale, Paris.

58. Breuning, p. 124.

59. Ley, "Ein Bild von Beethovens unsterblicher Geliebten?" *Atlantis*, 5 (1933), 766–67. See Solomon, "New Light on Beethoven's Letter to an Unknown Woman," *MQ*, 58 (1972), 585, n. 39.

60. Ley, *Wahrheit, Zweifel und Irrtum in der Kunde von Beethovens Leben* (Wiesbaden: B&H, 1955), pp. 24–25. See also *NBJ*, 6 (1935), 30–31; Ley, *Aus Beethovens Erdentagen* (Bonn: Glöckner, 1948), pp. 254–56.

61. Here and in the following I quote, without giving the source for each citation, from Frau Brentano's reminiscences as written down following two series of conversations with her on May 4, 1865, and January 25, 1866, by Karl Theodor Reiffenstein. These are partly reprinted in *Goethes Briefwechsel mit Antonie Brentano, 1814–21*, ed. Rudolf Jung (Weimar, 1896), pp. 5 ff., and *Frankfurter Beiträge Arthur Rickel gewidmet*, ed. Hubert Schiel (Frankfurt, 1933), pp. 68–72. The lengthy courtship correspondence of 1797–98 reveals that Birkenstock drove a hard bargain for his daughter's hand and also that he postponed the conclusion of the marriage arrangements for some months because he feared for his daughter's safety in the war-torn Rhineland. (I am grateful to Harry Goldschmidt for making extracts from this correspondence available to me.)

62. Henry Crabb Robinson, *Diary, Reminiscences, and Correspondence* (Boston, 1870), I, 55.

63. Letter of September 1, 1805, to Sophia Brentano, cited in Steig, *Achim von Arnim und Clemens Brentano* (Stuttgart, 1894), p. 144.

64. Wilhelm Schellberg and Friedrich Fuchs, eds., *Das unsterbliche Leben: unbekannte Briefe von Clemens Brentano* (Jena, 1939), p. 268.

65. Letter of August 10, 1805, cited in Heinz Amelung, ed., *Briefwechsel zwischen Clemens Brentano und Sophie Mereau* (Leipzig, 1908), II, 163.

66. Bettina von Arnim, *Werke und Briefe*, ed. Gustav Konrad (Frechen/Cologne, 1959–61), V, 265.

67. Letter of July 10, 1806, to Clemens Brentano (*GM*).

68. Letter of October 3 [no year] to Karl von Savigny (Deutsche Staatsbibliothek, Berlin/DDR, Handschriftenabteilung/Literaturarchiv, Nachlass Savigny [hereinafter *DSB*]).

69. Letter of June 21, 1808, to Gunda and Karl von Savigny (*DSB*).

70. Letter of December 14, 1808, to Joseph Merkel (*GM*).

71. Letter of November 21, 1808, to Merkel (*GM*).

72. Letter to Merkel (*GM*).

73. Antonie and the children arrived in Vienna at some time between September 1 and the middle of October 1809.

74. Thayer-Deiters-Riemann, III, 216.

75. Letter of November 22, 1799, to Sophia Brentano (*DSB*). Even before her marriage she complained of Franz's immersion in his work: "For such an unimportant person as I am, he will not undertake a journey [to Vienna], and then he is now so occupied with business" (quoted in letter from Franz to Sophia Brentano, October 4, 1797).

76. Letter of January 9, 1812, to Clemens Brentano (*GM*).

77. Letter to Merkel (*GM*).

78. Anderson no. 308 (to B&H, May 20, 1811). Trans. amended.

79. Letter of January 26, 1811, to Clemens Brentano (*GM*).

80. Thayer-Forbes, p. 492.

81. Adolf Sandberger, *Ausgewählte Aufsätze zur Musikgeschichte*, II, 255–56.

82. Letter of October 6, 1812, to Clemens Brentano (*GM*). Another letter from Franz to Clemens Brentano, written from Frankfurt and dated January 28, 1813 (*GM*), provides the *terminus ad quem*.

83. Maria Andrea Goldmann, *Im Schatten des Kaiserdomes. Frauenbilder* (Limburg, 1938), p. 100. A more detailed discussion of Frau Brentano, with an account of her later life and full bibliographical details, is in Solomon, "Antonie Brentano and Beethoven," *M&L*, 58 (1977), 153–69.

84. Kerst, II, 44; Sonneck, pp. 156–57.

85. Mircea Eliade, *Cosmos and History* (New York: Harper, 1959), p. 18.

86. Fanny Giannatasio, diary entry of June 15, 1817; cited in Thayer-Deiters-Riemann, IV, 540.

87. Leitzmann, II, 242 (no. 10); trans. Thayer-Forbes, pp. 549–50 (amended).

CHAPTER 16: THE MUSIC (MIDDLE PERIOD)

1. "At the same time," Tyson wrily comments, "it was a work calculated to entitle him to a Holy Week benefit concert at the Theater-an-der-Wien" (personal communication).

2. See Tyson, "Beethoven's Heroic Phase," *Musical Times*, 110 (1969), 141, in which he points to the time pressures under which the work was completed, and to the obsessive rewriting of the line "Take this cup of sorrow from me" in the March 1804 revision.

3. Newman, *Sonata in the Classic Era*, p. 27.

4. Alfred Einstein, *Music in the Romantic Era* (New York: Norton, 1947), p. 42.

5. Schenk, "Salieris 'Landsturm'-Kantate von 1799 in ihren Beziehungen zu Beethovens 'Fidelio,'" in *Colloquium Amicorum, Joseph Schmidt-Görg zum 70. Geburtstag*, ed. S. Kross and H. Schmidt (BB, 1967), pp. 338–54.

6. Schiller, "The Pathetic," in *The Works of Friedrich Schiller: Aesthetical and Philosophical Essays*, ed. N. H. Dole (New York, 1902), I, 142.

7. See Robert W. Corrigan, ed., *Comedy: Meaning and Form* (San Francisco, 1965), p. 126. From Langer's *Feeling and Form* (New York: Scribner's, ca. 1953), p. 333.

8. *High Fidelity*, December 1974, p. 98.

9. Riezler, *Beethoven*, pp. 247–48.

10. Beethoven perhaps first achieved this kind of effect in the opening of the Piano Sonata, op. 31 no. 2. Later, Beethoven utilized a similar technique in the first movements of the Fifth and Ninth Symphonies; the Fifth Piano Concerto; the Piano Sonatas, opp. 53 and 57; and the Overture to *Egmont*.

 In his celebrated essay on the Fifth Symphony, Tovey argues the absurdity of analyzing Beethoven's middle-period symphonies in terms of the development of motif cells, emphasizing that the first movement of the Fifth Symphony, for example, "is really remarkable for the length of its sentences rather than for the brevity of its initial figure" (*Essays*, I, 38).

11. Tovey, *Essays in Musical Analysis*, I (London: Oxford, 1935), 39. See also Curt Sachs, *Rhythm and Tempo* (New York: Norton, 1953), p. 329.

12. Hermann Scherchen, *The Nature of Music* (New York: Regnery, 1950), pp. 138–46.

13. Leonard G. Ratner, "Key Definition—A Structural Issue in Beethoven's Music," *JAMS*, 23 (1970), 483.

14. Czerny wrote: "Beethoven himself considered [opus 57] his greatest . . . ." (Thayer-Forbes, p. 407).

15. Tovey, *A Companion to Beethoven's Pianoforte Sonatas* (London: Associated Board of the Royal Schools of Music, 1931), p. 169.

16. See Otto Erich Deutsch, "Beethovens Theaterpläne," *Schweizerische Musikzeitung*, no. 3 (March 1, 1945), 76–78; Giovanni Biamonti, *Catalogo cronologico e tematico delle opere di Beethoven* (Turin, 1968), pp. 1062–68; Winton Dean, in Arnold and Fortune, eds., *The Beethoven Reader*, pp. 381–85.

17. Ernst Bücken, in *Der heroische Stil in die Oper* (Leipzig, 1924), p. 77, sees "Horror Opera" (*"Schreckensoper"*) as the primary category, with three subdivisions—"Rescue," "Outlaw," and "Revolutionary" opera. See also R. Morgan Longyear, "Notes on the Rescue Opera," *MQ*, 45 (1959), 49–66.

18. Thayer-Forbes, p. 381.

19. Freud, "A Special Type of Object-Choice," in *Collected Papers*, IV, 200; see also Karl Abraham, "The Rescue and Murder of the Father in Neurotic Phantasy-Formations," in *Clinical Papers and Essays on Psychoanalysis* (New York: Basic Books, 1955), pp. 68–75.

20. Kerst, II, 44; Sonneck, pp. 156–57.

21. See n. 2 above. Tyson observes that "the provision of bread and wine to

the starving prisoner Florestan also has sacramental (Eucharistic) overtones" (personal communication).

22. See Joseph Braunstein, *Beethovens Leonore-Ouvertüren* (Leipzig: B&H,
1927). The date of *Leonore* No. 1 is firmly established in Tyson, "The
Problem of Beethoven's 'First' *Leonore* Overture," *JAMS*, 28 (1975),
292–334. A further revision of *Leonore* No. 2 was sketched in 1814, but
abandoned. (See Tyson, "Yet Another Leonore Overture?" *M&L*, 58
[1977], 192–203.)

23. J. W. N. Sullivan, *Beethoven: His Spiritual Development* (London: Jonathan Cape, 1927), p. 160.

24. Thayer-Forbes, p. 400; N II, 89.

25. Kerman, *Beethoven Quartets*, p. 118.

26. Radcliffe, *Beethoven's String Quartets*, p. 50.

27. Anderson no. 132 (July 5, 1806).

28. Thayer-Forbes, p. 409.

29. Bekker, *Beethoven*, p. 122.

30. Thayer-Forbes, p. 410.

31. Roy Pascal, *The Growth of Modern Germany* (London: Cobbett, 1946),
p. 12.

32. Anderson no. 140.

33. N II, 262–63.

34. Schindler-MacArdle, p. 147.

35. Heinrich Schenker, *Beethoven: V. Sinfonie* (Vienna: Tonwille, n.d. [1925]),
p. 7.

36. Cited in Grove, *Beethoven and His Nine Symphonies*, p. 137.

37. Berlioz, *Beethoven's Symphonies*, trans. Edwin Evans (London: Reeves,
1958), p. 67.

38. Lang, *Music in Western Civilization*, p. 764.

39. Nottebohm, *Ein Skizzenbuch . . . aus dem Jahre 1803*, p. 55; N II,
369–71.

40. Grove, *Beethoven and His Nine Symphonies*, pp. 191–92.

41. F. E. Kirby, "Beethoven's Pastoral Symphony as a *Sinfonia caracteristica*,"
MQ, 61 (1970), 612 ff, with further references.

42. Riezler, *Beethoven*, p. 152.

43. N II, 375.

44. Edward J. Dent, "The Choral Fantasia," *M&L*, 8 (1927), 111–22.

45. For example, Neefe, Haydn, Lichnowsky, and Apponyi. Beethoven dedicated his Piano Sonata, op. 28, to a leading Mason, Joseph von Sonnenfels.
See Kerst, II, 187; Frimmel, *Handbuch*, I, 151–52; Schmitz, *Das romantische Beethovenbild*, pp. 86–88.

46. Alfred Einstein, *Essays on Music* (London: Faber & Faber, 1958), p. 247.

47. *Ibid.*, p. 248.

48. Lewis Lockwood, "The Autograph of the First Movement of Beethoven's Sonata for Violoncello and Pianoforte, Opus 69," *The Music Forum*, II, ed. W. J. Mitchell and Felix Salzer (New York and London: Columbia Univ. Press, 1970), 34.

49. Tovey, *Beethoven* (1944; rpt. London: Oxford, 1965), p. 88.

50. N II, 100.

51. Kinsky-Halm, p. 361.

52. N II, 446.

53. Kerman, *Beethoven Quartets*, p. 156.

54. S. Kierkegaard, *Either/Or* (Garden City, L.I.: Anchor, 1958), I, 68.

55. Friedrich Nietzsche, *The Birth of Tragedy* (Garden City, L.I.: Anchor, 1956), p. 46.

56. Cited in Michel Brenet, *Histoire de la symphonie* (Paris, 1882), pp. 146 f.; see also Prod'homme, *Les Symphonies de Beethoven*, pp. 332 f.

57. Bekker, *Beethoven*, p. 185; Newman, notes to the Klemperer recording (Angel H-3619).

58. See Robert C. Elliott, *The Shape of Utopia: Studies in a Literary Genre* (Chicago and London: Univ. of Chicago Press), 1970, pp. 12 ff; see also A. L. Morton, *The English Utopia* (London: Lawrence & Wishart, 1952), and Mikhail Bakhtin, *Rabelais and His World* (Cambridge: MIT, 1968).

59. *Group Psychology and the Analysis of the Ego*, in *Standard Edition*, XVIII, 131.

60. Notes to the Klemperer recording.

61. Richard Wagner, *Beethoven* (1870), trans. A. R. Parsons (New York: Schirmer, 1883), p. 65.

62. Riezler, *Beethoven*, p. 153.

63. Bakhtin, *Rabelais*, p. 89.

64. Frimmel, *Handbuch*, I, 156; Thayer-Deiters-Riemann, II, 311.

65. Thayer-Forbes, p. 575.

66. Thayer-Forbes, p. 576.

67. Sieghard Brandenburg, in *BJ*, 2nd ser., 9 (1977).

68. Sidney Finkelstein, notes to the Szigeti-Arrau recording (Vanguard VRS 1109/12).

CHAPTER 17: THE DISSOLUTION OF THE HEROIC STYLE

1. Anderson no. 383.

2. Anderson nos. 382, 384–90 (September 16–end of September 1812).

3. Anderson incorrectly places a letter (A 391) to Gleichenstein at "end of September, 1812" from Vienna—an impossible date for various reasons.

4. Thayer-Forbes, p. 542.

5. *Ibid.*

6. Thayer-Forbes, p. 543. For dates of these symphonies, see N II, 101–18; see also *NBJ*, 5 (1933), 45–46.

7. Anderson no. 394.

8. Anderson no. 402. Trans. amended.

9. Anderson no. 426.

10. See Leitzmann, II, 245 (no. 30): "Diagnosis of the doctors about my life. There is no further salvation, therefore must I use ° ° °?" Rolland comments: "The missing words have been suppressed. . . . [O]ne may ask himself whether Beethoven was not contemplating suicide" (Rolland, p. 1459). See also Leitzmann, II, 242 (no. 8): "Nothing must chain me to life."

11. Thayer-Krehbiel, I, 324; Schindler-MacArdle, pp. 101–104.

12. Nohl, III, 897. Beethoven and Röckel were in friendly contact during 1813 (see Anderson no. 413).

13. Anderson no. 407. The Sterbas were the first to note the implications of these references (Sterba, *Beethoven and His Nephew*, p. 110).

14. Anderson nos. 562 (October 16, 1815), 653 (September 5, 1816), and 681 (December 16, 1816).

15. Anderson no. 715 (1816; trans. from Kalischer-Shedlock, *The Letters of Beethoven*, II, 33); no. 597 (January 21, 1816); no. 846 (probably 1811 according to the watermark). See also Anderson nos. 333, 347, 349, and 368.

16. Leitzmann, II, 261 (no. 135).

17. Thayer-Forbes, p. 685.

18. Leitzmann, II, 262 (no. 150); Nohl, III, 828.

19. Schindler-Moscheles, p. 55; see also Schindler-MacArdle, pp. 164–65.

20. Thayer-Forbes, p. 590.

21. Schindler-Moscheles, p. 55.

22. For Malzel's and Beethoven's respective contributions to this work, see Hans-Werner Küthen, "Neue Aspekte zur Enstehung von *Wellingtons Sieg*," *BJ*, 2nd ser., 8 (1975), 73–92.

23. Thayer-Forbes, p. 565.

24. Thayer-Forbes, p. 566.

25. But see Ludwig Misch, "The Battle of Victoria," *Beethoven Studies* (Norman: Univ. of Oklahoma, 1953), pp. 153–62.

26. Anderson, Appendix H (6), III, 1438.

27. Thayer-Forbes, p. 571.

28. Leitzmann, II, 246 (no. 32).

29. *Der Sammler*, cit. Thayer-Forbes, p. 583.

30. Thayer-Forbes, pp. 586–87. Trans. amended.

31. Leitzmann, II, 245 (no. 26); Thayer-Forbes, p. 561. In 1827, Ferdinand Hiller heard Beethoven exclaim: "They say 'Vox populi, vox dei'—I have never believed in it" (Kerst, II, 229).

32. Thayer-Forbes, p. 565.

33. Schindler-Moscheles, p. 64.

34. See N II, 577; Anderson no. 1388 (to Haslinger, June 12, 1825).

35. Harold Nicholson, *The Congress of Vienna: A Study in Allied Unity* (New York: Viking, 1946; Compass Books, 1961), p. 160.

36. Barea, *Vienna*, p. 130.

37. Schindler-Moscheles, p. 64.

38. Schindler-MacArdle, p. 205.

39. M. H. Weil, *Les dessous du congrès de Vienne* (Paris, 1913); cited in Edouard Herriot, *The Life and Times of Beethoven* (New York: Macmillan, 1935), p. 217.

40. Anderson no. 540 (to J. N. Kanka, April 8, 1815).

41. Sullivan, *Beethoven*, p. 166.

42. Charles Rosen, *The Classical Style* (New York: Viking, 1971), p. 404.

43. Lewis Lockwood, "Beethoven's Unfinished Piano Concerto of 1815: Sources and Problems," *MQ*, 56 (1970), 626.

44. Geoffrey Bruun, *Europe and the French Imperium, 1799–1814* (New York: Harper Torchbooks, 1963), p. 202.

45. Thayer-Forbes, pp. 804 and 956.

46. Anderson no. 175 (fall 1808).

47. See W. S. Newman, *Sonata in the Classic Era*, p. 527.

48. Thayer-Forbes, pp. 577–78. Spohr's hostility to Beethoven should be taken into account.

CHAPTER 18: BEETHOVEN AND HIS NEPHEW

1. Viewed psychoanalytically, Beethoven at this time faced a "danger situation," which gave rise to a whole set of neurotic and even quasi-psychotic symptoms. According to Freud, "symptom formation . . . has the actual result of putting an end to the danger situation." It is a process "analogous to flight, by means of which the ego avoids a danger threatening from without [in] that it represents, indeed, an attempt at flight from an instinctual danger." Freud, *The Problem of Anxiety* (New York: Norton Library, n.d.), pp. 86–87.

2. Schünemann, III, 158.

3. Leitzmann, II, 255 (no. 82); Sterba, *Beethoven and His Nephew*, p. 51.

4. Nohl, III, 34; Thayer-Forbes, p. 551.

5. Nohl, III, 814; Sterba, p. 54.

6. Anderson, Appendix C (15), III, 1389.

7. Nohl, II, 482; according to Karl's wife, Caroline.

8. Hedwig M. von Asow, *Ludwig van Beethoven: Heiligenstädter Testament* (Vienna: Döblinger, 2nd ed. 1969), pp. 4–5.

9. Nohl, ed., *Neue Briefe Beethovens* (Stuttgart: Cotta, 1867), p. 243 n.; Kalischer-Shedlock, *Letters of Beethoven*, II, 304.

10. Dagmar Weise, ed., *Beethoven: Entwurf einer Denkschrift an das Appellationsgericht*. . . (BB, 1953), p. 31; Nohl, III, 849, n. 68.

11. Anderson no. 1009 (undated and unaddressed draft letter).

12. Thayer-Forbes, p. 624.

13. Thayer-Forbes, p. 625.

14. Anderson, Appendix C (1), III, 1360.

15. Anderson, Appendix C (2), III, 1361.

16. Anderson, Appendix C (3), III, 1362.

17. Anderson no. 607.

18. Kerst, II, 193.

19. Anderson no. 603 (to Giannatasio, February 1, 1816).

20. Anderson no. 611 (to Giannatasio, before February 20, 1816).

21. Leitzmann, II, 256 (no. 92); trans. Michael Hamburger, ed., *Beethoven: Letters, Journals, and Conversations* (Garden City, L.I.: Anchor, 1960), p. 139.

22. Anderson no. 633.

23. Leitzmann, II, 256 (no. 92).

24. Anderson no. 654 (September 6, 1816). Trans. amended.

25. Anderson no. 661 (September 29, 1816). Trans. amended.

26. Thayer-Forbes, p. 625.

27. Sterba, pp. 146 and 317.

28. Freud, *Standard Edition*, X, 239.

29. Freud, *Standard Edition*, XIX, 43.

30. Anderson no. 686.

31. Anderson no. 876 (to Giannatasio).

32. Anderson, Appendix C (6) (Contract between Johanna van Beethoven and Ludwig van Beethoven, May 10, 1817).

33. Anderson no. 793 (July 30, 1817).

34. Anderson no. 800 (to Giannatasio, August 14, 1817).

35. Anderson no. 904 (June 18, 1818).

36. Anderson, Appendix C (9) (to the Magistrat der Stadt Wien, February 1, 1819), III, 1375–76.

37. Anderson no. 658.

38. Anderson no. 660.

39. Anderson no. 672 (to Giannatasio, November 14, 1816).

40. Anderson no. 871.

41. Anderson no. 618 (to Archduke Rudolph, February 1816); Anderson no. 636 (to Neate, May 18, 1816).

42. Anderson no. 598 (to Giannatasio, end of January 1816).

43. Köhler-Beck, II, 156; Schünemann, II, 157; Sterba, p. 200.

44. Anderson no. 937 (to Bach, ca. February 1, 1819).

45. Breuning, pp. 77–78.

46. Anderson no. 937.

47. Anderson, *The Letters of Mozart,* 2nd ed., I, 340.

48. Sterba, p. 112.

49. Anderson no. 839 (December 28, 1817).

50. Anderson no. 866 (1817).

51. Anderson no. 860 (should be dated January 1818).

52. Anderson no. 841 (should be dated between January 13 and 25, 1818).

53. Anderson no. 885 (early January 1818).

54. Anderson no. 904 (June 18, 1818).

55. The relevant sections of her diary—cited below—are reprinted in Thayer-Deiters-Riemann, IV, 513–41, and in Nohl, *Eine stille Liebe zu Beethoven* (1875, 2nd. ed. Leipzig, 1902); further reminiscences are in Prod'homme, *Beethoven, raconté par ceux qui l'ont vu,* pp. 81–93.

56. Frimmel, *Beethoven Studien: Bausteine zu einer Lebensgeschichte des Meisters,* II (Munich and Leipzig: Müller, 1906), 116.

57. Anderson no. 632 (to Ries).

58. Anderson no. 633 (to Marie Erdödy, May 13, 1816).

59. Leitzmann, II, 261 (no. 139).

60. Sterba, p. 315.

61. The following citations from the court records appear in Thayer-Deiters-Riemann, IV, 550–54; Thayer-Forbes, pp. 708–11; and Sterba, pp. 311–13.

62. Thayer-Deiters-Riemann, IV, 554; Sterba, p. 148.

63. Schindler-Moscheles, pp. 70–71; see Schindler-MacArdle, pp. 220–21.

64. Anderson no. 979 (to Bach, October 27, 1819).

65. Schindler-Moscheles, p. 115.

66. Anderson, Appendix C (9), III, 1375–77.

67. Anderson, Appendix C (10), III, 1381.

68. Anderson no. 951 (to Bernard, early July 1819).

69. Anderson no. 954 (to Bernard, ca. July 20, 1819).

70. Anderson nos. 960 and 956 (to Bernard, August 19, 1819, and late July 1819).

71. Anderson no. 964 (to Bernard, August 1819).

72. Anderson, Appendix C (11).

73. Anderson, Appendix C (14), III, 1387–88.

74. Köhler-Herre, I, 115.

75. Anderson no. 1008 (should be dated November or December 1819); Anderson, Appendix C (15), III, 1400.

76. Sterba, p. 175; Thayer-Deiters-Riemann, IV, 563.

77. Sterba, pp. 185–86; Thayer-Deiters-Riemann, IV, 565.

78. Anderson no. 1007.

79. Anderson, Appendix C (15); the original, in facsimile and transcription, is in Dagmar Weise, ed., *Beethoven: Entwurf einer Denkschrift an das Appellationsgericht;* a translation from Kastner-Kapp is in Sterba, pp. 319–34.

80. See Weise, *Denkschrift,* p. 44, n. 1; Kastner-Kapp, pp. 553–54; and Sterba, p. 324; omitted from Anderson, III, 1393, apparently in error.

81. Anderson no. 1010.

82. Köhler-Herre, I, 330.

83. Anderson no. 941 (should be dated ca. February 1820).

84. Thayer-Forbes, p. 635; Anderson no. 611 (to Giannatasio, before February 20, 1816).

85. Sterba, p. 190; Köhler-Herre, I, 398.

86. Joseph Schmidt-Görg, personal communication.

87. Köhler-Beck, II, 153; Schünemann, II, 153.

88. Thayer-Forbes, p. 754.

89. Nohl, *Eine stille Liebe,* p. 124.

90. Thayer-Forbes, p. 644.

91. Czerny, *Proper Performance,* p. 16.

92. Frimmel, *Handbuch,* II, 265.

93. Sterba, p. 211. For a critique of this position, see Solomon, "Beethoven and His Nephew: A Reappraisal," *Beethoven Studies,* ed. Tyson, 2 (London: Oxford, 1977).

94. Kerst, I, 214.

95. Leitzmann, II, 260 (no. 130). Closing lines of *Die Braut von Messina.*

96. Leitzmann, II, 264 (no. 171).

97. Leitzmann, II, 265 (no. 174).

98. Sterba, p. 100.

99. Of course, on some level Beethoven knew well the difference between adoption and physical parentage; in his copy of *Othello,* he placed three question marks next to Brabantio's "I had rather to adopt a child than to get it" (Nohl, *Beethovens Brevier,* p. 3).

100. Anderson no. 979 (to Bach, October 27, 1819).

101. Abraham, *Clinical Papers,* p. 288.

CHAPTER 19: PORTRAIT OF AN AGING COMPOSER

1. Frimmel, *Handbuch,* I, 233.

2. Thayer-Forbes, p. 738.

3. Thayer-Forbes, p. 644.

4. Thayer-Forbes, p. 647.

5. Nohl, *Beethoven nach den Schilderungen,* p. 141.

6. Krehbiel, *Music and Manners in the Classical Period* (Westminster: Constable, 1898), p. 210; Frimmel, *Handbuch*, I, 237.

7. Schindler-Moscheles, p. 187.

8. Krehbiel, *Music and Manners*, pp. 199–200 and 209.

9. Thayer-Forbes, p. 944.

10. Thayer-Forbes, p. 965.

11. Thayer-Forbes, p. 803.

12. Kerst, II, 97–98.

13. Nohl, *Beethoven nach den Schilderungen*, p. 166; Breuning, p. 40.

14. Thayer-Forbes, pp. 800-801; Sonneck, pp. 123–24.

15. A. J. P. Taylor, *The Course of German History* (1946; rpt. New York: Capricorn, 1962), p. 54.

16. Köhler-Herre, I, 346.

17. Nohl, III, 609; Prod'homme *Cahiers de conversation de Beethoven* (Paris: Corrêa, 1946), p. 410. For a summary of Conversation Book materials of this nature, see Boyer, *Le "romantisme" de Beethoven* (Paris: Didier, 1938), pp. 400–405; see also Frida Knight, *Beethoven and the Age of Revolution* (London: Lawrence & Wishart, 1973), pp. 139–44.

18. Boyer, p. 405.

19. Köhler-Herre, I, 300.

20. Schünemann, III, 159. Trans. amended. See Boyer, p. 400.

21. Köhler-Beck, II, 279; Schünemann, II, 286.

22. Schünemann, III, 284.

23. Thayer-Forbes, p. 774.

24. Köhler-Beck, II, 172.

25. Thayer-Forbes, p. 775.

26. See Luigi Magnani, *I Quaderni di conversazione di Beethoven* (Milan and Naples: Ricciardi, 1962), *passim*.

27. Köhler, "Beethoven's Conversation Books," *High Fidelity*, January 1970, p. 59.

28. Köhler-Herre, I, 212.

29. Marie Pachler-Koschak received a few bars, "Das Schöne zum Guten," WoO 202, during a visit on September 27, 1823. And Beethoven intended to dedicate the Sonatas, opp. 110 and 111, to Antonie Brentano.

30. Anderson no. 1175 (April 1823).

31. Nohl, III, 828.

32. Köhler-Herre, I, 184 (the entry was partly obliterated). "Wollen Sie bey meiner Frau schlafen? Es ist so [sehr] kalt." One authority suggests it could be read: "Would you like to sleep over at my wife's place?" I find it difficult to accept this reading.

33. Rolland, p. 840.

34. Nohl, III, 828.

35. Schünemann, I, 205; Köhler-Herre, I, 207–208, attributes this line to Janitschek.

36. Köhler-Herre, I, 262.

37. I have dealt with this question at some length in "Beethoven and Religion," a paper presented to the Beethoven Symposium held jointly at the University of North Carolina at Chapel Hill and at Duke University in April 1977. (Report of the Symposium will be published by Univ. of North Carolina Press.)

38. Anderson no. 1054 (July 18, 1821).

39. N II, 151.

CHAPTER 20: RECONSTRUCTION

1. *AMZ*, 23 (1821), 539; cit. Schindler-MacArdle, p. 231.

2. Kerst, II, 72.

3. Anderson no. 1072 (February 12, 1822).

4. *AMZ*, 24 (1822), 310; cit. MacArdle, *Beethoven Abstracts,* p. 6.

5. Francis Toye, *Rossini: A Study in Tragi-comedy* (New York: Knopf, 1947), p. 86.

6. Thayer-Forbes, p. 802.

7. Thayer-Forbes, pp. 984 f.

8. Thayer-Forbes, p. 801.

9. Thayer-Forbes, p. 811.

10. Schindler-MacArdle, p. 237.

11. Anderson no. 1110.

12. Thayer-Forbes, p. 872.

13. Thayer-Forbes, p. 851.

14. Thayer-Forbes, pp. 897–98.

15. Schindler-MacArdle, p. 275.

16. Köhler-Herre, V, 122.

17. Prod'homme, *Cahiers de conversation de Beethoven,* p. 346.

18. Henry E. Dwight, *Travels in the North of Germany in the Years 1825 and 1826* (New York, 1829), p. 145.

19. Hegel, *The Philosophy of Fine Art,* trans. Osmaston (London: Bell, 1920), III, 417.

20. Thayer-Forbes, p. 767.

21. Anderson nos. 1098 and 1099.

22. Anderson no. 1152 (March 10, 1823).

23. Anderson no. 1226 (August 2, 1823).

24. Anderson no. 1136 (February 8, 1823). Trans. amended.

25. Anderson no. 1154 (shortly before March 15, 1823). Goethe did not reply; Cherubini's reply (Kerst, II, 184) has not survived.

26. Anderson no. 1217 (to Pilat, July 1823).

27. Anderson no. 1121.

28. Thayer-Forbes, p. 841.

29. See Anderson no. 1153 (to Simrock, March 10, 1823) and no. 1158 (to Peters, March 20, 1823).

30. Schindler-MacArdle, p. 241. Holz said flatly: "The story . . . is not true" (Kerst, II, 183).

31. Schindler-Moscheles, p. 81.

32. Schindler-MacArdle, p. 242.

33. Anderson no. 1271 (early March 1824).

34. Anderson no. 1292 (May 26, 1824).

35. Anderson no. 1407 (to Schott, August 2, 1825).

36. Anderson no. 1472; see reminiscences of Samuel Spiker in Prod'homme, *Beethoven raconté*, pp. 228–29.

CHAPTER 21: THE "RETURN" TO BONN

1. Anderson no. 1028 (August 5, 1820).

2. Anderson no. 1051 (March 14, 1821).

3. Frimmel, *Beethoven-Forschung*, 1 (1911), 27.

4. Köhler-Herre, I, 237; see also I, 225.

5. Anderson no. 1078 (May 1822).

6. Anderson no. 1247 (1823).

7. Anderson no. 1231 (August 19, 1823).

8. Anderson no. 1087 (July 31, 1822); trans. Thayer-Forbes, p. 799.

9. For details on this and what follows, see Schünemann, II, 307–308; III, 115–22.

10. Anderson no. 1259 (should be dated February or March 1823).

11. Anderson no. 1256 (should be dated February or March 1823).

12. Anderson no. 1257 (January 8, 1824).

13. Anderson no. 1316 (day after October 6, 1824).

14. Thayer-Forbes, p. 922.

15. Anderson no. 1359.

16. Thayer-Forbes, p. 945.

17. Anderson no. 1371 (May 13, 1825).

18. Thayer-Forbes, p. 947.

19. Anderson no. 1377.

20. Anderson no. 1379.

21. Anderson no. 1387 (June 10, 1825).

22. Anderson no. 1390 (June 15, 1825).

23. Anderson no. 1380. Anderson incorrectly assigns this letter to May 1825.

24. Anderson no. 1445 (after October 17, 1825).
25. Thayer-Forbes, p. 968.
26. Thayer-Forbes, p. 999.
27. Thayer-Forbes, p. 994.
28. Thayer-Forbes, p. 995.
29. Anderson no. 1489.
30. Thayer-Forbes, p. 991.
31. Thayer-Forbes, p. 995.
32. Thayer-Forbes, p. 1001.
33. Thayer-Forbes, p. 1003.
34. Thayer-Forbes, p. 1014.
35. Anderson no. 1534 (October 2, 1826).
36. Anderson no. 1535 (October 13, 1826).
37. Thayer-Forbes, p. 1015.
38. Thayer-Forbes, p. 999.
39. Sterba, p. 282; see also R. Gruneberg, "Karl van Beethoven's 'Suicide,'" *Musical Times*, 97 (May 1956), 270.
40. Thayer-Deiters-Riemann, V, 378; Thayer-Forbes, pp. 1003–1004; trans. Sterba, p. 286.
41. Anderson no. 1521 (September 9, 1826).
42. Thayer-Forbes, p. 1013.
43. Wawruch's history of Beethoven's last illness is cited from Thayer-Forbes, pp. 1016–18.
44. Anderson no. 1542 (December 7, 1826).
45. Anderson no. 1526 (ca. September 22, 1826).
46. Anderson, Appendix D (6) (September 1826).
47. Prod'homme, *Cahiers de conversation*, p. 426.
48. *Ibid.*, p. 427.
49. *Ibid.*, pp. 426–27.
50. Thayer-Deiters-Riemann, V, 369.
51. Anderson no. 1546 (December 1826).
52. Holz to Fanny Linzbauer, cit. Nohl, III, 749, and Nohl, *Beethoven, Liszt, Wagner*, p. 111. See also Holz to Jahn, in Kerst, II, 183.
53. Anderson no. 1547 (to J. B. Bach).
54. Thayer-Forbes, p. 1027.
55. Thayer-Forbes, p. 1022.
56. Breuning, p. 92; see also p. 103.
57. Thayer-Forbes, p. 1047.
58. Anderson no. 1552 (February 18, 1827).
59. Thayer-Forbes, p. 1036.
60. Breuning, pp. 98–99.

61. Kerst, II, 230; Sonneck, p. 218.

62. Prod'homme, *Beethoven raconté*, p. 245.

63. Hiller, cit. Thayer-Forbes, p. 1045.

64. Anderson no. 1564 (March 16, 1827).

65. Anderson no. 1569 (March 1827).

66. Anderson no. 1561 (March 10, 1827).

67. Schindler-MacArdle, p. 328.

68. Anderson no. 1568; Nohl, III, 781; facsimile in Stephan Ley, *Beethovens Leben in authentischen Bildern und Texten* (Berlin: Cassirer, 1925), p. 140.

69. Rudolf Stammler, "Rechtliche Verwicklungen Beethovens," *Welhagen und Klasings Monatshefte*, 43/2 (1929), 153; cit. MacArdle, "The Family van Beethoven," *MQ*, 35 (1949), 544, n. 9.

70. Ley, *Beethoven als Freund der Familie Wegeler-v. Breuning*, p. 236 (Schindler to Moscheles, letter of March 24, 1827); Thayer-Forbes, p. 1048.

71. Krehbiel, *Music and Manners*, p. 204.

72. Thayer-Deiters-Riemann, V, 490–91; Thayer-Forbes, pp. 1050–51.

73. Thayer-Forbes, p. 1051.

CHAPTER 22: THE MUSIC (LAST PERIOD)

1. C. H. H. Parry, *Style in Musical Art* (London: Macmillan, 1911), p. 95.

2. Rousseau, *Ecrits sur la musique* (rpt. Paris, 1838), pp. 288–89.

3. Cooper, *Beethoven*, p. 133.

4. Kerman, *Beethoven Quartets*, p. 196.

5. Rolland, pp. 527–28.

6. Kerman, "*An die ferne Geliebte*," *Beethoven Studies*, ed. Tyson, 1 (1973), 154.

7. Philip L. Miller, trans., *The Ring of Words* (Garden City, L.I.: Anchor, 1966), p. 147.

8. Rolland, p. 545; Hans Boettcher, *Beethoven als Liederkomponist* (Augsburg: Benno Filser, 1928), p. 67.

9. Thayer-Forbes, p. 984.

10. Nottebohm, *Beethoven's Studien*, p. 200.

11. Schindler-MacArdle, p. 212.

12. Ludwig Misch, *Neue Beethoven-Studien und andere Themen* (BB, 1967), p. 59.

13. See Kerman, *Beethoven Quartets*, pp. 270–72; d'Indy, *Beethoven*, p. 98; John V. Cockshoot, *The Fugue in Beethoven's Piano Music* (London: Routledge & Kegan Paul, 1959), pp. 145–78. See the comprehensive list

in Warren Kirkendale, *Fuge und Fugato in der Kammermusik des Rokoko und der Klassik* (Tutzing: Schneider, 1966), pp. 263–64.

14. See N II, 349 ff; Willy Hess, *Verzeichnis der nicht in der Gesamtausgabe veröffentlichten Werke Ludwig van Beethovens* (Wiesbaden, B&H, 1957), p. 24.

15. Wilhelm von Lenz, *Beethoven. Eine Kunst-Studie* (Hamburg: Hoffman & Campe, 1860), V, 32.

16. *Ibid.* For a summary of reported early performances, see W. S. Newman, "Some Nineteenth-Century Consequences of . . . Opus 106," *Piano Quarterly*, 67 (Spring 1969), p. 12.

17. Riezler, *Beethoven*, p. 227; for analyses of the fugue, see Cockshoot, *Fugue*, pp. 73–94, and Tovey, *A Companion to Beethoven's Pianoforte Sonatas*, pp. 230–42.

18. Cooper, *Beethoven*, p. 172.

19. Rolland, pp. 650–51.

20. Rosen, *The Classical Style*, pp. 406-33.

21. Anderson no. 939.

22. Tyson, *Authentic English Editions of Beethoven*, p. 102; Kinsky-Halm, p. 296.

23. But see also Cooper, *Beethoven*, p. 164, and Rolland, pp. 594–95.

24. Rosen, *The Classical Style*, p. 434.

25. See Kinsky-Halm, pp. 311–19, which is now somewhat out of date.

26. This and the following are from Blom, *Classics: Major and Minor* (London: Dent, 1958), pp. 49–51.

27. Thayer-Forbes, p. 620.

28. Thayer-Forbes, p. 851.

29. Schindler, *Biographie von Ludwig van Beethoven* (4th ed., Münster, 1871), I, 240; mistrans. in Schindler-MacArdle, p. 209.

30. Cited in Tovey, *Essays in Musical Analysis: Chamber Music* (London: Oxford, 1944), p. 124.

31. *Ibid.*, pp. 126–27.

32. Karl Geiringer, "The Structure of Beethoven's Diabelli Variations," *MQ*, 50 (1964), 496–503.

33. The Bagatelles, op. 119 nos. 7 and 8, have been regarded as spin-offs from opus 120.

34. Walker, *Beethoven*, p. 149.

35. Blom, *Classics: Major and Minor*, p. 78.

36. N II, 196.

37. Comment on a leaf of sketches of 1824, cit. Nohl, III, 512.

38. Schindler-Moscheles, pp. 179–80.

39. Weissenbach, cit. in MacArdle, "Beethoven and the Archduke Rudolph," *BJ*, 2nd ser., 4 (1962), 41; N I, 152.

40. J. F. Reichardt, *Vertraute Briefe*, ed. G. Gugitz (Munich: Müller, 1915), II, 95; Thayer-Deiters-Riemann, III, 189.

41. See Anderson no. 938 (to Ries, March 8, 1819), no. 939 (to Ries, ca. March 20, 1819), no. 948 (to Archduke Rudolph, early June 1819), and no. 1016 (to Rudolph, April 3, 1820).

42. See Anderson nos. 1134, 1135, and 1136 (all early February, 1823); Anderson no. 1292 (to Prince Galitzin, May 26, 1824).

43. Schmitz sees no contradiction here, because the oratorio is also one of the main forms of religious music (Schmitz, *Romantische*, pp. 100–101).

44. Anderson no. 1278 (to the censor, April 1824).

45. Anderson no. 1029 (August 30, 1820); see also Schmitz, *Romantische*, p. 100, n. 3.

46. Rolland, pp. 674 and 677.

47. Anderson no. 1307 (September 16, 1824).

48. Anderson no. 1248 (1823).

49. Cited in Warren Kirkendale, "New Roads to Old Ideas in Beethoven's *Missa Solemnis*," *MQ*, 56 (1970), 676.

50. Leitzmann, II, 265 (no. 177); Thayer-Forbes, p. 715.

51. Leitzmann, II, 263 (no. 167). C. P. E. Bach's "Zwei Litaneyen. . . für acht Singstimmen in zwei Chören," published in Copenhagen, 1786 (Nottebohm, *Ein Skizzenbuch von Beethoven aus dem Jahre 1803* [Leipzig: B&H, 1880], p. 77, n. 3).

52. Kirkendale, *op. cit.*, p. 666.

53. Anderson no. 1161 (March 25, 1823).

54. Lang, *Music in Western Civilization*, p. 768.

55. Anderson no. 1079 (to Peters, June 5, 1822).

56. Bekker, *Beethoven*, p. 274.

57. Ernest Newman, notes to the Toscanini recording (RCA LM 6013).

58. William Mann, notes to the Klemperer recording (Angel B-3679).

59. Anderson no. 85 (November 2, 1803).

60. Leitzmann, II, 260 (no. 126). The quotation is from Pliny, *Epistles*.

61. Schünemann, III, 160.

62. *Ibid.*

63. Riezler, *Beethoven*, p. 198.

64. Martin Buber, *Paths in Utopia* (Boston: Beacon, 1960), p. 7.

65. *BJ*, 1st. ser., 2 (1909), 331–32; Thayer-Forbes, pp. 120-21; letter to Charlotte Schiller, January 26, 1793.

66. Anton Bauer, *150 Jahre Theater an der Wien* (Zürich, Leipzig, and Vienna, 1952), pp. 80–82.

67. Boettcher, *Beethoven als Liederkomponist*, p. 45; Thayer-Forbes, p. 472.

68. N II, 282; Boettcher, pp. 44–45. Also the canons, WoO 163 and WoO 166.

69. Letter of September 13, 1803, *Simrock Jahrbuch*, 2 (1929), 26; Kinsky-Halm, p. 122; see Willy Hess, *Beethoven-Studien* (BB, 1972), pp. 113–14.

70. N I, 41; N II, 168.

71. N II, 328–29.

72. Cooper, *Beethoven*, p. 281.

73. D'Indy, *Beethoven*, p. 114.

74. Rudolph Reti, *The Thematic Process in Music* (New York: Macmillan, 1951), p. 22.

75. Tovey, *Beethoven's Ninth Symphony* (1922; rev. ed. London: Oxford, 1928), pp. 24 and 36.

76. *Ibid.*, p. 36.

77. N II, 189–90, with slight alterations based on A. C. Kalischer, "Die Beethoven-Autographe der Königl. Bibliothek zu Berlin," *Monatshefte für Musik-Geschichte*, 28 (1896), 19.

78. N I, 41.

79. Nietzsche, *The Birth of Tragedy*, p. 23.

80. Rolland, pp. 977 f.; see also Otto Baensch, *Aufbau und Sinn des Chorfinales in Beethovens neunter Symphonie* (Berlin and Leipzig: Walter de Gruyter, 1930), pp. 94–95.

81. Grove, *Beethoven and His Nine Symphonies*, p. 364; Kalischer, "Die Beethoven-Autographe. . . ," p. 19, lends itself to a different reading.

82. Thayer-Forbes, p. 888.

83. Kerman, *Beethoven Quartets*, p. 194.

84. Heinrich Schenker, *Beethovens neunte Sinfonie* (Vienna: Universal, 1912), p. 268.

85. Herbert Marcuse, *An Essay on Liberation* (Boston: Beacon, 1969), pp. 46–47.

86. Max Raphael, *The Demands of Art* (Princeton: Princeton Univ. Press, 1968), p. 187.

87. Anderson no. 1308 (to Schott's Sons, September 17, 1824).

88. Par. 83.

89. Schiller, *Letters on the Aesthetic Education of Man*, letter 9.

90. Hegel, *The Philosophy of Fine Art*, I, 208.

91. Schiller, *Letters on the Aesthetic Education of Man*, letter 2.

92. Thayer-Forbes, p. 815.

93. Anderson no. 1123. Due to Galitzin's later financial difficulties, Beethoven never received full payment for the dedications.

94. Anderson no. 1079. The earliest sketches of opus 127 contain the legend "Quartet for Peters" (Nohl, III, 512).

95. Rolland, p. 1030; Lenz, *Beethoven: Eine Kunst-Studie*, V, 221; see also Max Unger, "Neue Briefe an Beethoven," *Neue Zeitschrift für Musik*, 81 (1914), 409 ff.

96. Rolland, p. 1029.

97. Anderson no. 1144.

98. Anderson, Appendix G (17) (to Schlesinger, September 10, 1825).

99. Nohl, ed., *Letters of Distinguished Musicians,* p. 56.

100. Rolland, p. 1036.

101. Köhler-Herre, V, 120; see Schindler, *Biographie von Ludwig van Beethoven,* 2nd ed. (Münster: Aschendorff, 1845), pp. 63 f.; cit. Rolland, p. 1040.

102. Thayer-Forbes, p. 938 (from a Conversation Book of 1825).

103. Böhm, cit. Thayer-Forbes, p. 940.

104. Unpublished *Konversationshefte* (Deutsche Staatsbibliothek, Berlin), Heft 115, fol. 14ʳ and 14ᵛ.

105. Heft 117, fol. 12ᵛ.

106. Heft 124, fol. 10ᵛ and 11ʳ.

107. Heft 126, fol. 14ᵛ.

108. Heft 126, fol. 13ᵛ.

109. Nohl, III, 964.

110. Schindler-MacArdle, p. 307.

111. Lenz, *Beethoven: Eine Kunst-Studie,* V, 218.

112. See Ivan Mahaim, *Beethoven: Naissance et renaissance des derniers quatuors* (Paris: de Brouwer, 1964), II, 442–71, for performances to 1875.

113. Lenz, *Beethoven: Eine Kunst-Studie,* V, 216–17.

114. Cooper, *Beethoven,* p. 421.

115. Kerman, *Beethoven Quartets,* pp. 229, 265–66; see also Rolland, p. 1071.

116. Kerst, II, 188; Lenz, V, 217.

117. Kerman, *Beethoven Quartets,* p. 239.

118. *Ibid.,* p. 241.

119. Erich Schenk, "Barock bei Beethoven," in *Beethoven und die Gegenwart,* ed. Arnold Schmitz (Berlin and Bonn: Dümmler, 1937), pp. 210–16.

120. Lenz, V, 218–19.

121. Mahaim, p. 419. (I cannot locate an earlier source for this quotation.)

122. Kerman, *Beethoven Quartets,* p. 268.

123. Bekker, *Beethoven,* p. 331.

124. Thayer-Deiters-Riemann, V, 298; Sonneck, *Beethoven Letters in America* (New York: Beethoven Association, 1927), p. 79; Mahaim, p. 422.

125. Lenz, V, 219; Mahaim, p. 436, n. 11; see also Holz to Jahn, in Thayer-Deiters-Riemann, V, 298, n. 3.

126. Unpublished *Konversationshefte,* Heft 117, fol. 12ʳ.

127. Heft 117, fol. 31ᵛ and 32ʳ.

128. Lenz, V, 216.

129. Riezler, *Beethoven,* p. 239.

130. Kerman, *Beethoven Quartets,* p. 322; see also p. 374.

131. Cit. Mahaim, p. 417.

132. *The New York Review of Books,* September 26, 1968, pp. 3–4.

133. Radcliffe, *Beethoven's String Quartets*, p. 173.

134. Cooper, *Beethoven*, pp. 413–14; Antonio Bruers, *Beethoven: Catalogo storico-critico di tutte le opera*, 3rd ed. (Rome: Giovanni Bardi, 1944), p. 317.

135. Max Raphael, *Prehistoric Cave Paintings* (New York: Pantheon, 1945), p. 17.

136. Anderson no. 1068 (to Treitschke, 1821).

Selective Bibliography

I. BEETHOVEN'S WORKS AND WRITINGS

Collected Works

A new complete edition (21 vols., from 1961), *Werke*, ed. by the Beethoven Archiv, Bonn, until 1976 under the direction of Joseph Schmidt-Görg, is in progress. Pending its completion, the standard edition remains *Beethovens Werke. Kritische Gesamtausgabe*, 25 vols. (Leipzig: B&H, 1862–65, 1888). Omissions are listed in Willy Hess, *Verzeichnis der nicht in der Gesamtausgabe veröffentlichten Werke Ludwig van Beethovens* (Wiesbaden: B&H, 1957). Hess edited the *Supplemente zur Gesamtausgabe*, 14 vols. (Wiesbaden: B&H, 1959–71).

Sketches and Autographs

The publication, reconstruction, and analysis of Beethoven's sketches is the most active and fruitful field in current Beethoven scholarship. More than fifty sketchbooks survive, together with some 350 individual pages, bifolia, and sketch miscellanies. A provisional inventory of these is in Hans Schmidt, "Verzeichnis der Skizzen Beethovens," *BJ*, 2nd ser., 6 (BB, 1969), 7–128. An earlier list is in Joseph Braunstein, *Beethovens Leonore-Ouvertüren* (Leipzig: B&H, 1927), pp. 159–60. Gustav Nottebohm published commentaries with copious music examples of two sketchbooks (1865, 1880), including that of the *Eroica* Symphony, and provided more selective excerpts from a wide variety of sketches in shorter essays gathered into two seminal volumes, N I and the posthumous N II. Other significant early descriptions are in Nohl, *Beethoven, Liszt, Wagner* (Vienna: Braumüller, 1874), pp. 95–101, and two series of articles by J. S. Shedlock in *Musical Times*, 33–35 (1892–94). Transcriptions (sometimes accompanied by facsimiles) of about a dozen sketchbooks and autograph miscellanies have been published in the twentieth century, prepared by Cecilio de Roda, Arnold Schmitz, M. Ivanov-Boretsky, K. L. Mikulicz, N. L. Fishman, Wilhelm Virneisel, Dagmar Busch-Weise, Joseph Schmidt-Görg, and Joseph Kerman. A large-scale edition (BB) is under way. See Alan Tyson, "Sketches and Autographs," in *The Beethoven Reader*, ed. Denis Arnold and Nigel Fortune (New York: Norton, 1971); Tyson and Douglas Johnson, "Reconstructing Beethoven's Sketchbooks," *JAMS*, 25 (1972), 137–56; Lewis Lockwood, "On Beethoven's Sketches and Autographs: Some Problems of Definition and Interpretation," *Acta Musicologica*, 42 (1970), 32–47; and Joseph Kerman, "Beethoven's Early Sketches," *MQ*, 56 (1970), 515–38. A valuable interpretation is Paul Mies, *Beethoven's Sketches* (London: Oxford, 1929; rpt. New York: Johnson Reprint, 1969). See also Allen Forte, *The Compositional Matrix* (Baldwin, N.Y.: Music Teachers National Association, 1961; rpt. New York: Da Capo, 1974).

Letters

The standard English edition is *The Letters of Beethoven*, 3 vols., ed. and trans. Emily Anderson (London: Macmillan, 1961), which is the most comprehensive and accurate collection in any language. This superseded A. C. Kalischer, ed., J. S. Shedlock, trans., *The Letters of Ludwig van Beethoven*, 2 vols. (London: Dent, 1909); about 500 items omitted from Kalischer-Shedlock appear in *New Beethoven Letters*, ed. and trans. D. W. MacArdle and Ludwig Misch, (Norman: Univ. of Oklahoma, 1957) in accurate translation and with superb annotations. German collections include: A. C. Kalischer and Theodor Frimmel, eds., *Beethovens sämtliche Briefe*, 2nd ed., 5 vols. (Berlin and Leipzig: Schuster & Loeffler, 1908–11); Fritz Prelinger, ed., *Ludwig van Beethovens sämtliche Briefe und Aufzeichnungen*, 5 vols. (Vienna and Leipzig: C. W. Stern, 1907–11); and, without annotations, but the most complete and convenient German edition, Emerich Kastner and Julius Kapp, eds., *Ludwig van Beethovens sämtliche Briefe* (Leipzig: Hesse & Becker, [1923]). A reportedly complete German edition is being planned under the supervision of Schmidt-Görg. There are other important collections by Ludwig Nohl (1865, 1867), Leopold Schmidt (1909), Max Unger (1921), O. G. Sonneck (1927), and Schmidt-Görg (1957). The watermarks of numerous letters are described in Schmidt-Görg, "Wasserzeichen in Beethoven-Briefen," *BJ*, 2nd ser., 5 (BB, 1966), 7–74. Beethoven letters discovered since Anderson have appeared in recent auction catalogs of J. A. Stargardt (Marburg); Sotheby & Co. (London);

Schneider (Tutzing); in Tyson, ed., *Beethoven Studies*, 1 and 2: and in *MQ*, 49 (1963), 144.

Conversation Books

A complete edition, *Ludwig van Beethovens Konversationshefte*, ed. K.-H. Köhler, G. Herre, and D. Beck (Leipzig: VEB), is in progress. Of ten projected volumes, five have appeared: 1 (1972), 2 (1976), 4 (1968), 5 (1970), and 6 (1974). All are carefully annotated; vols. 4 and 5 lack indexes. An earlier edition of vols. 1–3 is Georg Schünemann, ed., *Ludwig van Beethovens Konversationshefte*, 3 vols. (Berlin: Hesse, 1941–43). In many instances, Schünemann's readings and handwriting identifications vary from those of Köhler-Herre. A French edition of excerpts from the entire range of conversation books is J.-G. Prod'homme, ed. and trans., *Cahiers de conversation de Beethoven, 1819–27* (Paris: Corrêa, 1946). All editions are marred by the inclusion of Schindler's falsified entries. There is no English edition. Schünemann, Prod'homme, and an earlier edition of vol. 1, ed. Walther Nohl (Munich: Allgemeine Verlaganstalt, 1924) are indexed in MacArdle, *An Index to Beethoven's Conversation Books* (Detroit: Information Service, 1962). Unsystematic excerpts from the conversation books appear in various biographical writings, especially those by Schindler, Nohl, Thayer, Kerst, Volkmann, and Kalischer. A loose commentary on some of the subjects discussed in the conversation books is Luigi Magnani, *I Quaderni di conversazione di Beethoven* (Milan and Naples: Ricciardi, 1962), German trans. (Munich: Piper, 1967).

Other Source Writings

The most important is the *Tagebuch, 1812–18*, from the Fischhof Manuscript (Deutsche Staatsbibliothek, Berlin). This exists in two, variant printed versions: Albert Leitzmann, ed., *Ludwig van Beethoven. . .* , 2nd ed. (Leipzig: Insel, 1921), II, 241–66, and Ludwig Nohl, *Die Beethoven-Feier und die Kunst der Gegenwart* (Vienna: Braumüller, 1871), pp. 52–74. An English edition is in preparation by the present author. The notebook which Beethoven kept from late 1792 to early 1794 is reprinted in Dagmar von Busch-Weise, ed., "Beethovens Jugendtagebuch," *Studien zur Musikwissenschaft*, 25 (Graz: Hermann Böhlaus, 1962), 68–88. A collection of Beethoven's excerpts and marked passages from his favorite authors (Homer, Goethe, Sturm, Shakespeare, etc.) is in Nohl, ed., *Beethovens Brevier* (Leipzig: Günther, 1870), and in Leitzmann. No systematic collection exists of Beethoven's prose notations written on autographs and leaves of sketches, but see N I, N II, and Kerst, *Beethoven im eigenen Wort* (Berlin: Schuster & Loeffler, 1904); Eng. trans. H. E. Krehbiel (New York: Huebsch, 1905). See also Hedwig Müller v. Asow, *Beethoven. Heiligenstädter Testament, Faksimile* (Vienna: Doblinger, 1969); Max Braubach, ed., *Die Stammbücher Beethovens und der Babette Koch. Faksimile* (BB, 1970); Dagmar Weise, ed., *Beethoven: Entwurf einer Denkschrift an das Appellationsgericht. . . Faksimile* (BB, 1953).

II. REFERENCE WORKS

Catalogs

Thematic catalogs of Beethoven's works, by B&H (1851), Lenz (1860), Thayer (1865), Nottebohm (1868), and Antonio Bruers (1951) were superseded by the standard work, Georg Kinsky and Hans Halm, *Das Werk Beethovens. Thematisch-Bibliographisches Verzeichnis...* (Munich: Henle, 1955). It contains a systematic, thematic list of all the completed published works, together with detailed descriptions of the autographs, early editions, and published arrangements as well as cross-references to the published sketches, correspondence, and critical literature. A more modest, but useful catalog is Giovanni Biamonti, *Catalogo Cronologico e Tematico delle Opere di Beethoven* (Turin: Industria Libraria, 1968). A valuable study is Alan Tyson, *The Authentic English Editions of Beethoven* (London: Faber, 1963).

For the various catalogs of Beethoven manuscript holdings, see, among others, Beethoven-Archiv, Bonn (Hans Schmidt in *BJ*, 2nd ser., 1969–70, 7 [1971]); Deutsche Staatsbibliothek, East Berlin (Eveline Bartlitz); Staatsbibliothek Preussischer Kulturbesitz, West Berlin (Hans-Günter Klein); Bibliothèque Nationale (Unger, in *NBJ*, 6); and British Library (Augustus Hughes-Hughes; Willetts). For the H. C. Bodmer collection, now in BB, see Unger, ed., *Eine schweizer Beethovensammlung: Katalog* (Zürich, 1939). For Beethoven manuscripts in the Soviet Union, see Nathan Fishman, *Avtografy L. Beethovena v khranilischchakh SSSR* (Moscow: Glinka Museum, 1959).

Handbooks

An invaluable work is Theodor Frimmel, *Beethoven-Handbuch*, 2 vols. (Leipzig: B&H, 1926). Largely derived from Frimmel, but useful, is Paul Nettl, *Beethoven Encyclopedia* (New York: Philosophical Library, 1956; 2nd ed., retitled *Beethoven Handbook* (New York: Ungar, 1967). A projected encyclopedia by D. W. MacArdle, incomplete at his death in 1964, is in the Library of Congress.

Bibliographies

No up-to-date cumulative bibliography of works about Beethoven exists. See Emerich Kastner, *Bibliotheca Beethoveniana* (1913), 2nd ed., enlarged by Frimmel (Leipzig: B&H, 1925), and listings in various vols. of *NBJ* and *BJ*, 2nd ser. Much of the periodical literature to ca. 1962 is suveyed in MacArdle, *Beethoven Abstracts* (Detroit: Information Coordinators, 1973). Further MacArdle abstracts of the book literature are on deposit at the Library of Congress, the British Library, and the New York Public Library. See also the Beethoven bibliographies in *Musik in Geschichte und Gegenwart*, I (1949–51), 1554–65; *Riemann Musik Lexikon*, I (1959), 129–30; *Grove's Dictionary of Music and Musicians*, 5th ed., I (1954), 573–75; *Grove's*, 6th ed. (1980).

Scholarly Series and Yearbooks

Frimmel, ed., *Beethovenjahrbuch*, 2 vols. (Munich and Leipzig: Müller, 1908–1909); Frimmel, ed., *Beethoven-Forschung, Lose Blätter*, 10 issues (Vienna, 1911–25); Ludwig Schiedermair, ed., *Veröffentlichungen des Beethoven-Hauses in Bonn*, 10 vols. (Bonn, 1920–34); Adolf Sandberger, ed., *Neues Beethoven-Jahrbuch*, 10 vols. (Augsburg, Braunschweig, 1924–42); Paul Mies and Joseph Schmidt-Görg, eds., *Beethoven-Jahrbuch*, 2nd ser., 9 vols. through 1977 (Bonn, 1954–77); Alan Tyson, ed., *Beethoven Studies*, 2 vols. through 1977 (London and New York, 1973–77); Schmidt-Görg, ed., *Veröffentlichungen des Beethovenhauses in Bonn, New Series, Schriften zur Beethovenforschung*, 7 vols. through 1976 (BB and Munich: Henle).

Special Issues and Symposiums

Special issues of the following: *MQ*, 13 (April 1927); *M&L*, 8 (April 1927); *La Revue Musicale*, 8 (April 1927); *JAMS*, 23 (Fall 1970); *MQ*, 56 (October 1970), in book form as Paul H. Lang, ed., *The Creative World of Beethoven* (New York: Norton, 1971); see MacArdle, *Beethoven Abstracts*, for special issues of other periodicals and for yearbooks of B&H, Peters, and Simrock. The leading symposiums include: Alfred Orel, ed., *Ein Wiener Beethoven Buch* (Vienna: Gerlach & Wiedling, 1921); *Beethoven-Zentenarfeier internationaler musikhistorischer Kongress* (Vienna: Universal, 1927); Gustav Bosse, ed., *Beethoven-Almanach der deutschen Musikbücherei* (Regensburg: Bosse, 1927); Arnold Schmitz, ed., *Beethoven und die Gegenwart* (Berlin and Bonn: Dümmler, 1937); Dagmar Weise, ed., *Festschrift Joseph Schmidt-Görg zum 60. Geburtstag* (BB, 1957). Siegfried Kross and Hans Schmidt, eds., *Colloquium Amicorum* (BB, 1967); Erich Schenk, ed., *Beethoven-Symposion Wien 1970* (Vienna: Böhlaus, 1971); Schenk, ed., *Beethoven-Studien* (Vienna: Böhlaus, 1970); H. A. Brockhaus and K. Niemann, eds., *Bericht über den internationalen Beethoven-Kongress 10.–12. December 1970 in Berlin* (Berlin: Neue Musik, 1971); Carl Dahlhaus, et al., eds., *Bericht über den internationalen musikwissenschaftlichen Kongress Bonn 1970* (Kassel: Bärenreiter, 1971).

Essays

Among the important collections by individual scholars are: Frimmel, *Neue Beethoveniana* (Vienna: Gerold, 1888); Frimmel, *Beethoven-Studien*, 2 vols. (Munich & Leipzig: Müller, 1905-06); A.C. Kalischer, *Beethoven und seine Zeitgenossen*, 4 vols. (Berlin: Schuster & Loeffler, n.d. [1908–10]); Adolph Sandberger, *Ausgewählte Aufsätze zur Musikgeschichte*, II (Munich: Drei Masken, 1924); Ludwig Misch, *Beethoven Studies* (Norman: Univ. of Oklahoma, 1953) and *Neue Beethoven-Studien* (BB, 1967); Willy Hess, *Beethoven-Studien* (BB, 1972); and Harry Goldschmidt, *Die Erscheinung Beethoven* (Leipzig: VEB, 1974). Also Hans Volkmann, *Neues über Beethoven* (Berlin and Leipzig: Seemann, 1904 [1905]); Max Reinitz, *Beethoven im Kampf mit dem Schicksal* (Vienna: Rikola, 1924); Stephan Ley, *Wahrheit, Zweifel und Irrtum in der Kunde von Beethovens Leben* (Wiesbaden: B&H, 1955); Ley, *Aus Beethovens Erdentagen* (Bonn: Glöckner, 1948). For presentations of comparative textual problems in Beethoven's autographs and original editions, see H. Unverricht, *Die Eigenschrift und die Originalausgaben von Werken Beethovens in ihrer Bedeutung für die moderne Textkritik* (Kassel: Bärenreiter, 1960); Paul Mies, *Textkritische Untersuchungen bei Beethoven* (BB, 1957).

Of great interest are the uncollected writings of Unger, Wilhelm Altmann, Kinsky, Leitzmann, Schünemann, Schiedermair, Otto Erich Deutsch, Schmidt-Görg, Racek, Virneisel, MacArdle, W. S. Newman, Kerman, and Tyson, among others.

III. LIFE

Reminiscences of Contemporaries

Apart from the numerous reminiscences printed in Thayer-Forbes, the only significant selections available in English are O. G. Sonneck, ed., *Beethoven: Impressions of Contemporaries* (New York: Schirmer, 1926), and H. C. Robbins Landon, *Beethoven: A Documentary Study* (New York: Macmillan, 1970). See also the imprecise translations in Michael Hamburger, ed., *Beethoven: Letters, Journals and Conversations* (rpt. Garden City, L.I.: Anchor, 1960). The most comprehensive, but incomplete, German editions are Friedrich Kerst, ed., *Die Erinnerungen an Beethoven*, 2 vols. (Stuttgart: Julius Hoffman, 1913), and Leitzmann. These may be augmented by J.-G. Prod'homme, *Beethoven, raconté par ceux qui l'ont vu* (Paris: Stock, 1927), and Nohl, *Beethoven nach den Schilderungen seiner Zeitgenossen* (Stuttgart: Cotta, 1877). (An English edition of Nohl [1880] is faultily translated.) The following are the most important separate volumes of individual reminiscences: Fischer; Wegeler-Ries; Schindler, various editions of his *Biographie von Ludwig van Beethoven;* Gerhard von Breuning, *Aus dem Schwarzspanierhause* (Vienna: Rosner, 1874); the diary of Fanny Giannatasio, in Nohl, *Eine stille Liebe zu Beethoven*, 2nd ed. (Leipzig: Seemann, 1902), in faulty English trans. as *An Unrequited Love* (London: Reeves, 1876); also in Thayer-Deiters-Riemann, IV, 513–41. See also the supplement to Ignaz von Seyfried, *L. v. Beethovens Studien* (Vienna: Haslinger, 1832), Eng. trans. H. H. Pierson (Leipzig: Schuberth, 1853). For Czerny, see "Recollections from My Life," *MQ*, 42 (1956), 302–17, and *On the Proper Performance of All Beethoven's Works for the Piano* (Vienna: Universal, 1970), pp. 4–18.

Biographies

There exists no documentary study of Beethoven comparable to those which have been done for Bach, Handel, Mozart, and Schubert, or to that which is currently under way for Haydn. The standard biography is Alexander Wheelock Thayer, *Ludwig van Beethovens Leben*, 3 vols. (Berlin: Schneider, 1866; Weber, 1872, 1879); 2nd ed., ed. and enl. Hermann Deiters and/or Hugo Riemann, 5 vols. (Leipzig: B&H, 1901–11); vol. I, 3rd ed., re-edited by Riemann (Leipzig: B&H, 1917). Thayer's original English manuscript, which carried the biography to ca. 1816, was completed by H. E. Krehbiel from Thayer's notes, 3 vols. (New York: Beethoven Association, 1921). This was scrupulously revised and updated as *Thayer's Life of Beethoven*, ed. Elliot Forbes, 2 vols. (Princeton: Princeton Univ. Press, 1964; rev. ed. 1967).

The pioneering biographical studies are Wegeler-Ries; Schindler, *Biographie von Ludwig van Beethoven*, 1st ed. (Münster: Aschendorff, 1840), Eng. trans. *The Life of Beethoven*, ed. I. Moscheles (London, 1841; Boston: Oliver Ditson, n.d. [1841]); Schindler, 3rd ed., 2 vols. (Münster: Aschendorff, 1860), Eng. trans., *Beethoven as I Knew Him*, ed. D. W. MacArdle (Chapel Hill: Univ. of North Carolina, 1966); and Nohl, *Beethovens Leben*, 3 vols. in 4 (Vienna: Markgraf & Müller, 1864; Leipzig: Günther, 1867–77), a pathbreaking work utilizing original sources. A 2nd edition of Nohl, ed. P. Sakalowski, 4 vols. (1909–13), tacitly omits 330 pages of valuable notes and close documentation. Prod'homme, *La Jeunesse de Beethoven* (Paris: Payot, 1920; Librairie Delagrave, 1927), and Ludwig Schiedermair, *Der junge Beethoven* (Leipzig: Quelle & Meyer, 1925), are the standard works on Beethoven's early years. Martin Cooper's *Beethoven: The Last Decade, 1817–27* (London: Oxford, 1970) and Editha and Richard Sterba's *Beethoven and His Nephew* (New York: Pantheon, 1954) are important studies of his final years. Romain Rolland, *Beethoven: Les grandes époques créatrices*, 5 vols. in 7 (Paris: Sablier, 1928–57), in 1 vol. as *Edition définitive* (Paris: Albin Michel, 1966), though incomplete, is a brilliant, wide-ranging study of the life and major works; there is an Eng. trans. of the first two vols. (New York: Harpers, 1929, 1931).

Numerous general biographies are of interest. A few can be singled out as either of historical importance or as containing some new information: A. B. Marx, *Ludwig van Beethoven. Leben und Schaffen*, 2 vols. (Berlin: Janke, 1859); Wilhelm von Lenz, *Beethoven. Eine Kunststudie*, vol. I (Cassel, 1855; new edition, A. C. Kalischer, ed., Berlin: Schuster & Loeffler, 1921) Alexandre Oulibicheff, *Beethoven, ses critiques et ses glossateurs* (Leipzig: Brockhaus; Paris: Gavelot, 1857); Victor Wilder, *Beethoven, sa vie et son oeuvre* (Paris: Charpentier, 1883); W. J. v. Wasielewski, *Ludwig van Beethoven*, 2 vols. (Berlin: Brachvogel & Ranft, 1888); Paul Bekker, *Beethoven* (Munich: Schuster & Loeffler, 1911), Eng. trans. (London: Dent, 1925); André de Hevesy, *Petites amies de Beethoven* (Paris: Champion, 1910); Hevesy, *Beethoven the Man* (London: Faber & Gwyer, 1927); E. Herriot, *The Life of Beethoven* (New York: Macmillan, 1935); Walter Riezler, *Beethoven* (Berlin; Atlantis, 1936; 9th ed. 1966), Eng. trans. (London: Forrester, 1938); Willy Hess, *Beethoven* (Zürich: Gutenberg, 1956); J. & B. Massin, *Ludwig van Beethoven* (Paris: Fayard, 1967); George Marek, *Beethoven: Biography of a Genius* (New York: Funk & Wagnalls, 1969). There are also worthy biographies by Richard Specht, W. A. Thomas-San-Galli, Gustav Ernest, Frimmel, Volkmann, Marion Scott, W. J. Turner, J. N. Burk, and Arnold Schmitz.

Among shorter studies, the most valuable remains George Grove, "Beethoven," in *Grove's Dictionary of Music and Musicians*, I (London: Macmillan, 1879), 162–209, reprinted in 2nd–4th eds. and in *Beethoven, Schubert, Mendelssohn* (New York: Macmillan, 1951). See also "Beethoven" entries in *Grove's*, 5th ed. (William McNaught); *Die Musik in Geschichte und Gegen-*

wart (Schmidt-Görg); *Encyclopaedia Britannica,* 11th ed. *et seq.* (Tovey); and, especially, *Grove's,* 6th ed. (Alan Tyson and Joseph Kerman, 1980).

Interpretative studies which have significantly shaped or altered the received view of Beethoven's life or character include: Richard Wagner, *Beethoven* (Leipzig: Fritzsch, 1870), Eng. trans. A. R. Parsons (New York: Schirmer, 1872); Rolland, *Beethoven* (Paris: Cahiers de la Quinzaine, 1903), Eng. trans. (London: Kegan Paul, 1917); Max Graf, *Die innere Werkstaat des Musikers* (Stuttgart: Ferdinand Enke, 1910), Eng. trans. and rev. ed., *From Beethoven to Shostakovich* (New York: Philosophical Library, 1947); Ernest Newman, *The Unconscious Beethoven: An Essay in Musical Psychology* (New York: Knopf, 1927); J. W. N. Sullivan, *Beethoven: His Spiritual Development* (London: Jonathan Cape, 1927); Arnold Schmitz, *Das romantische Beethovenbild* (Berlin and Bonn; Dümmler, 1927); Sterba, *Beethoven and His Nephew.* See also the present author's psychoanalytic study, "The Dreams of Beethoven," *American Imago,* 32 (1975), 113–44.

Special Studies

GENEALOGY AND FAMILY BACKGROUND. Raymond Van Aerde, *Les Ancêtres flamands de Beethoven* (Malines: Godenne, 1927); Joseph Schmidt-Görg, *Beethoven: Die Geschichte seiner Familie* (BB, 1964); MacArdle, "The Family van Beethoven." *MQ,* 35 (1949), 528–550, with definitive bibliography.

LODGINGS. Kurt Smolle, *Wohnstätten Ludwig van Beethovens von 1792 bis zu seinem Tod* (BB, 1970); Rudolph Klein, *Beethoven Stätten in Oesterreich* (Vienna: Lafite, 1970). See also Thayer-Forbes, pp. 1108–1109.

MEDICAL HISTORY. Waldemar Schweisheimer, *Beethovens Leiden* (Munich: Müller, 1922); Schweisheimer, "Beethoven's Physicians," *MQ,* 31 (1945), 289–98; Walther Forster, *Beethovens Krankheiten und ihre Beurteilung* (Wiesbaden: B&H, 1955); G. Bilancioni, *La Sordità di Beethoven* (Rome: Formíggini, 1921); Edward Larkin, "Beethoven's Medical History," in Cooper, *Beethoven,* pp. 439–66, with selective bibliography.

POLITICS AND IDEOLOGY. Schmitz, *Romantische;* Schiedermair, *Junge,* pp. 316–36; Cooper, *Beethoven,* pp. 86–98; Frida Knight, *Beethoven and the Age of Revolution* (London: Lawrence & Wishart, 1973); Sandberger, "Beethoven Stellung zu den führenden Geistern seiner Zeit in Philosophie und Dichtung," in *Ausgewählte Aufsätze zur Musikgeschichte,* II, 263–91; Prod'homme, "Beethoven's Intellectual Education," *MQ,* 13 (1927), 169–82; Hans Joachim Marx, "Beethoven als politischer Mensch," *Tagungsbericht des II. internationalen musikologischen Symposiums* (Piestany, 1970), pp. 173–85, with further bibliographical references; reprinted in *Ludwig van Beethoven 1770–1970* (Bonn: Inter Nationes, 1970), pp. 24–34. See also the present author's "Beethoven, Sonata, and Utopia," *Telos* no. 9 (Fall 1971), 32–47, and "Beethoven and the Enlightenment," *Telos* no. 19 (Spring 1974), 146–54.

ICONOGRAPHIES. Robert Bory, *Ludwig van Beethoven: His Life and Work in Pictures* (London: Thames & Hudson, 1966); Schmidt-Görg and Hans

Schmidt, *Ludwig van Beethoven* (New York: Praeger, 1970); H. C. Robbins Landon, *Beethoven: A Documentary Study* (New York: Macmillan, 1970). The best earlier collection was Stephan Ley, *Beethovens Leben in authentischen Bildern und Texten* (Berlin: Cassirer, 1925); Ley's definitive, multi-volume iconography remained unpublished at his death. The best survey of Beethoven portraits is Frimmel, *Beethoven im zeitgenössischen Bildnis* (Vienna: Karl König, 1925).

BEETHOVEN'S TEACHERS. General: Nottebohm, *Beethoven's Studien, vol. 1: Beethoven's Unterricht bei J. Haydn, Albrechtsberger und Salieri* (Leipzig & Winterthur: Rieter-Biedermann, 1873). Neefe: Irmgaard Leux, *Christian Gottlob Neefe* (Leipzig: Kistner & Siegel, 1925); Leux, "Neue Neefeiana," *NBJ*, 1 (1924), 86–114; Alfred Becker, *Christian Gottlob Neefe und die bonner Illuminaten* (Bonn: Bouvier, 1969); Schiedermair, *Junge*, 140–62; Neefe's "Autobiography," in Paul Nettl, *Forgotten Musicians* (New York: Philosophical Library, 1951), pp. 246–64. Haydn: Karl Geiringer, *Haydn: A Creative Life in Music* (New York: Norton, 1946); rev. ed., in collaboration with Irene Geiringer (Berkeley and Los Angeles: Univ. of Calif., 1968). Currently being published is H. C. Robbins Landon, *Haydn: Chronicle and Works*, 5 vols. (Bloomington: Indiana Univ. Press), of which vol. III, *Haydn in England, 1791–1795*, appeared in 1976. An excellent survey of current Haydn problems is Georg Feder, "Joseph Haydn als Mensch und Musiker," in Gerda Mraz, ed., *Joseph Haydn und seine Zeit* (Eisenstadt: Institut für österreichische Kulturgeschichte, 1972), pp. 43–56. See also Fritz von Reinöhl, "Neues zu Beethovens Lehrjahr bei Haydn," *NBJ*, 6 (1935), 35–47; for an able defense of Haydn's instruction, see Alfred Mann, "Beethoven's Contrapuntal Studies with Haydn," *MQ*, 56 (1970), 711–26; for Beethoven's relations with Albrechtsberger, Salieri, etc., see the entries in Frimmel, *Handbuch*. Albrechtsberger's three letters to Beethoven are in *Musica divina* (Jan.–Feb. 1921), pp. 10–11. See also Richard Kramer, "Notes to Beethoven's Education," *JAMS*, 28 (1975), 72–101.

RELATIONSHIPS WITH SIGNIFICANT INDIVIDUALS. These may most easily be consulted in Frimmel, *Handbuch;* Kalischer, *Beethoven und seine Zeitgenossen;* and the articles indexed in MacArdle, *Beethoven Abstracts*. Among MacArdle's own important special studies of such relationships, see esp. "Beethoven and the Czernys," *Monthy Musical Record*, 88 (1958), 124–35; "Beethoven and George Thomson," *M&L*, 37 (1956), 27–49; "Beethoven and Grillparzer," *M&L*, 40 (1959), 44–55; "The Brentano Family in Its Relations with Beethoven," *MR*, 19 (1958), 6–19; "Beethoven and the Archduke Rudolph," *BJ*, second ser., 4 (1962), 36–58; "Beethoven and Ferdinand Ries," *M&L*, 46 (1965), 23–34; "Anton Felix Schindler, Friend of Beethoven," *MR*, 24 (1963), 50–74; "Beethoven and Schuppanzigh," *MR*, 26 (1963), 3–14; and "Beethoven und Karl Holz," *Musikforschung*, 20 (1967), 19–29.

THE IMMORTAL BELOVED. The best summary of the problem is O. G. Sonneck, *The Riddle of the Immortal Beloved* (New York: Schirmer, 1927). The basic works are: W. A. Thomas-San-Galli, *Die unsterbliche Geliebte Beethovens:*

Lösung eines vielumstrittenen Problems (Halle: Otto Hendel, 1909); Max Unger, *Auf Spuren vom Beethovens "Unsterblicher Geliebten"* (Langensalza: Hermann Beyer, 1911); La Mara, *Beethovens Unsterbliche Geliebte: Das Geheimnis der Gräfin Brunsvik und ihre Memoiren* (Leipzig: B&H, 1909); La Mara, *Beethoven und die Brunsviks* (Leipzig: Siegel, 1920); Siegmund Kaznelson, *Beethovens ferne und unsterbliche Geliebte* (Zürich: Standard-Buch, 1954); Harry Goldschmidt, *Um die Unsterbliche Geliebte* (Leipzig, 1977). The present author's identification of Antonie Brentano first appeared in *The New York Times*, May 21, 1972, section 2, p. 19; see his "New Light on Beethoven's Letter to an Unknown Woman," *MQ*, 58 (1972), 572–87, and "Antonie Brentano and Beethoven," *M&L*, 58 (1977)`, 153–69.

INTERNATIONAL RECEPTION. Typical and exemplary studies include Leo Schrade, *Beethoven in' France: The Growth of an Idea* (New Haven: Yale, 1942); Nicholas Temperley, "Beethoven in London Concert Life, 1800–1850," *MR*, 21 (1960), 207–14; Otto Kinkeldey, "Beginnings of Beethoven in America," *MQ*, 13 (1927), 217–48, which is now superseded by Anne Chan, *Beethoven in the United States to 1865* (unpub. Ph.D. dissertation, Univ. of North Carolina at Chapel Hill, 1976); Luba Ballova, *Beethoven a Slovensko* (Osveta, 1972); Jan Racek, *Beethoven a České Země* (Brno, 1964); Victor Papp, *Beethoven és a Magyorok* (Budapest, 1927); O. E. Deutsch, *Beethovens Beziehungen zu Graz* (Graz: Leykam, 1907); and H. Volkmann, *Beethoven in seinen Beziehungen zu Dresden* (Dresden: Deutscher Literatur, 1942). For reception in and relation to other places, see the extensive listings in the bibliographies in *NBJ* and *BJ*, 2nd ser. For the growth of the Romantic image of Beethoven, see Schmitz, *Das romantiche Beethovenbild*, and Jean Boyer, *Le 'romantisme' de Beethoven* (Paris: Didier, 1938), with comprehensive bibliography.

RELIGION. Schmitz, *Romantische*, pp. 82–101; Boyer, *Le "romantisme" de Beethoven*, pp. 359–81; Cooper, *Beethoven*, pp. 105–19; Rolland, pp. 667–749; see also Schmitz, "Zur Frage nach Beethovens Weltanschauung und ihrem musikalischen Ausdruck," in Schmitz, ed., *Beethoven und die Gegenwart*, pp. 266–93; Schiedermair, *Junge*, pp. 327 ff; Schiedermair, *Die Gestaltung weltanschaulicher Ideen in der Vokalmusik Beethovens* (Leipzig: Quelle & Meyer, 1934).

IV. CRITICISM

Surveys

Two classic works are Riezler, *Beethoven*, and Bekker, *Beethoven*. Much of the music is analyzed in Tovey, *Essays in Musical Analysis*, 7 vols. (London: Oxford, 1935–44), *The Mainstream of Music* (Cleveland and New York: Meridian, 1959), and *Beethoven* (London: Oxford, 1944; rpt. 1965). For the early music, see Schiedermair, *Junge;* Prod'homme, *Jeunesse;* Thayer-Deiters-

Riemann; and specialized studies by Hans Gál, T. de Wyzewa, and H. Jalowetz. Cooper, *Beethoven*, offers an outstanding discussion of the late works. An intelligent and fresh survey is Denis Arnold and Nigel Fortune, eds., *The Beethoven Reader* (British title: *The Beethoven Companion*) (New York: Norton, 1971). Schmidt-Görg and Hans Schmidt, eds., *Ludwig van Beethoven*, contains useful but uneven essays on each genre. Thomas K. Scherman and Louis Biancolli, eds., *The Beethoven Companion* (Garden City, L.I.: Doubleday, 1972), is an uneven anthology of previously published criticism and program notes, some newly translated. See also the biographies by Marion Scott, J. N. Burk, and Willy Hess; also Karl Schönewolf, *Beethoven in der Zeitenwende*, 2 vols. (Halle: Mitteldeutscher, 1953). For recurrent patterns in the music, see Newman, *Unconscious Beethoven*, and Irving Kolodin, *The Interior Beethoven* (New York: Knopf, 1975). For a survey of the literature on Beethoven's "three styles" and suggestions for a new approach to periodization, see the present author's "The Creative Periods of Beethoven," *MR*, 34 (1973), 30–38; a more subtle approach to the style periods may be found in *Grove's*, 6th ed. A fine survey of the chamber music is Hans Mersmann, *Die Kammermusik*, vol. 2 (Leipzig: B&H, 1930); this continues the important series begun by Hermann Kretzschmar, *Führer durch den Konzertsaal*, 3 vols. (Leipzig, 1888 *et seq.*); a classic study is Vincent d'Indy, "Beethoven," in *Cobbett's Cyclopaedic Survey of Chamber Music* (London and New York: Oxford, 1929).

Symphonies

The standard monographs are George Grove, *Beethoven and His Nine Symphonies*, 3rd. ed., 1898 (New York: Dover, 1962); Prod'homme, *Les Symphonies de Beethoven* (Paris: Librairie Delagrave, 1906); and Karl Nef, *Die neun Sinfonien Beethovens* (Leipzig: B&H, 1928). See also, for the Third Symphony: Heinrich Schenker, "Beethovens 3. Sinfonie zum erstenmal in ihrem wahren Inhalt dargestellt," in *Das Meisterwerk in der Musik*, 3 (Munich, 1930); also Riezler, *Beethoven*, pp. 247–81, and Rolland, *Édit. Définitive*, pp. 49–80. For the Fifth Symphony: Elliot Forbes, ed., *Beethoven, Symphony no. 5 in C Minor* (New York: Norton, 1971), with essays by Schenker (excerpt), Tovey, Hoffmann, etc. Also Schenker, *Beethoven: V. Sinfonie* (Vienna: Tonwille, n.d. [1925]; 2nd ed. Vienna: Universal, 1970). For the Sixth Symphony: F. E. Kirby, "Beethoven's Pastoral Symphony as a *Sinfonia caracteristica*," *MQ*, 61 (1970), 605–23: Philip Gossett, "Beethoven's Sixth Symphony: Sketches for the First Movement," *JAMS*, 27 (1974), 248–84; Tyson, "A Reconstruction of the Pastoral Symphony Sketchbook," in Tyson, ed., *Beethoven Studies*, 1, 67–96. For the Ninth Symphony: Tovey, *Beethoven's Ninth Symphony* (London: Oxford, 1928); Schenker, *Beethovens Neunte Sinfonie* (Vienna: Universal, 1912; 2nd ed. 1969); Otto Baensch, *Aufbau und Sinn des Chorfinales in Beethovens neunter Symphonie* (Berlin and Leipzig: Walter de Gruyter, 1930); Rolland, *Édit. Définitive*, pp. 863–1024.

Quartets

The standard works are now Joseph Kerman, *The Beethoven Quartets* (New York: Knopf, 1967), and Philip Radcliffe, *Beethoven's String Quartets* (London: Hutchinson, 1965; New York: Dutton, 1968). The pioneering study is Theodor Helm, *Beethoven's Streichquartette*, 1885, 3rd ed. (Leipzig: Siegel, 1921). Ivan Mahaim, *Beethoven: Naissance et renaissance des derniers quatuors*, 2 vols. (Paris: de Brouwer, 1964), offers rich details on the performances and reputation of the late quartets in the nineteenth century. For further listings see Kerman, p. 384.

Piano Sonatas

For a detailed overview and bibliography, see W. S. Newman, *The Sonata in the Classic Era* (Chapel Hill: Univ. of North Carolina, 1963; 2nd ed. New York: Norton, 1972), pp. 501–43. Newman counts more than fifty separate books wholly devoted to the sonatas. Valuable pioneering works include Lenz, *Beethoven et ses trois styles*, 1852, new ed. (Paris: Legouix, 1909), and Wilibald Nagel, *Beethoven und seine Klaviersonaten*, 2 vols., 1903–5, 2nd ed. (Langensalza: Hermann Beyer, 1923–24). The most useful studies are Prod'homme, *Les Sonates pour piano de Beethoven* (Paris: Librairie Delagrave, 1937); Eric Blom, *Beethoven's Pianoforte Sonatas Discussed* (London: Dent, 1938; New York: Da Capo, 1968); and Tovey, *A Companion to Beethoven's Pianoforte Sonatas (Bar-to-bar Analysis)* (London: Assoc. Board of the Royal Schools of Music, 1931). For the last sonatas, except for opus 106, see Heinrich Schenker, ed., *Die letzten fünf Sonaten von Beethoven: Kritische Ausgabe mit Einführung und Erläuterung*, 4 vols. (Vienna: Universal, 1913–21; new ed., 1971–72).

String Sonatas

For background, see Theodor Müller-Reuter, *Lexikon der deutschen Konzertliteratur*, *Nachtrag* zu Band I, 1909 (Leipzig: C. F. Kahnt, 1921). Descriptive analyses are in J. H. Wetzel, *Beethovens Violinsonaten*, I (Berlin: Max Hesse, 1924), and Marcel Herwegh, *Technique d'Interprétation. . .* (Paris: Magasin Musical, 1926). See also Mersmann, *Die Kammermusik*, and Joseph Szigeti, *The Ten Beethoven Sonatas for Piano and Violin* (Urbana: American String Teachers Association, 1965).

Variations

There is no adequate modern study. See Henry Hadow, "Variation Form," *M&L*, 8 (1927), 127–31; Willy Hess, "Von Dressler bis Diabelli," *Beethoven-Studien*, pp. 72–79; Otto Klauwell, *Ludwig van Beethoven und die Variationenform* (Langensalza: Hermann Beyer, 1901); Blom, "Beethoven's Diabelli Variations," *Classics Major and Minor* (London: Dent, 1958), pp. 48–

78; Karl Geiringer, "The Structure of Beethoven's Diabelli Variations," *MQ*, 50 (1964), 496–503.

Fidelio

A scholarly model is Winton Dean, "Beethoven and Opera," in Arnold and Fortune, eds., *Beethoven Reader*, pp. 331–86. The standard work on the three versions is Willy Hess, *Beethovens Oper Fidelio und ihre drei Fassungen* (Zürich: Atlantis, 1953). Now superseded is Maurice Kufferath, *Fidelio* (Paris: Fischbacher, 1913). The texts of Bouilly's *Léonore* and Sonnleithner's adaptation are in Sandberger, *Ausgewählte Aufsätze*, II, 281–365. The classic study of the overtures is Joseph Braunstein, *Beethovens Leonore-Ouvertüren* (Leipzig: B&H, 1927), but see also Tyson, "The Problem of Beethoven's 'First' *Leonore* Overture," *JAMS*, 28 (1975), 292–334.

The Bonn Cantatas

The pioneering essay is Hanslick, "Zwei neu aufgefundene Cantaten von Beethoven," in *Suite: Aufsätze über Musik und Musiker* (Vienna: Prochaska, n.d. [1885?]); see also Elliot Forbes, "Stürzet nieder, Millionen," in *Studies in Music History: Essays for Oliver Strunk* (Princeton: Princeton Univ. Press, 1968), pp. 449–57; Kolodin, *The Interior Beethoven*, pp. 21–31; Jürgen Mainka, "Beethovens bonner Kantaten," in Brockhaus and Niemann, eds., *Bericht über den internationalen Beethoven-Kongress*, pp. 315–26.

Missa Solemnis

For a major study of its musical and liturgical sources, Warren Kirkendale, "New Roads to Old Ideas in Beethoven's *Missa Solemnis*," *MQ*, 56 (1970), 665–701, reprinted in Lang, ed., *Creative World*. Rolland, *Édit. Définitive*, pp. 667–750. Outstanding brief commentaries are in Bekker, Riezler, Cooper, and in Ernest Newman's notes to the Toscanini recording (RCA LM 6013 [1954]). See also T. W. Adorno, "Alienated Masterpiece: The *Missa Solemnis*," *Telos* no. 28 (Summer 1976), 113–24; Willy Hess, *Beethoven-Studien*, pp. 232–62.

Lieder

The standard work is Hans Boettcher, *Beethoven als Liederkomponist* (Augsburg: Benno Filser, 1928). See also the brief study by Henri de Curzon, *Les Lieder et airs détachés de Beethoven* (Paris: Fischbacher, 1905); Rolland, *Édit. Définitive*, pp. 527–569; Kerman, "An die Ferne Geliebte," in Tyson, ed., *Beethoven Studies*, 1, 123–57, and Lockwood, "Beethoven's Sketches for *Sehnsucht* (WoO 146)," in Tyson, ed., *Beethoven Studies*, 1, 97–122. For studies of Beethoven's folksong arrangements see Kinsky–Halm, pp. 627–28; see also Richard Hohenemser-Halensee, "Beethoven als Bearbeiter schottischer und anderer Volksweisen," *Die Musik*, 10 no. 6 (December 1910), 323–38.

Style

For specialized studies of Beethoven's styles and forms, see, e.g., Arnold Schmitz, *Beethovens 'zwei Prinzipe'* (Berlin and Bonn, 1923); Hans Mersmann, *Beethoven: Die Synthese der Stile* (Berlin: Julius Bard, n.d. [1922]); Walter Engelsmann, *Beethovens Kompositionspläne* (Augsburg: Benno Filser, 1931); Fritz Cassirer, *Beethoven und die Gestalt* (Stuttgart: Deutsche Verlags-Anstalt, 1925). See also writings by Baensch, Rolland, Walter Krug, G. Becking, August Halm, Tovey, Rudolph Reti, Hugo Leichtentritt, and T. W. Adorno. For a seminal essay on late Beethoven, see Ernest Newman, "Beethoven: The Last Phase," *Testament of Music* (London: Putnam, 1962), pp. 240–52. A classic monograph is C. H. H. Parry, *Style in Musical Art* (London: Macmillan, 1911).

General Background

For the record of Viennese concert life, see Eduard Hanslick, *Geschichte des Concertwesens in Wien* (Vienna: Braumüller, 1869). Among standard histories of music, see Paul Henry Lang, *Music in Western Civilization* (New York: Norton, 1941); Jules Combarieu, *Histoire de la Musique*, II, 2nd ed. (Paris: Armand Colin, 1920); H. Leichtentritt, *Music, History, and Ideas* (Cambridge: Harvard Univ. Press, 1947). An elegant sociology of the piano is Arthur Loesser, *Men, Women, and Pianos: A Social History* (New York: Simon & Schuster, 1954). For the evolution of the symphony orchestra, see Paul Bekker, *The Orchestra* (New York: Norton Library, 1963), and Adam Carse, *The Orchestra from Beethoven to Berlioz* (New York: Broude Bros., 1949). The standard history of the sonata, its styles, forms, and development, is W. S. Newman, *A History of the Sonata Idea*, 3 vols. (Chapel Hill: Univ. of North Carolina, 1959–69); see also Philip T. Barford, "The Sonata-Principle," *MR*, 13 (1952), 255–63. On Classicism and Romanticism, see Friedrich Blume, *Classic and Romantic Music* (New York: Norton, 1970); Charles Rosen, *The Classical Style* (New York: Viking, 1971); and Alfred Einstein, *Music in the Romantic Era* (New York: Norton, 1947). For several genres, see H. J. Moser, *Das deutsche Lied seit Mozart*, 2 vols. (Berlin and Zürich: Atlantis, 1937); Abraham Veinus, *The Concerto* (London: Cassell, 1948); and Karl Nef, *Geschichte der Sinfonie und Suite* (Leipzig, 1921). For a history of Bonn, see Edith Ennen and Dietrich Höroldt, *Vom Römerkastell zur Bundeshauptstadt: Kleine Geschichte der Stadt Bonn*, 3rd ed. (Bonn: Stollfuss, 1976), with further bibliography; see also Max Braubach, *Die erste Bonner Universität und ihre Professoren* (Bonn, 1947). Finally, a superb social and cultural history is Ilse Barea, *Vienna* (New York: Knopf, 1966).

Index of Compositions

The index contains a complete list of works with opus numbers along with a list of those works without opus number mentioned in this book. The index is preceded by a "classified list" of major compositions referring the reader to the relevant opus, WoO, or Hess numbers.

CLASSIFIED LIST

Ballets: *Die Geschöpfe des Prometheus* (op. 43); *Ritterballett* (WoO 1).

Concertos: For Piano: in E-flat (WoO 4); 1 (op. 15); 2 (op. 19); 3 (op. 37); 4 (op. 58); 5 (op. 73); unfinished concerto of 1815 (Hess no. 15). For Violin: in C, fragment (WoO 5); in D (op. 61). For Piano, Violin and Cello: (op. 56).

Cantatas, Oratorios, etc.: *Joseph* Cantata (WoO 87); *Leopold* Cantata (WoO 88); *Der glorreiche Augenblick* (op. 136); *Christus am Oelberge* (op. 85); "Choral Fantasia" (op. 80); "Meerestille und glückliche Fahrt" (op. 112); "Elegischer Gesang" (op. 115); "Germania" (WoO 94); "Ihr weisen Gründer" (WoO 95).

Chamber Music (Misc.): String Quintets (op. 4 and op. 29); Septet (op. 20); Octet (op. 103); Quartets for Piano and Strings (WoO 36); Rondino (WoO 25).

Lieder: Six Gellert Lieder (op. 48); Eight Songs (op. 52); Six Songs (op. 75); Three Goethe Songs (op. 83); *An die ferne Geliebte* (op. 98).

Masses: in C (op. 86); *Missa Solemnis* (op. 123).

Opera and Incidental Music: *Fidelio/Leonore* (op. 72); *Egmont* (op. 84); *Die Ruinen von Athen* (op. 113); *König Stephan* (op. 117); *Leonore Prohaska* (WoO 96); *Die schöne Schusterin* (WoO 91).

Overtures: *Coriolanus* (op. 62); *Egmont* (op. 84); *Fidelio* (op. 72); *Leonore* (opp. 72 and 138); *König Stephan* (op. 117); *Zur Namensfeier* (op. 115); *Prometheus* (op. 43); *Ruinen von Athen* (op. 113); *Weihe des Hauses* (op. 124).

Sonatas: For Piano: op. 2; op. 7; op. 10; op. 13 (*Pathétique*); op. 14; op. 22; op. 26 (*Funeral March*); op. 27 (*Quasi una Fantasia*); op. 28; op. 31; op. 49; op. 53 (*Waldstein*); op. 54; op. 57 (*Appassionata*); op. 78; op. 79; op. 81a (*Lebewohl*); op. 90; op. 101; op. 106 (*Hammerklavier*); op. 109; op. 110; op. 111; WoO 47 (*Electoral*); WoO 51. For Violin and Piano: op. 12; op. 23; op. 24; op. 30; op. 47 (*Kreutzer*); op. 96. For Cello and Piano: op. 5; op. 69; op. 102. For Horn and Piano: op. 17.

String Quartets: op. 18, 1–6; op. 59, 1–3 (*Razumovsky*); op. 74; op. 95; op. 127; op. 130; op. 131; op. 132; op. 135; *Grosse Fuge* (op. 133).

Symphonies: 1 (op. 21); 2 (op. 36); 3 (op. 55); 4 (op. 60); 5 (op. 67); 6

(op. 68); 7 (op. 92); 8 (op. 93); 9 (op. 125); *Wellington's Victory* (op. 91).

Trios: For Piano, Violin and Cello: op. 1; op. 70; op. 97; WoO 38; WoO 39. For Violin, Viola, and Cello: op. 3; op. 8; op. 9.

Variations: For Piano: On a March by Dressler (WoO 63); on a Swiss Air (WoO 64); on "Venni amore" (WoO 65); on "Es war einmal ein alter Mann"

(WoO 66); on a Theme by Count Waldstein (WoO 67); on "Quant' è più bello" (WoO 69); on a Russian Dance (WoO 71); on "La stessa, la stessissima" (WoO 73); on "God Save the King" (WoO 78); on "Rule Britannia" (WoO 79); on an Original Theme in C minor (WoO 80); Six Variations in F (op. 34); Fifteen Variations (*Eroica*) in E-flat (op. 35); on a Waltz by Diabelli (op. 120).

INDEX

General Index